STUDIES IN IMPERIALISM

general editor John M. MacKenzie

When the 'Studies in Imperialism' series was founded more than twenty-five years ago, emphasis was laid upon the conviction that 'imperialism as a cultural phenomenon had as significant an effect on the dominant as on the subordinate societies'. With more than ninety books published, this remains the prime concern of the series. Cross-disciplinary work has indeed appeared covering the full spectrum of cultural phenomena, as well as examining aspects of gender and sex, frontiers and law, science and the environment, language and literature, migration and patriotic societies, and much else. Moreover, the series has always wished to present comparative work on European and American imperialism, and particularly welcomes the submission of books in these areas. The fascination with imperialism, in all its aspects, shows no sign of abating, and this series will continue to lead the way in encouraging the widest possible range of studies in the field. 'Studies in Imperialism' is fully organic in its development, always seeking to be at the cutting edge, responding to the latest interests of scholars and the needs of this ever-expanding area of scholarship.

Science, race relations and resistance

Manchester University Press

SELECTED TITLES AVAILABLE IN THE SERIES

RACE AND EMPIRE
Eugenics in colonial Kenya
Chloe Campbell

ENDING BRITISH RULE IN AFRICA
Writers in a common cause
Carol Polsgrove

MARTIAL RACES
The military, race and masculinity in British imperial culture, 1857–1914
Heather Streets

CHILD, NATION, RACE AND EMPIRE
Child rescue discourse, England, Canada and Australia, 1850–1915
Shurlee Swain and Margot Hillel

'THE BETTER CLASS' OF INDIANS
Social rank, Imperial identity, and South Asians in Britain 1858–1914
Martin Wainwright

Science, race relations and resistance

BRITAIN, 1870–1914

Douglas Lorimer

MANCHESTER UNIVERSITY PRESS
Manchester and New York

distributed in the United States exclusively by
Palgrave Macmillan

Published by MANCHESTER UNIVERSITY PRESS
OXFORD ROAD, MANCHESTER M13 9NR, UK
and ROOM 400, 175 FIFTH AVENUE, NEW YORK, NY 10010, USA
www.manchesteruniversitypress.co.uk

Distributed in the United States exclusively by
PALGRAVE MACMILLAN, 175 FIFTH AVENUE, NEW YORK, NY 10010, USA

Distributed in Canada exclusively by
UBC PRESS, UNIVERSITY OF BRITISH COLUMBIA,
2029 WEST MALL, VANCOUVER, BC, CANADA V6T 1Z2

British Library Cataloguing-in-Publication Data
A catalogue record for this book is available from the British Library

Library of Congress Cataloging-in-Publication Data applied for

ISBN 978 0 7190 3357 5 hardback

First published 2013

Typeset in Trump Medieval by
Special Edition Pre-Press Services
www.special-edition.co.uk
Printed in Great Britain by TJ International, Padstow, Cornwall

CONTENTS

GENERAL EDITOR'S INTRODUCTION

Few issues in modern history have a greater purchase on contemporary concerns and attitudes than the questions surrounding race and racism. The very words raise problems of definition even before we develop the analyses relating to the historical dynamic through which these concepts have been framed, reframed, and endlessly discussed, notably by Europeans and by their dispersed populations in the 'neo-Europes' in the Americas, Australasia and enclaves elsewhere. Even if imperialism and colonialism do not have a wholly exclusive connection with matters of race, it is certainly the case that it was through the lens of imperial relationships, both in the sphere of rule (so-called 'dependent' empire) and in the sphere of settlement by white migrants from Europe, that they were debated and modified. In being so, a whole range of disciplines were called in as providing evidence, including most notably ethnography and anthropology, as well as archaeology, geography, climatology, anatomy, anthropometry, biology, eugenics, psychology, and in modern times sociology, history and genetics. To say that these questions are broadly based and richly textured is to deliver something of an understatement.

In this book, Douglas Lorimer brings to bear knowledge and insights that stem from almost a lifetime of study in the field. He examines the striking changes that took place in debates about race in the course of the nineteenth century, and the manner in which the twentieth century saw further significant developments in the field, before modern medical understanding put paid to many of the myths that had surrounded these questions. In the course of British imperial rule, a whole succession of policies, sometimes applied, sometimes merely proposed, were developed to attempt to cope with the racial questions that faced colonial rulers and settlers at every turn. Some of these policies contrasted ideas like assimilation and separate development. Others were concerned with planning across a spectrum from the extreme notion of the predicted evolutionary disappearance of some peoples, to an acceptance by whites of the inevitability, as they saw it, of colour prejudice, and on to a desire for the necessary amelioration of 'race relations'. Such debates had a very real basis in discussions of the supposedly varied 'races' of Europe, even of the British and Hibernian Isles, as derived from historic patterns of migration and the alleged characteristics of different ethnicities. 'Race' was a concept which very much embraced different forms of 'whiteness', as well as peoples of supposedly contrasting skin colours on a variety of continents.

These debates were expressed in many different formats and locations. Lorimer analyses scientific societies and the development of an institutionalised professional science in the later nineteenth century, as well as the many different books and popular publications through which such ideas were communicated to a wider public. Moreover, many concepts (such as social Darwinism) permeated aspects of popular culture, in exhibitions, shows, museums (where the connections with natural history could be profound), the theatre, photography and other visual representations, among others. In all of these, racial ideas were carried through a linguistic lexicon (or sets of visual tropes) which themselves underwent much expansion and modification. This language of race passed from the realm of what may be described as amateur and quasi-scientific theorists to politicians, administrators, academics, theologians and practitioners of modern scientific and medical disciplines. Moreover, racial dogmas (themselves always malleable) inevitably aroused resistance, and the forms and content of such oppositional movements also have to be understood. As Lorimer makes clear, the language of the emerging concept of 'race relations' owed much to the continuing traditions of the prominent anti-slavery movement, while much of the resistance to harder racial ideas was led by persons of colour resident in the United Kingdom. In all of this, the early twentieth century was something of a transition period, a watershed between the ideas and writings of the Enlightenment and post-Enlightenment eras and the rapid advances of the modern sciences. Throughout all of this discussion, as Lorimer cautions, we have to be wary of reading current perceptions and obsessions back into Victorian and Edwardian times.

But of course questions of race continued to be live issues, not least in discriminatory politics, right through the twentieth century, producing endless debate, political tensions and diplomatic controversy up to the period of decolonisation and after, in such places as the southern United States, apartheid South Africa, and the former colonies of settlement. Although contexts change dramatically, nevertheless questions of race are still with us. There are also many matters of mutual racial attitudes as between the peoples of the world generally. They, however, must be the subject of other studies. As it is, this work will surely take its place as a landmark study in Western attitudes to race, as was the case with Lorimer's earlier book *Colour, Class and the Victorians*.

John M. MacKenzie

ACKNOWLEDGEMENTS

The exploration of the three constituent elements of this narrative of racism – science and race, the language of race relations, and historically limited forms of resistance – has been a lengthy process during which I have had the good fortune to make frequent visits to archives and libraries in the United Kingdom. This research would not have been possible without funds from the Social Science and Humanities Research Council of Canada and Wilfrid Laurier University. In locating and studying a range of not necessarily readily available sources, librarians and archivists at the following institutions have been unstinting in their assistance: the National Archive, the British Library including the Additional Manuscript collection and the newspaper library at Colindale, Rhodes House Library, Oxford, with its indispensable anti-slavery papers, Friends House Library, London, for the *Anti-Caste* and information on the Impey family, the London School of Economics for the Morel Papers, Imperial College for the Huxley Papers, University College, London, for the Galton Papers and records relating to Professor A. H. Keane, the Royal Anthropological Institute for its archival records, and librarians at Wilfrid Laurier University for assistance in obtaining sources not readily available locally.

As this research developed, I received encouragement and helpful suggestions from colleagues with an interest in the theme of racism and race relations. Before my fellow historians at the universities of Guelph, Waterloo and Wilfrid Laurier I floated various trial balloons at our annual Tri-University history conferences. Some of these ideas proved of sufficient interest to become papers presented at conferences in the United Kingdom and Canada. In particular, my project gained appreciably from the support and suggestions of the following scholars, conference conveners and editors: Phillip Buckner, Ian Duffield, Gretchen Gerzina, Jagdish Gundara, Brian Kelly, Bernard Lightman, Paul Rich, Charles Swaisland and Shearer West. I also had the good fortune to work at Wilfrid Laurier University with John Laband and Richard Fuke, two scholars of related histories in the late nineteenth century. As I slowly came to realise that South Africa had an important place in the narrative, John with great patience and understanding answered my novice's queries about its rich and complex history. Dick Fuke and I have had a thirty-year conversation about British and American history post-1865. He also read the manuscript and offered helpful observations. I also benefited from a most patient editor, John

MacKenzie, an old friend from graduate student days at the University of British Columbia, who never gave up on my project and supported its development through various stages. Last and certainly not least, I owe more than I can say to Joyce, who suffers the double burden of fellow historian and spouse. No longer able to cling to a narrative of liberation, I found the topic at times distressing, and Joyce had to endure my bouts of frustration with the work and its progress. In the end her editorial expertise helped bring the manuscript to completion. In addressing a large and complex theme, there are no doubt errors and omissions, and for these I alone am responsible.

ABBREVIATIONS

AF	*Aborigines' Friend*
APS	Aborigines' Protection Society
ASR	*Anti-Slavery Reporter*
BFASS	British and Foreign Anti-Slavery Society
BL	British Library
CO	Colonial Office
CRA	Congo Reform Association
JAI	*Journal of the Anthropological Institute*
NOED	*New Oxford English Dictionary*
NODNB	*New Oxford Dictionary of National Biography*
OHBE	Oxford History of the British Empire
RAI	Royal Anthropological Institute
RH	Rhodes House, Oxford
SRBM	Society for the Recognition of the Brotherhood of Man
TNA	The National Archive, London

PART I

Introduction

CHAPTER ONE

Rethinking Victorian racism

Our received narrative of the ideology of race needs to be reconsidered. It misconstrues the relationships between nineteenth-century science, race and culture, it overlooks the Victorian language of race relations which constitutes the most substantial legacy of the nineteenth century for the racism of the present, and it has no place for the dissenting voices of resistance among persons of colour in the United Kingdom and among a few British radicals and philanthropists. In addition to these distortions and omissions, in accounting for racism and anti-racism in the more recent past, our received narrative relies upon significant discontinuities. Between 1850 and 1950, racism, often attributed to the influence of science, attained a dominant place in the constructions of the world's peoples. Following the Second World War, scientists and the international community engaged in a retreat from scientific racism, and the achievements of the civil rights and colonial nationalist movements in the next two decades marked a substantial rejection of the racism of the past. Nonetheless, racial inequalities and conflicts persisted, and since the 1970s, a reinvention of racism has occurred under the 'new imperialism' and neo-liberalism of the late twentieth and early twenty-first centuries.[1]

This historical synopsis is obviously over-simplified. Part of the problem stems from the origin of the term 'racism' itself, which was coined in the 1930s by critics of Nazi doctrines of racial supremacy.[2] This originating context gave racism its most common yet most historically restrictive definition as a belief that human beings could be categorised into distinct, unequal racial types whose attributes and status were biologically determined. In the nineteenth century, scientists – even Charles Darwin and his generation – had confused ideas about biological as distinct from environmental explanations for inheritance. The legacy of nineteenth-century science for the scientific racism of the 1920s and 1930s may not be as straightforward as our narrative suggests. The scientists shared the confused notions of race

[3]

and culture commonplace in the nineteenth century. Our scholarly quest for the historical roots of a biologically determined racism, as Peter Mandler has argued, may well have overlooked the role and utility of ideas about culture and civilisation in constructing national character and world inequality.[3] The scientists' discourse was unavoidably informed by colonial conquest, the clash of cultures, and the construction of unequal relations between peoples of diverse origins living within colonial jurisdictions including former slave societies.[4] In fact, cultures, according to the thinking of the time, defined distinct essences of peoples, and the scientists through comparative anatomy and other methods searched for a biological explanation for those presumed cultural essences. The retreat of scientific racism in the 1930s first involved the rejection of Jews and European ethnicities as races. Whether such an analysis applied to British subjects of colour still was a contentious issue among the scientists.[5]

Other elements in the presumed discontinuity in the mid-twentieth century (c. 1950–1970) also need to be addressed. Colonial nationalism and the civil rights movement have roots in the nineteenth century. Their pioneering advocates participated in the racial discourse of late Victorian and Edwardian Britain. As historical actors, they do not belong solely in the pages of black or colonial nationalist history, for they engaged in an intellectual and political struggle within the imperial metropole against the hegemonic racism of the time.[6] Equally important and yet missing altogether from our histories of the ideology of race is the rich nineteenth- and early twentieth-century literature on race relations. Conventional wisdom attributes the birth of the sociology of race relations to Robert Park and the Chicago School in the early 1920s, whereas our language of race relations was largely a Victorian invention. Its authors included discerning colonial administrators, abolitionists and humanitarians assessing the outcome of emancipation and the impact of the new imperialism on colonised peoples, and Africans and persons of African descent who faced directly the growing intensity of racial prejudice and discrimination. The United States of America was the pioneer among modern states with a past of race slavery, an industrialising economy and a democratic polity in institutionalising racial subordination and segregation. Developments there were watched with intense interest from across the Atlantic. The term 'race relations' came into use around 1910, probably originating in the United States, but having particular resonance for the British Empire. For a decade, British politicians, journalists and humanitarian lobbyists had discussed the post-war settlement in South Africa. In the end, white South Africans – British settlers and Boers – were victorious, for in 1909 the Imperial Parliament approved a race-based constitution for the new union. There were now two templates for modern multi-racial states: the United States and South Africa, and developments in these two countries would have profound influence on the discourse race relations in the twentieth century.[7] As Laura Tibili has eloquently pointed out, 'race is a relationship and not a thing'. It is the overlooked 'language of race relations' which provided the longer-term legacy of the nineteenth century for the ideology of race post-1950.[8]

While post-colonial studies and the linguistic turn more generally have fuelled a virtual explosion in studies of Victorian race and culture, I have nagging concern that some of these studies are as much a celebration of the present as an effort to understand the past. Our new methods with their sensitivity to the manifold bipolar constructions of racial identities, while exposing the Victorians to reveal something about ourselves, may also be engaged in colonising the Victorians. By constructing the Victorians as archetypical 'racists', we implicitly celebrate our own freedom from racism.[9] This book is written from the point of view that racism is alive and well in the twenty-first century. In a different historical context, our racism may well be differently constituted from that of the past, but to understand that difference we need a better representation of the complexity, diversity and sophistication of the nineteenth-century discourse on race. The richest studies address the aftermath of the abolition of slavery and how by the 1860s the tide seemed to have turned against earlier abolitionist commitments. Strangely enough, apart from the literature on African and Asian history, until recently, far less attention has been given to changes in racial discourse in the metropolitan culture under the new imperialism, 1870–1914.[10]

Beyond the possibility that we might be colonising the Victorians, our new methods may encourage us to focus on individual texts or authors and extrapolate a larger significance from them without a full appreciation of the historical context. In some ways, this approach is similar to the older history of ideas once common in the history of science. It is an invitation to practice what W. L. Burn called 'selective Victorianism'. I am always uncomfortable dealing with a solitary author or source (though at times by necessity I have had to do so), and more comfortable in dealing with a variety of sources from the same historical context, yet expressing differing views. The task then is to establish the meaning of the sources, to assess their differences and weigh their historical significance.[11] It may be that I am 'splitter' rather than a 'lumper' when it comes to historical analysis. I must admit I am extremely sceptical about any claim that a single author is representative of larger body of opinion on questions of race. I hope the book will demonstrate that, just as it is for us, from 1870 to 1914, race was contested territory.

While not a believer in any way in the adage that history repeats itself, there is an eerie parallel between the nineteenth and twentieth centuries. Between the 1830 and the 1860s, an international anti-slavery movement, led by abolitionists in Britain and the United States, including the resistance of slaves themselves and the leadership of black abolitionists, overthrew colonial slavery, and, through civil war, slavery in the American republic. While a notable historic achievement in the record of liberation from racial oppression, it was an incomplete emancipation. Worse still, as the nineteenth century advanced into the twentieth, the supposed failure of the mighty experiment of abolition justified new coercive practices, the so-called 'new slaveries' in Africa, and in the most modern of multi-racial societies instituted racial segregation and subordination in the law and in everyday life.[12]

Following the Second World War, the long-term economic boom and the creation of the welfare state eventually produced a significant improvement in living standards in the West. It also led to migration of peoples of colour from the colonies to supply the labour needs of the metropole. The exposure of the contradictions in American democracy opened space for successful protests by African-Americans. The success of the civil rights movement had not just an American but an international impact, setting new standards for racial equality under the law. A parallel but not unrelated development occurred in the old colonial empires. The Second World War had stimulated rapid urbanisation in some colonies, and rising expectations among those soldiers and civilians who had contributed to the war effort. When those expectations could not be fulfilled, the tinder existed for colonial nationalist movements to confront colonial rule. The old colonial empires facing the costs of post-war reconstruction, a new cold war, and the claims of the colonised for political and social justice, decided it was better to withdraw.[13] The gains made by civil rights movement in America and elsewhere and the process of decolonisation, like the emancipation moment of the nineteenth century, were unfinished or incomplete liberations. It is no longer possible to construct a narrative of liberation into the twenty-first century. The celebrated victories of the colonial nationalists have not lived up to expectations. The gains in legal equality achieved by the civil rights movement did not necessarily translate into social and economic gains. In Britain, governments continued to wrestle with immigration, race relations and the redefinitions of citizenship never managing to embrace fully the multi-racial legacy of an imperial past. More recently, the dominant neo-liberal agendas of governments dismantle the power to the state to intervene, and tax and economic policies widen the gap between rich and poor. Among the latter class racialised minorities are over-represented, and yet the successors to the civil rights movement have not managed to develop a political strategy to protect the erosion of gains made almost fifty years ago.[14]

This recent manifestation of racism exists apparently without its pre-1945 ideological buttress. It is measured by the consequences of policies and culturally informed practices that reward white privilege and disadvantage persons of colour. As a concept, 'race' has no meaning in biological science, and 'race', 'racial identities' and 'race relations' persist as historically informed, social and cultural constructions subject to change over time. This racism without ideology has received various labels including 'structural', or 'institutional', or 'pragmatic' racism. Some authors are more willing to see discriminatory outcomes not as unintended but as deliberate consequences of white power and privilege. This more recent form of racism has been variously termed simply 'new racism', or 'racism without race', or 'hegemonic racism', or 'born again racism'.[15] Racism's revival should at least make us wary of the arrogance of the present as we approach those Victorians and Edwardians contending with the erosion of their own principles of racial justice. In 1906, P. E. Cheal wrote to H. R. Fox Bourne of the Aborigines' Protection Society (APS) complaining of the failure of the New Zealand Government to recognise the 'natural and political rights' of 40,000 Maoris as 'natural born British Subjects'. Appealing to the past precedent of the Native Rights Act of 1865, Cheal observed, 'often the greatest condemnation of the present state of affairs is found in the record of the past'.[16] A more comprehensive view of racism a century ago, when the old certainties of human equality were under attack, might be instructive about how tried certainties wither under concerted assault.

The problem then is to provide a more comprehensive study of racial discourse between 1870 and 1914 which will come to terms with the contested territory of this discourse, i.e., deal with sources in conflict rather than in agreement. I have followed a strategy of Georges Duby, a French *annaliste*, who suggested that to study changes in an ideology over time one should trace the working out of its contradictions.[17] To address the problem of selective Victorianism, I have relied on bibliographies compiled in the 1920s and 1930s. Essential to this task were the bibliographies of Evans Lewin, the librarian of the Royal Empire Society. He produced in pamphlet form a bibliography 'illustrating relations between Europeans and Coloured Races' in 1926, and it was incorporated with revisions into the published *Subject Catalogue of the Royal Empire Society* in 1930. These bibliographies have the additional advantage of citing authors and articles in Victorian and Edwardian periodicals.[18]

Since institutions establish continuity over time and may represent in some measure authority within their specialties, I have looked in the first instance to the publications of institutions with a special interest in race and race relations. In Part II, on science, I have studied the publications of the Anthropological Institute founded in 1871 out of the controversies of the 1860s. As a way of looking at how the findings of professional scientists about race were presented to a larger (if educated) public, I have followed the journal *Nature* over the same period. In their quest for natural or primitive man, preferably untouched by western colonialism, the anthropologists had surprisingly little to say about the construction of race relations. For Part III, on race relations, and for Part IV, on resistance, I have relied upon the publications and papers of the British and Foreign Anti-Slavery Society (BFASS) and the APS. Here the rich, under-utilised, and essential source has been the anti-slavery papers at Rhodes House Library, Oxford. These organisations more directly addressed the legal status and conditions of the increasing numbers of peoples subject to colonial authority. The abolitionists focused their attention on people caught up in the slave trade and slavery in Africa, and kept a watch on former slave populations in the Americas. The APS addressed the status of indigenous peoples facing what C. A. Bayly has termed the 'White Deluge' (1840–90). These peoples were pushed to the margins of new societies created by mass influx of European settlers with their own political and legal institutions which defined the place and status of indigenes in the new colonial order.[19]

These humanitarian organisations had an active membership and funding roughly equivalent to the organisations of professional scientists, but had more extensive networks through churches, chapels and local associations, and including nation-wide circles of friendship among their female supporters. Their publications had larger circulations than those of the professional scientists, though not so large as some commercial, popular science publications. Nonetheless, the standing of science as compared to the credibility of philanthropy had undergone a significant change in the course of the nineteenth century. Scientific organisations and their members were producers of 'knowledge', whereas the humanitarian organisations, even their studies of how legitimate commerce stimulated the slave trade and slavery in Africa, or of how colonial development relied upon new forms of coerced labour, produced not knowledge, but 'sentiment'.

As racialism intensified toward the end of the nineteenth century, individuals who thought that the principle of racial equality had been established by the anti-slavery movement moved to defend this principle against the tide now clearly running against them. Having experienced the alliance of abolitionists with fugitive slaves and African-American abolitionists, in the campaign against American slavery twenty years earlier, they recognised the importance of giving voice to persons of colour with direct experience of race prejudice and discrimination. This new direction began with Catherine Impey, a Quaker spinster, in 1888, with her publication of the *Anti-Caste*. It maintained a circulation of 3,500 copies considerably larger than that of the *Journal of the Anthropological Institute*, the *Anti-Slavery Reporter*, and the *Aborigines' Friend*. Impey teamed up with Isabella Fyvie Mayo, a Scottish novelist and journalist, and Celestine Edwards, a black lay preacher, temperance advocate, and editor from the West Indies. They formed the Society for the Recognition of the Brotherhood of Man and sponsored the tours (1893–94) of Ida B. Wells, an African-American journalist who lectured on lynching in the United States. The society's magazine, *Fraternity*, initially edited by Celestine Edwards, offered a critical perspective on institutionalised racism in the United States, on the economic and political impediments imperial policy and white privilege put in the way of development in the West Indies, on colonialism in Africa, especially the appropriation of land and dislocation of peoples by Cecil Rhodes and the British South Africa Company, and on British rule in India, following and supporting the Indian National Congress. The Society for the Recognition of the Brotherhood of Man had a relatively short life, troubled in part by internal divisions, but there was a continuity in the people engaged in this dissenting movement with the next significant initiative of H. Sylvester Williams who founded the African Association in 1897. From that association, Williams organised the Pan-African Conference in London in 1900.

From this range of sources, it might be possible to put together a more comprehensive, though not nearly complete, range of opinion to constitute the discourse on race in 1870–1914. It might be tempting to describe a range of opinion from extreme to moderate to radical, but such a scheme would not adequately capture the way contemporaries characterised this discourse. As will be explored in Chapter 2, the established position, consistent with the liberal civilising mission of the empire, articulated by the abolitionist movement and by the missionary societies, was one of assimilation. Over time, the world's peoples would come to adopt the culture of the most civilised and progressive of nations. Liberal imperialism and its goal of assimilation, as Udah Singh Mehta has argued, embraced the need for authoritarian rule in the empire. Its goal of assimilation presumed a ranked global hierarchy of peoples and cultures.[20]

INTRODUCTION

In the last two decades of the nineteenth century, as liberal imperialism did not seem to be advancing colonised peoples along the path to assimilation, some liberals, especially in the response to developments in India and South Africa, began to explore what they perceived as the contradiction between liberalism at home and authoritarian imperial rule abroad. Others, including some advocates of the 'new liberalism', simply rejected the old pieties of the anti-slavery movement and openly proposed a path of separate development for the non-European peoples of the empire. Assimilation and separate development were binary concepts in the sense that they were related elements in a system of race-thinking. Nonetheless, they were not polar opposites but two variants in the construction of world inequality. What our received historical narrative of racism overlooks is that in the longer term assimilation proved the more enduring and politically credible ideological buttress for institutional or structural forms of racism.

The late Victorian and Edwardian discourse on race was a contested territory. The older liberalism of assimilation was eventually overtaken by a newer language of exclusion and separate development. This description of late Victorian and Edwardian racial discourse as a contest between assimilation and separate development has one important advantage – it is the language of participants in discussion of the 'native' or 'colour' question. Furthermore, this language also had consequences in the lives of Africans, persons of African descent, and other colonised persons of colour who constructed and reconstructed their own identities within the context of colonial rule. The transition from assimilation to separate development constituted a 'betrayal' of those creole elites who had bought into the promise of a colour-blind empire, and now found themselves excluded and treated as a racially subordinate caste. This betrayal provoked a new critique of empire and its racialist ideology, and informed the rise of colonial nationalism.[21]

The political engagement over separate development versus assimilation was not in the first instance over the science of race but over the construction of race relations. The discourse on race relations was about the management of racial inequality under the historically unprecedented conditions of multi-racial societies with dominant white populations living under modernising democratic or representative governments, or subordinate peoples of colour living under colonial rule by European administrators and white elites. It may be well to keep in mind that just as we find the conditions of the most recent phase of globalisation unprecedented, taxing our analysts in their attempts to forecast outcomes, and testing the limits of our received political wisdom and practice, so too just over a hundred years ago as the twentieth century dawned, observers knew that the new century would be unlike the old. History provided little guidance, as a minority struggled to find answers to forms of racial oppression and injustices inherited from the past, and now being reinvented for the new century.

Ultimately, the discourse on race was a political discourse. It was about the unequal distribution of power and status, of privileges and entitlements, and of wealth and opportunity based upon the racialised identities of subjects or citizens. This unequal distribution of power and resources was governed both by the informal realm of social and cultural conventions shaping everyday life and by the formal structures and administrative practices of political institutions and the law.[22] In the grosser inequalities of multi-racial colonial states, this distribution of power and status weighted the balance of authority in favour of coercion over consent.

In the western political tradition of the metropole, the principle of equality was far more problematic in its meaning and application, and far poorer in its elaboration, than the principle of individual freedom or liberty. Although some late Victorians expressed themselves committed to the principle of political equality and even racial equality, it is not clear what they meant. As citizenship broadened with the extension of the vote following the Reform Act of 1867, it still was restricted by class, gender and, by implication, culture or ethnicity.[23] At the beginning of the twentieth century, women still struggled for the vote, and under the provisions of the Reform Act of 1884, forty per cent of adult males did not have the vote because they were not heads of households or failed to meet residency requirements. The discourse on race was about what forms of racial inequality were legitimate and what forms lacked legitimacy according to the conventions of the political culture. These considerations took on a bewildering variety of forms at the beginning of the twentieth century, and in the process transformed the terms of the discourse on race and race relations. The post-war settlement in South Africa brought a regressive resolution to these developments. It weakened the humanitarian agencies that failed in their efforts to protect and advance the legal and political status of Africans, Indians and coloureds. It further marginalised those early colonial nationalists who had believed in the capacity of the imperial state to preserve past commitments to a colour-blind empire. It liberated the scientists who could claim, free from alternative dissenting voices, that their apolitical, objective expertise sanctioned the inequality of peoples identified as distinct races.

The book is organised in four parts, with an introductory first part followed by discussions of science and race in Part II, race relations in Part III and resistance in Part IV. Chapter 2 sets out the terms of the discourse on the theme of assimilation and separate development, and traces the regressive direction of this discourse towards the end of the nineteenth and the beginning of the twentieth century.

In Part II, Chapter 3 examines professional science as represented largely through the proceedings of the Anthropological Institute and the leading science magazine, *Nature*. It raises questions about what biological determinism might mean for Victorian scientists, and it explores the mix of culture and biology in constructions of race, and how the colonial encounter shaped the scientists' enquiries. Strangely enough, although a great deal of weight has been given to the influence of scientific racism, few studies show how the racial scientists came to have such an influence. Chapter 4, on race and popular science, discusses how non-scientific, cultural influences were incorporated into popular characterisations of racial groups. The chronology of developments in popular science was also significant, for rather than at the mid-century, successful popular science publications established a market for their publications after state schooling spread literacy, and the reduction of printing costs made magazines, often illustrated with photographs, available to a wider reading public by the end of the nineteenth century. Apart from exceptional individuals like Charles Darwin, whose anti-slavery opinions *The Anti-Slavery Reporter* quoted, and who supported the APS petition to protect the Cape coloured franchise, scientists had very little to say about the relations between the human types they designated as races.[24]

Yet, these racial types supposedly depicted real people living within multi-racial colonial regimes, subject not only to colonial officials, European traders and missionaries, but in many cases to the influx of peoples from afar. The empire was a great engine for transforming the distribution of the world's peoples and creating new multi-racial communities. These migrants were not just European settlers but indentured and other labourers transported in great numbers and at great distances. In Part III, Chapter 5 examines the Victorian invention of our language of race relations, which originated with the anti-slavery movement, was adapted and extended by colonial administrators, and was subjected to the criticism of dissenting voices that objected to the spread of various forms of racial inequality and coercive practices in the late Victorian empire. By the beginning of the twentieth century, the 'native question' or the 'colour question', as discussed in Chapter 6, became a matter of intense scrutiny partly in response to developments in South Africa, but also in response to the restrictive immigration policies of the white dominions, and to signs of intensifying racial conflict in the United States. Although largely overlooked in our received narrative of race, this language of race relations, elaborated by extensive commentary over a decade and refined to become politically sensitive to the realities of power, provided the longer-term and more substantial legacy for the politics of race and empire.

Part IV on resistance looks at those critical or dissenting voices which tried to resist those ascendant forces giving new sanction and legitimacy to the systemic and institutional practices of racial inequality and oppression. The two surviving and active organisations from the 1830s, the BFASS and the APS, still worked within the imperial framework of the civilising mission and attempted to lobby against innovations which in their thinking deviated from established principles. More radical groups less engaged in lobbying governments and more interested in shaping the broader public discourse offered a more critical view of the culture of empire and its ideological and institutional constructions of racial inequality. Included in this group were some early colonial nationalists whose confidence in the imperial state to oversee the excesses of colonial administrations and white-dominated legislatures was tested to the limit.

I have preferred to identify these dissenting voices as engaging in the politics of resistance rather than as early expressions of anti-racism. By using the familiar term resistance, I am not suggesting there was an alternative set of collaborators waiting in wings. Imperial, colonial nationalist and African historiography has moved beyond the crude resistance/collaborator dichotomy and beyond the Eurocentric presumption that the language of political rights and social justice were simply borrowings from western culture.[25] I am more hesitant about the term 'anti-racism' which, if introduced into the period before the First World War, to my mind seems anachronistic. Resistance describes a broader church inclusive of those who, as colonial reformers, were critical of colonial practices but still hoping to revive the integrity of the civilising mission, and also a more radical minority despairing about the empire and on the verge of seeing independence and self-government as the only route forward. Whether such voices would pass the test of a post-1970s anti-racism hardened by disillusionment with the incomplete liberations of the 1950s and 1960s is doubtful.[26] In the early twentieth century, the test for the dissenting voices of resistance was South Africa. Here, not only did the humanitarian lobbyists fail to influence the final outcome, but the imperial parliament abandoned its historic role of protecting the interests of all British subjects regardless of race, and bowed to white power in South Africa. This failure had both immediate and longer-term consequences for the newly amalgamated Anti-Slavery and Aborigines Protection Society, for the alienation of early colonial nationalists, and for the capacity of dissenting voices to resist the mobilisation of white citizens and their governments in defence of a global colour line.[27]

To understand the dimensions of the Victorian discourse on race and how it changed in the course of the nineteenth century, the place to begin is 1837. In that year, Queen Victoria's accession began a long reign in which she came to personify the era, and perhaps more modestly, the APS began its long struggle against the destructive impact of empire on the world's peoples.

Notes

1 Elazar Barkan, *The Retreat of Scientific Racism: Changing Concepts of Race in Britain and the United States between the World Wars* (Cambridge: Cambridge University Press, 1992); David T. Goldberg, *The Threat of Race: Reflections on Racial Neoliberalism* (Malden, MA: Wiley-Blackwell, 2009); Marilyn Lake and Henry Reynolds, *Drawing the Global Colour Line: White Men's Countries and the International Challenge of Racial Equality* (Cambridge: Cambridge University Press, 2008); Kenan Malik, *The Meaning of Race: Race, History and Culture in Western Society* (New York: New York University Press, 1996); Howard Winnant, *The World is a Ghetto: Race and Democracy since World War Two* (New York: Basic Books, 2001).

2 There was no entry for 'racism' in the 1933 edition of the Oxford English Dictionary; citations from 1926 through the 1930s link racism not to colonialism but to European nationalism and fascism, *NOED* [www.oed.com]; Ruth Benedict, *Race, Science and Politics* (New York: Modern Age, 1940), republished in the United Kingdom as *Race and Racism* (London: George Routledge, 1942), provides an early effort at a formal definition and history.

3 Peter Mandler, *The English National Character: The History of an Idea from Edmund Burke to Tony Blair* (New Haven, CT: Yale University Press, 2006); see also Douglas Lorimer, 'Race, science and culture: historical continuities and discontinuities, 1850–1914', in Shearer West (ed.), *The Victorians and Race* (Aldershot: Scolar Press, 1996), pp. 12–33.

4 For an exploration of the role of constructions of culture in the context of South Africa and its implications for colonial rule in Africa as a whole, see Mahood Mamdani, *Citizen and Subject: Contemporary Africa and the Legacy of Late Colonialism* (Princeton, NJ: Princeton University Press, 1996).

5 Barkan, *Retreat*, pp. 237–45.

6 R. J. M. Blackett, *Building the Anti-Slavery Wall: Black Americans in the Atlantic Abolitionist Movement, 1830–60* (Baton Rouge: Louisiana State, 1983); Gretchen H. Getzina (ed.), *Black Victorians/Black Victoriana* (New Brunswick, NJ: Rutgers University Press, 2003); Jonathan Schneer, *London 1900: The Imperial Metropolis* (New Haven, CT, and London: Yale University Press, 1999).

7 Lake and Reynolds, *Drawing the Global*; John W. Cell, *The Highest Stage of White Supremacy: The Origins of Segregation in South Africa and the American South* (Cambridge: Cambridge University Press, 1982).

8 Laura Tabili, 'Race is a relationship not a thing', *Journal of Social History*, 37 (2003), 125–30; Douglas Lorimer, 'From natural science to social science: race and the language of race relations in late Victorian and Edwardian discourse', in Duncan Kelly (ed.), *Lineages of Empire: The Historical Roots of British Imperial Thought*, Proceedings of the British Academy, 155 (Oxford University Press/The British Academy, 2009), pp. 181–212.

9 Douglas Lorimer, 'From Victorian values to white virtues: assimilation and exclusion in British racial discourse, c. 1870–1914', in P. Buckner and D. Francis (eds), *Rediscovering the British World* (Calgary: University of Calgary Press, 2005), pp. 109–34; for a more general commentary on post-colonialism and history see: Catherine Hall, 'Introduction: thinking the post-colonial, thinking the empire', in Hall (ed.), *Cultures*

of Empire: Colonizers in Britain and the Empire in the Nineteenth and Twentieth Centuries (New York: Routledge, 2000), pp. 1–33; Frederick Cooper, *Colonialism in Question: Theory, Knowledge, History* (Berkeley, CA: University of California Press, 2005).

10 Catherine Hall, *Civilising Subjects: Metropole and Colony in the English Imagination, 1830–1867* (Cambridge: Polity, 2002); Thomas Holt, *The Problem of Freedom: Race, Labor, and Politics in Jamaica and Britain, 1832–1938* (Baltimore, MD: John Hopkins University Press, 1992); Seymour Drescher, *Abolition: A History of Slavery and Antislavery* (Cambridge: Cambridge University Press, 2009); for the later period, Robert A. Huttenback, *Racism and Empire: White Settlers and Colored Immigration in the British Self-Governing Dominions, 1830–1910* (Ithaca, NY: Cornell University Press, 1976); Paul B. Rich, *Race and Empire in British Politics* (Cambridge: Cambridge University Press, 1986); Saul Dubow, 'Race, civilisation and culture: the elaboration of segregationist discourse in the inter-war years', in Shula Marks and Stanley Trapido (eds), *The Politics of Race, Class and Nationalism in Twentieth-Century South Africa*, (London: Longman, 1987); Lake and Reynolds, *Drawing the Global*.

11 W. L. Burn, *The Age of Equipoise: A Study of the Mid-Victorian Generation* (London: Unwin, 1968), pp. 8–10, 26–37; on selection of evidence and problems in cultural history, see Peter Mandler, 'The problem with cultural history', *Cultural and Social History*, 1 (2004), 94–117.

12 Seymour Drescher, *The Mighty Experiment: Free Labor Versus Slavery in British Emancipation* (Oxford: Oxford University Press, 2002); Eric Foner, *Nothing but Freedom: Emancipation and its Legacy* (Baton Rouge: Louisiana State, 1983); Kevin Grant, *A Civilised Savagery: Britain and the New Slaveries in Africa, 1884-1926* (London: Routledge, 2005); Raymond T. Smith, 'Race, class and gender in the transition to freedom', in F. McGlynn and S. Drescher (eds), *The Meaning of Freedom: Economics, Politics and Culture after Slavery* (London and Pittsburgh, PA: University of Pittsburgh, 1992), pp. 257–90.

13 Cooper, *Colonialism in Question*; R. F. Holland, *European Decolonization, 1918–1981* (London: Macmillan, 1985).

14 Paul Gilroy, *Against Race: Imagining Political Culture beyond the Color Line* (Cambridge, MA.: Belnap, 2000); Thomas Holt, *The Problem of Race in the 21st Century* (Cambridge, MA: Harvard University Press, 2000); Kathleen Paul, *Whitewashing Britain: Race and Citizenship in the Postwar Era* (Ithaca, NY: Cornell University Press, 1997); Goldberg, *Threat*; Winnant, *Ghetto*.

15 E. Balibar, 'Is there a "Neo-Racism"?', in E. Balibar and I. Wallerstein, *Race, Nation, Class: Ambiguous Identities* (London: Verso, 1991), pp. 17–28; Antonio Darder and Rodolfo Torres (with Robert Miles), 'Does race matter? Transatlantic perspectives on racism after "Race Relations"', in Darder and Torres, *After Race: Racism after Multiculturalism* (New York: New York University Press, 2004), pp. 25–46; Barbara J. Fields, 'Whiteness, race and identity', *International Labor and Working-Class History*, 60 (2001), 48–56; Robert Miles, *Racism after 'Race Relations'* (London: Routledge, 1993), pp. 1–23; Goldberg, *Threat*, pp. 23–5; Winnant, *Ghetto*, pp. 305–8.

16 Rhodes House (RH) Brit Emp S18. Anti-Slavery Papers. C150/163 P. E. Cheal to H. R. Fox Bourne, 25 June 1906.

17 Georges Duby, 'Ideologies in social history', in J. Le Goff and P. Nora (eds), *Constructing the Past: Essays in Historical Methodology* (Cambridge: Cambridge University Press, 1985), pp. 151–65.

18 Evans Lewin, *Select Bibliography of Recent Publications in the Library of the Royal Colonial Institute illustrating the Relations between Europeans and Coloured Races* (London: Royal Colonial Institute, 1926) and *Subject Catalogue of the Library of the Royal Empire Society: Volume One: The British Empire Generally and Africa* (London: Royal Empire Society, 1930).

19 C. A. Bayly, *The Birth of the Modern World, 1780–1914* (Oxford: Blackwell, 2004), pp. 432–50; Julie Evans, Patricia Grimshaw, David Philips and Shurlee Swain, *Equal Subjects, Unequal Rights: Indigenous Peoples in British Settler Colonies, 1830–1910* (Manchester: Manchester University, 2003).

20 Uday Singh Mehta, *Liberalism and Empire* (Chicago, IL: University of Chicago Press, 1999).

21 Sean Hawkins and Philip D. Morgan, 'Blacks and the British Empire: an introduction', pp. 1–34, and Vivian Bickford-Smith, 'The betrayal of the creole elites', pp. 194–227, in P. D. Morgan and S. Hawkins (eds), *Black Experience and the Empire*, OHBE Companion Series (Oxford: Oxford University Press, 2004); see also the pioneering study of persons of colour in Britain, Peter Fryer, *Staying Power: The History of Black People in Britain* (Atlantic Highlands, NJ: Humanities Press, 1984).

22 On racism and everyday life, see Thomas C. Holt, 'Marking: Race, race-making, and the writing of history', *American Historical Review*, 100:1 (1995), 1–20; on race and the economy of authority, see David Theo Goldberg, 'The social formation of racist discourse', in Goldberg (ed.), *Anatomy of Racism* (Minneapolis, MN: University of Minnesota, 1990), pp. 295–318.

23 Catherine Hall, Keith McClelland and Jane Rendall, *Defining the Victorian Nation: Class, Race and Gender and the Reform Act of 1867* (Cambridge: Cambridge University Press, 2000); Douglas Lorimer, *Colour, Class and the Victorians: English Attitudes to the Negro in the Mid-Nineteenth Century* (Leicester: Leicester University Press, 1978); Keith McClelland and Sonya Rose, 'Citizenship and empire, 1867–1928', in Catherine Hall and Sonya Rose (eds), *At Home with the Empire: Metropolitan Culture and the Imperial World* (Cambridge: Cambridge University Press, 2006), pp. 275–97.

24 'Charles Darwin on slavery', *Anti-Slavery Reporter* (*ASR*), 4th ser., vol. 2 (1882), 221–2; 'Native rights in South Africa', *The Colonial Intelligencer* (September, 1877), 413–17; Adrian Desmond and James Moore, *Darwin's Sacred Cause: Race, Slavery, and the Quest for Human Origins* (London: Allen Lane, 2009).

25 Ronald Robinson, 'Non-European foundations of European imperialism' in E. R. Owen and B. Sutcliffe (eds), *Studies in the Theory of Imperialism* (London: Longman, 1972), pp. 117–42; Terence Ranger, 'African initiatives and resistance in the face of partition and conquest', in A. Adu Boahen (ed.), *Africa under Colonial Domination, 1880–1935, General History of Africa* (London: Heinemann/UNESCO, 1985), vol. 7, pp. 45–62; Shula Marks, 'Southern Africa, 1867–1886', *Cambridge History of Africa*, vol. 6 (Cambridge histories online@CUP, 2008), pp. 399–405; Timothy H. Parsons, 'African participation in the British Empire', in Morgan and Hawkins (eds), *Black Experience*, pp. 257–85.

26 Alastair Bonnett, *Anti-Racism* (London: Routledge, 2000); Gilroy, *Against Race*, pp. 6, 50–3, 334–6; on the meaning and historical origins of anti-colonialism see Stephen Howe, *Anticolonialism in British Politics: The Left and the End of Empire, 1918–1964* (Oxford: Clarendon, 1993).

27 Lake and Reynolds, *Drawing the Global*.

CHAPTER TWO

Imperial contradictions:
assimilation and separate development

In 1837, the year of Queen Victoria's accession, a group of abolitionists led by members of the Society of Friends established a new society for the protection of the rights of aboriginal peoples. Triumphant in their recent victory over slavery and buoyed by the Report of the Select Parliamentary Committee on Aborigines, the founders of the APS initiated their work with a strident condemnation of European colonialism:

> It is a melancholy fact that the intercourse of Europeans with the un-civilized Aboriginal Tribes has, in almost all cases, been characterized by injustice on the one side, and suffering on the other. By fraud and violence, Europeans have usurped immense tracts of native territory, paying no regard to the rights of the inhabitants. In close alliance with the process of usurpation, has been that of extermination ... There is scarcely a tribe that has had communication with what are called the Civilized Nations which is not the worse for the intercourse.[1]

While they were gravely aware of the magnitude of the task before them, they were equally confident in their capacity to transform the world. Within their own nation, the founding Address announced, they had witnessed enormous change and improvement, and externally they had struggled to establish the liberties of man in [their nation's] colonial possessions, by the abolition of negro slavery'.[2] Under their motto, 'Ab uno sanguine', proclaiming their common kinship with the world's peoples, the founders of the APS had little idea that imperialism and racism would be far more intractable obstacles than the institution of chattel slavery.

In 1901, at the conclusion of Queen Victoria's reign, the members of the APS, struggling with limited finances and an ageing and declining membership, recognised that their founders' mission had not been fulfilled. Furthermore, they realised that the need to transform colonialism was no less urgent, but it now seemed an insurmountable task.

[17]

With the ending of the South African War, the most pressing concern was the protection of the rights and interests of the African population. The members of the APS stood ready to champion the cause, but they had little confidence in their ability to shape its outcome.

Like the abolitionists before them, their one weapon was the mobilisation of public opinion. The late Victorian and Edwardian public, unlike its radical and evangelical forebears of the 1830s and 1840s, was now largely indifferent or even hostile to the philanthropists' call for action against colonial injustice. In addressing the Annual Meeting of the APS in 1901, Sir Charles Dilke shared with his audience the common experience of an increasing isolation within a community enthusiastic for empire and contemptuous of the rights of persons of colour. Noting 'the retrograde character of the change in public opinion … which had taken place in the lifetime of many of them', Dilke observed that in the previous year they had not 'even arrested the decline in public sentiment on those evils which all of them deeply deplored and regretted'. He was particularly pessimistic about the response of Members of Parliament, and reminded his audience that 'it was their duty to make a desperate effort to arouse the national conscience'. He concluded with the scarcely cheering warning of 'the futility of their meeting and passing resolutions unless they tried to arouse active public interest in these questions'.[3]

Imperial ideology and race

The historical task of understanding how the constructions of 'race' and 'race relations' changed from the early Victorian period to the early twentieth century requires the assessment of a dual transformation. On the one hand, in the external sphere of the empire, late nineteenth-century imperialism had created a new global order characterised by the political subordination and economic dependency of much of the non-western world. This process also initiated an ongoing transformation of colonial societies in making new forms of institutionalised inequality with a significant racial dimension. In 1901, the Victorians simply observed a different world from that of their predecessors in 1837. The second transformation occurred within the metropolitan society. Simply put, the Victorians of 1901 were not the same Victorians as those of 1837. The focus of this study will be upon this second transformation. It will explore how changes in the metropolitan society and culture influenced the changing character of British constructions of race and race relations between 1870 and 1914.

To Victorian observers the march of civilisation and progress went hand in hand with the advance of European economic and political dominance over the world's peoples. The Victorians looked out upon a world in which the inequalities in wealth, status and power of human groups designated as races seemed self-evident. As the nineteenth century progressed the reality of European power became even more apparent with the extension of informal and especially formal imperialism. This imperial progress involved the exercise of power to transform the economic, political, social and cultural life of colonised peoples.[4] The penetration of non-European economies by western capital and technology and the weakening of indigenous customs and institutions by European military action and political intervention sparked wars of resistance. From the secure and remote distance of the British Isles news of these colonial wars confirmed the presumption of the natural inequality of human groups, and indicated that inevitably when peoples of differing cultures met the result was conflict, with the victory going to the stronger and superior power.

By analogy to natural selection and to recent works on social evolution, Walter Bagehot, in *Physics and Politics* (1872), applied military prowess as his readiest test of civilised progress. Unlike the ancients, modern states had no need to fear barbarian armies, 'since the monopoly of military inventions by cultivated states, real and effective military power tends to confine itself to those states'.[5] Citing the familiar examples of the Maoris' loss of land in New Zealand, the decline in the Australian Aborigine population, and the extermination of the Tasmanians, Bagehot drew a commonplace conclusion that 'Savages in the first year of the Christian era were pretty much what they were in the 1800th; and if they stood the contact of ancient civilised men, and cannot stand the contact of ancient civilised men, and cannot stand ours, it follows that our race is presumably tougher than the ancient.'[6] Although he referred to the authority of modern science for the observation that European diseases decimated many non-European populations, care needs to be exercised in citing Bagehot or similar comments from other Victorian observers as instances of social Darwinism or other scientific theories.

Bagehot appealed as much to his readers' general knowledge of colonialism and its impact as he did to Darwin, and the instances of racial conflict were real enough. The Tasmanians were exterminated, and colonialism imposed drastic change if not genocide upon many cultures. Ronald Segal's phrase, a 'race war', is not an altogether exaggerated description of imperialism in the late nineteenth century. The Victorians' language, and particularly the prevalence of notions of `survival of the fittest', a term coined by Herbert Spencer in 1864 and later adopted by Darwin in 1869, reflected the reality that racial conflict was part and parcel of colonial relationships.[7] The Victorians' error lay in using an analogy to Darwinian natural selection to describe this conflict as a natural and not as a historical process resulting from human agency.

Even in the unlikely case that colonies were acquired in an absence of mind by reluctant imperialists, the extraordinary arrogance involved in the imposition of external control and change over alien cultures required justification. Colonialism gained legitimacy from the belief that societies and cultures were at differing and unequal stages of development. Furthermore, it was the duty of the most developed cultures to impose progressive change on the undeveloped. In his best selling work, *Social Evolution* (1894), Benjamin Kidd asserted: 'the last thing our civilization is likely to permanently tolerate is the wasting of the resources of the richest regions of the earth through the lack of the elementary social efficiency in the races possessing them.'[8] When taking up this theme again in *The Control of the Tropics* (1898), Kidd stressed that this obligation to develop the tropics was 'a trust for civilization', and 'if our civilization has any right there at all, it is because it represents higher ideals of humanity, a higher type of social order'.[9] Victorians like Kidd pioneered our language of 'development' and 'undevelopment'. Though they often expressed this idea in the now archaic language of the 'civilising mission', they also laid the foundations of theories of modernisation and development trusting in science, technology and western expertise as the keys to progress.[10]

Coupled with this belief in the civilising mission was a conviction that the British were by nature and historical experience peculiarly gifted for the task of governing. Through the traditions of their jurisprudence, administrative practice and cultural inheritance, commentators from a diverse range of political allegiance and social rank claimed Britain's imperial rule struck the appropriate balance between the economic interests of the colonisers and those of the colonised, and between the need for law and order and the just treatment of subject peoples. In his preface for the volume on Asia for *Stanford's Compendium of Geography and Travel* (1882), Sir Richard Temple, after more than three decades of administrative experience in India, including service as Lieutenant Governor of Bengal and Governor of Bombay, described, in stereotypical orientalist language, the unprogressive and deficient character of Asian peoples and cultures from Arabia to Japan. Summing up the state of Asia as a whole, he commented:

> She [Asia] is, in short, unable to attain moral or spiritual enlightenment by any strivings of her own, or to propel herself onward in the path of progress by spontaneous energy. Decrepitude has long been stealing over her, and old age has supervened without any future in hopeful prospect, unless she shall be rendered amenable to external influences.[11]

Those external influences would obviously come from Europe; and in particular the British in India, according to Temple, had served by 'enriching a vast population materially, and striving to elevate the upper classes morally and intellectually by enlightened legislation, by honest administration, and by national education'.[12]

To understand the relationship of imperialism and racism, we should resist the temptation to view the belief in a civilising mission as merely a rhetorical device to disguise crude self-interest and overt racial oppression. In their rehabilitation of J. A. Hobson's thesis of the metropolitan financial roots of imperialism, P. J. Cain and A. G. Hopkins emphasise the common set of values which underlay British presumption of leadership in a global economy. Rooted in the links between the City and the landed interest originating in the late seventeenth century, and in the connections between this interest and the political elite of both parliamentarians and the civil service, this culture of 'gentlemanly capitalism' had the capacity to change with the transformation of the global economy and with reforms in the domestic polity. Recognising the fusion of economic, political and cultural contexts, Cain and Hopkins argue that 'Imperialism, then, was neither an adjunct to British history nor an expression of a particular phase of its industrial development but an integral part of the configuration of British society, which it both reinforced and expressed.' The alliance represented by gentlemanly capitalism sought to preserve 'property and privilege at home in an age of social upheaval and revolution', and sought allies and collaborators abroad 'in a global campaign to subdue republicanism and democracy by demonstrating the superiority of the liberal ideal of improvement'. The civilising mission and the cultivation of loyalty and patriotism through the symbols of an imperial monarchy meant that 'the most pervasive images of imperialism and empire were those which projected gentility rather than industry'.[13] Ironically, the most thoroughly urbanised and industrial of societies at the end of the nineteenth century identified its weaknesses with cities and their inhabitants, and its strengths, especially its vitality as an imperial race, with the country and its idealised hierarchy of landed gentlemen and dependent but robust labourers.[14]

The presumption of British leadership in civilisation and progress had to contend with a nineteenth-century world undergoing change at an unprecedented rate, and in ways that even the best informed British observers could not anticipate. The accelerated growth of European populations and their outward migration to the Americas, Australasia and southern Africa between 1840 and 1890 – what C. A. Bayly terms the 'White Deluge' – decimated so-called 'native' populations of largely nomadic hunters and gatherers. White settlers and their military and political agents appropriated their land and pushed them to the margins of white rural and urban communities engaged in forms of market and industrial production and linked by the revolution in communications and transport to a world economy.[15] Concurrent with these longer-term trends, events as geographically and culturally distant as the Taiping Rebellion (1851–62), the Indian Mutiny and Rebellion (1857–59) and the American Civil War (1861–65) had, according to Bayly, global repercussions for trade and commerce and for the political and military challenges and opportunities of European and non-European empires. One contingent consequence of these events was on the supply and price of raw cotton on the world market. The decline in cotton prices after 1867 depressed conditions for rural producers in India and Egypt in the 1870s and 1880s.[16] With ambitious plans for modernisation including the financing of the Suez Canal, and with the threatened bankruptcy of the Ottoman Empire, the Khedive of Egypt found himself in the midst of an international financial and political crisis. The initial British and French financial and political intervention had far-reaching unanticipated consequences in the British military occupation of Egypt in 1882, followed by the crisis of the Mahdi's rising in the Sudan, and the subsequent demands of European diplomats for their share of colonial territory in the partition of Africa at Berlin in 1885.[17]

The sense of an accelerated pace of change, both from longer-term movements of populations, technological innovation and the growth and development of world markets, and from shorter-term crises, wars and rebellions, created a sense of a world order in crisis, out of which a new world order would emerge. Imperial rule, under formal or informal empire, depended upon the participation of colonised populations, and involved a process of cultural, economic and political exchange and adaptation, often on unequal terms, but nonetheless engaging the active agency of the colonised often in ways outside of the direction and control of the colonial authority. These relationships were subject to arrangements negotiated between indigenous elites and the local administrative agents of the colonial power. Dependent on the historical contingency of internal developments and on external events within the region or as far away as the metropolitan centre itself, these relationships between local populations and the agents of the imperial power were vulnerable to crisis, breakdown and conflict. In the last three decades of the nineteenth century, these systems of collaboration with indigenous communities broke down under the intensified impact of western political, economic and cultural influences. In response, proto-nationalist resistance movements attempted to check or throw off the alien western presence. The crisis of the periphery, intensified by the political and economic imperatives of the metropolis, made racial conflict endemic in colonial relationships, and informed late Victorian perceptions of race and race relations.[18]

The confidence in assimilation or conversion of an earlier generation of abolitionists and of the evangelical champions of foreign missions now seemed simplistic. Participants in these humanitarian causes found that their interventions overseas rarely met expectations. At times their philanthropy had unanticipated consequences creating conflict and harm, as in the case of the Xhosa in South Africa. Beyond these disappointments and unanticipated outcomes overseas, back home the radical turmoil of the 1840s and the stability of the mid-Victorian equipoise moderated enthusiasms for reform.[19] The 'civilised' conditions identified with conversion to Christianity, the rule of law and the rational self-interest of individuals in the market-place, including the sale of free labour, were no longer 'natural' but now required the artificial interventions of a colonial administration. Some observers doubted whether these conditions were suited for some 'backward' races, and thus special, innovative forms of subordination, unlike the tried certainties of Victorian civilised life, needed to be created.

In the global context of rapid and unanticipated change, the British project of empire, as John Darwin has recently described, was necessarily pluralistic: externally from its global reach and the local particularities of relations between the coloniser and the colonised; and internally from the heterogeneous nature of British society and culture itself.[20] As varying ethnic, regional, economic, social and political interests identified their place in the project of empire, they offered competing versions of how the imperial mission defined Britain's global role at the vanguard of modernity, ethical conduct and good governance. Some variant of this civilising vision, which changed form between 1870 and 1914 in adaptation to developments in the colonial sphere and in the metropolitan culture, informed the views not simply of the advocates of empire but also of its critics. Humanitarian opponents of colonial policy, anti-imperialist free traders, little Englanders, and even pro-Boers did not advocate the dismemberment of the empire; they simply decried the betrayal of their version of the imperial mission.[21]

Though not singular in its construction and therefore open to differing priorities, imperial ideology, nonetheless, provided a sense of the larger purpose and moral legitimacy of Britain's project of empire. Commenting on European imperialism in general, Michael Adas observed: 'That ideology gave Europeans the sense of righteousness, self-assurance, and higher purpose which as much as the firepower of their Maxim guns made it possible for them to dominate most of humankind through much of the nineteenth century.'[22] Thus, as the pace of colonial acquisition intensified as the nineteenth century wore on, the champions of empire claimed that, unlike their buccaneering forefathers, they acquired colonies not for loot or profit but reluctantly, even in an absence of mind, and as a trust for the benefit of the colonised. For Victorians of diverse social classes espousing differing political loyalties, even for members of the metropolitan subject classes, the imperial ideology provided a common vision and a shared sense of historical destiny. Given the purposes of such a world view, it provided a particular interpretation, or deformation, of relations between the colonisers and the colonised, yet its exponents were supremely confident in the realism of their vision.[23] Its premises – the superiority of Victorian civilisation and the concomitant sense of right and duty to transform the world – were not subject to dispute but rather had become, as Gramsci characterised such hegemonic beliefs, matters of common sense.[24]

Even if this imperial vision of a world system under British leadership was part of a broad consensus crossing differences of region, class and politics in the metropolitan culture, the pluralism of the empire with its diverse political forms, economic relations and cultures frustrated any attempt by Victorian commentators, and subsequent generations of historians, to treat the empire as a unified whole. Consequently, there was always tension between the imperial vision informed by the ethnocentric presumptions of the metropolitan culture and the policies and practices in the distant colonial or imperial locality. There agents of empire and the subjects of colonial rule negotiated a balance of coercion and consent that differed according to the contexts of place and time in each locality. For those in the metropolitan culture whose imperial vision encompassed a 'civilising mission' or the transformation of the world to Victorian notions of modernity, metropolitan values and imperial practices often stood in contradiction to one another.

In his influential effort to come to terms with these evident contradictions and the place of empire in the British historical narrative, J. R. Seeley in *The Expansion of England* (1883), presented two contrasting series of lectures to describe two empires. The empire of settlement, where British migrants and their descendants were dominant, were 'ultra-English' in the practice of self-government, whereas the empire of rule, principally India, and by implication all colonial dependencies with 'alien races', were subject to 'un-English' authoritarian rule under laws, policies and officialdom sanctioned by Westminster. In Seeley's view, the contradictory nature of the empire of rule 'bewildered' public opinion in England which

> looks with blank indignation and despair upon a Government which seems utterly un-English, which is bureaucratic and in the hands of a

ruling race, which rests mainly on military force, which raises revenue, not in the European fashion, but by monopolies of salt and opium and by taking the place of a universal landlord, and in a hundred other ways depart from the traditions of England.[25]

The tensions, not to say contradictions, within the British world of the United Kingdom and its imperial domains, became even more apparent with the dramatic changes occurring towards the end of the nineteenth century and the beginning of the twentieth.

The metropolitan perspective at the level of the 'official mind' which formulated policy and at the level of imperial visions in elite and popular culture reacted to the initiatives and conflicts occurring in the particular colonial locale. Most dramatically, events such as the Indian Mutiny in 1857 and the Jamaica Insurrection of 1865 provoked controversial reactions and unsettled confidence in the assumed fairness and justice of British rule overseas. These controversies weakened the appeal of humanitarian visions of a benevolent empire, and after 1870, a preference for free wage labour established by the abolitionists' victory over slavery gave way to various forms of coerced labour under the pressures of colonial development, including the construction of railroads, the plantation production of crops for export and the mining industry.[26] Despite the claims of an imperial vision projecting a new and better future under British leadership, these changes were more often than not unanticipated developments, and certainly were not the working out of some coherent theory of empire. The pluralism of the empire itself together with the pace of unanticipated change both globally and within the metropolitan society gave credence to Seeley's famous dictum: 'We seem ... to have conquered and peopled half the world in a fit of absence of mind.'[27] In 1912, Sir Charles Lucas, a senior member of the colonial office, celebrated the pragmatism of British imperial rule by suggesting that the key to the 'practical constructiveness' of the empire was the 'British instinct, the instinct of wise opportunism'.[28]

This celebration of pragmatism accommodated the diversity of imperial rule and its contradictions, and consequently, if even imperial ideology had attained the hegemonic status of common sense, it functioned very imperfectly. The contradictions between the imperial ideology of the civilising mission and the racialism of colonial practice were abundantly evident to the subject peoples who supposedly benefited from empire. Neither Charles Dilke nor J. R. Seeley had any illusions that the Queen's Indian subjects were fond of British rule.[29] The contradictions between the proclaimed ideal, the practice of colonialism and the signs of disaffection among the colonised troubled those Victorians who championed the civilising mission and who saw the conduct of their imperial agents overseas as an expression of the national will and character.[30]

Imperial ideology appears weakest in its capacity to gain the consent of the colonised to the legitimacy of British authority. Despite efforts to design forms of rule according to their imagined constructions of local customs, colonial administrators had little capacity to either direct or control the adaptations of their subjects to their alien western presence.[31] Colonial rule was subject to breakdown at crisis points of social protest and rebellion, and even in times of relative social peace it required a measure of consent and not affection from the populations subject to its authority. More importantly, imperial ideology defined the legitimate exercise of authority by the colonisers, and in so doing defined the forms of legitimate resistance by colonised subjects. For example, the ideology of the rule of law in the eighteenth century provided opportunities for some social dissidents and members of the labouring poor to gain redress against the rich and the powerful. Most importantly for colonial developments, the ideology of the rule of law enabled black slaves in England to set in motion the process by which they not only achieved their own liberation but also launched the abolitionist movement. The anti-slavery movement itself and its allied defenders of aboriginal peoples similarly exploited the conventions of the rule of law to expose the practices of slave traders, colonial planters and settlers.[32]

The ideology of imperialism in a similar way helped shape the forms and the opportunities for resistance by Asians and Africans. In so far as the governance of the empire relied upon some form of cooperation with indigenous elites, they gave a measure of consent to this vision, but they were also in a position to exploit its contradictions to their own advantage. African and Asian nationalists, with a western education and in many cases trained as barristers, appealed to the ideology of the rule of law, an important element in the civilising mission itself, as a means to expose the failings of governance in the locality. In the longer term, the contradictions within the ideology became irreconcilable, and the process of decolonisation after the Second World War represented a collapse of the ideology of imperialism. This crisis of legitimacy had its roots in the pervasive racism of the late nineteenth and early twentieth centuries.

Racism, as an ideology justifying racial inequality, develops in the course of the nineteenth century as a subset of this broader imperialist ideology, and served to reconcile, in a very imperfect fashion, the contradictions between the hegemonic vision of the civilising mission and the colonial practice of racial subordination. Imperialism and racism did not fit together as hand in glove. Racism gave legitimacy to the exercise of imperial authority over peoples racialised and classified as 'inferior' by the constructions of the metropolitan culture. It also helped create a 'British' identity between the ruling and subordinate classes within the United Kingdom and within the colonies of white settlement.[33] Despite its utility in enhancing the solidarity of the white citizens of the empire, racism also exposed the illusionary pretences of the civilising mission. For example, the discriminatory immigration policies of the self-governing dominions directly challenged the imperial pretence that in policy and in the law the empire was colour-blind. Beyond creating awkward political questions for the colonial office, the dominions' racism alienated persons of colour who were subjects of the crown, and it aggravated relations with non-western governments anxious to secure the standing of their states and citizens in the international arena. Protests by the governments of Japan, China and India against the discriminatory immigration laws led the colonial office, urged on by the foreign and India offices, to attempt to moderate the language if not the substance of the most arbitrary and abusive regulations.[34] In the late nineteenth-century, the racialism which conformed to common sense within the metropolitan culture turned assimilated colonial subjects, educated in the ideals of Victorian Christianity and civilisation at mission schools, into colonial nationalists.[35]

The civilising mission seeking to convert the peoples of the world to superior Victorian ways was a doctrine of assimilation. In its most discriminatory form, racism, separating 'kith and kin' from the 'lesser breeds without the law', was a doctrine of exclusion and separate development. The dogmas of an assimilating civilising mission and of an exclusionary racism were only partly compatible. Both presumed an unequal relationship. The tension between these two strands of race-thinking provided the framework within which the Victorians constructed a modern discourse of 'race' and 'race relations'.

Sir Charles Dilke: assimilation within Greater Britain

No better instance of the ambiguities and complexity of the liberal racialism of assimilation can be found than in the case of Sir Charles Dilke (1843–1911). Dilke, who coined the phrase 'Greater Britain', was an influential spokesperson for the imperial ideal, and a parliamentarian who was a prominent spokesperson on colonial policy and an advocate of the interests and rights of colonial subjects of colour. In 1866, at the age of twenty-two, having just ended his successful undergraduate studies at Cambridge, Dilke set out to tour the United States, then in the immediate aftermath of its Civil War. Proceeding across

America to the Pacific coast, the young traveller decided to continue westward around the world, visiting New Zealand, Australia, and India on his way back to England. Upon his return home, and just at the time of his election to Parliament as the Member for Chelsea in 1868, Macmillan published *Greater Britain*, the highly successful account of his global travels enlivened by his political commentary on the state of the English-speaking world.[36]

His phrase 'Greater Britain' caught the political imagination of his contemporaries. It enhanced the global stature of Great Britain by treating the possessions of the empire – including the self-governing colonies of white settlement, the crown colonies and dependencies, India, and most importantly the United States – as sharing a common 'English' culture and tradition, especially in language and in politics. In addition to making 'Greater Britain' geographically and politically the predominant influence in the world, Dilke gave his observations a decidedly racist twist by describing this Anglo-American predominance in terms of the ascendency of the 'Saxon' race. By bringing the term 'Greater Britain' into common usage, Dilke and his best-selling book have been attributed with having a formative influence on the growth of Anglo-Saxon racism in Britain and in America during the last three decades of the nineteenth century. Following Dilke's invention of 'Greater Britain', the idea took on a life of its own. In the United States and among imperial federalists in Britain it meant more than the common cultural heritage that Dilke intended it to mean; it came to apply exclusively to white populations of British ancestry.[37]

The success of *Greater Britain* gave Dilke a brilliant start for what promised to be an equally brilliant political career in the Liberal Party. He more than fulfilled those expectations, serving – despite his radicalism and even republican sentiments – in Gladstone's ministry of 1880–85 as undersecretary at the Foreign Office and then as president of the Local Government Board. Dilke and his friend and rival Joseph Chamberlain were touted as possible successors to the Grand Old Man, but then Dilke was named as a correspondent in one of the century's most sensational divorce cases, which ruined his prospects of high office.

He returned to Parliament in 1892, sitting as a prominent and respected backbencher, where he often acted as an independent voice, sometimes challenging the policies of his own party. From 1892 until his death in 1911, he took a special interest in questions of colonial policy and racial injustice, organising parliamentary support for the agitation against atrocities in the Congo, challenging the colonial office under Chamberlain and subsequently under the Liberals in defence of the rights of coloured subjects of the crown, and leading a parliamentary rump in defence of African rights under the new constitution of the Union of South Africa.[38] The author of *Greater Britain*, with its Anglo-Saxon racism, and the outspoken parliamentary defender of the rights of persons of colour hardly seem to be the same person. In fact, Dilke in his youth and in his senior years was quite consistent.

Dilke proved to be a poor witness in the Crawford divorce proceedings; his statements on race, in both *Greater Britain* and its sequel, *The Problems of Greater Britain* (1890), were equally ambiguous if not incriminating. In its confusion of cultural heritage and biological inheritance, his use of the language of race was typical of his time. He identified both the English settlers in America and their transplanted political institutions and beliefs as products of the 'Saxon' race, and similarly classified Irish immigrants as Celts and associated their presence in American cities such as New York with a high incidence of pauperism and of crime.[39]

He took a particularly harsh view of the Native Americans of the plains and warned his English readers against a smug condemnation of the American treatment of 'native races'. Noting the failure of English efforts to civilise India and to convert the Maoris, as well as the destruction inflicted on the Tasmanians and Australian Aborigines, Dilke pronounced: 'if the [American] Indian is mentally, morally, and physically inferior to the white man, it is in every way for the advantage of the world that the next generation that inhabits Colorado should consist of whites instead of reds.' He hoped that the process would not inflict cruelties upon Native Americans, but drew the brash conclusion that 'The gradual extinction of the inferior races [was] not only a law of nature, but a blessing to mankind'.[40]

In common with other Victorian travellers, Dilke generalised freely about racial groups. Encountering Chinese in California, he confirmed the conventional opinion that they were 'all alike', and extended this observation, noting: 'The same, however, may be said of the Sikhs, the Australian natives, of most coloured races.'[41] Accepting conventional opinion about the superabundance of nature and the consequent indolence of the human inhabitants of warmer climates, he speculated on the industry and productivity and on the fitness for civilisation and self-government of the brown and black populations of the tropics.[42] At times, Dilke contrasted the 'cheap' and the 'dear' races, forecasting an international proletariat of coloured labour supervised by white managers. Noting the changing character of the merchant marine, he observed:

the ships are manned with motley crews of Bombay Lascars, Maories [*sic*], Negroes, Arabs, Chinamen, Kroomen, and Malays … But there is nothing to regret in this: Anglo-Saxons are too valuable to be used as ordinary seamen where Lascars will do nearly, and Maories [*sic*] quite as well. Nature seems to intend the English for a race of officers, to direct and guide the cheap labour of the Eastern peoples.[43]

He concluded *Greater Britain* with a rising call to the Saxon race as the predominant force in the world. Its mission, Dilke affirmed, was to spread the use of the English language and culture, and to foster political freedom by the spread of British conventions and institutions.[44]

This mix of racial pride and strident liberalism, trenchantly asserted in Dilke's quotable prose, entices the historian to focus on his appeal to race without due regard for his radicalism. This confusing mix also puzzled some of Dilke's more astute contemporaries. John Stuart Mill wrote to Dilke congratulating him on his book and predicting that the young author had a promising parliamentary career ahead of him. Mill offered, though, a significant criticism of Dilke's use of racial explanations, observing, 'that (in speaking of the physical and moral characteristics of the populations descended from the English) you sometimes express yourself almost as if there were no sources of national character but race and climate'. Mill then commented on the other, and to his mind more acceptable, forms of explanation which Dilke provided:

> But as you show, in many parts of your book a strong sense of the good and bad influence of education, legislation, and social circumstances, the only inference I draw is, that you do not, perhaps, go so far as I do myself in believing these last causes to be of prodigiously greater efficacy than either race or climate, or the two combined.[45]

Following from this letter, Dilke struck up a close friendship with Mill, who attracted the young politician's reverential respect.[46] Even on the question of race, the two shared more in common than might at first appear.

When *Greater Britain* and its sequel, *The Problems of Greater Britain* are examined more closely, Dilke's later role as defender of the interests of persons of colour does not seem such a departure from his views as a young confident traveller. At Cambridge, Dilke had supported the North in the Civil War, and he planned his trip to America, landing in Virginia, partly out of interest in the outcome of emancipation. He acknowledged that opinion in England was changing on the question of slavery, observing, 'if it is still impossible openly to advocate slavery in England, it has, at least, become a habit persistently to write down freedom. We are no longer told that God made the blacks to be slaves, but we are bade to remember that they cannot prosper under emancipation.'[47] He provided a thorough-going defence of the black population, testifying to the necessity of a Northern occupation to keep the former slave masters under control. He argued that the right to vote and their acquisition of land were essential defences of the ex-slaves' new free status. In 1890, he reiterated his defence of African-American political rights, but noted the regression in their status due to the vehemence of white prejudice. The question of the outcome of emancipation in the United States invited comparisons to the experience of the British West Indies. In *The Problems of Greater Britain*, Dilke, somewhat out of keeping with opinion of the day and in contrast to the observations of J. A. Froude, defended the Jamaican peasantry against the charge of having squandered the benefits of emancipation, and argued for greater political representation for the black population.[48]

In his travels west, Dilke went as far as the railroad would take him, and then journeyed through 'Indian' country by coach and horses. On that journey he was genuinely frightened by an encounter with Plains Indians, but what distressed him most was the appalling conditions of native people living in western towns such as Denver. He had little sympathy for the idea of preserving a nomadic and hunting way of life, but hoped for an assimilation of Native Americans by the creation of settled agricultural communities neighbouring similar white communities, and contemplated the possibility of intermarriage between whites and Native Americans. Given the prejudices of the whites and the magnitude of the change such a plan would force upon Native Americans, he saw that continued conflict rather than peaceful assimilation was the more likely outcome.[49] Applying this logic to analogous situations in Australasia, he observed that English settlers were as prejudiced as white Americans, but, by 1890, he thought that in New Zealand whites and Maoris had established peaceful, settled conditions. On the other hand, he viewed the aboriginal peoples of Australia as being depleted in number and isolated geographically. Consequently, Australia was 'virtually without a native race'.[50]

He also observed that the treatment of Chinese labourers in California and Australia was very similar. He defended the Chinese as industrious labourers and objected to their arbitrary and brutal treatment by the authorities and the white communities.[51] For Dilke, the root of the issue was economic. White miners and agricultural workers feared cheaper immigrant labour and acted as a trade union attempting to control the labour market by exclusion. He understood that reasoning and suggested, in 1890, that legislation against pauper immigration in general rather than against specific racial groups, such as the Chinese, would be a fairer way to deal with the issue.[52]

In Queensland, he encountered coerced coloured labourers in production on tropical plantations. For economic reasons and for reasons of climate, he thought that coloured labour would always have an advantage over white labour under these conditions. Such a situation, though, was fraught with political dangers. It engendered a servile, undignified and inefficient labour force and, worse still, led to an idle aristocratic planter class. Both classes were unsuited to the values and practice of democracy. Similarly in Ceylon, he advised against following the Dutch practice of government advances to planters, for it gave the state a vested interest in the exploitation of labour. To remedy the degradation of coloured labour in plantation production, in Queensland at least, Dilke suggested that the workers form a cooperative. He recognised, though, that such a solution would face severe opposition, for 'there [could] be little hope of the general admission of coloured men to equal rights by English settlers'.[53]

In his world tour as a young man and in his later reflections on the problems of empire, Dilke was quite consistent. He had little tolerance for aboriginal cultures, for he saw the transition to 'modern' or 'civilised' conditions of settled, market agriculture and forms of wage labour production within a legal and political framework modelled on British institutions as both progressive and inevitable. At the same time, in Dilke's view, the transition to modern conditions was often effected by the excessive brutality which settlers inflicted on indigenous peoples. That violence also denied those peoples rights which were among the supposed benefits of modern British legal institutions. Dilke's eurocentric perspective was less of a hindrance in his treatment of peoples working and living under conditions of a market, wage-labour economy. He defended the freed slaves of the United States and the black peasantry of the West Indies, and criticised systems of coerced migrant labour in Queensland and Ceylon. He thought that Chinese immigrants in California, British Columbia, and Australia suffered intolerably abusive conditions. At the root of the conflict lay the economic competition between dearer white labour and cheaper migrant labour, and in Dilke's view the answer lay not in exclusionary legislation but in the prevention of the exploitation of labour. In short, Dilke's remedy to racial conflict was assimilation. Because he believed in the capacity of assimilation among racialised groups, this answer was quite consistent with his advocacy of the superiority and global predominance of 'Greater Britain' and 'Saxon' institutions and culture.

The greatest test of Dilke's belief in assimilation was India. There he had to confront the demographic reality of a population of 250–300 million ruled over by a tiny Anglo-Indian elite who viewed themselves not as a community of settlers but as temporary residents destined to return to the United Kingdom. In addition, Dilke recognised that India represented a tremendous diversity in geographic regions, in political organisation and institutions, in religion and culture, and in caste and class. Furthermore, the Indian people, according to Dilke, saw the British as alien and largely disliked intruders. Yet despite these obstacles, Dilke advocated a policy of assimilation and foresaw that the end of British rule in India would come with self-government modelled on 'Saxon' institutions and practice.[54]

As a traveller, Dilke was suitably impressed by the wonders of India, but had little appreciation for the traditions and cultures he observed. He advised his readers that the popular images of India which pictured the grandeur of splendid palaces and exotic temples, and no less splendid and exotic princes, ignored the grimmer realities of Indian life: 'When he [the English traveller] lands and surveys the people he finds them naked barbarians, plunged in the densest ignorance and superstition, and safe only from extermination because the European can not dwell permanently in the climate of their land.' He identified various peoples within India as barbarians and savages, and compared them with other peoples he had encountered on his travels, observing that 'of the purely native races the Rajpoots are only fine barbarians, the Bengalese mere savages, and the tribes of Central India but little better than the Australian aborigines or the brutes'.[55]

In 1868, but less so in 1890, Dilke was quite critical of Anglo-Indian rule, seeing the inflated size of the army as a burden on the Indian population. He objected in particular to the arrogant and brutal treatment of the population at the hands of Anglo-Indian officialdom.

> We profess to love them, and to be educating them for something they can not comprehend, which we call freedom and self-government; in the mean time, while we do not plunder them, nor convert them forcibly, after the wont of the Mogul emperors, we kick and cuff them all round, and degrade the nobles by ameliorating the condition of humbler men.[56]

With the Indian ruling class undermined, he claimed that all that remained was 'the slave-class, and little else'. From this class came 'our policemen and torturer-in-chief', as well as the soldiers who serve as 'our guards and the executioners of their countrymen'. Consequently British rule in India managed to 'reduce the government to a mere imperialism, where one man rules and the rest are slaves'.[57]

Writing in 1868, Dilke retained the notion of imperialism as a form of authoritarian government as practised in continental Europe, especially France, but now applied it in a new way to British rule in India. He offered a new definition of 'imperialism' itself: 'not only is our government in India a despotism, but its tendency is to become an imperialism, or despotism exercised over a democratic people, such as we see in France, and are commencing to see in Russia.'[58] As a young radical, Dilke saw that this 'imperialism' in India, especially the existence of a large army without effective control by Parliament, threatened the liberties of Englishmen. 'It is hard to believe', he observed, 'that men who have periodically to go through such scenes as those of 1857, or who are in daily contact with a cringing dark-skinned race, can in the long run continue to be firm friends to constitutional liberty at home.' Despite these reservations and despite his critique of Anglo-Indian administration, Dilke thought British rule in India both necessary and 'very modern', for 'it [was] progress toward imperialism, or equality of conditions under paternal despotism'.[59]

He recognised that the rigid imposition of western notions often led to a worsening of conditions. He claimed that British principles of equality before the law offended members of the higher castes by the treatment accorded to the lower. Nonetheless, he saw that in the long term British institutions and practices would prevail, and advocated greater efforts at education, insisting as emphatically as Macaulay before him, that the education should be in the English language. He criticised Anglo-Indian reluctance to employ qualified Indians in positions of higher status and responsibility, for ultimately British rule rested upon the consent of the governed. Eventually, as India changed so too would the day of Indian self-government come closer to fulfilment.[60] In 1890, in *Problems of Greater Britain*, he was less optimistic than in 1868. He remained a critic of the Anglo-Indian administration, but also thought the Indian National Congress did not represent the population as a whole. He saw India in a stage of transition, thought that the British should work with Congress, called for greater representation of the Indian population in government councils, especially at the local level, and yet defended the continuation of British rule.[61]

While by 1890 Dilke had become more cautious, he remained an advocate of representative and self-government as the fulfilment of Britain's imperial mission. In 1868, in *Greater Britain*, this vision mixed the language of Anglo-Saxon racism with a strident liberalism which affirmed the value of freedom for all peoples regardless of race:

> There is much exaggeration in the cry that self-government, personal independence, and true manliness can exist only where the snow will lie upon the ground, that cringing slavishness and imbecile submission follow the palm-belt around the world. If freedom be good in one country it is good in all, for there is nothing in its essence which should limit it in time or place.[62]

He affirmed that once freedom was established, the peoples of the tropics would fight as determinedly to retain that freedom as any other people. He saw, though, that freedom could only be established gradually over time as people became prepared for it. He observed that it would 'take years to efface the stain of a couple of hundred years of slavery in the negroes of America', and then predicted that 'it may take scores of years to heal the deeper sores of Hindustan'. Nonetheless, he remained confident that 'history teaches us to believe that the time will come when the Indians will be fit for freedom'.[63]

Dilke concluded *Greater Britain* with the recognition that in the future global predominance lay not with the United Kingdom. Rather, global influence would be exerted through the combined influence of English-speaking peoples led by the United States whose size in territory, population and wealth gave it a preeminent role. What historians have missed in Dilke's appeal to this Anglo-Saxon union was his assignment of a special global role to the British Empire. His conclusion reviewed the global struggle between races, and he affirmed the dominance of what he termed the 'dearer' over the 'cheaper' races. 'The result of our survey', he observed, 'is such as to give us reason for the belief that race distinctions will long continue; that miscegenation will go but little way toward blending races; that the dearer are, on the whole, likely to destroy the cheaper people, and that Saxondom will rise triumphant from the doubtful struggle.'[64] Certain that within this 'Saxondom' America and potentially Australia would surpass the British Isles, Dilke placed a special emphasis on British imperial possessions outside of the areas of English settlement. India gave the British 'that element of vastness of dominion which, in this age, [was] needed to secure width of thought and nobility of purpose.' He then extended this purpose to encompass a newly defined global role: 'to the English race our possession of India, of the coasts of Africa, and of the ports of China offers the possibility of planting free institutions among the dark-skinned races of the world.'[65] For Dilke this vision was more than the liberal idealism of a young traveller with political ambitions. In 1870, just two years after the publication of *Greater Britain*, Dilke chaired the annual general meeting of the APS and began a life-long engagement with the principal lobby for the subjects of colour within the empire.[66]

Two decades later, in *Problems of Greater Britain*, Dilke reaffirmed this global role. He thought that being part of a global empire served to stem the growth of a 'hopeless provincialism' which he saw as a danger among the inhabitants of the British Isles and among settler communities in Australasia, Canada and South Africa.[67] He also defended Britain's special role in regard to the peoples in dependencies outside areas of British settlement. He saw that the partition of Africa was a product of the rivalry with France and Germany, and queried whether Europeans had any right to intervene in Africa. He feared that the high-sounding principles of the Berlin Conference in 1885 might open the way to a new exploitation of Africans.[68] He saw that South Africa presented the most complex problem in the British Empire, and stressed the special role of the British Government in the defence of the interests of Africans. Nonetheless, as he noted with regard to South Africa and elsewhere, 'to induce Parliament to adequately protect in all parts of the world native interests for which we are morally responsible has hitherto been found impossible, and there is no reason to think that it will be more easy as time goes on'.[69] Despite the acknowledged difficulty of the task, he dedicated much of his last twenty years in Parliament to the protection of what he termed 'native interests'.

Dilke used the language of Anglo-Saxon racism to express his belief that economic and social relations within the framework of British laws and institutions best exemplified universal liberal principles. He believed that those principles, under the assimilating agency of the empire, would eventually apply to all peoples and places, and thus he confidently preached that the sole justifiable and the inevitable long-term goal of British imperialism was to institute equality before the law and to establish representative self-government. He was an ideologue of empire in the sense that, for him, these claims were not mere rhetoric to disguise the exercise of British power. The young traveller of the 1860s and the senior parliamentarian of the 1890s shared a common vision. The elder statesman, though, was a far more isolated figure. This isolation was not simply a question of the tragedy of the divorce scandal; rather, his liberal vision of assimilation had been undermined by the exercise of imperial authority and by the growth of a more strident and exclusive racism.

Imperial contradictions

The contradiction between the belief in the benevolence of British imperialism and the character of colonial racial strife and oppression was not simply a consequence of liberal conventions running into conflict with colonial experience and imperial needs. Underpinning this conflict was the contrast between the theory and practice of social and political inequality within late Victorian Britain and the forms of racial inequality in the empire.

This contrast between the metropolitan society and the form of colonial administration in India and other tropical dependencies was a commonplace theme of both the advocates and the critics of empire. Charles Dilke advised his readers: 'England in the East is not the England that we know. Flousy Britannia, with her anchor and ship, becomes a mysterious Oriental despotism.'[70] As noted earlier, Seeley presented the colonies of British settlement and British rule in India as polar opposites: 'Whatever political maxims are most applicable to one, are most inapplicable to the other.' He set out to explain how British policy could 'be despotic in Asia and democratic in Australia'.[71] In Benjamin Kidd's opinion, Britain's relations with its tropical dependencies were 'incompatible with both the spirit and forms of modern civilization'. Colonial policy in tropical dependencies had erred in trying to apply the lessons of the self-governing colonies, where England had 'put forth vigorous reproductions of herself in the white man's lands of the world'. Kidd doubted if British institutions could 'be reproduced in the twentieth century in Africa and similar regions of the earth'.[72] From the perspective of an imperial administrator, Sir Evelyn Baring, Lord Cromer, warned of the dangers to the empire of 'democratic tyranny' at home. He doubted whether Anglo-Saxon institutions based on the 'more complex conception of ordered liberty' could be reproduced in the empire, and feared that a western education would only produce Indian or Egyptian 'demagogues' seeking to impose their own despotism in place of a more benevolent if bureaucratic British rule.[73]

Cromer's observations were, of course, the very substance of the fears of the critics of empire who supported the imperial mission but thought that authoritarian imperial practice threatened democratic values at home. In 1908, H. M. Hyndman, the founder of the Social Democratic Federation and an imperialist despite his socialism, wrote to Sir Charles Dilke commenting on the external and internal problems facing the British government. Recognising the need for a strong navy, Hyndman was concerned about the strength of the army in light of new commitments on the continent and of the possibility of social unrest at home. 'I have been of opinion for many years,' he commented, 'that our predatory Imperialism is played out & that we cannot have democracy & a citizen army at home & exercise tyranny, as in India aboard ... I am satisfied you cannot do both: act the despot in Africa & Asia and come forward to champion free development & national rights in Europe.'[74] Writing in 1904 in the aftermath of the South African War, L. T. Hobhouse identified imperialism with the forces of reaction threatening democratic advances in the United Kingdom. In his statement of a long-standing radical argument, he claimed that the imperial idea was liberal and Cobdenite in origin, spreading the benefits of British liberty and governance by free trade, peace and colonial self-government. Citing J. A. Hobson on the growth of empire in the previous twenty years, Hobhouse associated the new imperialism with militarism, the abuses of servile labour, and denial of the rights of citizens. Imperialism had an equally disastrous impact domestically. At a time when the advance of democracy promised social reform and peace, Hobhouse observed that the forces of reaction were ascendant, appealing to patriotism, appropriating state funds from social reform to military expenditure, encouraging the House of Lords and judiciary to attack the rights of trade unions, and weakening the democratic voice of elected Members of Parliament by enhancing the power of the cabinet. Pointing to developments in South Africa, Hobhouse affirmed: the 'spirit of domination which rejoices in conquest is by nature hostile to the idea of racial equality, and indifferent to political liberty'.[75]

While espousing a similar critique of imperial rule in India and elsewhere, the Fabian Society paid less attention to democracy at home and more to contradictions in imperial rule overseas. Its election manifesto for the khaki election of 1900, *Fabianism and Empire* edited by George Bernard Shaw, reminded readers that most subjects of the empire were neither white nor Christian. Distrusting the capacity of the white citizens of self-governing democracies to provide just government for persons of colour and claiming that non-Europeans were not suited to democracy, the pamphlet condemned all parties engaged in the contradictory policies of empire. A source of dispute within Fabian ranks, the manifesto asserted: 'the Empire cannot be governed on either Liberal or Conservative, democratic or aristocratic principles exclusively; and cannot be governed on Church of England or Nonconformist principles at all.'[76] While the Fabians placed greater trust in bureaucratic solutions, Ramsay MacDonald reiterated the older radical antithesis between democracy and empire. In his effort to develop an imperial policy for the Labour Party in 1907, he observed that 'the Imperialist movement' was 'in declared hostility to democracy'. Questioning a policy of assimilation and preferring to leave indigenous peoples and institutions alone, the Labour MP saw colonial despotism as a threat to British democracy:

> For, so long as we regard the native as someone whom *we* [emphasis in original] must rule, we are attempting the palpable impossibility of ruling democratically at home and despotically abroad. The result will be that our own democracy will be tainted, and our democratic systems will crumble, eaten to the heart of their supports by the autocracy of our dependency rule.[77]

Aware of the contrast between the political values of the metropolis and the practice of colonial administration, much of the commentary by advocates and critics of empire, including commentary on race and race relations, addressed the question of how this contradiction could be reconciled.

At times, this contrast in two differing worlds of the metropolis and the empire could force a dramatic alteration. In the early nineteenth century, the anti-slavery crusade, as a form of cultural imperialism, imposed the new ethos of an emerging industrial society upon colonial slave societies.[78] In the late nineteenth century, a mature industrial society with a free labour ideology, a legalised trade union movement, and an enlarged mass, if not fully democratic, electorate witnessed an imperial process which destroyed indigenous cultures, forcefully incorporated non-Europeans into market economies using coercive forms of labour, and created a colonial polity resting on authoritarian administrative rule. In spite of the apparent contradictions between developments in the colonial world and practices within British society, no crusade on the scale of the earlier anti-slavery movement existed in the late nineteenth century. Part of the explanation for this apparent anomaly is the emergence of a pervasive racist ideology which claimed that non-whites were unsuited by nature to British institutions and practices.

In part, the tension between the metropolitan and colonial spheres was a conflict between past and present. In the early nineteenth century, evangelical and radical reformers had succeeded in their assault on the racial oppression of chattel slavery, had laid the foundations for the missionary movement, and had launched a campaign for the protection of aboriginal peoples against colonial abuses. This historical record, especially the campaign against slavery, gave British imperialism its sense of moral purpose and legitimacy. As early as the 1850s and certainly from the 1860s onwards, this moral idealism no longer seemed suited to a colonial present reliant on military force to extend and stabilise turbulent frontiers, and on various forms of coercion to supply indigenous and migrant labour to produce goods for a world economy. In interpreting this record of imperial advance and racial conflict, the Victorians were not free agents. Their responses to some degree were shaped by their recent and not forgotten past. Just as the majesty of empire inflated patriotic pride, so did the past record of the crusade against the slave trade and slavery inspire the belief in the benevolence of British rule overseas.[79] What is important is that Victorians of a broad range of social origins and political affiliations believed in the `positive good' of British imperialism. In the period between 1870 and 1914, the tension between a moralised imperial past and an insistent colonial present shaped the British racial discourse between two options – a liberal creed of assimilation and an exclusionary doctrine of separate development.

Separate development

Within the historical limitations of their time and place, the Victorians had two options, and both choices were implicitly racialist. They were racialist in the sense that there was an assumption that British agencies, including not only the state but also commercial enterprises, immigrant settlers and philanthropic and missionary organisations, had a right to impose their order upon other peoples' lives. Within this imposed order a racial hierarchy would exist with whites in command of non-whites. The first option was the liberal racialism of assimilation most clearly articulated by anti-slavery, missionary and humanitarian reformers. This tradition, which was ascendant in the early and mid-Victorian periods and persisted in the late nineteenth century, was interventionist and pro-imperialist in seeking to reshape the world to conform to British ways by the agencies of Christianity, civilisation and commerce. This liberal imperial vision was rooted in the values and conventions of the hierarchical ordering of the metro-politan society by class and gender. This prescribed social order when translated to the multi-racial world of colonial dependencies gave the accepted hierarchies of class and gender a significant racial dimension articulated in various ways according to the contingent circumstances of relations between the British colonisers and the resident population and its culture.[80] In the post-emancipation West Indies, the emergence of a three-tiered structure of a white elite, coloured middle class and black peasantry appeared to conform to the expectations of liberal reformers. They were suspicious of efforts to create a system that explicitly discriminated on grounds of race either by administrative policy or by special legislation. They rejected this tampering with the 'natural' order of liberal individualism, and appealed to the principle of equality of the law despite the inequities the law and jurisprudence placed on gender and class. Confident that persons with talent would rise to the top, the advocates of assimilation by and large expected that the 'races' would find their natural place in the social hierarchy.[81]

The second option the Victorians contemplated was that of separate development or global apartheid. The advocates of this view thought that the goal of assimilation was simply wrong-headed. The slave-traders, West Indian planters, and their defenders had first presented this position, but were simply overwhelmed by the evangelical and reforming energies organised and made potent by the anti-slavery movement between the 1770s and the 1850s. In the second half of the nineteenth century, the belief in assimilation lost favour and the case for separate development gained credibility until it attained the ascendant position. Within the metropolitan culture, the construc-tions of race by professional scientists secularised Victorian racial discourse and gave new authority to constructions placing humans as part of nature, subject to 'natural laws' constructed by scientists, and separated into defined racial types differentiated by biologically determined and unequal characteristics.

Much of the scholarship on Victorian race-thinking has focused on this development of scientific racism. As a result, the ideology of racism has its clearest, yet most restrictive, definition as a form of biological determinism. This well-established historical narrative will be reconsidered in Part II of this book. Some attention needs to be paid to differing views among scientists about their conceptions about race, and to the chronology of the popularisation of scientific racism which was more concurrent with the new imperialism of post-1870 than is sometimes claimed. Within this revised chronology, the institutionalised inequalities in multi-racial post-slave societies, the last stages of the cultural encounter and colonial conquest of indigenous peoples, and the administrative structures and social conventions that developed in colonial regimes in Asia and Africa clearly informed the scientific discourse. This broader context makes problematic the definition of racist ideology as being dependent on ideas of biological determinism, for constructions of race and race relations never relied solely on the ideas or authority of science. Constructions of race gained their hegemonic status from the particular historical context of the second half of the nineteenth century, and their power and utility from the ambiguous mix of science and culture. Out of this toxic mix, visions of separate development gained the ascendancy over the older doctrines of assimilation.

By the beginning of the twentieth century, various commentators had little doubt that the older liberal imperial project of assimilation should be rejected and a new direction of separate development should guide thinking about Britain's imperial and global role. Writing in 1910, Lord Cromer sought to explain why assimilation had been a more marked feature of ancient as distinct from modern empires. He observed that the British in 'habits are insular, and our social customs render us ... somewhat unduly exclusive.' Nonetheless, according to Cromer, the failure of assimilation in Asia and Africa was not simply due to British attitudes. In contrast to the Romans, the British had taken on a far greater task in ruling peoples of vastly different cultures. Consequently, assimilation had failed in the past and would fail in the future: 'There has been no thorough fusion, no real assimilation between the British and their alien subjects, and, so far as we can now predict, the future will in this respect be but a repetition of the past.'[82] Cromer's views grew out of his experience in India and Egypt and his own autocratic style of administration, but his rejection of the assimilating cultural imperialism of the past also accommodated a new more sophisticated cultural relativism.

With increased interest in and understanding of non-European

[41]

cultures, traditions, and social and political practices, there developed a more relativistic stance which cautioned against the ethnocentric and destructive impact of the assimilating efforts of missionaries and philanthropists. Spokespersons for this position were largely contemptuous of western-educated Asians and Africans, and praised those indigenous peoples and customs least affected by western influences.[83] On the other hand, this cultural relativism was tied to policies of colonial development that left political direction in the hands of colonial administrators and economic policy in the hands of traders and investors. Together they instituted policies in the administration of justice, in the limits placed on the participation of the governed in the political process, and in the implementation of labour codes that contravened British practice. These policies of separate development were defended by imperial advocates such as Benjamin Kidd, E. D. Morel and Mary Kingsley. In South Africa, modernising liberals, influenced by the experience of the Southern United States and anxious to protect African culture through reserve lands, defended a policy of segregation. In West Africa, cultural relativism provided a defence of the forms of separate development which ultimately materialised through the practical experience of colonial administration in Lugard's ideas of trusteeship and indirect rule.[84]

The cultural relativist rejection of assimilation and defence of separate development took place within the context of a more aggressive, exclusionary racialism. The new young men of the 1890s, who thought of themselves as espousing a 'new humanitarianism' free of the cant of out-moded philanthropy, willingly advocated the exercise of imperial power as the means to fulfil the national destiny. George W. Steevens, a journalist for Harmondsworth's *Daily Mail* and author of popular travel and war stories in colonial settings, contrasted his 'new humanitarianism' with the hypocrisy of the old:

> The naked principle of our rule is that our way is the way that shall be walked in let it cost what pain it may. Meantime our humanitarians preach exactly the contrary. And if they are right we have two courses before us. Either we may go on, as now, conducting our empire by force, and pretend that we do so by charity and meekness; or we may cease to conduct it by force, and try to do so by charity and meekness. In the first case we shall finally engrain hypocrisy as the dominant trait of our national character; in the second we shall very soon have no national character or national self-esteem or national existence to lose.[85]

Steevens' unreserved advocacy of force in fulfilment of the imperial mission was in keeping with the reassessment of the humanitarian causes of the past and with the expression of a new strident racialism in both the elite and the popular press.

[42]

To some degree, Steevens' 'new humanitarianism' reaffirmed the older polarities of Thomas Carlyle, whose attack on West Indian blacks and British abolitionists identified sentiment and philanthropy with women's work and feminine weakness, and in contrast associated force and action, including Governor Eyre's use of martial law in Jamaica, with white masculine virtues.[86] J. A. Froude, Carlyle's friend and acolyte, gave his mentor's opinions a new currency both in his historical writing on Britain's imperial past and, more specifically, in his *English in the West Indies*, an account of his brief tour of the Caribbean published in 1888. Froude was no lover of democracy in general and specifically warned of the dangers of black self-government in the West Indies. In Froude's view, the rights of active citizenship had to accord with the dictates of nature, and nature had decreed that such rights belonged exclusively by race, gender and class to white males. Observing that 'Nature had made us unequal, and Acts of Parliament cannot make us equal', Froude declared that 'Some must lead and some must follow'. In defence of this principle, he observed: 'There may be authority, yet not slavery: a soldier is not a slave, a sailor is not a slave, a child is not a slave, a wife is not a slave; yet they may not live by their own wills or emancipate themselves at their own pleasure from positions in which nature has placed them, or into which they have themselves voluntarily entered.'[87] Froude declared that black West Indians were 'not yet disobedient children', but self-government would only return them to the savagery of their African ancestry 'from which the slave trade was the beginning of their emancipation'.[88] In the 1840s or even the 1860s, these views belonged to acerbic sages aiming to excite controversy; by the 1890s professional journalists felt free to express similar opinions for the breakfast reading of respectable middle-class men and women.

Without fear of a lingering humanitarian critique and without concern for unsettling genteel decorum, many late Victorian and Edwardian journalists expressed an unreserved contempt for alien races and an uninhibited conceit in their sense of white masculine superiority. This changed sense of the proprieties of racial discourse from the gentler and perhaps hypocritical language of their early and mid-Victorian forebears grew out of the experience of colonialism and the observation of racial conflict in which privileged whites defended their interests against the assertions of subjugated non-Europeans. The new language made a much more direct appeal to white male phobias about a presumed sexual threat black males posed to white females, who were themselves subordinate to and possessed by their white fathers and husbands.

These more explicit sexual references were particularly evident in the reassessment of the consequences of emancipation in the United States, but over time were applied to racial conflicts within the British Empire, and even to the imagined danger of an alien immigration into the United Kingdom. Out of their own presuppositions and from their white American sources, British journalists commonly accepted the view that Reconstruction and its efforts at black political emancipation had failed. In 1889, the *Standard*, a Conservative morning newspaper, used the occasion of a political crisis in Haiti to warn of the dangers of a return to savage African conditions in the British West Indies and in the Southern United States. From its American sources, the *Standard* repeated the familiar stereotype of 'that strange mixture of indolence, childishness, and latent ferocity which is the essential characteristic of the Negro'. Asserting that the former slaves had degenerated since emancipation, the *Standard* informed its readers that African-Americans had little regard for chastity and that Southern white women were 'circumscribed in their comings and goings, and [had] to practise as much caution, as if they were actually in an enemy's country'. Such assaults inflamed white opinion and made the outbreak of lynchings in the South shocking but comprehensible.[89]

By the 1890s, the prejudices of the white South had become the commonplace truths of respectable British newspapers. In a more extended review of race relations in the Southern States, *The Times* commissioned W. Laird Clowes to tour the South, and published his report as ten letters between November 1890 and January 1891. White Southerners had paid for their loss in the Civil War and for their sin of slavery by Reconstruction in which 'the black, ignorant, unscrupulous, dissolute, and corrupt, was to enslave them'. Advising English readers that they had little appreciation of the conditions of 'the long-suffering South', Clowes claimed: 'the race prejudice which is prevalent with all white races, ... has kept the Anglo-Saxon race pure and has preserved its institutions, civilisation, and free government'.[90] Describing a state of race war in the Southern States comparable to the Bulgarian atrocities, *The Times'* correspondent observed: 'no white woman is safe, from hour to hour, in those black country districts. It was because the race war on the black man's side is waged largely, though not exclusively, against the whites who are least capable of self-protection, and whose safety is held most precious by those to whom they are near and dear.'[91] By the beginning of the twentieth century, the lessons taught by white America had become commonplace and were applied not only to the mounting crisis in South Africa but even to the British Isles. In 1901, the *Spectator*, a Liberal Unionist weekly, addressed the issue of 'The Negro Problem in America' on the occasion of Theodore Roosevelt's invitation to Booker T. Washington to lunch at the White House. The

Spectator claimed that the President had erred in his invitation, 'because we do not believe that the recognition of a nonexistent equality between the races is the way to kill out the white prejudice against the black one'.[92] T. E. S. Scholes, a Jamaican medical doctor and missionary living in London and an outspoken critic of the pervasive racialism of the early twentieth century, claimed that influential British newspapers championed racial supremacy, and gave both the *Spectator* and the *Daily Telegraph* as examples.[93]

Such advocacy necessitated a reassessment of the legacy of the anti-slavery movement. On 29 August 1902, sixty-nine years after the act abolishing slavery had passed Parliament, the *Daily Telegraph*, a Unionist daily, reflected on the lessons learned since the days of Wilberforce. Citing the experience of the West Indies and the American South, and of colonialism in Africa in general and South Africa in particular, the newspaper asserted: 'The potential equality of the typical African with the white people, as we now know, never has existed, and never can exist. No black race is capable of assimilating the higher spirit or of mastering the political and economic mechanism of modern civilisation.'[94] As attentions turned to developments in South Africa, the British press proved as responsive to white South Africa as it had been to white America.

In 1907, Lord Elgin, the Colonial Secretary, asked Sir Charles Lucas, a senior colonial office civil servant, to write a discussion paper on 'the Native Races in the British Empire' in preparation for the forthcoming parliamentary debates on the reconstruction of the new South African Union.[95] Lucas, who had experience with the self-governing dominions' discriminatory policies on immigration, remained attached to the older gentlemanly ethos of mid-Victorian assimilating liberalism. In his paper, issued as a confidential print for the colonial office on 31 December 1907, Lucas recognised that newer, harsher views favoured a more exclusionary policy. These contending perspectives would be the focus of 'native policy' in the new South African Union, and he perceptively recognised that the outcome of this most complex of imperial problems would have broader implications for the entire empire.[96] Lucas contrasted his own, or what he called 'the traditional English view ... that colour shall not be a bar to citizenship; and that the goal to be aimed at is political equality of races' with the contrary doctrine of racial separation most clearly but not solely evident in the Transvaal.[97] Even in the Cape with its more liberal tradition, in the self-governing colonies generally, and within British public opinion as well, Lucas was aware that racial exclusiveness not assimilation was the dominant trend:

it seems to me that the attitude which is now openly and very generally adopted towards the coloured races, as regards their political status in the lands into which white men came and which they now consider their own is, I suppose, largely economic, but it is also part and parcel of a general tendency to racial exclusiveness. It is only another step, in lands where the coloured men are at home and hold their own numerically, to keep them as a separate element in the community and to oppose their rise to citizenship.[98]

To underscore the importance of the choices being negotiated for the new Union, he predicted that Africans 'must become ordinary citizens or they must become slaves'.[99]

Believing in assimilation to the universal norms of the British metropole, Lucas had no doubt that the long-term objective of policy should be equality of citizenship regardless of race. Not unlike the APS, his concern was to develop policy for the transition of Africans, coloureds and Indians to 'civilised' conditions requisite for equality of citizenship.[100] The most difficult, even intractable, political challenge, as Lucas observed, was to effect this transition in ways that would be acceptable to Boer and British settlers fearful that a black and brown majority would 'swamp the whites'.[101] Recognising the political weight behind a settlement between the two white communities to the exclusion of all others, he thought that the limited coloured franchise in Cape Colony needed to be protected, and despite the long-term risks, he was prepared to advocate setting aside native reserve lands as 'no more than a temporary makeshift, unsound in principle because stereotyping exclusiveness and non-citizenship'.[102] These reserve lands, under the governance of residents modelled on Malaysia, or with native chiefs as government officials modelled on Lugard's innovations in Nigeria, would serve to facilitate assimilation to civilised conditions.[103]

Lucas's gravest fear, and realistic forecast of a more likely outcome, was that native reserve lands would become permanent, would entrench separation and exclusion, and would make Africans a subordinate, oppressed class living under economic, political and legal conditions determined by a white electorate and its representatives.[104] Lucas's fears were soon realised. The new constitution of the Union of South Africa received approval from the Imperial Parliament in 1909, and subsequent South African legislation, most notably the Lands Act of 1913, instituted racial segregation in the law long before apartheid became the official state doctrine in 1948.

In retirement, Lucas became more reconciled to the power of white democracy as evident in the settlement of the South African Union and as expressed by the nationalism of the other self-governing dominions. In his comparison of the Roman and British empires, *Greater Rome and Greater Britain* published in 1912, he dismissed the 'mischievous characteristic of Englishmen at home to assume that the laws and institutions which are good for Englishmen in England must necessarily be good for all other races under all conditions', and in the task of ruling an empire noted: 'the British character has not brought any special power of assimilation'.[105] Adopting the new language of 'race instinct', Lucas affirmed that, unlike the Spanish Empire with its 'hybrid populations' and 'constant revolutions', British rule was based on 'the instinct for fair play, common sense, and practical constructiveness'. The colonised subjects of the dependencies had gained 'security for life and property, justice between man and man, immunity from extortion, law instead of caprice', and consequently the ruled had 'unmistakable evidence that they [had] derived material advantage from the rulers'.[106] Like J. R. Seeley before him, Lucas recognised there were two empires within one, and these two parts were 'mutually exclusive spheres, which may be distinguished as the sphere of rule and the sphere of settlement'. In the sphere of rule, in tropical lands with 'coloured races', the 'English' administered and ruled 'wholly alien peoples'.[107] In the sphere of settlement, white settlers, largely from the British Isles, reproduced British forms of self-governance, and retained links to the mother country through self-interest and patriotism based on ties of kinship, culture and race.[108] In the sphere of rule in crown colonies or other dependencies, colonial administrators ruled by a mix of force and good government.[109] According to Lucas's description, separate development had become institutionalised with the structure of the empire itself.

Lucas was not alone in reassessing past visions of assimilation. The failure to mobilise public support and to defend the interests of Africans and other persons of colour in South Africa between 1901 and 1910 led humanitarian lobby groups, most notably the newly amalgamated Anti-Slavery and Aborigines Protection Society, to reassess its long-standing commitment to assimilation and equality before the law.[110] In so far as the press was an indication of changing public attitudes, there was no doubt that the humanitarian agencies faced not only a less interested but a more hostile public. Already experienced in recounting white racial phobias from the Southern States, British newspapers, in the immediate aftermath of the creation of the self-governing union, publicised stories of a 'Black Peril' in South Africa.

According to some newspaper accounts the sexual threat of black males to white females had reached crisis proportions in South Africa. In 1911, the *Standard*, the *Daily Telegraph*, the *Daily Express*, and the *Star*, relying uncritically on their South African sources, reported that daily white women faced the 'Black Peril' in the new dominion and in its colonial neighbour, Rhodesia.[111] Alarmed by these South African reports, which in his view had all the signs of the racial hysteria and lynchings then common in the United States, W. T. Stead in a public letter to his white South African friends warned of the danger of failing to provide legal protection and due process for the African majority. From recent labour unrest in England and from reports of passive resistance by Indians in South Africa, he predicted, in 1911, that the white minority by its failure to provide fundamental legal rights could face a general strike by the black majority.[112]

The 'Black Peril', some journalists claimed, even threatened the peace and order of the British Isles. In May 1906, the *People's Journal* of Dundee headlined a special report on 'A "NEGRO" INVASION – Britain's New Racial Problem – White Women and Blacks.' The report described the marked increase in the number of blacks in London, in university towns and in ports. It traced this 'influx of "niggers"' to the Diamond Jubilee', and warned particularly of the danger threatening young British girls unaccustomed to the advances of black men. The reception Africans gained in Britain, the article claimed, led them to become dissatisfied and demand changes in South Africa. Under the headline of 'Objections to Niggers in Public Places', the paper advised its readers that 'So serious is the evil becoming that steps are soon to be taken to enlighten the public on this matter, and returned colonists are arranging concerted action by way of protests against the presence of negroes of whatever rank in restaurants, public vehicles, and in general assemblies.'[113] The special report concluded by advocating racial exclusion as the only solution to the black presence. This special report in the *People's Journal* would appear to have had a South African origin, but there is evidence that such prejudices were more evident in the United Kingdom. T. E. S. Scholes reported that despite a reputed absence of prejudice in Britain, black visitors and residents more frequently faced discrimination.[114] Even those with a reputation as defenders of Africans were not free of phobias about the 'Black Peril'. E. D. Morel, a leader in the campaign against the atrocities of King Leopold's Congo and a defender of indigenous tradition and practice in West Africa, led the cry of 'Horror on the Rhine' when the French used African troops in Germany in 1920.[115]

Press reports of the 'Black Peril' were part of the effort to excite fears of immigration and its accompanying racial contamination within the British Isles. This panic about immigration chiefly involved European Jewish immigrants subjected to anti-Semitic stereotyping and new restrictive immigration laws. Fears about immigration grew out of a broader social pessimism which linked the decline in British power overseas with urban degeneracy within the metropolitan society. Such pessimism had a significant imperial and racial dimension. In 1893, Charles Pearson warned of the threat that socialism and feminism posed to the manly and competitive qualities of an imperial race. He foresaw a world where the demographic preponderance and political awakening of the peoples of Asia and Africa would end European dominance:

> The day will come, and perhaps is not far distant, when the European observer will look round to see the globe girdled with a continuous zone of the black and yellow races, no longer too weak for aggression or under tutelage, but independent, or practically so, in government, monopolising trade of their own regions, and circumscribing the industry of the European.[116]

Pearson saw that this transformation would have an impact within Europe, as citizens of colour from these states now equal in the international arena would 'throng the English turf, or the salons of Paris, and ... be admitted into intermarriage'. This humiliation would mark the end of the supremacy of 'the Aryan races', he claimed; 'We shall wake up to find ourselves elbowed and hustled, and perhaps even trust aside by peoples whom we looked down upon as servile, and thought of as bound always to administer to our needs.'[117] Pearson's sole consolation was his own mortality, as he anticipated these changes would not happen in his own lifetime.

Pearson's pessimism made a strong impact upon B. L. Putnam Weale, a pseudonym for Bertram Lennox Simpson, who published *The Conflict of Colour* in 1910. Writing from Beijing, he paid particular attention to the ascendancy of Japan in Asia, to the unrest among the peoples of China, and to the signs of nationalist insurgency in India and Egypt. Despite the objections of his black correspondents, he identified Africans and their descendants as in a state of 'arrested development', but nonetheless differences of race created conflict in both Africa and America. He predicted a black challenge to white supremacy out of a transatlantic coalition of Africans and their New World descendants, and within Africa from an Islamic alliance of Africans and Arabs. Although still using commonplace racist stereotypes, Weale did not fully endorse Pearson's pessimism, and offered a liberal solution to racial conflict.

Believing that racial prejudice was a natural instinct expressed in the discriminatory policies of the white dominions, Weale foresaw a new regional separation and global balance of power in accordance with the racial divisions of the world's peoples. In this new multi-racial, separate but more equal world order, the task was to come to some new understanding and mutual respect based on a measure of devolution of political power and resistance to the appeals of protectionism. Weale's fear was that existing colonial policies and race relations, products of the expediency of cabinet ministers and bureaucrats, and dependent on the crude exercise of power, profoundly alienated non-European peoples and created the possibility of global racial conflict. In this light, he called upon his readers to recognise that 'never [had] there been any period of the world's history in which racial problems were invested with such consummate interest as they now [were]'. Since Britain's political and economic ascendency from the eighteenth century rested on colonial possessions in the Americas, Asia and Africa, Weale forewarned: 'the problem of colour becomes finally an almost British problem', and consequently 'the question of colour is the rock on which the Empire must split, or on which may be builded [sic] the greatest edifice the world has ever seen.'[118] Like Charles Dilke before him, Weale saw a special role for Britain and its empire in relation to non-European peoples. In contrast to the elder statesman's continued trust in assimilation, Weale sought to reconcile separate development with a new mutuality between races and nations under the continued economic and political leadership of Great Britain.

The older advocates of assimilation and the younger and ascendant advocates of separate development shared a common belief in the superiority of British civilisation. A more comprehensive narrative of race needs to include both these visions, but it also needs to recognise that the struggle of ideas in the contested territory of race was not only an unequal struggle but also one that became more unequal over time. A transformation in the production of knowledge, especially the institutional basis for its production, gave less space for the amateur opinions and lobbying of philanthropists, dissenters and radicals. Correspondingly, this transformation gave enhanced authority to professional experts. Among those speaking with professional authority were scientists attached to established professions and academic disciplines such as medicine and biology, and to the newer fields such as anthropology, psychology, geography, and in its modern academic form, history. In some form all these fields used the language of 'race' and 'race relations'. The power and utility of this language lay in its ambiguous, but nevertheless potent and pervasive, mix of science and culture.

Notes

1 British and Foreign Aborigines Protection Society (APS), 'Address', *Regulations of the Society and Address* (London: 1837), p. 3.
2 APS, 'Address', p. 4.
3 *Aborigines' Friend* (*AF*), new series, 6 (April 1901), 3–5.

4 For a definition of imperialism stressing the exercise of power in expansion see P. J. Cain and A. G. Hopkins, *British Imperialism: Innovation and Expansion, 1688–1914* (London: Longman, 1993), pp. 42–6.

5 Walter Bagehot, *Physics and Politics* [1872] in *The Collected Works of Walter Bagehot, Volume VII: Political Essays* (Aylesbury, Bucks.: The Economist, 1974), p. 44, see also p. 135.

6 Bagehot, p. 45; on colonial warfare and race-thinking see James Belich, *The Victorian Interpretation of Racial Conflict: The Maori, the British, and the New Zealand Wars* (Montreal and Kingston: McGill Queens, 1989), pp. 322–7.

7 Ronald Segal, *The Race War* (Harmondsworth: Penguin, 1967); in an earlier statement of the idea if not the phrase 'survival of the fittest', Spencer discussed the colonial encounter between aboriginal peoples and Europeans (H. Spencer, 'A theory of population deduced from the general law of animal fertility', *Westminster Review* [1852] in *Herbert Spencer on Social Evolution*, ed. J. D. Y. Peel (Chicago, IL: University of Chicago Press, 1972), pp. 33–7; Greta Jones, *Social Darwinism and English Thought: The Interaction between Biological and Social Theory* (Brighton: Harvester, 1980), pp. 42–4, 157–9.

8 Benjamin Kidd, *Social Evolution* (New York: Macmillan, 1895), p. 347.

9 Benjamin Kidd, *The Control of the Tropics* (London: Macmillan, 1898), pp. 53–4, see also pp. 80–91, and *Social Evolution*, pp. 338–49.

10 Michael Adas, *Machines as the Measure of Men: Science, Technology, and Ideologies of Western Dominance* (Ithaca, NY, and London: Cornell University Press, 1989), pp. 199–241; M. P. Cowen and R. W. Shenton, *Doctrines of Development* (London: Routledge, 1996); on imperial history and theories of development, A. G. Hopkins, 'Development and the utopian ideal, 1960–1999', in R. Winks (ed.), *Historiography*, Oxford History of the British Empire (OHBE) (Oxford: Oxford University Press, 1999), vol. 5, pp. 635–49.

11 Sir Richard Temple, 'Preface', *Asia* in *Stanford's Compendium of Geography and Travel* (London: Edward Stanford, 1882), p. xv.

12 Temple, 'Preface', p. xii.

13 Cain and Hopkins, *British Imperialism*, pp. 45–6.

14 These themes were commonplace among promoters of imperialism, e.g., Lord Rosebery's address to the students of the University of Glasgow, 16 November 1900 reprinted in *Miscellanies: Literary and Historical* (London: Hodder and Stoughton, 1921), vol. 2, pp. 229–63, and Rider Haggard, *Rural England* (1902); H. J. Field, *Toward a Programme of Imperial Life: The British Empire at the Turn of the Century* (Westport, CT: Greenwood, 1982); M. J. Weiner, *English Culture and the Decline of the Industrial Spirit* (Cambridge: Cambridge University Press, 1981).

15 Bayly, *Modern World*, pp. 432–50.

16 Bayly, *Modern World*, pp. 148–69.

17 John Darwin, *The Empire Project: The Rise and Fall of the British World-System, 1830–1970* (Cambridge: Cambridge University Press, 2009), pp. 69–75.

18 Parsons, 'African participation', pp. 257–85; T. C. McCaskie, 'Cultural encounters: Britain and Africa in the nineteenth century', in Andrew Porter (ed.) *The Nineteenth Century*, OHBE, vol. 3, pp. 644–89, reprinted in Morgan and Hawkins (eds) *Black Experience*, pp. 166–93; an older historiography emphasised the crisis of the periphery but gave less scope for the agency of colonised peoples: R. Robinson, 'Non-European foundations of European imperialism', pp. 117–42; A. E. Atmore, 'The extra-European foundations of British imperialism: Towards a reassessment', in C. C. Eldridge (ed.), *British Imperialism in the Nineteenth Century* (London: Macmillan, 1984), pp. 106–25; D. K. Fieldhouse, *Economics and Empire, 1830–1914* (London: Weidenfeld and Nicolson, 1973), pp. 459–77.

19 Richard Price, *Making Empire: Colonial Encounters and the Creation of Imperial Rule in Nineteenth-Century Africa* (Cambridge: Cambridge University Press, 2008); Andrew Porter, *Religion versus Empire? British Protestant Missionaries and Overseas Expansion, 1700–1914* (Manchester: Manchester University Press, 2004), pp. 163–90; Susan Thorne, *Congregational Mission and the Making of an Imperial*

Culture in Nineteenth-Century England (Stanford, CA: Stanford University Press, 1999); Lorimer, *Colour, Class.*

20 Darwin, *Empire Project,* pp. 1–20; see also Laura Tabili, 'A homogeneous society? Britain's internal others", 1800 – present', in Hall and Rose (eds) *At Home with the Empire,* pp. 53–76.

21 A. P. Thornton, *The Imperial Idea and Its Enemies* (London: Macmillan, 1959); C. C. Eldridge, *England's Mission: The Imperial Idea in the Age of Gladstone and Disraeli, 1868–1880* (London: Macmillan, 1973), pp. 234–55; Miles Taylor, 'Imperialism and libertas? Rethinking the radical critique of imperialism during the nineteenth century', *Journal of Imperial and Commonwealth History,* 19 (1991), 1–23; Stephen Howe, *Anticolonialism in British Politics,* pp. 27–52; Nicholas Owen, 'Critics of empire in Britain', in Judith Brown and Wm. Roger Louis (eds) *The Twentieth Century,* OHBE, vol. 4, pp. 188–92. See also Chapter 7.

22 Adas, *Machines,* p. 268.

23 J. R. Seeley, *The Expansion of England* [1883], ed. John Gross (London and Chicago, IL: University of Chicago, 1971), pp. 12–13, 189–200, 239–41; Bernard Porter, *The Absent-Minded Imperialists* (Oxford: Oxford University Press, 2004) has challenged the claim of the empire's formative influence of British society by cultural and post-colonial analysts; for alternative and critical views see Andrew Thompson, *The Empire Strikes Back: The Impact of Imperialism on Britain from the Mid-Nineteenth Century* (London: Longman, 2005); Catherine Hall and Sonya Rose, 'Introduction: being at home with the empire', *At Home with the Empire,* pp. 1–31; Darwin, *Empire Project,* p. 15.

24 Antonio Gramsci, *Selections for the Prison Notebooks,* ed. and trans., Quintin Hoare and Geoffrey Nowell Smith (New York, International Publishers, 1971), pp. 416–25, 447–8; Walter L. Adamson, *Hegemony and Revolution: A Study of Antonio Gramsci's Theory of Hegemony and Revolution* (Berkeley and Los Angeles: University of California, 1980), p. 149; Joseph V. Femia, *Gramsci's Political Thought* (Oxford: Clarendon, 1981), pp. 43–5.

25 Seeley, *Expansion,* pp. 151–2.

26 Hall, *Civilising Subjects;* Hugh Tinker, *A New System of Slavery: the Export of Indian Labour Overseas, 1830–1920* (London: Institute of Race Relations and Oxford University Press, 1974); Kay Saunders (ed.), *Indentured Labour in the British Empire, 1834–1920* (London: Croom Helm, 1984); Kevin Grant, *A Civilised Savagery.* See also Chapter 7.

27 Seeley, *Expansion,* p. 12.

28 C. P. Lucas, *Greater Rome and Greater Britain* (Oxford: Clarendon, 1912), pp. 162, 176.

29 Charles Dilke, *Greater Britain: A Record of Travel in English-Speaking Countries during 1866 and 1867* (New York: Harper, 1869), pp. 481–2, 529; Seeley, *Expansion,* pp. 216–20.

30 *AF,* new series, 5 (May 1897), 143–60, a special meeting on the decline in public support.

31 Susan Bayly, 'The evolution of colonial cultures: nineteenth-century Asia', in Porter (ed.), OHBE, vol. 3, pp. 447–69; Adas, *Machines,* p. 268, doubts if most colonised populations even knew of let alone consented to the idea of the civilising mission, and for this reason rejects the use of Gramsci's concept of hegemony in colonial relationships.

32 Douglas Hay, 'Property, authority and the criminal law', in D. Hay, P. Linebaugh, J. G. Rule, E. P. Thompson, C. Winslow (eds), *Albion's Fatal Tree* (Harmondsworth: Penguin, 1977), pp. 16–64; E. P. Thompson, *Whigs and Hunters* (Harmondsworth: Penguin, 1977), pp. 21–4, 219–69; Douglas Lorimer, 'Black slaves and English liberty: a re-examination of racial slavery in England', *Immigrants and Minorities,* 3 (1984), 121–50; R. Anstey, *The Atlantic Slave Trade and British Abolition* (London: Macmillan, 1975); D. B. Davis, *The Problem of Slavery in the Age of Revolution* (Ithaca, NY: Cornell, 1975), pp. 373–85, 427–53; on hegemony and the rule of law see also Eugene Genovese, *Roll, Jordan, Roll: The World the Slaves Made* (New

York: Pantheon, 1974), pp. 25–31. In a much broader scope, Robin Blackburn, *The Overthrow of Colonial Slavery, 1776–1848* (London: Verso, 1988), deals with the contradictions between capitalism, slavery and abolition.

33 Andrew Porter, 'Introduction', in A. Porter (ed.), OHBE, vol. 3, pp. 19–25.

34 The National Archive, London (TNA), CO886/1 Dominions No. 1. Confidential. The Self-Governing Dominions and Coloured Immigration, July 1908; and Dominions No. 2. Very Confidential. Suggestions as to Coloured Immigration into the Self-Governing Dominions, July 1908; CO886/4 Dominions No. 26. Confidential. The Self-Governing Dominions and Coloured Immigration, July, 1910; Huttenback, *Racism and Empire*; Lake and Reynolds, *Drawing the Global*.

35 Bickford-Smith, 'Betrayal', pp. 192–227; J. F. Ade Ajayi, *Christian Missions in Nigeria: The Making of a New Elite, 1841–91* (London: Longmans Green, 1965); A. E. Ayendele, *The Missionary Impact on Modern Nigeria, 1842–1914* (London: Longman, 1966).

36 Roy Jenkins, 'Dilke, Sir Charles Wentworth, second baronet (1843–1911)', *New Oxford Dictionary of National Biography (NODNB)* (2008); Roy Jenkins, *Sir Charles Dilke: A Victorian Tragedy* (London: Fontana, 1968).

37 Duncan Bell, *The Idea of Greater Britain: Empire and the Future of the World Order, 1860–1900* (Princeton, NJ: Princeton University Press, 2007); E. H. H. Green, 'The political economy of empire, 1880–1914', in Porter (ed.), OHBE, vol. 3, pp. 356–7, 365–7; Reginald Horsman, *Race and Manifest Destiny: The Origins of American Anglo-Saxon Racism* (Cambridge, MA: Harvard University Press, 1981); Richard Koebner and Helmut Dan Schmidt, *Imperialism: The Story and Significance of a Political Word, 1840–1960* (Cambridge: Cambridge University Press, 1964), pp. 87–91.

38 S. Gwynn and G. M. Tuckwell, *Life of Sir Charles Dilke* (London: John Murray, 1917), vol. 2, pp. 368–86.

39 Dilke, *Greater Britain*, pp. 42–6.

40 Dilke, *Greater Britain*, pp. 98–100.

41 Dilke, *Greater Britain*, p. 192.

42 Dilke, *Greater Britain*, pp. 32–4, 291–2, 391, for examples of this persistent theme.

43 Dilke, *Greater Britain*, p. 194, see also p. 545.

44 Dilke, *Greater Britain*, pp. 545–6.

45 British Library (BL), Add MS 43897, fols 2–4. Dilke Papers. J. S. Mill to Charles Dilke, 9 February 1869.

46 Jenkins, *Dilke*, pp. 42–4.

47 Dilke, *Greater Britain*, p. 31.

48 Dilke, *Greater Britain*, pp. 32–5, and *Problems of Greater Britain* (London: Macmillan, 1890), vol. 1, pp. 173–8, and vol. 2, pp. 195–208.

49 Dilke, *Greater Britain*, pp. 92–3, 97–100.

50 Dilke, *Greater Britain*, pp. 97, 271–8; *Problems*, vol. 1, p. 414–15, 428.

51 Dilke, *Greater Britain*, pp. 193–4, 301–2.

52 Dilke, *Greater Britain*, pp. 332–6; *Problems*, vol. 2, pp. 305, 311.

53 Dilke, *Greater Britain*, pp. 291–2, 398–401.

54 Dilke, *Greater Britain*, pp. 414–25, 447–9, 481–2.

55 Dilke, *Greater Britain*, p. 519.

56 Dilke, *Greater Britain*, pp. 481–2, see also pp. 470–4; *Problems*, vol. 2, pp. 12–14, 38–43.

57 Dilke, *Greater Britain*, p. 520.

58 Dilke, *Greater Britain*, p. 528; Koebner, *Imperialism*, pp. 23–4.

59 Dilke, *Greater Britain*, pp. 474, 529.

60 Dilke, *Greater Britain*, pp. 422–3, 491–3, 521–9.

61 Dilke, *Problems*, vol. 2, pp. 93–104, 114–47; see also Dilke, *The British Empire* (London: Chatto and Windus, 1899), pp. 18–32.

62 Dilke, *Greater Britain*, p. 530.

63 Dilke, *Greater Britain*, p. 530.

64 Dilke, *Greater Britain*, p. 545.

65 Dilke, *Greater Britain*, p. 546.
66 H. C. Swaisland, 'The Aborigines Protection Society and British Southern and West Africa', Oxford DPhil (1968), p. 396.
67 Dilke, *Problems*, vol. 2, p. 581.
68 Dilke, *Problems*, vol. 2, pp. 158–72; see also *The British Empire*, pp. 114–19.
69 Dilke, *Problems*, vol. 1, p. 574; see also 517–34, 563–78.
70 Dilke, *Greater Britain*, p. 525.
71 Seeley, *Expansion*, pp. 140–1, 147–8, 151–2.
72 Kidd, *Control of the Tropics*, pp. 23–4, 29–30.
73 Sir Evelyn Baring, 'The government of subject races', in *Political and Literary Essays, 1908–1913* (London: Macmillan, 1913), pp. 20–8, 50–3.
74 BL, Add MS 43920 fols 142–5. Dilke Papers. H. M. Hyndman to Sir Charles Dilke, 25 August 1908.
75 L. T. Hobhouse, *Democracy and Reaction* [1904] ed. P. F. Clarke (Brighton: Harvester 1972), p. 36, and pp. 13–57.
76 G. B. Shaw (ed.), *Fabianism and Empire: A Manifesto of the Fabian Society* (London: Grant Edwards, 1900), pp. 15–16.
77 J. Ramsay MacDonald, *Labour and Empire* [1907], reprint in *From Serfdom to Socialism; Labour and the Empire*, ed. Robert F. Dowse (Warbury, NJ: Associated Universities, 1974), pp. 14–15, 102–3; on radical tradition and empire see Taylor, 'Imperialism and libertas?', 1–23.
78 The question of the precise relationship between colonial slavery, industrial capitalism, and the abolitionist movement is itself the subject of an immense historiographical literature debating the original thesis of Eric Williams, *Capitalism and Slavery* (1944); for example: David Brion Davis, *Slavery and Human Progress* (London: Oxford University Press, 1984), pp. 168–226; Blackburn, *Overthrow of Colonial Slavery*, pp. 419–72; Barbara L. Solow and Stanley L. Engerman, (eds) *British Capitalism and Caribbean Slavery: The Legacy of Eric Williams* (Cambridge: Cambridge University Press, 1987); Cedric J. Robinson, 'Capitalism, slavery, and bourgeois historiography,' *History Workshop Journal*, 23 (1987), 122–40.
79 Most famously Lecky in his *History of European Morals*, cited by Kidd as proof of altruism in *Social Evolution*, p. 49, see also pp. 178–81, 325–35; Both Seeley, *Expansion*, pp. 108–9, 239, and Baring, 'Government of subject races', pp. 10–18, emphasise philanthropy as an imperial motive.
80 Catherine Hall, 'Of gender and empire: reflections on the nineteenth century', in P. Levine (ed.), *Gender and Empire*, OHBE Companion Series (Oxford: Oxford University Press, 2004), pp. 46–76; Thorne, *Congregational Mission*; Lorimer, *Colour, Class*.
81 Raymond T. Smith, 'Race and class in the post-emancipation Caribbean', in Robert Ross (ed.), *Racism and Colonialism* (The Hague: Martinus Nijhoff, 1982), pp. 93–119; W. A. Green, 'Was British emancipation a success? The abolitionist perspective', in David Richardson (ed.), *Abolition and its Aftermath: The Historical Context, 1790–1916* (London: Frank Cass, 1985), pp. 183–202; Foner, *Nothing but Freedom*, pp. 14–38; Davis, *Slavery and Human Progress*, pp. 217–26; Lorimer, *Colour, Class*, pp. 122–8; on Cape liberalism, Stanley Trapido, '"The friends of the natives": merchants, peasants and the political and ideological structure of liberalism at the Cape, 1854–1910', in Shula Marks and Anthony Atmore (eds) *Economy and Society in Pre-Industrial South Africa* (London: Longman, 1980), pp. 247–74.
82 Evelyn Baring, Earl of Cromer, *Ancient and Modern Imperialism* (London: John Murray, 1910), pp. 73, 88–90.
83 Peter Burroughs, 'Institutions of empire', in Porter (ed.), OHBE, vol. 3, pp. 182–3.
84 Bernard Porter, *Critics of Empire: British Radical Attitudes to Colonialism in Africa* (London: Macmillan, 1968); Mamdani, *Citizen and Subject*; Cell, *Highest Stage of White Supremacy*; William Beinhart and Saul DuBow (eds), *Segregation and Apartheid in Twentieth-Century South Africa* (New York: Routledge, 1995); Mary Kingsley, *Travels in West Africa* [1897] (London: Virago, 1982), pp. 653–80; Rich, *Race and Empire*, pp. 29–39.
85 George W. Steevens, *Things Seen* quoted in Field, *Programme of Imperial Life*, p.

187 (see also pp. 88–93).

86 Catherine Hall, 'Competing masculinities: Thomas Carlyle, John Stuart Mill and the case of Governor Eyre', *White, Male and Middle-Class: Explorations in Feminism and History* (New York: Routledge, 1992), pp. 255–95.

87 J. A. Froude, *The English in the West Indies* (London: 1888), p. 235 (see also pp. 49–51, 79–81, 98–9, 348–9); also his *Oceana* (London: 1886), pp. 153, 391–2; W. H. Dunn, *James Anthony Froude, a Biography* (Oxford: Oxford University Press, 1963), vol. 2, pp. 314–16, 613.

88 Froude, *English in the West Indies*, p. 236; for contemporary criticism of Froude see: George Murray, 'Two voyages to the West Indies,' *The Academy*, 33 (February 1888), 108; N. Darnell Davis, *Mr. Froude's Negrophobia* (London: 1888).

89 'The relapse of the negro', *Standard* (20 September 1889), 3a; the editorial writer may have been Robert Brown, a journalist for the *Standard* and the author of popular geographic surveys promoting colonialism and racialism (see Chapter 4).

90 W. Laird Clowes, *Black America: A Study of the Ex-Slave and his Late Master* [1891] (Westport, CT: Negro Universities, 1970), p. 72 (also pp. vii–iii, 16–17, 31).

91 Clowes, *Black America*, pp. 130–2.

92 'The negro problem in America', *Spectator* (26 October 1901), 595–6.

93 T. E. S. Scholes, *Glimpses of Past Ages* (London: John Long, 1908), vol. 2, pp. 230–2.

94 'The yellow and black difficulty', *Daily Telegraph* (29 August 1902), 6g.

95 R. Hyam, *Elgin and Churchill at the Colonial Office, 1905–1908: The Watershed of the Empire-Commonwealth* (London: Macmillan, 1968), pp. 367–8.

96 TNA, CO885/19. Miscellaneous. No. 217. Confidential. Native Races in the British Empire [C. P. L.] (31 December 1907); Robin Butlin, 'Lucas, Sir Charles Prescott Lucas (1853–1931)', *NODNB* (2004–6).

97 TNA, CO885/19, p. 26.

98 TNA, CO885/19, p. 27.

99 TNA, CO885/19, p. 27.

100 Anticipating the end of the South African War and the need to address post-war reconstruction, as early as 1900, the APS issued a 'Charter of Native Rights' including a transition to civilised status, APS [H. R. Fox Bourne], *The Native Question in South Africa* (London, 1900). See also Chapter 7.

101 TNA, CO885/19, p. 10.

102 TNA, CO885/19, p. 12.

103 TNA, CO885/19, pp. 11–16.

104 TNA, CO885/19, p. 26. See also Chapter 6.

105 Lucas, *Greater Rome*, pp. 161–2.

106 Lucas, *Greater Rome*, pp. 162–3; on 'race instinct', pp. 106, 108, 172.

107 Lucas, *Greater Rome*, p. 41; Lucas's ideas about empire were strongly influenced by Seeley; both men lectured at the Working Men's College, Great Ormond Street, London (Butlin, *NODNB*).

108 Lucas, *Greater Rome*, pp. 165–72.

109 Lucas, *Greater Rome*, p. 161.

110 See Chapter 7.

111 *Standard* (25 May 1911); *Daily Telegraph* (6 June 1911); *Daily Express* (30 June 1911); *Star* (26 August 1911); on the analysis of 'Black Peril' see Ann Laura Stoler, *Carnal Knowledge and Imperial Power: Race and the Intimate in Colonial Rule* (Los Angeles, CA: University of California Press, 2002), pp. 58–60.

112 'To My White Friends and Readers in Africa – A Frank and Friendly Open Letter by W. T. Stead', *Review of Reviews*, 44 (July–December 1911), 385–7.

113 *People's Journal* (Dundee), 12 May 1906, RH, Brit. Emp. S18. Anti-Slavery Papers. J1. APS newspaper clippings, p. 87.

114 Scholes, *Glimpses*, vol. 2, pp. 232–6.

115 E. D. Morel, *Horror on the Rhine* (London: Union for Democratic Control, 1920); Catherine A. Cline, *E. D. Morel, 1873–1924: The Strategies of Protest* (Belfast: Blackstaff, 1980), pp. 126–8; Robert C. Reinders, 'Racialism on the left: E. D. Morel and the "Black Horror on the Rhine",' *International Review of Social History*, 13

(1968); Fryer, *Staying Power*, pp. 316–19.
116 Charles H. Pearson, *National Life and Character: A Forecast* (London: Macmillan, 1893), p. 84; Lake and Reynolds, *Drawing the Global*, pp. 75–94.
117 Pearson, *National Life*, p. 85.
118 B. L. Putnam Weale [Bertram Lennox Simpson], *The Conflict of Colour: Being a Detailed Examination of Racial Problems throughout the World with Special Reference to English-Speaking Peoples* (London: Macmillan, 1910), pp. 85, 320.

PART II

Science and race

CHAPTER THREE

From institutional foundations to applied anthropology, 1871–1914

Our historical and cultural studies of the construction of racial identities look back to nineteenth-century science for the foundations of modern racist ideology. In this narrative, a leading role is given to Victorian anatomists and anthropologists whose science constructed classifications of humans by racial type, and depicted these discrete races as having distinct and unequal characteristics determined by their biological inheritance. The elusive attempt to define 'racism' as an ideology often incorporates this narrative by making the belief in racial inequality dependent on a biological determinism derived from science. From the 1930s through to the 1950s developments in science, particularly human genetics and anthropology, led to a retreat from scientific racism and its biological determinism. After the Second World War, a new international consensus articulated in the United Nations declarations on human rights and racial equality, the process of decolonisation prompted by colonial nationalist revolt, and advances in civil rights spearheaded by the political mobilisation of racialised peoples promised a new order free of the racism of the past. Nonetheless, forms of racial inequality, discrimination, exclusion and oppression have persisted.[1]

The persistence of race as a marker of difference and inequality has led to a reconsideration of the linkages between race and culture. While 'race' as a biological category is largely discredited, differences, even essentialised characteristics, assigned to culture as a product of language and history retain their currency. Regardless of how race and culture in their more recent post-1960s manifestations are characterised, the received narrative explains the origins of modern racist ideology from schemes of racial classification originating in the eighteenth-century enlightenment. Although scientific racism was not fully articulated until the mid-nineteenth century, this history of ideas about race forms the basis for the claim that science represented the dominant mode of thinking about race. It is time to reconsider this narrative, for it misrepresents the Victorian discourse on race.

The linking of the ideology of racism with biological determinism is problematic, for ideas about a fixed biological inheritance are historically more limited in time than the constructions of racialised identities from the colonial encounter and its associated forms of racial prejudice, discrimination, conflict and oppression. The term 'racism' itself came into use in the 1930s in journalists' reports of Nazi ideology. The use of the term in academic circles gained currency with Ruth Benedict's *Race, Science and Politics* (1940), co-authored with Franz Boas to challenge Nazi race theories and to awaken social scientists to the presence of analogous myths built into their own disciplines.[2] In its original use, the linking of racism and biological determinism made sense, but with the retreat of scientific racism since the 1930s and the development of opposition to racial injustice, the definition and usage of the term 'racism' itself has been recast. 'Racism' has come to describe all those practices in which individuals and groups are racialised (i.e., given a racial identity), and subject to prejudice, discrimination, subordination, exclusion and other forms of oppression.

In this fashion, racism has been delinked from its scientific roots, and applied back in time to historic practices which may or may not be dependent on science or biological determinism. Just as the linkage between racism and biological determinism is problematic in the twenty-first century, so too is it problematic for earlier periods of history including the nineteenth century. Victorian scientists, even such a careful observer of wild species and the breeding of domesticated animals as Charles Darwin, had no adequate explanation of biological inheritance. Many eminent Victorians, for example Herbert Spencer in his evolutionary sociology and comparative psychology of racial types, accepted Lamarck's theory of the inheritance of acquired characteristics.[3] No doubt one can find Victorian scientists who advanced ideas about the biologically determined character of racial traits. Robert Knox, the Edinburgh anatomist, advocate of polygenesis and believer in transcendental anatomy – a deterministic doctrine if there ever was one – fits the mode. Nonetheless, Knox was an outsider, his ideas were contentious, and, as will be discussed below, historians and others have inflated his influence partly because he fits so well into the received narrative of scientific racism.

This received narrative has paid insufficient attention to two important elements in the scientific constructions of race: first, the ambiguous relationship of race and culture, and second, the imperial dimension of Victorian science. By focusing our attentions on the scientific aspect of the constructions of racial types – for example, comparative anatomy and its use of measurements of skull shape and size – we have over-looked the cultural component of those typologies. These racial types invariably had two components: their physical and anatomical features, and their cultural traits in terms of intelligence, personality, behaviour and values. The point of racial science was to build a correspondence between biological and cultural traits, and to claim that the former determined the latter. In this construction, the given or assumed, even unquestioned, knowledge was the non-biological or cultural part of the racial type, whereas the new knowledge scientists hoped to establish addressed the anatomical or biological traits and their significance. What was the source then of the scientists' untested knowledge of the non-biological features of the racial types? Obviously, the source was the common culture informed by the colonial encounter. Even more specifically, as recent scholarship has shown, knowledge within this common culture expressed the power of the coloniser over the colo-nised and incorporated the colonial rule of difference.[4] Here, bipolar constructions compared the native or colonial other with the self of the metropolitan British culture usually defined in terms of upper- or middle-class and invariably male caricatures epitomising Victorian values. In the high culture of scholarship, as Edward Said famously set out, orientalist discourse defined the occident by its contrast with the imagined orient.[5] In missionary and anti-slavery literature and polem-ics, evangelicals constructed bipolar images of black and white, sinner and Christian, and savage and civilised. The racial types constructed by the scientists incorporated these bipolar constructions, but by the mid-century made them secular. As a result, the black sinner as savage remained, but the evangelical promise of conversion was eliminated.[6] The literature of travel and exploration, sponsored by learned socie-ties such as the Royal Geographical Society, was accepted as scientific knowledge. These books and lectures contained much more in the way of descriptions of cultural differences than strictly biological knowl-edge. In more popular forms, the descriptions in science publications borrowed extensively from and were indistinguishable from travel literature.[7]

Consequently, not only is it difficult to specify when the racial types of the scientists were grounded specifically in a theory of biological determinism, but it is also misleading to draw a sharp distinction between scientific knowledge and the common culture of colonial discourse. Recent studies of the imperial dimensions of Victorian sci-ence have documented the role of scientific institutions and scientists in the administration and commerce of the empire.[8] Older treatments of the history of scientific racism explore the European ancestry of ideas of race, but outside the world of ideas they pay little attention to four centuries of the enslavement of Africans in the Americas, and in the development of nineteenth-century race-thinking they pay insufficient attention to the global transformations associated with the new imperialism of post-1870.[9] Within this context, scientists – professionalised in status and method – claimed to be producers of 'knowledge' in contrast to the 'sentiment' of humanitarian causes of the past and associated with the accepted public sphere of women's activity in the present. In the dialogue between assimilation and separate development, science added its weight behind defining differences of race and culture and on the side of separate development. The originating society dedicated to studies of race and culture, the Ethnological Society of London, was an offshoot of the APS founded by Quaker abolitionists in 1844. After 1870, with the notable exception of Charles Darwin, no members of the Anthropological Institute or other eminent scientists were members or supporters of the APS.[10]

Even though science became one of the principal sources of knowledge, we need to go beyond the particular ideas promoted by individual scientists to make sense of what biological determinism might mean in Victorian science. In terms of a broader cultural influence not only on the established natural sciences but on the new social sciences, the appeal of 'scientific naturalism' provides a better sense of how scientific modes of thinking came to be authoritative on questions of race. This scientific naturalism treated human beings not as separate from but as part of nature, and presumed that human and historical developments over time were analogous to processes in nature.[11] Human beings became objects of scientific study, and natural processes such as Darwinian evolution had application to fields outside of biology, including culture, politics and economics. Francis Galton's phrase 'nature versus nurture' best captures the Victorian sense of the tension and ambiguity between the aspects of humanity under the rule of nature and those belonging to the domain of culture. Galton coined the phrase in 1874 as a subtitle to his book on *Englishmen of Science*, a study of the role of inheritance in the lives of eminent scientists. Galton's actual wording was 'nature and nurture'. Although he advanced the case for the primacy of nature, suggesting that in a competition when all other things were equal nature triumphed over nurture, his phrase captures the interplay and tension between biology and the environment, and specifically between race and culture, more aptly than does a cruder biological determinism.[12] That does not mean that the community of Victorian scientists was any less convinced of the superiority of the metropolitan culture and the inferiority and appropriate subordination of colonised peoples in the empire; it only means that Victorian scientists' construction of race was not exclusively a result of their science, for their science itself was informed by the metropolitan imperial culture. Of course, the scientists also informed that culture, but their influence came not out of the controversial ideas of the 1860s but from the professionalisation of science and its authoritative place in the production of knowledge.

Robert Knox, the Edinburgh anatomist and author of *The Races of Men* (1850), is usually identified as the founder of modern scientific racism within Britain. Knox, who studied comparative anatomy in Paris, had a promising career as a professor of anatomy in Edinburgh ruined by his association with the murderers and grave-robbers Burke and Hare. After his professional disgrace, he struggled to make a living practising medicine in London and as a lecturer and author on the applications of what he termed 'transcendental anatomy'. Knox wanted to prove that his anatomy lessons, in which anatomical features signified inherited traits of intelligence, personality and character, could be used to assess ethnic differences within the British population. In his anatomy lessons, Knox, who had served in the British army at the Cape and lived for a time in South Africa, drew upon the history of colonial racial conflict. From his comparative anatomy, Knox claimed that the races constituted separate species with separate origins. His polygenesis challenged existing ethnological thinking still dominated by James Cowles Prichard and the theory of monogenesis or common origins which was compatible with Biblical teaching and the humanitarian outreach of the abolitionist and missionary movements. Aware of the mortality of Europeans in West Africa and of African military resistance to European encroachments in southern Africa, Knox warned that visions of the conversion of Africans under European rule was contrary to the scientific laws of his comparative anatomy.[13]

As Knox recognised in his preface, he was an outsider at odds with the prevailing opinions still attached to the anti-slavery cause and still committed to a civilising mission. Knox published a revised edition of *The Races of Men* in 1862.[14] A year later, James Hunt, a young speech therapist, broke with the Ethnological Society and its philanthropic connections, and established the Anthropological Society of London. Under the newly named science of anthropology, Hunt promoted the Scottish anatomist's racial theories and aroused intense controversy. Defending Knox's comparative anatomy with its treatment of races as fixed and separate species, Hunt and his followers rejected Darwin and evolution, and ridiculed missionaries and abolitionists. Hunt's Anthropological Society also championed the political applications of the new science by defending slavery and the Confederacy in the American Civil War, and by supporting Governor Eyre and his use of martial law to quell protests in Jamaica. To the friends and supporters of Charles Darwin and members of the influential X-Club led by T. H. Huxley, Hunt was a charlatan, and his society a scandal threatening the reputation of the scientific community. After the death of Hunt in 1869, Huxley led the negotiations that resulted in the amalgamation of the rival Anthropological and Ethnological Societies.[15]

This union in the new and respectable Anthropological Institute, established in 1871, represented, according to George Stocking, a compromise which accommodated within an evolutionary paradigm both the older ethnological interest in cultures and the new approaches to man as part of nature, including the origin and distribution of human racial varieties. Scarred by the controversies of the 1860s, the members of the Anthropological Institute avoided engaging in political questions, even though the objects of their science were invariably persons of colour subject to western imperial interventions in Asia, the South Pacific and Africa.[16]

In the last three decades of the nineteenth century, Knox was largely forgotten, and his rehabilitation as the founder of modern British scientific racism began with the new scholarly interest in the history of racist-thinking in the 1960s. For his influential work on *Images of Africa* (1964), Philip Curtin saw Knox's *Races of Men* as a culmination of the paradoxical process of an increasingly negative view of Africans during a period of greater European contact with the continent. Scholars less concerned with the mid-Victorian encounter with Africa and more interested in placing Knox in the history of racist thought have ascribed greater significance to the Scottish anatomist, and have exaggerated his popular influence. Certainly too much weight has been given to Knox's acolyte, James Hunt and his notorious pamphlet on 'The Negro's Place in Nature' (1863). It had a print run of 500, but only sold 230 copies. In contrast, Catherine Impey's *Anti-Caste*, an anti-racist magazine, circulated 3,500 copies or more per month for more than four years between 1888 and 1892. Undoubtedly, there were a range of influences and ideas at work contesting abolitionist and missionary views of Africans and their New World descendants, and it is ill-advised to attribute too much influence exclusively to one particular author.[17] In his comprehensive work on Victorian anthropology, George Stocking notes that Knox 'is marginal to the mainstream of British anthropological thought'.[18]

After the controversies of the 1860s, beyond the occasional reference to the historical disputes over race, there are few citations to Knox in the proceedings of the Anthropological Institute or in *Nature*, the leading scientific journal aimed at a broader educated readership. Even the leading publicist of texts and popular readers on race and anthropology at the end of the nineteenth century, Professor A. H. Keane, who as a linguist retained a preference for distinct racial types with separate origins, identified Knox with the discredited school of American comparative anatomists.[19] Knox and Hunt, the promoter of his polygenetic science, had their moment of fame in the controversies of the 1860s. In the aftermath of these exciting contests of science, religion and politics, and with the compromise established by the amalgamation of the ethnologists and anthropologists in their new institute, anthropology made its first step toward joining the learned societies and the British Association. Under this new institutional foundation, the anthropologists participated in the professionalisation of the production of knowledge, and this process proved more significant in establishing the authority of racial science than the controversies of the 1860s.

Professionals and amateurs, 1871–85

Changes in the intellectual and institutional context between 1870 and 1914 gave scientific racism greater credibility and acceptance. In the last two decades of the nineteenth century, a world transformed at home and abroad called for a newly constructed narrative to explain and justify western technological advances, global economic and political dominance, and intensified conflict with non-European peoples most dramatically through colonial wars and more generally as subjects brought under colonial rule. Scientific racism offered one such narrative incorporating hierarchies of race and culture, promoting science in the project of empire, and presenting an apartheid vision of the world critical of humanitarian initiatives of the past and premised on strategies of separate development in the future. For the period after 1871 (the year of the publication of Darwin's *Descent of Man*, and of the formation of the Anthropological Institute), the emergence of professional science provided the institutional base for a more certain scientific orthodoxy in the 1880s.[20] Informed in part by Galton's promotion of nature over nurture, professional scientists attempted to give this reinvigorated scientific racism a practical, political application, and to disseminate its message through the new opportunities afforded by the development of state education and a market for cheaper, popular, illustrated books, encyclopaedias and magazines.

Through its *Journal*, the Anthropological Institute provides a year-by-year record of late Victorian scientific discourse on race. Information about the Institute's membership and organisation permits some analysis of the background of the subscribers to the *Journal* and allows some insight into the social as well as the intellectual context of late Victorian race-thinking. In addition, as a periodical aiming to present developments in science to an educated public, *Nature*, through its editor's selection of articles and of books to review, provides some indication of which scientists spoke with authority and of which books were worthy of note. While precursors of modern scientific racism propounded their views in the 1850s and 1860s, the proceedings of the Anthropological Institute and the contents of *Nature* indicate that a scientific orthodoxy on the racial question was only established in the 1880s. By this time, the professionalisation of science gave enhanced authority to trained experts, increased their isolation from the criticisms of an educated lay public and created the institutional framework for the spread of scientific racist ideas.

From at least the 1830s, the various sciences became professionalised both in the training of their practitioners and in the opening up of salaried positions with government agencies or in institutions of higher education usually connected with the professional training of medical doctors or engineers.[21] Although this process began in the early nineteenth century, the mid-Victorian scientific community, aware of the more advanced professional standing and opportunities of their colleagues in France, Germany and the United States, expressed great concern about the limited public role of science and limited professional opportunities for scientists in Great Britain. Advocates of science such as Lyon Playfair, Thomas Henry Huxley, John Lubbock and Norman Lockyer, the editor of *Nature*, attempted to enhance public awareness of science, to expand its place in the reformed university curricula and at the newly founded civic universities and colleges, and to make it part of the recently established and expanding system of state education.[22]

The demand for a more specialised and research-orientated pursuit of science in the early nineteenth century led to the creation of various learned societies each devoted to a particular science and to the foundation of the British Association for the Advancement of Science in 1831. These organisations opened scientific pursuits to a broader but largely middle-class public, but at least until the 1870s the number of participants who were scientists by profession remained a minority. The learned societies attracted a well-educated, respectable and even genteel following, and the devotees of ethnology, or anthropology as it was newly named in the 1860s, struggled to achieve scientific respectability by founding their own learned society and by attempting to gain recognition by the British Association. Greater respectability was established with the foundation of the Anthropological Institute in 1871, but this respectability rested on shaky foundations. In a rancorous dispute over the elections to the Institute's council from January 1872 to February 1873, members of the influential X-Club (Huxley, Lane Fox, Lubbock and Professor George Busk) rescued the council from a rump of Hunt's Anthropological Society under the titular leadership of Captain Richard Burton. The defeated rump seceded to form the new London Anthropological Society devoted to the study of race and psychology, but this division was short-lived, and within two years the secessionists rejoined the Institute to participate in its saner if duller discussions.[23] The formation of the Anthropological Institute, now under the control of respected professional scientists, and the foundation of *Nature*, according to Robert Young, were symptomatic of the larger process of the secularisation of knowledge, the increased specialisation in science and the breakup of a common intellectual context.[24]

As a consequence of its origin in the amalgamation of two feuding societies, the Anthropological Institute began with an inflated membership of 585 fellows, but soon a more rigorous maintenance of membership lists reduced the Institute's size to between 440 and 480 fellows for most of the 1870s and 1880s.[25] A further decline in numbers in the 1890s reduced the society to 363 members by 1900. Only a minority of members, from twenty to fifty in the 1890s, attended meetings in London.[26] The membership lists, which were in effect lists of subscribers to the *Journal of the Anthropological Institute (JAI)*, gave the addresses for almost all of the fellows, and for one-third of the names included some additional information about social rank or occupation.[27] Of the 638 addresses on the membership lists for 1879 and 1881–85, just under half were in London, thirty-five per cent were in the 'provinces', and the remainder were in overseas locations (chiefly the colonies and particularly India with over forty subscribers). The 203 members for whom social position, education or occupation was listed included thirty-three titled gentlemen and fourteen Members of Parliament. There were more than twenty members of the Royal Society, and at least seventy of the fellows belonged to one or more of the other learned societies, with the Royal Geographical Society and the Royal Geological Society being the most common, followed by the Linnean and Zoological Societies. Of the members whose professional affiliation was given, the most numerous were the sixty-three medical doctors, followed by forty-three army officers, thirty-six scientists or other academics, and thirty clergymen. Forty per cent of the army officers listed colonial or Indian addresses, and about one-third of these served as doctors. Most of the handful of naval officers in the Institute were also medical men. If the military officers are combined together with those who served in the foreign, colonial and civil services, some seventy-four fellows, or over one-third of those whose occupation is known, were employed by some branch of the government. By 1900, the number of army officers and clergy had declined to less than ten in each category. Their place had been taken up to some extent by an increase in the number of of academics and scientists affiliated with colleges, universities or museums. Most of this group, now numbering forty-four, had training in medicine or biological science. This change in membership reflected the decline in the participation of interested amateurs and the growth of the specialised academic and scientific professions by the end of the century.

As with other learned societies, the Institute was dominated by the London-based professional middle class, and within this group a significant minority had some training in medicine or the biological sciences. As indicated by the remarks of several of the Institute's presidents, these professionals believed in social advancement by merit and not by patronage, but at the same time they saw social rank as indicative of inherited potential. Thus they believed in the value of education, but thought that the existing social system protected the aristocracy from the process of social selection, and worried that excessive democracy would cause the inherited ability of the educated middle class to be swamped by the mediocrity of the masses.[28] The combination of these elitist assumptions with a strong orientation towards medicine and natural science makes it hardly surprising that these late Victorian members of the Institute, a significant number of whom had military or colonial connections, should look for biological explanations for the geopolitical reality of European dominion over much of the world. The formation of the Anthropological Institute in 1871, and its calmer deliberations of the 1870s and 1880s, marked the successful institutionalisation of anthropology within the British scientific community.[29] It would be premature, however, to think that this step marked the arrival of anthropology as a professional, independent discipline. As late as 1900 only three fellows held teaching positions as ethnologists or anthropologists. In contrast, no fewer than seven Institute members held chairs in anatomy.[30]

One important outlet for the communication of the proceedings of the Institute to a larger public was the science periodical, *Nature*. After the demise of *The Reader*, a short-lived but promising review of literature and science in the mid-1860s, *Nature* first appeared in November 1869 with the aim of publicising new discoveries in science and of advancing public awareness of the role of science in the community. Under the editorship of Norman Lockyer, with the backing of leading scientists, and dependent on the financial support of its publisher, Alexander Macmillan, *Nature* proved to be an intellectual rather than a financial success. Some of the journal's founders, including its editor Lockyer, saw the need for greater professionalism and specialisation, but at the same time other supporters – for example T. H. Huxley –

feared the compartmentalisation of science, its alienation from literary and humanistic learning, and the inevitable fragmentation of cultural interests and concerns.[31] The magazine attracted many of the leaders of professional science to its columns, but it had fewer than 900 subscribers, and until 1899 it failed to earn a sufficient amount in sales and advertising revenue to pay for its cost of production.[32] Even though it aimed to reach the general reader, *Nature*, by the 1890s if not before, had lost sight of that readership as articles became more technical and its readers increasingly consisted of professional scientists interested in the activities of their colleagues in their own specialty or in other scientific disciplines.[33]

The professionalisation of science enhanced the standing and authority of those who claimed an expert knowledge of race, but the field never became the exclusive preserve of physical anthropologists and craniologists. Within the imperial metropolitan culture, the question of race was of too great an interest and of too great an importance to be left to the scientists. Unlike continental scientists' concern with the tangled ethnic history of European populations, British scientists' discussion of race was global rather than domestic in focus. Interest in the ethnic composition of the British population, despite the tensions of the Irish question and concerns about alien (largely Jewish) immigration at the end of the century, played a secondary role to the comparison of European and non-European populations observed within the colonial context. Given the scope of their chosen mandate, the anthropologists faced a fair degree of scepticism about their pretence to a privileged expertise. In part, they faced the rival expertise of the colonial administrators, military officers, missionaries, traders and travellers with direct experience of the colonial encounter. The professional scientists and this interested lay public participated together in the scientific discussions of race, sharing a common presumption in favour of the inequality of racial groups.

Only rarely did colonial experience challenge the prevailing assumption that racial differences were real and significant. For example, in 1874, W. Lauder Lindsay reported to *Nature* the findings of his friend, Mons. J. C. Houzeau, in testing the intelligence of Jamaican school children. While he identified individual differences in ability, these differences were not as great as he had assumed, and more significantly, the teacher concluded: 'I see nothing – at least nothing clearly and unmistakably discernible – that can be referred to differences of race.'[34] Houzeau realised his findings contradicted the prevailing scientific opinion, and in his report to *Nature*, Lindsay was quick to dissociate himself from his friend's conclusions. Lindsay noted that with different races, as with the varying ability of the sexes, the inferior groups often compete successfully at a young age, and thereafter: 'In subsequent intellectual development proper, man, as a rule, far surpasses woman.'[35]

This report was exceptional, for through the 1870s, *Nature* presented commentaries on race largely through reviews of the literature of exploration and travel. Following the lead of the Royal Geographical Society, the magazine paid greatest attention to Africa, and particularly to the fate of Dr Livingstone and the exploits of Henry Stanley.[36] The primary interest here, beyond the personal adventures of the explorers, was the mapping of the geographical features of Central Africa. The ethnography of various African cultures took a secondary place, and descriptions of Africans tended to mirror the diverse, contradictory, and at times extremely derogatory opinions of the travellers' accounts.[37] In faithfully reproducing the unsystematic yet commonplace prejudices of its literary reviewers, *Nature* differed little from the popular illustrated natural histories and collections of travel literature produced for curious, self-improving readers with an amateur interest in geography and exploration.[38]

The proceedings of the Anthropological Institute similarly reflected the mix of amateur and professional interests of its members. On the one hand, there were those interested in prehistoric archaeology and in exotic cultures. For the large contingent of clergymen, army officers and colonial officials who fell within this category, the Anthropological Institute fulfilled a purpose like that of the Royal Geographical Society. It enabled travellers and officials to report their observations or to read about individuals with similar experiences to their own. In this way the Institute and the Royal Geographical Society became important channels for the dissemination of information about outposts of the empire.[39] Authors of these papers had little training in human biology and anatomy, and their reports rarely attempted to relate observations to a larger theoretical framework of human physical or cultural evolution.

The anthropologists prided themselves on being able to attract large audiences, including in particular clergymen and some adventuresome women, to their sessions at the British Association.[40] Although these enthusiasts for accounts of exotic cultures were not trained professionals, they nonetheless thought their study had a profound moral and political purpose. In his report on the British Association meetings in 1872, Augustus Lane Fox (1827–1900), an officer in the Grenadier Guards, a landed gentleman, and collector of ethnographic artefacts, claimed that 'a nation which from its vast colonial possessions [was] placed more continuously in contact with savage races than any other' had a special responsibility to promote anthropology. According to Lane Fox, there was an urgent need for anthropological studies, for 'the manners and customs of uncivilised races [were] changing with a rapidity unprecedented in the world's history, and ... the continued existence of some of these races [was] becoming a question of only a few years.'[41] This sense of urgency did not always stem from a concern for the plight of the indigenous populations faced with the impact of European colonialism. In the case of Lane Fox, his interest in the collection of cultural artefacts from around the globe was both archival and theoretical. At an Institute meeting in 1877, he observed: 'The English race has done more than any other to destroy all these races and obliterate their culture. As a nation we are bound to keep some scientific record of that which we destroy.'[42]

Late Victorian anthropologists were very aware of the speed and magnitude of changes being effected by European imperialism on the world's peoples and cultures. In a review for *Nature* of a travel book on New Guinea in 1880, Alfred Russel Wallace (1823–1913) observed:

> Are we still, notwithstanding all our wretched failures, to go on in the old way, and allow these interesting and now happy people to be first ruined morally by the teaching of the dregs of our Australian and Pacific traders, and then physically deteriorated by the forced introduction of a form of civilisation utterly unsuited to them? ... Here is perhaps the last chance we have to preserve one remnant of the better class of savages from being crushed under the Juggernaut car of our high-pressure civilisation and mad struggle for wealth.[43]

Wallace's critical remarks were exceptional, for more typically, members of the Anthropological Institute supported imperialism. According to John Beddoe (1826–1911), a president of the Institute, the audience who attended a session of the Anthropology Section of the British Association in 1890 responded warmly to a defence of the empire.[44] In his President's Address in 1880, Major-General Pitt-Rivers (formerly Augustus Lane Fox) argued for the practical utility of anthropology especially in the task of colonial administration. As a man of science, he scorned both party politics and the excesses of representative government which meant that 'knowledge [was] swamped by ignorance'. He pointed with pride to the participation of colonial governors and other administrators in the Institute's proceedings as proof of the practical applications of anthropology, and called for greater public support for the science of man.[45]

When presidents of the Anthropological Institute attempted to define the scope of their discipline in their annual addresses, their statements encompassed both physical and cultural anthropology.[46] The members of the Institute who had a more secure scientific standing were those who brought some technical expertise in human biology to their subject. These medical doctors and biologists, whose interest in anthropology was an offshoot from their primary professional responsibilities, expressed dissatisfaction with the casual observations of travellers, distrusted conclusions drawn from cultural or linguistic evidence, and looked to comparative anatomy for a more scientific assessment of the differences between racial groups.[47] These practitioners of comparative anatomy had the advantage of being able to examine skeletal remains at home in England without venturing overseas to see the living specimens, but nevertheless their science had its drawbacks. Beyond the difficulties that there was no clear-cut way to distinguish acquired from inherited characteristics and no adequate theory of biological inheritance, the physical anthropologists had established no consensus about the forms of measurement or about the significance of their results.

The physical anthropologists claimed that their findings about inherited characteristics revealed differences in intellectual and moral attributes between racial groups, but they gave little consideration to what the ethnographers had to say about the customs, values and practices of the living representatives descended from the skulls measured in the laboratory. Similarly, while the ethnographers seemed to accept the physical anthropologists' claim that races were unequal in inheritance, their diligent pursuit of a unilinear evolution of weapons, boats, games and intoxicants, and their readiness to use living cultures as evidence of Stone Age life in Europe, presumed the psychic unity of human beings.[48] The usual pattern for Institute proceedings was for an ethnographic paper by a visitor from overseas to be followed by a shorter detailed technical description of specimen crania of the racial group in question (the Royal College of Surgeons had at hand more than 3,000 such specimens from around the world). On special occasions, living specimens of exotic peoples were examined at the meeting.[49] Occasionally, Institute presidents, for example, John Evans (1823–1908) and E. B. Tylor (1832–1917), expressed concern that papers on physical anthropology were under-represented. By 1890, John Beddoe, despite his enthusiasm for craniology, had to 'acknowledge the far greater and higher interest of the psychological side of our science, with its bearings on sociology, mythology, and so forth'. Smarting from the fact his own anthropometric work, *The Races of Britain* (1885), never sold as well as anticipated, he petulantly added: 'there is no fear … that ethnography will ever lack cultivators'.[50]

There was a measure of truth in this complaint. An examination of the *Journal of the Anthropological Institute* for 1871–1900 reveals that craniology and anthropometry always represented a minority of the papers given. In the 1870s, presentations on prehistoric archaeology and on early historic migrations in Europe outnumbered those on ethnography and craniology combined, whereas during the 1880s ethnography had become the dominant field in the *Journal*. At no time during this period did the total number of papers on comparative anatomy, craniology and anthropometry, and the occasional broad racist treatise, outnumber ethnographic papers, and only in 1887 did presentations on physical anthropology surpass the number of historical or archaeological papers. This dominance of cultural studies occurred even when, from 1884 to 1891, the presidents were anatomists or anthropometricians.[51] From a comparative perspective, the professional gentlemen in the Anthropological Institute were more accepting of Darwinian evolution, and put less emphasis on comparative anatomy and polygenesis, than their colleagues in France, Germany and the United States.[52]

The presentations before the Anthropological Institute, some of which were reprinted in *Nature*, as well as extracts of papers before the British Association and lectures by leading authorities, revealed the confidence of late Victorian scientists in their belief in racial inequality and their uncertainty about the scientific demonstration of the precise nature and significance of racial differences. Unlike the 1850s and 1860s, when polygenists such as Knox and Hunt proclaimed their strident certainties about fixed racial types, scientists in the 1870s and 1880s attempted in a more tentative fashion to work within the framework of Darwinian evolution, which saw natural species not as fixed entities but as continuously changing forms. The experience of Victorian travellers and their accounts of encounters with exotic peoples had increased awareness of the diversity of human cultures. Faced with the contradictory claims of travellers' impressionistic accounts, scientists could not so readily classify humanity into four or five primary types and assign uniform distinctive characteristics to each group.

In a review in *Nature* in 1876, Alfred Russel Wallace complained of the 'chaotic state of the infant science of anthropology'. Faced with the complexities of racial intermixture and with the need to draw hasty, impressionistic conclusions about racial characteristics, Wallace remarked: 'the passing traveller is altogether deceived as to the characters of the race, and any observations he may make are of little value'. In spite of these difficulties, Wallace remained confident that a trained anthropologist living in close contact with a people for considerable time would be able 'to disentangle the complexities they present[ed], and determine with some approach to accuracy the limits of variation of the pure or typical race'.[53] Many late Victorian biologists and anthropologists shared Wallace's frustration with the current state of their science and his confidence that more careful observation and measurement would establish accurate, verifiable knowledge about racial distinctions.

Race and culture in Victorian anthropology

The agenda for the anthropologists' discussion of race in the 1870s was set by T. H. Huxley's paper at the Ethnological Society in 1870. Huxley provided a classification scheme of racial types based on skin colour, hair colour and texture, eye colour, skull shape and body stature. Using this range of criteria, and not a single measure such as skull shape or size, Huxley identified five main races: the Australoid; the Negroid; the Xanthochroi (fair whites of Europe); the Melanochroi (dark whites of Europe, North Africa, Asia Minor and Hindustan, including Irish, Celts, Bretons, Spaniards, Arabs and Brahmins); and the Mongoloid (including the peoples of Asia, Polynesia and the Americas).[54] In many ways Huxley's paper revived the procedure of James Cowles Prichard who, according to E. B. Tylor, was the founder of ethnology in Great Britain.[55] By basing his classification scheme on a variety of characteristics and by plotting their geographical distribution, Huxley, like Prichard, emphasised the wide variation in physical features within his five classes and pointed to the many intermediate gradations in human phenotype. For Huxley the five major classes of race were not 'pure' types and, unlike with the mid-century polygenist typologies, his scheme pointed to the intermingling and intermixture of racial groups. His conclusion suggested that the next question to be resolved was why a similarity of physical type existed in the Americas whereas a wide diversity of forms characterised the people of the Pacific Islands.[56]

Huxley's global perspective on the distribution and mixed character of human races led to an enlarged discussion of human diversity which tested the limits of existing racial typologies and engaged the newer approaches to the evolution of culture. Edward Burnett Tylor not only gave new focus to ethnological studies but enriched the emerging meanings of 'culture' itself. His *Primitive Culture* (1871) began with his famous enlarged definition of culture as 'that complex whole which includes knowledge, belief, art, morals, law, custom and any other capabilities and habits acquired by man as a member of society'. Tylor's enlarged concept of culture enabled anthropologists to conduct new kinds of studies of the exotic cultures of the colonised, but Tylor was not a cultural relativist. The new approaches to cultural evolution still implicitly used the metropolitan culture as a standard of civilisation and progress, and forged new links between culture and imperialism.[57] Consequently, the confused association of race and culture not only persisted but was magnified. Out of this ambiguity racism did not diminish but gained potency in its flexible capacity to address the diversity of the global parameters of the empire and its constructions of colonial knowledge.

Huxley may have identified the diversity of human varieties of the Indonesian Archipelago and Australasia as the question which would most puzzle late Victorian anthropologists, but the Institute did not immediately take up the issue. Attention began to focus on this problem only in the mid-1870s. Foreign rivalry from France, Germany and the United States, and controversy over migrant labour practices, prompted English planters and missionaries, as well as colonial legislators in New Zealand and Australia, to press for direct intervention by a reluctant British government. As a result, Fiji became a colony in 1874, and in Malaya a colonial war led to the establishment of British rule through a Resident in 1875. Meanwhile, reports of first encounters between Europeans and remote island societies in the Pacific excited the anthropologists' interest. For the decade from the mid-1870s to the mid-1880s, numerous papers on the various groups and subgroups in the area of the Indian and Pacific Oceans – on a north–south axis from the Andaman Islands to New Zealand, and on an east–west axis from the Hawaiian Islands to Madagascar – appeared in the *JAI*, making this topic the most extensive debate on race between 1870 and 1900.

The issue at stake was the distribution, origin and affinities of those groups identified as black (Australian Aborigines, Papuans, Melanesians, and Negritos) and those identified as brown (chiefly Polynesians, but also Indonesians and Malayans).[58] One side argued that the brown and black varieties shared a common and probably black ancestor, and subsequent change had occurred most commonly by migration and intermixture with other groups, and rarely by geographical isolation and adaptation. The other side argued for a classification of Papuans and Polynesians (or more broadly blacks and browns) as two distinct groups sharing no physical or linguistic affinities except in cases where obvious intermixture had occurred. Among those who argued for a common origin and closer linguistic connections were Alfred Russel Wallace, C. Staniland Wake, and two missionary linguists with long residence in the area, R. H. Codrington and George Brown. The theory of distinct races was advanced by several authors, but most notably by Augustus Keane (1833–1912), who argued that the region included representatives of the black, yellow and white races.[59]

In the short term, the anthropologists' deliberations on the Oceanic races proved inconclusive. The physical anthropologists laid claim to being the most scientific, yet they felt hampered in their contributions.

Travellers' accounts, even those based upon the Institute's *Notes and Queries on Anthropology* (1874; revised 1892) or other such guides for collecting data, rarely provided a sufficient range of reliable measurements, and anatomical specimens in England were too few in number to make a base for generalisation. More importantly, the anatomists recognised the diversity of peoples in the area, and since the available data failed to fit into a clear pattern of racial types, they drew the conclusion that the region was one of great racial intermixture.[60] Philology proved no more conclusive than comparative anatomy. The philologists did not accept language as an indication of race as readily as they had done between 1840 and 1870, but occasionally there was a suggestion (usually put forward by those arguing for two distinct peoples) that in the midst of evidence of physical diversity and intermixture, language demonstrated a stronger fixity of type.[61] Lane Fox and Tylor, both skilled in the art of tracing cultural evolution by the comparative method, recommended that more attention be paid to cultural affinities in the region, as evidenced by tools, artefacts, customs and beliefs.[62] Nonetheless, there was some resistance to this evidence because of the problem of distinguishing cultural borrowings from independent inventions.[63]

Although the participants still thought in terms of racial types and debated problems of classification, they described racial groups not as distinct species but rather as outcomes of evolution including migration and intermixture. Even though the evolutionary synthesis was accepted as a given, the discussion was not in a precise sense Darwinian. Few references were made to Darwin's work, and although authors, out of intrinsic interest in the subject, paid attention to the sexual practices of various cultures, no one attempted a Darwinian study of sexual selection to explain racial varieties. Nor did the concept of natural selection enter prominently into the discussion.[64] Since the physical environment in the region was accepted as common to all groups, there was little sense in attempting to explain particular traits – for example, long-headedness as against broad-headedness – as adaptations for survival. Although there were some suggestions that geographically isolated groups – for example the Andaman Islanders or Tasmanians – might be 'living fossils' representing an earlier form of man, there was no systematic attempt to trace an evolutionary progression of physical types in the region, with more 'advanced' forms evolving out of more 'primitive' ones. The cultural, linguistic and physical mix of peoples of the region, as constructed by most participants, resulted from a long history of waves of migration mixing new migrants and previously settled peoples.

Eventually the anthropologists' interest in the diversity of racial groups in the Indian and south Pacific Oceans diminished as other areas, especially Africa, came into prominence after the mid-1880s. As a rule, late Victorian anthropologists described lighter-complexioned Polynesians in more favourable terms than darker Papuans and Melanesians. This bias was not simply a product of the contrast in skin colour or culture between Melanesians and Victorian middle-class professionals, but was the result of an established association growing out of Europe's long-term historical links with Africa and the enslavement of its peoples. By the 1880s, the *JAI* strengthened these negative associations between blacks, savagery and backwardness by publishing sensationalised accounts of African peoples and cultures by travellers, missionaries and officials promoting European penetration of the 'Dark Continent'.[65]

Between 1879 and 1885, two leading members of the Institute attempted to sum up the current position of science on race. The first was Edward B. Tylor, the foremost student of cultural evolution, and the second was William H. Flower (1831–99), Hunterian Professor at the Royal College of Surgeons, president of the Zoological Society (1879–99), president of the Anthropological Institute (1883–85), director of the Natural History Museum (from 1884), and the leading late Victorian authority on comparative anatomy.[66] *Nature*, equally interested in giving its readers an up-to-date scientific view of race, also reprinted extensive extracts from the papers and lectures of these two eminent authorities.

E. B. Tylor, from a wealthy London Quaker family, attributed his original interest in ethnology to a chance encounter in 1856 in Cuba with Henry Christy, a Quaker active in the Ethnological Society. Tylor travelled with Christy to Mexico, where he developed his interest in ancient civilisations and primitive religion. Attaching less significance to physical differences than to learned behaviour or culture, he argued in *Primitive Culture* (1871) that it was 'both possible and desirable to eliminate considerations of heredity in varieties of races of men, and to treat mankind as homogeneous in nature, though placed in different grades of civilisation'.[67] Similarly, in a paper presented before the Institute in 1889, arguing for a statistical approach to the study of culture, he claimed:

> the institutions of man are as distinctly stratified as the earth on which he lives. They succeed each other in series substantially uniform over the globe, independent of what seem the comparatively superficial differences of race and language, but shaped by similar human nature acting through successively changed conditions in savage, barbaric, and civilised life.[68]

Tylor was not always consistent. His textbook *Anthropology* (1881) gave greater scope to racial determinism by classing differences in intelligence and temperament as racial traits, and by suggesting that subsequent generations of racial crosses reverted to primary types.[69] In writing an introductory text, Tylor had to deal with physical as well as cultural anthropology, and his inconsistency reflected the lack of synthesis between the two branches within the discipline. Tylor's treatment of physical anthropology was heavily dependent on the work of Huxley and Flower. Ironically Flower, in an otherwise favourable appraisal, criticised the cultural evolutionist for not giving due weight to comparative anatomy in classifying races.[70] In contrast, Wallace, in his review for *Nature*, praised Tylor's insistence upon human unity 'in the wonderful similarity and often identity, of habits, customs, ideas, beliefs, and religions among all savages, and the curious way in which traces of these can be found in the very midst of modern civilised society'.[71]

In 1879, in his President's Address before the Anthropological Institute and in an address before the British Association, Tylor gave a historical account of developments since Prichard's studies in ethnology. He noted: 'there lies between Prichard's time and ours the period of popularity and decline of the Polygenist doctrine'. Admitting that polygenesis had helped gain acceptance for the great extension of human history required by evolution, he saw the task of anthropologists as to record the development of human varieties by 'the effects of the intermarriage of races, and their change under altered condition of life'.[72] Before the British Association, he affirmed that 'the close resemblance of all men in body and mind, and the freedom with which races intercross' made it probable that mankind descended from 'one original stock'.[73]

In his inaugural lectures at the University Museum in Oxford, extracted in *Nature* in 1883, Tylor drew a link between Prichard's monogenetic studies and Darwin's theory of evolution. The evidence for the racial and linguistic intermixture of peoples both in Europe and in the Pacific confirmed, according to Tylor, this link between monogenesis and evolution.[74] When he turned to cultural evolution, he affirmed the mental unity of the human species:

> For my own part, when I look at the utter likeness of the working processes of the mind among the races, most different in skin, and when I see the resemblance of rude ideas and customs throughout the inhabited world, I cannot but think that much of the thought and habit of mankind not only goes back to the remote Palaeolithic age, but that it may be older than the divisions of race which separate us from the Chinese or the Negro.[75]

Tylor assumed a continuity of human nature over the vast period of time required for the evolution of significant physical and cultural differences. Anthropologists, in his view, attempted to reconstruct the historical migration of races by looking for the centre from which various physical and cultural varieties dispersed. He speculated that the black races originated in New Guinea and later some branches migrated west to Africa, because Africans were at the 'barbaric stage' with a culture 'higher than New Guinea' in its 'primitive savage state'.[76] This conception of evolutionary stages of development over an extended period of time reconciled the claim of the unity of the human races with a hierarchical ranking of cultures.[77]

Tylor's concept of cultural evolution led him to reconsider the conventional view of the role of Europeans in the development of civilisation. At the British Association in 1879, he claimed that civilisation began among non-white people, and remarked that the ancient Egyptians were probably 'a mixed race, mainly of African origin'.[78] In his Oxford lectures, he pondered whether 'there ever were any White savages', and asserted that whites developed relatively recently in human history. Consequently, he claimed, it may well be that a pre-white civilisation 'with its improved supply of food, its better housing and clothing, its higher intellectuality, was the main factor in the development of the White type'.[79] This account of the emergence of civilisation, Tylor advised his audience, 'may moderate our somewhat overweening estimate of our powers to remember that the white races cannot claim to be the original creators of literature and science, but from remote antiquity they began to show the combined power of acquiring and developing culture which has made them dominant among mankind'.[80] Tylor wished to make culture rather than race the engine of human development. Even though he insisted upon the mental similarity of all human beings and advocated the comparative study of cultures, Tylor's cultural explanation for progressive and therefore unequal development persisted in placing whites at the top of a rank-ordering of racial groups.

For the cultural evolutionists, progress did not come from the evolution of a superior type in physical or mental endowment but from the accumulated experience and knowledge transmitted culturally from one generation to the next. As Wallace explained in his review for *Nature* of Tylor's *Anthropology*, archaeological remains for prehistoric man 'show us in no case any important deviation from the existing human type, nor any indication that his mental status was lower than (if so low as) that of many living races'. By analogies to recent progress in western science and a comparison of the Victorians and the ancient Greeks, Wallace tried to demonstrate that progress came not from increased intelligence but from learning; or in his words, 'arts are a growth and have little relation to the mental status of the artificer'.[81] As sensible as this observation might be, the cultural evolutionists still had to contend with simpler and more obvious explanations of human differences.

To present an authoritative statement of a biologist's view of race, the Anthropological Institute and *Nature* relied upon Professor William H. Flower. A life-long friend of Thomas Huxley, he had first gained recognition by his public and effective support of evolution during the 1860s. Flower was as an innovator in making museums centres of public education and research, especially in the design of exhibits on evolutionary principles, and an active and popular lecturer on the evolution of human races.[82] In a series of articles for *Nature* in 1879 and 1880 based on his lectures before the Royal College of Surgeons, Flower provided a technical anatomical description of the primary racial types, identifying their distinguishing characteristics and variations within each type, and paying particular attention to measurements of skull shape and size. Reviewing past explanations for the origin of races, he commented that the theory of polygenesis was 'not held by many scientific men of the present day'.[83] Both the *JAI* and *Nature* printed Flower's opening address to the Anthropology Section of the British Association meetings of 1881. The eminent zoologist began by complimenting Tylor for his recent text *Anthropology*, but suggested that the work paid insufficient attention to racial differences. In contrast, Flower quoted from the late departed Lord Beaconsfield: 'Language and religion do not make a race – there is only one thing which makes a race, and that is blood.' Consequently, in Flower's view, an understanding of race had practical, political applications, and yet anthropology of any sort was not taught at a single institution of higher learning in the United Kingdom. For this study, the biologist gave priority to the study of comparative anatomy; next in importance was the study of 'moral and intellectual characters'; and least important because least reliable was the study of social institutions and culture.[84]

According to Flower, human racial varieties were a product of evolution acting through the process of natural selection. He noted that all races were fertile with one another and thus did not constitute separate species, and he claimed that science had moved beyond the contentious rivalry of monogenesis and polygenesis. He thought that human beings probably had a common origin, but the process of natural selection had acted over a vast period of time to produce variations in response to differing external environments. Geographical isolation led to the formation of distinctive physical traits, and he asserted that 'In the same way different intellectual and moral qualities would be gradually developed and transmitted in different groups of men.'[85] Given this fluid picture of human evolution, Flower then took the unusual step of admitting that the term 'race' itself had no adequate definition: 'any theory implying that the different individuals composing the human species can be parcelled out into certain definite groups, each with its well-marked and permanent limits separating it from all others, has no scientific foundation'.[86] Flower also questioned the value of craniology, which he described as an attempt 'to make use of what appear trivial characters, and compensate for their triviality by their number'. Nonetheless, he held out the hope that improvements in measurement would lead to more definite conclusions.[87]

In subsequent statements about the place of race in anthropology, Flower gave a less restrained view. In his President's Address before the Institute in 1884, he again insisted on the primacy of comparative anatomy above philology and cultural comparisons. He asserted that physical distinctions 'are probably always associated' with differences in 'temper and intellect', and claimed as a consequence that anthropology had important lessons for politicians seeking to govern the diverse peoples not only within the empire but even within the British Isles. He argued, for example, that policies suitable

> to mitigate the difficulties and disadvantages under which the English artisan classes may suffer in their struggle through life, would be absolutely inapplicable, for instance, to the case of the Egyptian fellaheen. It is not only that their education, training and circumstances are dissimilar, but that their very mental constitution is totally distinct.[88]

In cases where contact occurs between races even more dissimilar, as between Englishmen and Africans, American Indians, Australian Aborigines or Pacific Islanders, the result, the anatomist claimed, 'generally ends in the extermination of one of them'.[89]

Flower admitted that the science of comparative anatomy had one serious limitation. Inevitably, anatomical measurement required knowledge of human anatomy and its terminology, and consequently the study was limited to trained experts.[90] In his President's Address for 1885, Flower outlined his scheme of racial classification. Once again he admitted that any classification scheme would contain inadequacies because of the existence of many intermediate gradations and because of the frequency of intermixture. Although he used a variety of physical traits and measurements to classify groups, his threefold primary division of blacks, yellows and whites clearly rested upon skin colour.[91] He followed Huxley in dividing whites into the 'blonds' and the 'darks', but in contrast to Tylor, he claimed that the ancient Egyptians were 'nearly pure Melanochroi' with some traces of

Ethiopian ancestry. In concluding his presentation, Flower observed that the general features of his classification scheme, in spite of a vast increase in knowledge, 'scarcely differ[ed] from that of Cuvier nearly sixty years ago'.[92] To Flower this continuity confirmed its essential truthfulness. Consequently, Flower like his fellow scientists still thought in terms of a racial typology in spite of Darwin's transformation of the significance of species, and in spite of abundant evidence of racial intermixture.

The persistence in typological thinking reflected an important element of continuity in Victorian racism, but this sense of continuity needs to be balanced against significant discontinuities in the intellectual and institutional context of late nineteenth-century science. In the period after 1870, the most important development was the professionalisation of science. This new institutional framework established conditions for the emergence of a scientific orthodoxy and for the dissemination of its message. A transformation of this order did not occur as a consequence of a singular event, but it was a long-term process with origins prior to 1870, and it was not fully established until the end of the nineteenth century. With the formation of the Anthropological Institute in 1871, respected leaders among professional scientists secured control over the direction of anthropological studies and began the process of securing its academic respectability. To convert ethnology from the amateur pursuit of travellers, philanthropists, antiquarians, transcendental anatomists and other eccentric hobbyists into a credible form of knowledge, the newly named study of anthropology had to be made into a science. The process began with the claim that human beings were part of nature and thus subject to the methods and findings of the scientists. The scientific study of human beings most obviously applied to human biology. While biologists took the lead both in professional standing and in the promotion of scientific naturalism, the scope of their enquiries could not be limited to biology. Even the leading advocates of evolution, Wallace and Huxley for example, realised that biology or biological processes could not encompass the whole of the human sciences.[93]

Human beings were not simply part of nature; they were also the creators of culture. Just as human beings displayed a wide diversity in physical form and feature, so they exhibited an even greater diversity and complexity in social organisation and cultural forms. The new science of anthropology encompassed both biological and cultural studies, and consequently, the confused association between race and culture was institutionalised in the learned societies and university curricula. Reflecting the growing specialisation in the sciences, physical and cultural anthropology coexisted as related but unassimilated forms of enquiry. The cultural evolutionists such as Tylor and Wallace attempted to advance non-biological explanations for cultural differences, but nonetheless their evolutionary perspective incorporated a racial and cultural hierarchy. As systematic students of culture, they laid claim to being scientific, and had theoretical support from the adherents to Comte's positivism and from other luminaries such as John Stuart Mill and Herbert Spencer.[94] Nonetheless, in professional standing and in academic prestige, the students of culture retained the stigma of the amateur and the dilettante. The representatives of the natural sciences had a firmer professional standing within the learned societies, the universities and the training hospitals. When anthropology achieved a measure of recognition with the creation of its own section at the British Association in 1884, it had not yet established itself as an academic discipline within the universities. Its recognition as a science came largely through the prestige of William Flower, Francis Galton, and other natural scientists among its practitioners.

Through the 1870s and early 1880s, despite the continued confusion between race and culture, the physical and cultural anthropologists had added greatly to the knowledge of the diversity of humans in physical feature and social organisation, and of their affinity through their biological and cultural evolution. More aware of how human racial and cultural diversity and intermixture posed problems for crude racial typologies, some leaders of the scientific community – for example Flower – paused to consider what they meant by race. This was only a pause, however, for racist thinking under the leadership of professional scientists experienced a revival in the 1880s. This revival was not simply a rebirth of mid-Victorian polygenesis. In contrast to the 1860s, there existed by the 1880s the institutional framework of professional science for the development and dissemination of a more technically sophisticated and authoritative scientific racist orthodoxy.

Nature over nurture: from race types to psychology

Under the leadership of Francis Galton (1822–1911), president of the Anthropological Institute from 1885 to 1889, a pioneer of new statistical techniques and a promoter of eugenics, biological determinism gained new credibility. Galton's own phrase, 'Nature versus Nurture', came to characterise the late Victorian debate on the relationship between heredity and environment. Strengthened by the new forms of statistical analysis, scientists applied this reinvigorated biological determinism to differences of class, gender and race. This late nineteenth-century social biology inspired the eugenics movement and came to influence the emerging social sciences of anthropology, human geography, sociology and psychology. Entrenched within the scientific community in the period from 1880 to 1914, this revitalised scientific racism came to have an influence on government policy in colonial administration, education and social welfare after the First World War.[95] In the light of this chronology, the mature development of Victorian racism under the auspices of professional science occurred in the late nineteenth century when imperial expansion intensified conflict with non-European indigenous and migratory populations of the empire.

This revival of theoretical racism in the mid-1880s resulted in part from innovations in anthropological method. After a period of criticism of the sheer tedium, confusion and inconsequence of craniology, a new international agreement on the cephalic index in 1886 led to greater certainty about skull measurements.[96] The new science of anthropometry shifted the emphasis away from measurement of skull shape and size alone to the entire skeleton, and even more importantly began to measure the sensory and motor functions.[97] These developments depended upon innovations in statistical analysis. Francis Galton pioneered many of these new methods which allowed data to be handled in a more sophisticated manner, including the use of range rather than mean as a standard of comparisons, the employment of percentiles and curves of normal distribution, and the concepts of standard deviation and regression analysis. Galton was extremely active in promoting new methods to improve the quantifiable and – in his view – the scientific presentation of anthropological data.[98]

Galton's particular interest in the 'nature versus nurture' question first became apparent in *Tropical South Africa* (1853), an account of his travels in South-West Africa in 1850–52. He claimed that innate characteristics explained both the differences between various peoples in South-West Africa and the supposed inferiority of Africans to Europeans. In spite of his earlier travels and of his role as honorary secretary to the Royal Geographical Society during the exciting search for the Nile, he showed little interest in the ethnography of peoples outside the British Isles. His first studies of inheritance, 'Heredity Talent and Character' (published in *Macmillan's Magazine* in 1865), and his book *Hereditary Genius* (1869) used the common acceptance of racial inequality of non-Europeans to demonstrate the importance of inherited characteristics among all peoples including the British population. In the 1860s, he had to contest environmental explanations for human differences, but by the 1880s his ideas found a more receptive audience.[99] By this time he had also come to play a leading role in the Anthropological Institute, where his presentations dealt largely with the application of statistical methods to human populations.[100]

Galton and other advocates of anthropometry shared a sense that the study of physical anthropology, including the identification of racial types within British society, received neither the interest nor the respect accorded to similar studies in France, Germany, Russia and the United States. In 1882, the Anthropometric Committee of the British Association, including Professor W. H. Flower, Francis Galton, and Dr John Beddoe, claimed that anthropometry would provide a more precise measure of racial 'tendencies and proclivities'. Rejecting the view that the history of migration and resultant intermixture made it impossible to find pure racial types, the committee claimed that 'eminent anthropologists admit a natural law, through the operation of which a complete reversion takes place, under favourable circumstances, to original types'. This reversion to type was so complete that among the population 'prehistoric characteristics exist at the present day'.[101] The language here was reminiscent of the racial typology of Robert Knox and the Anthropological Society of London in the 1860s, but by the 1880s its authors were not eccentrics on the fringes of the scientific community. Flower and Galton were respected leaders of Victorian science and their committee carried the authority of the British Association. Galton also made an effort to publicise his new methods. At the International Health Exhibition in South Kensington in 1884, he found more than 9,000 individuals who were willing to be measured in his tiny anthropometric laboratory.[102] In 1887, under the sponsorship of the Anthropological Institute, Galton gave a series of public lectures at the South Kensington Museum, but he lectured not on the science of anthropology but on his favourite topic of 'Heredity and Nurture'.[103]

Galton's own presentations before the Institute and promotional activities only occasionally addressed anthropology and the empire. In a presidential address dealing with populations in the colonies, he observed that in temperate zones where Europeans had settled, the aboriginal inhabitants faced 'rapid diminution' and thus 'their peculiarities [were] losing present interest and [were] becoming historical and archaic'.[104] He then expressed a greater sense of urgency about the study of British populations, particularly those living in tropical colonies. For the heat, Galton recommended air conditioning using new techniques of refrigeration, and for the more difficult obstacle of disease, he thought that natural selection itself would lead to the survival and reproduction of the minority of whites with immunity.[105] Ever attentive to opportunities to advance his science, Galton organised an Anthropological Conference on the Native Races of the British Possessions at the Colonial and Indian Exhibition in 1886. This series of lectures and exhibits, including both some artefacts and some live specimen 'savages', offered presentations by white colonists and officials. In contrast to Galton's emphasis on statistical studies, these papers offered generalised descriptions of indigenous peoples and impressions about the decline of these populations and the disintegration of their cultures. They depicted colonial administrators as providing benevolent protection, and some speakers used the occasion to engage in the promotion of colonial development and described the 'natives' as a pool of productive labourers.[106]

During the 1890s, after his terms as president of the Institute, Galton remained an important patron of anthropological studies. A. C. Haddon (1855–1940), the founder of anthropological studies at Cambridge, sought Galton's assistance in placing anthropological articles in the periodical press. Haddon, who had recently returned from his first visit to the Torres Straits, and whose interests were shifting from zoology to anthropology, sought to establish his credentials in England and to escape from political and academic isolation in Ireland.[107] Galton also supported Tylor in his struggles at Oxford to establish a professorship in anthropology against the opposition of classicists and theologians.[108] Nonetheless, Galton's primary interest in the statistical study of the British population always ranked second to the ethnographic interests of the members of the Anthropological Institute.

Now in his eighties and in failing health, he dedicated the last years of his life and his personal fortune to the promotion of eugenics. By this time, Auguste Weismann's theory of the continuity of the germ plasm and Mendel's rediscovered work on genetics had advanced theories of biological inheritance. In inviting Galton to give the Huxley Memorial Lecture and to receive the Huxley Memorial Medal from the Institute in 1901, Haddon acknowledged Galton's distinguished leadership in putting 'biological data on a firm mathematical basis'.[109] At the Huxley Lecture, Galton spoke on the role of eugenics and turned to the same topic again before the Sociological Society in 1904. He founded a research fellowship in eugenics in 1905, and, in 1907, established a Eugenics Laboratory at the University of London under the direction of Karl Pearson, a fellow mathematician who took up and extended Galton's work in the statistical study of heredity. The Eugenics Education Society, established in 1907, drew support largely from the professional middle class with a significant representation from scientists and university lecturers.

With the intellectual defences of biological determinism refortified, and in a climate of self-doubt about Britain's world leadership and about the vitality of the national fibre in the aftermath of the South African War, Galton found fertile ground for his new eugenic science. In so far as the eugenists took an interest in the question of race, they warned against sentimental humanitarianism and reiterated the now conventional opinion of the superiority of European, and especially British stock.[110] Up until 1914, the Anthropological Institute continued to have an interest in anthropometry, and many of its practitioners were supporters of eugenics. Even though Karl Pearson identified eugenics as a form of 'applied anthropology', Galton's leadership in eugenics, and the foundation of a new science of sociology, ironically strengthened the identification of anthropology with the study of culture, especially of non-European peoples.[111]

Concurrent with the new interest in biological inheritance and with the origins of eugenics, there was a revival of some of the more extreme speculations about the origin and nature of racial groups. The most notable example was the revised version of the Aryan theory in the late 1880s. A. H. Sayce (1845–1933), professor of philology at Queen's College, Oxford, and Isaac Taylor (1829–1901), Canon of York, followed recent continental works in arguing for an Aryan homeland in northwestern Europe against the established convention of a central Asian origin linking Indian and European peoples through a common linguistic heritage. Although Taylor's paper received a largely hostile reception before the Institute, especially from orientalists with experience in Asia, the revival of the debate also reintroduced the confused connection between race and language.[112]

Led by Dr John Beddoe, there also were renewed efforts to identify the composition of the British population by race, and a revival of the idea of fixed types that persisted in spite of historical evidence of a mixed ancestry. Beddoe took an interest in the relationship of class and ethnicity, identifying 'Anglo-Saxons' and 'Celts' by class and region, and concluded in a paper delivered to the Institute in 1882: 'There has been as yet nothing like a complete amalgamation in blood of the upper, middle and lower classes.'[113] He was particularly harsh on the Irish, claiming that as an immigrant group they had experienced 'very little mixture of Irish with English or Scottish blood', and hardly any upward social mobility. With the crisis of Home Rule, these claims took on a new nationalistic twist. Some leading scientists, for example T. H. Huxley and Sir John Lubbock, wrote to *The Times* advising its readers not to confuse race and nationality, and denying that the British populations could be classified into several distinct races. Lubbock, a Liberal MP, opposed Home Rule and broke with Gladstone in 1886.[114]

Even though Galton's innovations in quantitative methods for the study of populations and his advocacy of nature over nurture gave biological determinism new authority, his leadership pushed the scientific study of heredity away from anthropology and away from culture. Concurrent with these developments in biology and eugenics, the anthropologists' primary focus remained with exotic peoples and cultures, still thought of as the uncivilised living in or close to a state of nature. Out of the inconclusive studies of the races, languages and cultures of the Indonesian archipelago and the Pacific region, the focus on identifying racial types revived, and this revival had a longer-term outcome in the presentations of race and culture to a wider public in the first three decades of the twentieth century. A. H. Keane, professor of Hindustani at the University of London, took the lead in developing a theory of the origin and migration of modern racial types out of this region, and until the First World War was the principal publicist for this popularised scientific racism.

As an active participant in the Institute, Keane gained recognition as a prolific author of geographical and anthropological texts, reference works and illustrated books which advanced an extreme racist position. Keane was a linguist, acknowledged as having an exceptional expertise in the world's languages. Born in 1832, at Cork, Ireland, he received his training in foreign languages at the College of Propaganda in Rome while training for the priesthood. Deciding not to enter the church, he became a teacher and tutor in classics and foreign languages, including Hindustani, which he taught to students preparing for the Indian Civil Service. A translator of German and French geographies and grammars, and particularly skilled in compiling comparative vocabularies of foreign languages, Keane assisted A. R. Wallace in producing the volume on *Australasia* (1879) for *Standford's Compendium of Geography and Travel*.[115] From this work, Keane developed his theory of the origins of human varieties in a paper entitled 'On the Relations of the Indo-Chinese and Oceanic Races and Languages'. This paper, presented before the Anthropological Institute in 1879 and reprinted as a four-part article in *Nature* in 1880–81, dealt with the complicated puzzle of the physical characteristics, linguistic variety and cultural diversity of the peoples of the Indonesian Archipelago, Australia and the islands of the Pacific. Out of the racial and ethnic diversity of the area many late Victorian scientists, including Keane, Wallace and Tylor, thought they had located the probable place of origin of the human races.[116] His colleagues at the Anthropological Institute thought his paper was interesting but rather speculative. Nonetheless, it was this paper and his work on vocabularies for Stanford's series on geography and travel which established his scholarly credentials for the professorship of Hindustani at University College, London, in 1883.[117]

Like other philologists such as Max Müller and A. H. Sayce, Keane denied that linguistic groups were 'races', but nonetheless he claimed that each language was the creation of a particular cast of mind, and thus language was a key sign of difference and lay behind unequal levels of development. While denying the connection between race and language, Keane saw in language a means to trace back the genealogies of human races to their origins.[118] Rejecting the orthodox monogenists' quest for a single original pair, but also rejecting 'orthodox polygenesis' which looked for fixed types originating at independent centres, he described his theory as 'unorthodox monogenism' relying not on an original pair but on 'one evolutionary centre'. He displayed his lack of training in biology by ignoring the usual test of species, the ability to produce fertile offspring, and claimed that 'species or race' were 'terms practically identical when used with scientific precision'. This confusing use of species, race and language allowed Keane to claim that he remained attached to monogenesis, that he had incorporated the fluidity of evolutionary biology, and that nonetheless he could confidently identify three distinct types – the Dark, the Caucasian, and the Mongolian. For Keane, the cultural evolutionists had not proven that similarity of customs indicated affinity or contact, for he only admitted that human beings having originated in a common centre revealed similarities 'in the infantile or underdeveloped stage'.[119]

Drawing second-hand from works of comparative anatomy and from ethnographic and travel literature, Keane contributed his facility as a linguist in constructing succinct psychological and cultural profiles of entire populations. To his colleagues at the Institute, his most dubious claim was the description of a distinct 'Caucasian Type' of fair and brown-skinned peoples, including Khmers or Cambodians, Indonesians and eastern Polynesians, as one of the original groups in the Southeast Asia and Oceanic region.[120] He described eastern Polynesians as 'one of the finest races of mankind, Caucasian in all essentials', and concluded by praising their 'cheerful joyous temperament, a frank and truthful disposition and kindly nature, and you have a type as different as it is possible to imagine from the Mongolian'.[121]

Keane was the most important of the speculators about the history of racial types. From an unknown centre in the Eastern Archipelago, or on an adjacent lost submerged continent linking now distinct land masses, he speculated that an 'infantile type', possibly a 'primitive Negrito race', migrated both eastward into the South Sea Islands and westward to Africa, and in these new locations subsequent adaptations produced new dark varieties. From the original centre there was also a migration north by the original dark type, and 'moving thence over the Asiatic continent, they became under more temperate climes differentiated, first probably into the yellow Mongol, and then through it into the fair Caucasian type'.[122] Other presentations to the Institute – some by survivors from Hunt's Anthropological Society of London – offered similar speculative accounts of the origin of races.[123]

In the most analytical of his popular texts, *Ethnology* (1896), Keane reviewed the findings of the physical anthropologists and noted that the evidence of the fertility of racial crosses and the fact that almost all existing races were of mixed ancestry confirmed the specific unity of man. Although he disavowed any link with Robert Knox or the discredited mid-Victorian polygenists, his speculations on the genealogies of races inclined towards a theory of separate origins.[124] He argued that existing races 'are to a certain extent of diverse origin, that is to say, descend in diverging, converging or parallel lines from their several pleistocene precursors'.[125] In a letter to Alfred Russel Wallace in 1899, his insistence upon the autonomy of the white race and its independent origin was expressed more frankly:

> My theory of the evolution of black, white and yellow, not one from the other, but *independently* from their several pleistocene precursors (the generalised human type) seems to meet such cases as these. The white man is thus, not a late arrival on the scene, but of equal antiquity with the others, and so starts *simultaneously* with them on his life history [emphasis in the original].[126]

Keane managed to retain the language of fixed physical and mental attributes by claiming that he described only 'ideal types'.[127] Consequently, in another popular text, *Man: Past and Present* (1899), he had no hesitation in claiming that the 'Saxon' remained an identifiable type in spite of the mixing of various peoples that made up the British population. Reiterating his neat summary of racial character, Keane confirmed that 'The Saxon also still remains the Saxon, stolid and solid, outwardly abrupt but warm-hearted and true, haughty and even overbearing through an innate sense of superiority, yet at heart sympathetic and always just, hence a ruler of men.'[128] His work on the Oceanic languages and races and his appointment as a professor of Hindustani established his academic credentials. He became a member of the Institute's council and then served as its vice-president (1886–90). As a recognised authority, he published a prolific range of textbooks, and periodical and encyclopaedia articles designed to educate the public about the science of race.[129]

While Keane led the way in the speculative accounts of the origin and migration of racial types, other more established authorities using the new methods for measuring populations strengthened confidence in the validity of racial types and their origins in the distant past. Out of an interest in the role of geographic isolation in evolution, Professor Flower pursued his studies of short varieties of black populations, including Andaman Islanders and Akkas of Central Africa, to develop a theory that these people were the primitive and childlike stock out of which Africans and Melanesians evolved.[130] H. H. Risely, of the Bengal Civil Service, undertook an anthropometric study of caste and occupation. His three-year study, commissioned by the Government of Bengal, strengthened the idea of a north–south racial division by arguing that the caste system originated as a division by race, not by social function or occupation. He claimed that physical distinctions were perpetuated by exogamy, and that dark Dravidians from the south composed the lower castes as opposed to the higher-caste Aryans from the north. In fashioning this more sophisticated and influential branch of colonial knowledge, Risely's study became the basis of the official government census in 1901, and consequently, the new science of anthropometry had greater impact in India than in the United Kingdom. The linking of caste to race in India would also have an influence on British thinking about what came to be known as 'race relations' in other parts of the empire. Risely gave a warning about the superficial observations in travel books and the sweeping generalisations of armchair anthropologists, and claimed that only persons able to make direct observations over time could establish reliable conclusions.[131] Although at first seen as speculative ventures, these attempts to deduce an evolution of racial types, strengthened by the work of such authorities as Flower and Risely, became entrenched in standard texts on ethnology and human geography.

As a lecturer in ethnology at Cambridge struggling to make ends meet on an annual salary of fifty pounds, A. C. Haddon published *The Study of Man* in 1898. In this and other general texts he made extensive use of the issues of the *JAI* and included descriptions of racial groups similar to those developed by Keane.[132] In *The Races of Man and their Distribution* (1912), he admitted that the definition of race itself and the identification of racial types were fraught with difficulties: 'these demarkations are perfectly arbitrary, and are employed merely to facilitate comparison and classification.'[133] Despite these reservations, Haddon's works relied on conventional stereotypes in describing racial groups. With A. H. Quiggin, Haddon reissued Keane's *Man, Past and Present* in 1920, and Haddon's own *The Races of Man and their Distribution* appeared in revised form in 1929. These later editions, while more cautious about the classification of racial groups, did not substantially alter the stereotypical descriptions and accounts of racial evolution of earlier versions. In this fashion, the post-1885 generalisations about race, entrenched in general texts on anthropology in the 1890s, passed on to a new generation of students after 1918.[134]

Even when they were first published, and certainly after the First World War, the popular texts of Keane and Haddon represented an older form of race-thinking. The pursuit of nature over nurture had moved on from anthropology to new developments in psychology. As early as 1875, the Anthropological Institute through its Psychology Committee had invited Herbert Spencer to present a paper on 'The Comparative Psychology of Man'. Proceeding in his customary deductive manner, Spencer compared the mind of the adult and the juvenile as being analogous to the mind of the civilised and the savage.[135] He pointed out that his deductions on comparative psychology, especially the precocious yet arrested development of savages, had been thoroughly established by many travellers. He concluded his paper with a call for anthropologists to shift their attentions away from physical character- istics to the study of psychological traits. In Spencer's absence, F. W. Rudler, the Institute's secretary, read his paper, and a lively discussion followed. Speakers praised Spencer's methods and conclusions, and then digressed on to anecdotes about their own encounters with the savage mind. Yet despite the immediate interest Spencer excited, in the proceedings of the Institute, few authors took up his challenge or followed his method.[136]

By the late 1880s, new developments in psychology, under the influ- ence of Alexander Bain and particularly David Ferrier's localisation of functions of the brain, opened up the possibility of comparing the brains of civilised and savage peoples to demonstrate unequal mental develop- ment.[137] The first serious effort using the new methods of psychology in the field occurred on the Cambridge Anthropological Expedition to the Torres Straits in 1898. Under the leadership of Haddon, anthropo- metric measurements of sensory and motor functions and other psy- chological observations were undertaken by W. H. R. Rivers, William McDougall, C. S. Myers, and C. G. Seligman. All these investigators later had distinguished careers in anthropology and psychology. Rivers and McDougall contributed to the growing interest in 'instinct' as an explanation of human behaviour, noting variations between cultures. Rivers, a nephew of James Hunt, attributed his early interest in anthro- pology to the bequest of his uncle's library. In his *History of Anthro- pology*, Haddon identified Hunt with the discredited negrophobia and polygenesis of the 1860s, but recognised him as having been one of the first anthropologists to take an interest in psychology.[138] As a psy- chologist at Oxford, McDougall, a member of the Eugenics Education Society, took an interest in intelligence testing, and encouraged Cyril Burt, his student, to develop means to test school children.[139]

In contrast to Hunt and mid-Victorian polygenists, the Torres Straits Expedition and other investigations came to more sober conclusions. In 1910, Professor R. W. Woodworth summarised their findings, ob- serving, 'We are probably justified in inferring that the sensory and motor processes and the elementary brain activities, though differing in degree from one individual to another, are about the same from one race to another.'[140] Although he cited this observation with favour,

[92]

Haddon and other anthropologists were still uninhibited in their sweeping generalisations about racial groups. While Haddon noted that most studies only observed European populations, he saw the statistical methods and eugenist studies of Galton and Pearson promised 'race improvement'. Like Spencer, Haddon looked to childhood development to provide clues to adult traits, and like his fellow populariser A. H. Keane, he readily incorporated psychological profiles into his classification of racial groups.[141] Consequently, the new interest in psychological studies did not challenge existing generalisations but gave a new authority to conventional stereotypes. By the early twentieth century, partly through the leadership and patronage of Galton, the frontier of the study of nature versus nurture had moved away from anthropology. Yet anthropology, now associated more closely with the study of man in nature, in other words non-European peoples belonging to 'uncivilised' or 'primitive' cultures, had lessons to teach.

Applied anthropology and empire

At the close of the nineteenth-century, the students of anthropology, including the practitioners of the physical, cultural and psychological approaches to the subject, felt sufficient confidence in their science to launch a sustained effort to gain full recognition of the academic respectability and utility of their studies. In anticipation of the conclusion of the South African War, on 12 June 1900, the Anthropological Institute and the Folklore Society prepared a memorial to Joseph Chamberlain, the colonial secretary, urging him to establish a committee to investigate conditions of the 'native races' of the Transvaal and the Orange River Colony. The memorial noted that the black population, unlike other aboriginals, was 'prolific' and thus did not die from contact with Europeans. Incorporating the insights from their science, the memorial affirmed:

> That the natives are, for savages, in a somewhat advanced social state, having a tribal organisation, religious institutions and a morality of their own; that contact with civilisation tends to break up their organisation, to destroy their customs and to set them free from many of the old moral restraints without imposing new ones, and generally to render them difficult of management by a European Government.[142]

This situation was made worse by colonial administrators' ignorance of native customs, and this ignorance, the memorial observed, rather than 'wilful disregard' was the source of difficulties between Europeans and natives. Consequently there was a great need for the systematic collection of information about native customs:

That while some of such customs and institutions are of a character not to be tolerated by a civilised government, careful enquiry is necessary before deciding on any legislation, so as to ascertain the precise meaning and consequences of the customs which it may be proposed to abolish or to modify, and how to deal with them so as to cause the least disturbance of tribal customs.[143]

The memorial concluded with an appeal for the establishment of a commission of investigation for practical and humanitarian reasons of sound administration and for the scientific purpose of preserving a record of the cultures of peoples under British rule. In contrast to the Institute's appeal, with its emphasis on stability and the preservation of indigenous customs, colonial office civil servants and the APS looked for an orderly transition involving the assimilation of Africans to conditions of modernity and to legal and political equality.[144]

The appeal was unsuccessful, and independent of the Anthropological Institute a group of humanitarian lobbyists, including the APS, put together a committee to investigate conditions in South Africa. In his review in *Man*, the Institute's new magazine, E. S. Hartland complimented the South African Native Races Committee for its avoidance of rhetoric and its straightforward description. Hartland, a leading promoter of the Institute's proposal of a government commission, drew a commonplace distinction between scientific and political questions, and consequently found the first section of the report, which described the indigenous populations and their customs, of most interest. He was less impressed with the section that dealt with 'land tenure, the labour question in its various phases, the pass laws, education, taxation, the franchise, and the liquor laws'. Though the impact of civilisation on native cultures was a matter of scientific study, these topics were, he observed, 'of interest rather to the statesmen than to the anthropologist'.[145]

Unsuccessful in their bid to be part of a government commission on South Africa, the anthropologists were more successful in gaining academic and public recognition. In 1907, an announcement in *Man* stated that Edward VII had graciously awarded the title 'Royal' to the Anthropological Institute. It reiterated the practical benefits of anthropology for colonial administration, particularly 'when the "Native Question" [was] assuming formidable proportions in many of our colonies'. Observing that anthropology had established itself at Oxford and Cambridge, and that it was part of the education of many aspiring colonial administrators, the notice concluded by affirming the academic and practical importance of the new science: 'Anthropology is not merely an academic science, appealing to a few experts; it has a real practical application, and, moreover, an imperial function to perform, in the promotion of the well-being of the colonies, the further-ance of missionary endeavours, the increase of trade, and the general advancement of civilisation.'[146] Shortly after the Anthropological Insti-tute was made royal, the BFASS lost its royal patron. Queen Victoria, who sympathised with the abolitionist cause, had initiated the crown's patronage of the society, but in 1910, the new King George V ended the royal connection. The abolitionists, now amalgamated with the APS, had put the king in a politically difficult position by criticising the racial policies of the South African Government.[147] As scientists, the anthropologists claimed to be objective observers, detached from such political entanglements. In the long struggle of the primacy of know-ledge over sentiment, beginning at least from the critical reappraisal of slave emancipation in the 1840s, this transfer of royal favour recog-nised that science had triumphed over humanitarianism.

Under a constitutional monarchy, royal titles conveyed prestige, but more significant recognition belonged with the elected government. In 1909, a deputation from the Royal Anthropological Institute appealed to Prime Minister Asquith to establish a government-funded Bureau of Ethnology. This appeal had really commenced a year earlier with the publication of an amusing yet informative article in the *Nineteenth Century* by one of the Institute's more renowned members, Sir Harry Johnston. The African traveller, administrator and popular author began his essay on 'The Empire and Anthropology' with a striking contrast between 400 million people of the empire and the limited resources of Institute. The society charged with the scientific study of these diverse peoples was housed in one and a half rooms in Hano-ver Square, had a membership of about 500, and an annual budget of £500.[148] He observed that once anthropology was seen as 'a boring fad', but it was now recognised as such an important subject that he pre-dicted it would become a required subject for the colonial service. In keeping with the new respect accorded to science, Johnston appealed for government funding on behalf of the Institute, claiming: 'the time has come – if we are going to be governed intelligently by intelligent people – when scientific research will have to be heavily endowed; in the same way that a Church or a religion was endowed with properties and tithes in order to place it above penury and the risks of popular indifference and vacillating support'.[149]After reviewing the range of racial problems throughout the empire and the paltry state of know-ledge, Johnston concluded by affirming that anthropology teaches that 'all men are brothers under their skins'. It therefore served to rectify 'intolerance, cruelty, racial arrogance, and narrow-minded conceit', and consequently was 'the science of kings and rulers'.[150]

The memorial to Asquith did not quite reach these dizzy heights, but it did once again stress the utility of anthropology for colonial administrators, missionaries and traders. Their colonial rivals, the Germans, according to the memorial, spent substantial sums on ethnology which led to success in trade 'not only with primitive and barbaric races, but also in China and Japan'. It also mentioned the domestic applications of anthropometry in studying children and army recruits and in investigating the question of the physical deterioration of the British population.[151]

The memorial was of less interest for its rhetoric than for the role and organisation of the proposed bureau. Using as models the Royal Society and the Royal Geographical Society, the memorial proposed that the bureau be administered by the Royal Anthropological Institute and be established in London with a library and meeting rooms. It would act as an information and research centre, receiving reports from the foreign, colonial, and war offices as well as from colonial and dominion governments. For the accumulation and dissemination of knowledge, the bureau would act as coordinating centre for university faculty and students. It proposed diplomas for those who passed examinations, and in accordance with the university curricula, training included practical exercises with the instruments of anthropometry and the identification of racial types from photographs.[152] March 1909 was a poor time to ask the government for money as David Lloyd George was preparing his 'People's Budget' with its costly dreadnoughts and old age pensions. In turning down the request, Asquith suggested that the Institute should seek private funding.[153]

The Institute revived the scheme again in 1911 at the Imperial Conference. It appealed to the dominion premiers gathered in London to sponsor an Imperial Bureau of Anthropology. Once again the proposal stressed the role of the bureau in coordinating information, and foresaw an imperial network of 'Governments of the British Dominions, of the India and Colonial Offices, and of those Universities in Great Britain, in India and the Colonies and Dependencies of the Empire where anthropology is systematically studied'.[154]

Unsuccessful in its appeals to the heads of governments, the Royal Anthropological Institute had greater success in organising the professional academic community. At the British Association in 1914, Sir Richard Temple (1850–1931), the president of the Anthropology Section, an army officer and colonial administrator, and an advocate of applied anthropology for prospective officials, reported on initiatives dealing with the teaching of anthropology at the universities.[155] As chair of a committee of the British Association working in cooperation with a similar committee of the Royal Anthropological Institute, he noted that a recent report on university education had observed that officials in 'parts of the Empire inhabited by non-European races' required knowledge of their languages and of 'their racial characteristics'. The committee called for a coordinated effort on the part of the British Association, the Royal Anthropological Institute, government departments, and the universities to develop facilities for the study of anthropology.

At the Worshipful Company of Drapers on 19 February 1914, a meeting was held to consider the committee's recommendations. The distinguished speakers reiterated the importance of anthropology for the administration of the empire. Sir Henry Craik, MP, observed that the universities needed to prepare their 'men' for the task of carrying 'the white man's burden'. He noted the problems of dealing with the various races of the empire and recognised 'the enormous pluck, the tact, the inborn qualities of our race, that enable so many of our young men to overcome these difficulties'. He then called upon his distinguished audience to fulfil 'our duty both as leaders in educational work and as responsible for our share in the work of the State, to help them further, to give them those ideas which they might get in an atmosphere where this was pursued as a science'.[156] The message was familiar, but it now had the impressive backing of leading political and academic figures. Of the fifty-nine invited guests, sixteen were titled gentlemen and six were MPs. In attendance, besides members of the Royal Anthropological Institute, were representatives from the Royal Asiatic Society, the India Council, the Royal Society of Arts, the British Science Guild, the Royal Geographical Society, the British Museum, the African Society, the Colonial Office and the London Chamber of Commerce. Just under half of the invited guests came from the university community, including both professors and senior administrators. The largest representation came from London, Cambridge and Oxford, but representatives from the Scottish and newer civic universities were also in attendance, including faculty from University, King's, and Bedford Colleges (London), the London School of Economics, Bristol, University College Wales, Liverpool, Manchester, Glasgow, Dundee, and Aberdeen.[157]

The advocates of anthropology, especially the promoters of its application to colonial administration and the 'native question', had envisioned a network of universities to provide research and teaching facilities. In the period following the birth pangs of anthropology in the controversies of the 1860s, and especially in the period since 1880, scientific racism managed to establish its academic credentials. It did so within the context of the late nineteenth-century imperialism and the intensification of global racial conflict. At the same time, the institutional basis of the production of knowledge had been transformed.

This new institutional context of the modern university, staffed by middle-class professionals ready to serve the interests of state and empire, gave the new scientific racist orthodoxy its authority.

The professionalisation of science, initially the medical and bio-logical sciences and subsequently anthropology itself, gave writers and lecturers greater authority by comparison with the old-fashioned morality and casual impressions of clergy, philanthropists and travel-lers. The development of a technical vocabulary and the application of statistical methods added to the professional mystique and auth-ority of the scientists. Specialised publications, such as the *JAI*, or a magazine such as *Nature* for the broader community of professionals, kept scientists informed about innovations in anthropometry and new ideas about the origin and diversity of human racial varieties. With greater professionalism also came increased specialisation and protec-tion from potential sources of criticism. By this time, the founders of British sociology, such as Patrick Geddes and L. T. Hobhouse, began to query the weight given to biological determinism.[158] But just as the comparative anatomists and the ethnographers in the Anthropological Institute never attempted to reconcile their approaches and findings, so too the sociologists and biological determinists each pursued their own specialty independent of the other.

These institutional elements may explain why the scientific racists spoke with a more authoritative voice from the 1880s, but they do not explain why they spoke with a more acceptable voice. Many of the principal ideas of scientific racism had been current since the late eighteenth century, but prior to the 1880s the exponents of these ideas had either been on the fringes of scientific community, or even, in some cases, notorious eccentrics. This description certainly applied to Edward Long, Henry Home [Lord Kames] and Charles White in the late eighteenth century, and equally applied to Robert Knox, James Hunt and Richard Burton in the mid-Victorian period, but it hardly suited William Flower or Francis Galton. In one sense racism as an ideology was a pseudo-science in the 1850s and 1860s, but an established science from the 1880s onwards.

By the 1880s, promoters of scientific racism no longer met outraged shouts at the British Association, nor did anthropologists rail against radical philosophers or naive believers in human rights. In the last two decades of the nineteenth century, members of the professional middle class were confident in the realism of their vision, and yet foresaw a future full of worrisome change and potential decline. The national destiny seemed threatened externally by powerful foreign rivals and internally by an urban mass culture incapable of generating the talent needed to sustain the national character, let alone Britain's world leadership. In the empire, international rivalry and indigenous resistance to western imperialism forced the pace of formal colonisation, and from the metropolitan perspective the problem was how to administer a multi-racial empire inhabited by peoples of exotic appearances and strange habits, and apparently unsuited to the advanced practices of Victorian civilisation.

Late Victorian scientists, as evidenced by the membership of the Anthropological Institute and the contents of its *Journal* and of *Nature*, helped forge link between the domestic and imperial crises. This link informed the work and patronage of Galton and other scientists engaged in anthropology in the 1880s and supportive of the eugenics movement in the Edwardian period. Similarly, a continuity existed between the anthropometry of the 1880s and psychometrics of the 1920s. By the 1880s, at least for the professional specialists who saw themselves as natural scientists, environmentalism was on the losing side of the nature/nurture argument.[159] It was weakened in part by the assaults of the pseudo-scientists, the polygenetic racial typologists of the 1850s and 1860s, but the strength of nature over nurture derived more from the changed social, political and intellectual context of the late nineteenth and early twentieth centuries.

To their credit the professional scientists and others who took an interest in the question of race recognised that they were witnesses of a fundamental transformation of relations between the world's peoples. From the position of scientific authority within the universities and from their organisational basis within the Royal Anthropological Institute and other learned societies, they attempted to explain and justify the evident inequalities of global power and status. The ideology of their science led them to see this new world order as a product of nature independent of human agency. The professional scientists then compounded their error by offering their knowledge in service to the state and empire. Biological determinism offered simple and universal explanations for complex historical changes, and by analogy to nature favoured winners and survivors over losers and victims. Furthermore, from the 1880s onwards, these ideas carried the professional authority of science and had at hand its institutional apparatus for the dissemination of its message.

Notes

1 See Chapter 1 and literature cited in notes 1, 14 and 15.
2 Barkan, *Retreat*, pp. 332–4; Chapter 1 above.
3 Desmond and Morris, *Darwin's Sacred Cause*; R. M. Young, Darwinism *is* social', in David Kohn (ed.), *The Darwinian Heritage* (Princeton, NJ: Princeton University Press, 1982), pp. 609–38; Herbert Spencer, *On Social Evolution*, ed., J. D. Y. Peel

(Chicago, IL, and London: University of Chicago Press, 1972); George W. Stocking, Jr., *Victorian Anthropology* (New York, Free Press, 1987); Jones, *Social Darwinism*.

4 Catherine Hall, 'Histories, empires and the post-colonial moment', in Ian Chambers and Lidia Curti (eds), *The Post-Colonial Question* (London: Routledge, 1996), pp. 65–77, and 'Introduction: thinking the post-colonial', pp. 1–33; Nicholas B. Dirks, 'Introduction: Colonialism and Culture', in N. Dirks (ed.), *Colonialism and Culture* (Ann Arbor, MI: University of Michigan Press, 1992), pp. 1–12.

5 Edward Said, *Orientalism* (1978) (Harmondsworth: Penguin, 1985).

6 Douglas Lorimer, 'Science and the secularization of Victorian images of race', in B. Lightman (ed.), *Victorian Science in Context*, (Chicago, IL: University of Chicago, 1997), pp. 213–14, and *Colour, Class*, pp. 75–81.

7 See Chapter 4.

8 Richard Drayton, *Nature's Government: Science, Imperial Britain and the Improvement of the World* (New Haven, CT: Yale University Press, 2000); Robert Stafford, "Scientific exploration and empire', in Porter (ed.), OHBE, vol. 3, pp. 294–319; John MacKenzie (ed.), *Imperialism and the Natural World* (Manchester: Manchester University Press, 1990).

9 Ivan Hannaford, *Race: The History of an Idea in the West* (Washington, DC: Woodrow Wilson Centre, 1996); Michael Banton, *The Idea of Race* (London: Tavistock, 1977).

10 In 1876, out of his personal commitment to the anti-slavery cause, Charles Darwin supported the APS petition in defence of the coloured franchise in the Cape, *The Colonial Intelligencer* (September 1877), 413–17; on Darwin's support of abolition see Desmond and Moore, *Darwin's Sacred Cause*.

11 Evelleen Richards, 'The "Moral Anatomy" of Robert Knox: The inter-play between biological and social thought in Victorian scientific naturalism', *Journal of the History of Biology*, 22 (1989), 373–436; Frank M. Turner, *Between Science and Religion: The Reaction to Scientific Naturalism in late Victorian England* (New Haven: Yale University Press, 1974); Lorimer, 'Science and secularization', pp. 214–18.

12 Francis Galton, *Englishmen of Science: Their Nature and Nurture* (London: Macmillan, 1874), pp. 12–16.

13 Clare L. Taylor, 'Knox, Robert (1791–1862), anatomist and ethnologist', *NODNB* (2004–6); George W. Stocking, Jr., *Victorian Anthropology*, pp. 64–5; Philip Curtin, *The Image of Africa: British Ideas and Action, 1780–1850* (London: Macmillan, 1964), pp. 368–9, 377–82.

14 Robert Knox, *The Races of Men: A Philosophical Enquiry into the Influence of Race over the Destinies of Nations* (London: Henry Renshaw, 1862), pp. v–vi, 23–8.

15 J. W. Burrow, *Evolution and Society: A Study in Victorian Social Theory* (Cambridge: Cambridge University Press, 1970), pp. 118–36; Ronald Rainger, 'Race, politics and science: The Anthropological Society of London in the 1860s', *Victorian Studies*, 22 (1978), 51–70; George W. Stocking, Jr., 'What's in a Name? The origins of the Royal Anthropological Institute (1837–71)', *Man*, n.s., 6 (1971), 369–90, and *Victorian Anthropology*, pp. 246–57; Lorimer, *Colour, Class*, pp. 137–61.

16 Stocking, *Victorian Anthropology*, pp. 269–73.

17 Curtin, *Image of Africa*, pp. 377–80; one of the first histories of racist-thinking, Jacques Barzun's *Race: A Study in Superstition* (1937) (New York: Harper, 1965), refers to some British scientists but makes no mention of Knox; on Hunt's pamphlet, BL. British Publishers' Archive, micro. reel 25, vol. 2, fol. 123 Kegan, Paul, Trench, Trubner (1858–1912); on Catherine Impey, see Chapter 7; Hall, *Civilising Subjects*, pp. 48–49, 276–84; Christine Bolt, *Victorian Attitudes to Race* (London: Routledge and Kegan Paul, 1971); George Mosse, *Toward the Final Solution: A History of European Racism* (New York, 1978), and Nancy Stepan, *The Idea of Race in Science: Great Britain, 1800–1960* (Hamden, CT: Archon, 1982), assign greater significance to Knox and Hunt; for a more sceptical view see Lorimer, 'Science and secularization', pp. 214–17; Mandler, 'The problem with cultural history', 96–103 and *English National Character*, pp. 74–5, 84–5.

18 Stocking, *Victorian Anthropology*, p. 65.

19 A. H. Keane, *Ethnology* (Cambridge: Cambridge University Press, 1896), pp. 165–6.

20 The discussion that follows is based in part on two earlier articles: Douglas Lorimer, 'Theoretical racism in late Victorian anthropology, 1870–1900,' *Victorian Studies*, 31 (1988), 405–30, and *'Nature*, racism, and late Victorian science', *Canadian Journal of History*, 25 (1990), 369–85.

21 T. W. Heyck, *The Transformation of Intellectual Life in Victorian England* (New York: St. Martin, 1982); Colin Russell, *Science and Social Change, 1700–1900* (London: Macmillan, 1983); Adrian Desmond, *Archetypes and Ancestors: Palaeontology in Victorian London, 1850–1875* (Chicago, IL: University of Chicago Press, 1984); Stocking, *Victorian Anthropology*, pp. 257–69; Lorimer, 'Theoretical racism', 406–11, 428–30.

22 Heyck, *Transformation*, pp. 155–89. There are no reliable statistics for the number of students in secondary education prior to 1900, but the number of children in attendance in inspected day schools grew from 2,751,000 in 1880 to 4,666,000 in 1900 (C. Cook and B. Keith, *British Historical Facts, 1830–1900* (London : Macmillan, 1975), p. 195. In 1900–1, there were 20,000 students in universities and 5,000 in teacher training colleges (D. Butler and A. Sloman, *British Political Facts, 1900–1979* (London: Macmillan, 1979), p. 313.

23 Royal Anthropological Institute (hereafter RAI) Archives, A10(1) Council Minutes, 1 January 1872 – 4 February 1873; Lorimer, *Colour, Class*, pp. 158–9; Stocking, *Victorian Anthropology*, pp. 256–7. Huxley, Lubbock and Busk were all members of the influential X-club, Ruth Barton, 'X Club (act.1864–1892)', *NODNB* (2006). During this dispute A. R. Wallace and E. B. Tylor became Council members.

24 Robert M. Young, 'Natural theology, Victorian periodicals, and the fragmentation of a common context', *Darwin's Metaphor: Nature's Place in Victorian Culture* (Cambridge: Cambridge University, 1985), pp. 155–60.

25 Report of the Council for 1871, *The Journal of the Anthropological Institute of Great Britain and Ireland* (hereafter cited as *JAI*), 1 (1871–2), 379.

26 Published list of members *JAI*, 30 (1900), pp. 1–12; RAI Archives, A14 (1), 'Attendance books, Ordinary meetings, 1892–'.

27 RAI Archives, A20 and A31 [membership lists]; also list published in *JAI*, 30 (1900), 1–12; Henrika Kuklick, *The Social History of British Anthropology, 1885–1945* (Cambridge: Cambridge University Press, 1991).

28 A. Pitt-Rivers, *JAI*, 11 (1881–2), 507; Francis Galton, *JAI*, 15 (1885–6), 497–9, and 18 (1888–9), 406–7; John Beddoe, *Memories of Eighty Years* (Bristol: J. W. Arrowsmith, 1910), p. 312.

29 Stocking, 'What's in a Name'; Rainger, 'Race, politics and science'.

30 *JAI*, 30 (1900), 1–12; Meyer Fortes, 'Social anthropology at Cambridge since 1900', in R. Darnell (ed.), *Readings in the History of Anthropology* (New York: Harper and Row, 1974), pp. 429–33; Stocking, *Victorian Anthropology*, pp. 257–69.

31 Roy M. Macleod, 'Centenary review, 1869–1969', *Nature*, 224 (1 November 1969), 417–76; David A. Roos, 'The aims and intentions of *Nature*', in James Paradis and Thomas Postlewait (eds), *Victorian Science and Victorian Values: Literary Perspectives*, Annals of the New York Academy of Science, vol. 360 (New York: New York Academy of Science, 1981), pp. 159–80; Sir Norman Lockyer, 'Valedictory memories', *Nature*, 104 (6 November 1919), 189–90; Lorimer, '*Nature*, racism', 371–2.

32 Macleod, 'Centenary', 442–3, has evidence of 970 subscribers in 1913 and puts the number as low as 300–500 before 1895; T. Mary Lockyer and Winifred L. Lockyer, *Life and Work of Sir Norman Lockyer* (London: Macmillan, 1928), pp. 45–50, 114, 153, 173.

33 Roos, 'Aims and intentions', 173–6.

34 W. Lauder Lindsay, 'Mental potentiality in children of different races', *Nature*, 10 (6 August 1874), 272.

35 Lindsay, 'Children', 272.

36 *Nature*, 6 (20 June 1872), 137–8, and (8 August 1872), 288–9; 7 (5 December 1872), 81–3; 9 (24 December 1874), 142–5 and (7 January 1875), 182–4; 17 (14 February 1878), p. 297; 18 (13 June 1878), 178–9.

37 For examples see Lorimer, '*Nature*, racism', 372–3.

38 See Chapter 4.
39 Dorothy O. Helly, '"Informed" opinion on tropical Africa in Great Britain, 1860–1900', *African Affairs* 68 (1969), 195–200; David N. Livingstone, '"A sternly practical pursuit": geography, race and empire', *The Geographical Tradition* (Oxford: Blackwell, 1992), pp. 216–59; Robert Stafford, 'Scientific exploration and empire'.
40 *JAI*, 2 (1872–3), 359–60; *JAI*, 5 (1875–6), 348, 485–6.
41 A. Lane Fox, 'Report on anthropology at the British Association', *JAI*, 2 (1872–3), 360; later reports in *JAI*, 5 (1875–6), 348, 485–6; 6 (1876–7), 167, 178; 11 (1881–2), 507–8.
42 *JAI*, 6 (1877), 178. Lane Fox organised his collection to demonstrate stages of cultural evolution. In 1882, after a number of unsuccessful attempts, he (as Pitt-Rivers) found a home for his collection at Oxford University. A. Lane Fox, 'On the principles of classification adopted in the arrangement of his anthropological collection, now exhibited in the Bethnal Green Museum', *JAI*, 4 (1874–5), 293–308; David K. van Keuren, 'Museums and ideology: Augustus Pitt-Rivers, anthropological museums, and social change in later Victorian Britain', *Victorian Studies*, 28 (1984), 171–89.
43 A. R. Wallace, 'New Guinea', *Nature*, 23 (23 December 1880), 176.
44 Beddoe, *Memories*, p. 315.
45 Maj-Gen. A. Pitt-Rivers, 'President's address', *JAI*, 11 (1881–2), 507–8.
46 A. Lane Fox, *JAI*, 5 (1875–6), 470; E. B. Tylor, *JAI*, 9 (1879–80), 443–58; W. H. Flower, *JAI*, 13 (1883–4), 488–500.
47 George Busk, remarks on G. W. Leitner, 'Siah Posh Kafirs', *JAI*, 3 (1873–4), 368–9; W. L. Distant, 'On the term religion used in anthropology', *JAI*, 6 (1876–7), 60–3; H. H. Risely, 'The study of ethnology in India', *JAI*, 20 (1890–1), 235–49.
48 A. Lane Fox, 'On the principles of classification', *JAI*, 4 (1874–5), 293–308, and 'On early modes of navigation', *JAI*, 4 (1874–75), 399–437; A. Pitt-Rivers (Lane Fox), 'On the Egyptian boomerang and its affinities', *JAI*, 12 (1882–3), 454–63; E. B. Tylor, 'On the game of patolli in ancient Mexico and its probably Asiatic origin', *JAI*, 8 (1878–9), 116–31; A. W. Buckland, 'Ethnological hints afforded by the stimulants in use among savages and among the ancients', *JAI*, 8 (1878–9), 239–54; on kinship systems, for example, A. W. Howitt, 'The Dieri and other kindred tribes of central Australia', *JAI*, 20 (1890–1), 42, 98–104.
49 H. H. Prince Roland Bonaparte, 'Note on the Lapps of Finmark (in Norway)', A. H. Keane, 'The Lapps: their origin, ethnical affinities, physical and mental characteristics, usages, present status, and future prospects', and J. G. Garson, 'On the physical characteristics of the Lapps', *JAI*, 15 (1885–6), 210–38; R. A. Cunningham, 'Exhibition of natives of Queensland', *JAI*, 17 (1887–8), 83–4; on the Royal College of Surgeons collection, W. H. Flower, 'On the aims and prospects of the study of anthropology', *JAI*, 13 (1883–4), 497–8.
50 Beddoe in *JAI*, 19 (1889–90), 490; Evans in *JAI*, 7 (1877–8), 529–30, and 8 (1878–9), 419; Tylor in *JAI*, 9 (1879–80), 453; Beddoe, *Memories*, pp. 306, 321–2.
51 Presidents' reports in the early 1870s classified papers by topic, and I have used this scheme for contributions to the *Journal* from 1871 to 1900. My count differs from Stocking's – we agree on the prevalence of archaeological papers, but my count has a higher proportion of ethnographic papers, Stocking, *Victorian Anthropology*, pp. 257–62; J. Beddoe, 'President's address', *JAI*, 19 (1889–90), 481–90, and *JAI*, 20 (1890–1), 349–55, and *Memories*, pp. 321–2.
52 George W. Stocking, Jr., 'The persistence of polygenist thought', *Race, Culture and Evolution: Essays in the History of Anthropology* (Chicago, IL: University of Chicago Press, 1982), pp. 42–68, relies on French anthropologists; John S. Haller, *Outcast from Evolution: Scientific Attitudes of Racial Inferiority* (Urbana, IL: University of Illinois Press, 1971).
53 A. R. Wallace, 'Peschel's `Races of Man', *Nature*, 15 (28 December 1876), 174.
54 T. H. Huxley, 'On the geographical distribution of the chief modifications of man', *Journal of the Ethnological Society*, n.s., 2 (1869–70), 404–12.
55 E. B. Tylor, 'President's address', *JAI*, 9 (1879–80), 443–7; George W. Stocking, Jr., 'From chronology to ethnology: James Cowles Prichard and British anthropology, 1800–1850', in James Cowles Prichard, *Researches into the Physical History of Man*

(Chicago, IL: Chicago University Press, 1973).

56 Huxley, 'Geographical distribution', 409; his old antagonist, Professor Richard Owen, sharply criticised Huxley's paper, in 'Contributions to the ethnology of Egypt', *JAI*, 4 (1874–5), 231; also *JAI*, 8 (1878–9), 323. Huxley's friends came to his defence: George Busk, *JAI*, 4 (1874–5), 478–91; Lane Fox, *JAI*, 4 (1874–5), 414–16.

57 E. B. Tylor, *Primitive Culture* (London: John Murray, 1871), vol. 1, p. 1; Chris Holdworth, 'Sir Edward Burnett Tylor, *1832–1917)'*, *NODNB* (2006); Stocking, *Victorian Anthropology*, 302–14; Raymond Williams, *Culture and Society, 1780–1950* (Harmondsworth: Penguin, 1963); Edward Said, *Culture and Imperialism* (New York: Alfred A. Knopf, 1993).

58 S. J. Whitmee, 'The ethnology of Polynesia', *JAI*, 8 (1878–9), 261–75, and 'A revised nomenclature for the inter-oceanic races of man', *JAI*, 8 (1878–9), 360–9; Lorimer, 'Theoretical racism', 411–16.

59 C. S. Wake, 'Notes on the Polynesian race', *JAI*, 10 (1880–1), 109–23, and 'The Papuans and Polynesians', *JAI*, 12 (1882–3), 197–222; R. H. Codrington, 'On the languages of Melanesia', *JAI*, 14 (1884–5), 31–43; George Brown, 'Papuans and Polynesians', *JAI*, 16 (1886–7), 311–27; A. H. Keane, 'On the relations of the Indo-Chinese and Inter-Oceanic races and languages', *JAI*, 9 (1879–80), 254–89; W. L. Ranken, 'South Sea Islanders', *JAI*, 6 (1876–7), 223–44; Francis A. Allen, 'The original range of the Papuan and Negrito races', *JAI*, 8 (1878–9), 38–50.

60 H. O. Forbes, 'On the ethnology of Timor-Laut', *JAI*, 13 (1883–4), 8–31, and J. G. Garson, 'On the cranial characters of the natives of Timor-Laut', *JAI*, 13 (1883–4), 386–402; H. N. Moseley, 'On the inhabitants of the Admiralty Islands', *JAI*, 6 (1876–7), 382–7; E. H. Man, 'On the aboriginal inhabitants of the Andaman Islands', *JAI*, 12 (1882–3), pt. 1, 69–75, and 'The Nicobar Islanders', *JAI*, 18 (1888–9), 354–94; W. H. Flower, 'On the osteology and affinities of the natives of the Andaman Islands', *JAI*, 9 (1879–80), 108–35, and 'On the cranial characteristics of the natives of the Fiji Islands', *JAI*, 10 (1880–1), 153–4, 171; see also 'Feature: Representing the Andaman Islands', *History Workshop Journal*, 67 (Spring 2009), 147–207.

61 *JAI*, 6 (1876–7), 227; 12 (1882–3), 492–3; 14 (1884–5), 40–3; Lorimer, 'Theoretical racism', 415–16.

62 A. Lane Fox, 'Observations on Mr. Man's collection of Andamanese and Nicobarese objects', *JAI*, 7 (1877–8), 444–5, 450–51; E. B. Tylor, 'Notes on Asiatic relations of Polynesian culture', *JAI*, 11 (1882–3), 401–5; Henry Yule, 'Notes on analogies of manners between the Indo-Chinese races and the races of the Indian Archipelago', *JAI*, 9 (1879–80), 290–304.

63 Ranken, 'South Sea Islanders', 230; Keane on Wake's 'Notes on the origin of Malagasy', *JAI*, 11 (1881–82), 32; Flower, 'Aims and prospects of the study of anthropology', *JAI*, 13 (1883–4), pp. 491–2.

64 The question of what is 'Darwinian' is problematic. Some authors use the term broadly: Gertrude Himmelfarb, *Victorian Minds* (London: Weidenfeld and Nicolson, 1968), pp. 314–32; Jones, *Social Darwinism*. Others prefer, as I do, to limit the term to specific ideas advanced by Darwin, chiefly natural selection; see R. J. Halliday, 'Social Darwinism: a definition', *Victorian Studies*, 14:4 (1971), 389–405. On Darwin and sexual selection: Charles Darwin, *The Descent of Man, and Selection in Relation to Sex* (London: John Murray, 1871), vol. 1, pp. 248–51; Desmond and Moore, *Darwin's Sacred Cause*; Nancy Stepan, *Race in Science*, pp. 59–65; Lorimer, *Colour, Class*, pp. 142–5.

65 H. H. Johnston, 'On the races of the Congo and the Portuguese colonies in western Africa', *JAI*, 13 (1883–4), 461–79, and 'The people of eastern equatorial Africa', *JAI*, 15 (1885–6), 3–15; see also C. E. Conder, 'The present conditions of the native tribes in Bechuanaland', *JAI*, 16 (1886–7), 76–96; R. C. Philips, 'The lower Congo. a sociological study', *JAI*, 17 (1887–8), 214–29; James Macdonald, 'Manners, customs, superstitions and religions of South African tribes', *JAI*, 19 (1889–90), 264–96, and 20 (1890–91), 13–40; H. A. C. Cairns, *Prelude to Imperialism: British Reactions to Central African Society, 1840–1890* (London: Routledge Kegan Paul, 1965); Patrick Brantlinger, *Rule of Darkness: British Literature and Imperialism, 1830–1914* (Ithaca, NY, and London: Cornell University Press, 1988), 173–97.

66 Kate Fletcher, 'Flower, Sir William Henry (1831–1899)', *NODNB* (2004).
67 Tylor, *Primitive Culture*, vol. 1, pp. 6–7; Chris Holdsworth, 'Tylor, Sir Edward Burnett (1832–1917)', *NODNB* (2004).
68 E. B. Tylor, 'On a method of investigating the development of institutions applied to laws of marriage and descent', *JAI*, 18 (1888–9), 269; this paper was the occasion of the statisticians' 'Galton question' when Sir Francis Galton asked how one established statistically valid co-relations.
69 E. B. Tylor, *Anthropology: An Introduction to the Study of Man and Civilization* (London: Macmillan, 1881), pp. 56, 74–5, 80–1.
70 Flower, *JAI*, 11 (1881–2), 185.
71 A. R. Wallace, 'Anthropology', *Nature*, 24 (14 July 1881), 243.
72 Tylor, 'President's address', *JAI*, 9 (1879–80), 444; see also Tylor, *Anthropology*, pp. 5–7.
73 Tylor, 'Address to the Department of Anthropology at the British Association', *JAI*, 9 (1879–80), 235–6.
74 Tylor, 'Anthropology', *Nature*, 28 (3 May 1883), 8–10.
75 Tylor, *Nature*, 28 (3 May 1883), 10; see also Tylor, *Anthropology*, pp. 5–7.
76 Tylor, *Nature*, 28 (3 May 1883), 11; see also 'Address to the Department of Anthropology', *JAI*, 9 (1879–80), 239, and *Anthropology*, pp. 112–13.
77 Stocking, *Victorian Anthropology*, pp. 228–37.
78 Tylor, *JAI*, 9 (1879–80), 240–1.
79 Tylor, 'Anthropology', *Nature*, 28 (3 May 1883), 11; Tylor, *Anthropology*, pp. 112–13.
80 Tylor, *Nature*, 28 (3 May 1883), 11.
81 *Nature*, 24 (14 July 1881), 243.
82 Fletcher, 'Flower, Sir William Henry'.
83 W. H. Flower, 'Comparative anatomy of man', *Nature*, 22 (20 May 1880), 60. See also *Nature*, 20 (3 July 1879), 222–5; 20 (10 July 1879), 244–6; 20 (17 July 1879), 267–9; 22 (20 May 1880), 59–61; 22 (27 May 1880), 78–80; 22 (3 June 1880), 97–100.
84 Flower, 'Opening address, Section D, Report of the British Association', *Nature*, 24 (8 September 1881), 436–7.
85 Flower, *Nature*, 24 (8 September 1881), 437; see also Flower, 'Address to the Department of Anthropology at the British Association', *JAI*, 9 (1879–80), 188–9.
86 *JAI*, 11 (1881–2), 189–90; see also *Nature*, 14 (8 September 1881), 437, and *JAI*, 9 (1879–80), 128.
87 *JAI*, 11 (1881–2), 190–2.
88 Flower, 'On the aims and prospects of the study of anthropology', *JAI*, 13 (1883–4), 491–3; see also 'Aims and prospects of anthropology', *Nature*, 29 (31 January 1884), 320.
89 *JAI*, 13 (1883–4), 493.
90 Flower, *Nature*, 29 (31 January 1884), 320.
91 Flower, 'President's address', *JAI*, 14 (1884–5), 379–82.
92 *JAI*, 14 (1884–5), 391–3.
93 T. H. Huxley, *Man's Place in Nature* (1863) and *Evolution and Ethics* (1893); A. R. Wallace, 'The origin of the human races and the antiquity of man deduced from the theory of "natural selection"', *Journal of the Anthropological Society of London*, 2 (1864), clviii–clxx, reprinted in Michael D. Biddiss (ed.), *Images of Race* (Leicester: Leicester University Press, 1979), pp. 37–54.
94 J. S. Mill, 'Of the Inverse Deductive or Historical Method', reprinted from *System of Logic* (1843) in G. L. Williams (ed.), *John Stuart Mill on Politics and Society* (London: Fontana, 1976), pp. 56–77; Herbert Spencer, *Social Statics* (1851), and 'The comparative psychology of man', *JAI*, 5 (1875–6), 301–15; Burrow, *Evolution and Society*, pp. 101–18, 179–227; Stocking, *Victorian Anthropology*, pp. 38–41, 128–37, 171–2.
95 Stepan, *Race in Science*; Jones, *Social Darwinism*; G. R. Searle, *Eugenics and Politics in Great Britain, 1900–1914* (Leyden: Noordhoff International, 1976); Rich, *Race and Empire*, pp. 92–119.
96 George Busk, 'President's address', *JAI*, 3 (1873–4), 509, 520–5; J. Beddoe, 'On the anthropological colour in phenomena in Belgium and elsewhere', *JAI*, 10 (1880–1),

374–80; Paul Topinard, 'Observations on the methods and processes of anthropom-etry', *JAI*, 10 (1880–1), 212–14, 223–4; J. G. Garson, 'The Frankfurt Craniometric Agreement with critical remarks thereon', *JAI*, 14 (1884–5), 64–83; and 'The cephalic index', and 'The international agreement on the classification and nomenclature of the cephalic index', *JAI*, 16 (1886–7), 11–17.

97 'Extracts from the report of the Anthropometric Committee of the British Asso-ciation', *JAI*, 9 (1879–80), 345–51; Francis Galton, 'On recent designs of anthro-pometric instruments', *JAI*, 16 (1886–7), 2–9; British Association, *Anthropometric Investigation in the British Isles* (London: Royal Anthropological Institute, 1909).

98 Francis Galton, 'President's address', *JAI*, 18 (1888–9), 401–19; Gould, *Mismeasure*, pp. 75–7.

99 Ruth S. Cowan, 'Galton, Sir Francis (1822–1911)', *NODNB* (2004); Raymond E. Francher, 'Francis Galton's African ethnology and its role in the development of his psychology', *The British Journal of the History of Science*, 16 (1983), 67–79; R. S. Cowan, 'Nature and Nurture: The interplay of biology and politics in the work of Francis Galton', in W. C. Coleman and C. Limoges (eds), *Studies in the History of Biology* (Baltimore, MD: John Hopkins University Press, 1977), vol. 1, pp. 133–208; D. W. Forrest, *Francis Galton: The Life and Work of a Victorian Genius* (New York: Taplinger, 1974).

100 Galton, 'On recent designs', 2–9; 'President's address', *JAI*, 15 (1885–6), 489–499; 'President's address', *JAI*, 18 (1888–9), 406–7; and 'On the head growth in students at the University of Cambridge', *JAI*, 18 (1888–9), 155–6.

101 Report of the Anthropometric Committee of the British Association', *Nature*, 26 (7 September 1882), 463.

102 Galton, 'Anthropometric laboratory', *JAI*, 14 (1884–5), 205, and Galton, 'President's address', *JAI*, 17 (1887–8), 346–55.

103 *JAI*, 17 (1887–8), p. 79. In 1889, Institute members offered public lectures on the more conventional topics of physical and cultural evolution, *JAI*, 19 (1889–90), 441–2.

104 Galton, 'President's address', *JAI*, 16 (1886–7), 392.

105 *JAI*, 16 (1886–7), 394–402; otherwise he thought some intermixture with blacks (illustrated by an analogy of mixing black and white fluids to various shades of coffee to demonstrate the mathematical laws of heredity) would produce a breed of whites capable of survival.

106 Conference proceedings in *JAI*, 16 (1886–7), 174–236.

107 University College, London. Galton Papers. Haddon to Galton, 1 December 1891; A. H. Quiggin, *Haddon, the Head Hunter* (Cambridge: Cambridge University Press, 1942), pp. 56–80, 93–5.

108 University College, London. Galton Papers. Tylor to Galton, 29 May 1895, 7 June 1895, 18 June 1895.

109 University College, London. Galton Papers. Haddon to Galton, 24 June 1901.

110 Searle, *Eugenics*, pp. 4–44.

111 Searle, *Eugenics*, p. 39; Philip Abrams, *The Origins of British Sociology, 1834–1914* (Chicago,, IL: Chicago University Press, 1968), pp. 88–100, 149–50.

112 Isaac Taylor, 'The origin of primitive seat of the Aryans', *JAI*, 17 (1887–8), 238–69, and responses to it, 269–75; A. H. Sayce, 'Address to the Anthropological Section of the British Association', *JAI*, 17 (1887–8), 166–77; C. R. Conder, 'The races of modern Asia', *JAI*, 19 (1889–90), 30–43; J. Beddoe, 'President's address', *JAI*, 19 (1889–90), 491–3. Tony Ballantyne, *Orientalism and Race: Aryanism in the British Empire* (Basingstoke: Macmillan, 2002), deals with the emergence of Aryanism and its trans-cultural influences, and not this later manifestation which was partly a rejection of orientalism's trans-racial links.

113 J. Beddoe, 'English surnames from an ethnological point of view', *JAI*, 12 (1882–3), 238, and *The Races of Britain: A Contribution to the Anthropology of Western Europe* (London: 1885); see also J. Park Harrison, 'On the survival of certain racial features in the population of the British Isles', *JAI*, 12 (1882–3), 243–55; A. L. Lewis, 'On the evils arising from the use of historical national names as scientific terms', *JAI*, 8 (1878–9), 325–35.

114 Beddoe, 'English surnames', p. 236; Imperial College, London. Huxley Papers. 33.190. T. H. Huxley to the editor of *The Times* (12 October 1887); Huxley's comments, *Nature* 18 (29 August 1878), 479–80; Sir John Lubbock, 'The nationalities of the United Kingdom: Extracts from letters to *The Times*', *JAI*, 16 (1886–87), 418–22. Lubbock (1834–1913), a banker, was MP for the University of London, and even after 1886 a committed free trader, see Timothy L. Alborn, 'Lubbock, Sir John, first Baron Avebury (1834–1913)', *NODNB* (2006).

115 Edward Brabrook, 'A. H. Keane', *Man*, 12 (1912), 53; *Who Was Who, 1897–1915* (London: Adam and Charles Black), 389; *The Times* (5 February 1912), 11d. See also Chapter 4.

116 Keane, 'On the relations of the Indo-Chinese and Inter-Oceanic races and languages'; and 'The Indo-Chinese and Oceanic Races – types and affinities', *Nature*, 23 (30 December 1880), 199–203, 23 (6 January 1881), 220–3, 23 (13 January 1881), 247–51, 23 (20 January 1881), 273–4.

117 University College, London, Archives. Testimonials for A. H. Keane and Report of the committee on lectureships in the vernacular languages of India, read to Senate, 12 April 1883, and read to Council, 14 April 1883; Keane's Appendices in *Stanford's Compendium of Geography and Travel*, volume for *Australasia* (1879), and for *Asia* (1883).

118 A. H. Keane, 'The science of language', *Nature*, 22 (22 May 1880), 49–52; A. H. Sayce, 'Asia', *Nature*, 26 (3 August 1882), 317–18; see also Keane, *Nature*, 23 (6 January 1881), 222–3, and 23 (13 January 1881), 247.

119 Keane, *Nature*, 23 (30 December 1880), 199.

120 *Nature*, 23 (6 January 1881) 220, 222–3.

121 *Nature*, 23 (13 January 1881), 249; on the application of Aryanism in Australasia see, Ballantyne, *Orientalism and Race*.

122 *Nature*, 23 (20 January 1881), 274.

123 James Dallas, 'On the primary divisions and geographical distribution of mankind', *JAI*, 15 (1885–6), 304–30. W. S. Duncan, 'On the probable origin of man's evolution', *JAI*, 12 (1882–3), 513–25; G. Bertin, 'The races of the Babylonian Empire', *JAI*, 18 (1888–9), 104–20. For a recent account using archaeological finds and DNA genetic markers, see Stephen Oppenheimer, *Out of Eden: The Peopling of the World* (London: Robinson, 2003), who dates the migration of modern humans out of Africa about 80,000 years ago.

124 Keane, *Ethnology*, pp. 142–3, 150–6, 165–6.

125 Keane, *Ethnology*, p. 162; see also pp. 223–9, 239–40.

126 British Library. Wallace Papers, Add. MS 46437, fols 67–8. A. H. Keane to A. R. Wallace, 22 November 1899.

127 Keane, *Ethnology*, pp. 223–9; Haddon referred to Keane's claim in his own text, *History of Anthropology* (London: Watts, 1910), p. 95.

128 A. H. Keane, *Man: Past and Present* (Cambridge: Cambridge University Press, 1900) p. 532.

129 For Keane's popular works see Chapter 4.

130 Flower, 'On the osteology and affinities of the natives of the Andaman Islands', 127–32; 'Descriptions of two skeletons of Akkas, a pygmy race from Central Africa', *JAI*, 18 (1888–9), 3–19; 'The pygmy races of man, a lecture at the Royal Institution', *JAI*, 18 (1888–9), 72–91.

131 H. H. Risely, 'The study of ethnology in India', *JAI*, 20 (1890–1), 235–63; Nicholas B. Dirks, *Castes of Mind: Colonialism and the Making of Modern India* (Princeton, NJ: Princeton University Press, 2001).

132 Quiggin, *Haddon*, pp. 112–14; A. C. Haddon, *The Study of Man* (London: Bliss, Sands, 1898).

133 A. C. Haddon, *The Races of Man and Their Distribution* (Halifax: Milner [1912]), p. 5, and discussion pp. 1–6.

134 Keane, *Ethnology*, pp. 221–41; Haddon, *The Races of Man and Their Distribution* (Cambridge: Cambridge University Press, 1929), pp. 139–56.

135 Herbert Spencer, 'The comparative psychology of man', *JAI*, 5 (1875–6), 301–15;

reprinted from *Popular Science Monthly* (1876) in Biddiss (ed.), *Images of Race*, pp. 187–204.

136 Spencer, 'Comparative psychology', 304; one paper argued savages had regressed because they were less rational than children, Hon. Lady Welby, 'An apparent paradox in mental evolution', *JAI*, 20 (1890–1), 304–29.

137 D. Ferrier, 'On the functional topography of the brain', *JAI*, 17 (1887–8), 26–31, and H. D. Rolleston, 'Description of the cerebral hemispheres of an adult Australian male', *JAI*, 17 (1887–8), 32–42; Alexander Bain, 'The scope of anthropology and its relation to the science of mind', *JAI*, 15 (1885–6), 380–8.

138 Haddon, *History of Anthropology* (1910), pp. 53, 64–8, 79–80, 86, and (1934), pp. 40, 44–5, 60–1; Quiggin, *Haddon*, pp. 95–108; on 'instinct' in psychology, see Jones, *Social Darwinism*, pp. 125–39.

139 Searle, *Eugenics*, pp. 12–13, 52; Gould, *Mismeasure*, pp. 234–9, 273–96.

140 R. W. Woodworth, *Science*, 31 (1910), p. 179, quoted in Haddon, *History of Anthropology* (1910), p. 86 and (1934), pp. 63–4.

141 Haddon, *History of Anthropology* (1910), pp. 81–7, and (1934), pp. 31–2; *The Study of Man*, pp. xxv–xxix, pp. 16–29; *The Races of Man* [1912], pp. 24, 28, 34–5, 60–1, 70–6, 80–2, 101–2.

142 RAI Archive. A10(3) Council Minutes, 12 June 1900, 'The Memorial of the Anthropological Institute of Great Britain and Ireland and of the Folklore Society to Joseph Chamberlain, Secretary of State for Colonies'.

143 RAI Archive, A10(3) Council Minutes, 12 June 1903.

144 See Chapters 5 and 7.

145 E. S. Hartland, 'Review of *The Natives of South Africa; their Economic and Social Condition*', *Man*, 1:72 (1901), 90–1; The South African Native Races Committee, *The Natives of South Africa: their Economic and Social Condition* (London: John Murray, 1901).

146 'Anthropological Institute: Augmentation of title', *Man*, 7:70 (1907), 112.

147 RH. Brit. Emp. S.18. Anti-Slavery Papers. E2/12, British and Foreign Anti-Slavery Society Minute Book, #1798, 5 August 1910; #1811, 7 October 1910; #1830, 4 November 1910.

148 H. H. Johnston, 'The empire and anthropology', *The Nineteenth Century*, 64 (1908), 133–5; reprinted in Johnston's *Views and Reviews* (London: 1912).

149 Johnston, 'Empire and anthropology', p. 137.

150 Johnston, 'Empire and anthropology', p. 146.

151 RAI Archives, A10(3) Council Minutes, 5 May 1908; *JAI*, 38 (1908), 489–92; *Man*, 9: 55 (1909), 85–7; *The Times* (10 March 1909), 10d; Adam Kuper, *Anthropologists and Anthropology: The British School, 1922–72* (Harmondsworth: Penguin, 1975), pp. 125–7.

152 RAI Archive A10(3) Council Minutes, 5 May 1908; *The Times* (10 March 1909), 10d; C. H. Read, Anthropology at the universities', *Man* 6:38 (1906), 56–9, and 6:57 (1906), 85–6.

153 *The Times* (12 March 1909), 10d; *Man*, 9 (1909), 85–7.

154 RAI Archive A56, 'Memorial on Imperial Bureau of Anthropology', printed copy, no date; *JAI*, 42 (1912), 5; *Man*, 11:95 (1911), 157.

155 'Proceedings of societies – anthropological teaching in the universities', *Man*, 14:35 (1914), 57–72; Sir Richard Temple, 'The value of a training in anthropology for the administrator', *Man*, 14:19 (1914), 34–6.

156 *Man*, 14 (1914), 61–2.

157 *Man*, 14 (1914), 59–60.

158 Abrams, *Origins of British Sociology*, pp. 149–50.

159 Beddoe, *Memories*, p. 312 suggested that scientific opinion including 'a great many anthropologists' supported Galton and nature over nurture.

CHAPTER FOUR

Race, popular science and empire

Studies of imperialism and popular culture have richly documented the pervasive presence of the symbols and rituals of empire in late Victorian and Edwardian Britain. This celebration of British global pre-eminence included not just the formalised theatrics of monarchy and empire, most notably in the Golden and Diamond Jubilees in 1887 and 1897, but also the more mundane world of school athleticism, juvenile literature, the music hall, billboard and newspaper advertising, and the packaging of Imperial tobacco, Lipton's tea and Cadbury's chocolates.[1] What these signs of the empire's presence in the metropolis may mean has become a matter of dispute, with Bernard Porter's *Absent-Minded Imperialists* challenging the notion of a metropolitan imperial culture. Though he is not prepared to accept the existence of a common 'British' culture committed to a dominating imperialism, Porter concedes the omnipresence of the signs of empire in the metropolis between the 1880s and 1914.[2] The chronology of scientific racism in Chapter 3 and its popular dissemination explored in this chapter suggest that this later age of imperialism gave scientific representations of race a more prominent place within the metropolitan culture. The dramatic controversies of the 1860s had at most an uncertain outcome resting on the continued ambiguities of race and culture rather than upon an authoritative biological determinism. Developments between the 1880s and 1914 on the other hand, internally within the metropole and externally in the global context of the new imperialism, created conditions for the ascendancy of scientific-racist thinking.

There is no denying that the imperial presence in the metropolitan culture had a decidedly racial component. It came in the form of news reports of colonial conflict, in the ceremonial rituals of the massed troops of the imperial monarchy, in the minstrels on the music-hall stage, and in the smiling dark faces of the advertisements for the exotic groceries of the tropics.[3] Whether these ephemera of empire translated into a commitment to imperialism shared across the lines of class, region, religion and ethnicity is more difficult to ascertain. Responses to specific events, most notably the South African War, provide signs of identification with struggles and victories of British arms overseas. Support for the war proved short-lived, for as the British military failed to meet expectations for an easy victory and resorted to the 'methods of barbarism' against Boer guerrilla tactics, anti-war opinion gained support.[4] In the aftermath of the war, E. D. Morel and his Congo Reform Association, supported by John and Alice Harris and their illustrated 'atrocity' lectures at Nonconformist chapels, mounted a successful campaign against King Leopold's abusive exploitation of Africans engaged in the rubber harvest in the Congo. On the other hand, Sir Charles Dilke, H. R. Fox Bourne and the APS failed in their efforts to mount a public campaign in support of African rights in the new Union of South Africa. Their failure was not simply a matter of their methods of propaganda, but was due to the more substantial political obstacle of white racism and public indifference, and even antipathy at home.[5]

The social history of minorities in the United Kingdom also provides troubling evidence of popular attitudes. In the period from the 1860s to 1919, a popularly rooted xenophobia prompted outbursts of anti-Irish feeling, jingoistic mobs, anti-alien agitation against Jewish immigrants, and anti-Chinese and anti-black riots in Liverpool and Cardiff.[6] The immediate cause of these attacks on minorities was straightened economic circumstances which intensified competition for jobs and housing. These assaults stemmed from the scapegoating of minority groups as the cause of deeper social and economic ills, and this process of scapegoating in itself relied upon stereotypes firmly established within the popular culture. The correlation between popular identification with white privilege in the empire, antipathy toward immigrant groups at home, and the scientific orthodoxy of theories of racial inequality have created a presumption that professional science had a hand in shaping popular attitudes. However, this view is not much more than a presumption, for the process by which a professional elite came to have such an impact remains largely unexplored.

Questions of the influence of ideas are notoriously difficult to deal with, and perhaps the most notorious instance is the grossly overworked concept of 'social Darwinism'.[7] The success of Darwin's theory of evolution by natural selection lay in its deeply rooted origins in the social and cultural matrix of his age. In a culture pervasively informed by the political economy of Adam Smith and David Ricardo, and out of the specific influence of Malthus's *Essay on Population* (1798), Darwin was not alone in seeing the evolution of species as an outcome of competition. Most notably, Richard Chambers in his *Vestiges of Creation* (1844), and Alfred Russel Wallace, the co-author of the idea of natural selection, worked independently from Darwin, but were influenced by a common cultural context. Distinct from the biological realm, theories of social evolution had roots in the Scottish enlightenment of the eighteenth century and, quite independently of *The Origin of Species* (1859), developed contemporaneously with the long-term germination of Darwin's thought. Herbert Spencer, for example, developed his evolutionary sociology in the 1840s and 1850s and coined the phrase 'survival of the fittest' in 1864. Darwin, perhaps mistakenly, incorporated Spencer's phrase into later editions of *The Origin of Species*.[8]

Considering the roots of the theory of natural selection in this broad social and intellectual matrix, it is not surprising that Victorian observers drew connections between biological theories and evidence of racial conflict in the colonies. The danger of too readily ascribing these observations to the influence of Darwin, or of science in general, is that the events which prompted the observation in the first place get overlooked. For nineteenth-century observers the most readily recalled instances of genocide all derived from the history of colonialism: namely, the fate of the Caribs, Aztecs and Incas before the Spanish Conquistadors, and within the British Empire, the decimation of the Beothuk of Newfoundland and the extermination of the Tasmanians. In the latter case, the death of the last Tasmanian, Truganini, in 1876, was an event both anticipated and reported in the press.[9] The danger of applying a 'social Darwinian' label to the Victorian perception of these events is that we reduce what some contemporaries found a profoundly disturbing colonial reality to a scientific theory.

The task, then, of establishing what precisely constitutes an instance of the influence of science upon popular attitudes is not as straightforward as it might at first seem. This task is further complicated because we are not dealing with an ignorant population, in the sense of people with blank minds, but rather with an informed or misinformed public with a set of ideas which were then subject to new influences. During the whole of the nineteenth century, no range of secular or scientific sources can match the sustained production of anti-slavery and missionary publications preaching a common humanity regardless of race. Even more specifically, for the majority of children of the middle class and respectable working class, at least until the First World War, attendance at Sunday school formed part of their education.[10] Recognising the racial stereotyping of its principal characters, it is nonetheless significant that Harriet Beecher Stowe's *Uncle Tom's Cabin* was by far and away the best-selling novel in Britain and the empire from its original publication in 1852 to 1914. Its narrative of liberation from slavery was much more than a plain tale of the escape of black American slaves, for part of its appeal lay in how that romance of liberation from slavery readily translated into the Victorian child's growth into adulthood, or the adult's struggle to sustain individual autonomy and respectability.[11]

In the contested terrain of racial discourse, the appeal of the abolitionist and missionary movement needs to be considered, for it is not at all clear why the multiple meanings of its narrative of liberation should collapse when confronted with a biological determinism constructed by science. Nor should we confuse the Christian and humanitarian belief in a common humanity and a narrative of liberation with a commitment to racial equality. If it had any substance at all, that equality was not actual but potential, and realised by conversion, or liberation, or assimilation to the norms and practices of British, Christian, civilised, respectable life. Such a conversion or liberation implied some form of pre-existing or even natural condition. The equation of an uncivilised or savage state with a life led in sin, commonplace both in missionary publications and in the secular representations of popular science, informed the common culture in a more pervasive way than did the theories of mid-Victorian science. The most significant influence of science on these pre-existing representations of race may not be from the specific theories of the scientists but from the secularisation of representations of sin, and scientific naturalism's denial of the narrative of conversion or liberation to a civilised condition both ethnocentric in its construction and universal in its application.[12]

The quest for the intellectual origins of racism in the mid-nineteenth century has focused on polygenetic speculators such as Robert Knox and James Hunt, and upon the Anglo-Saxonism in some historical works, for example Thomas Arnold's *Lectures on Modern History* (1841) and Charles Kingsley's *The Roman and the Teuton* (1864).[13] Certainly an older scholarship too readily constructed a mid-Victorian identity of English national character in which the cherished historical foundations of the 'liberties of Englishmen', including individual liberty, equality before the law, and representative government, once a historical gift to humanity under British leadership, had become a privileged inheritance belonging exclusively to the white Anglo-Saxons of the British Empire and its prodigal daughter, the United States of America. Part of the confusion here, as in the case of Charles Dilke's *Greater Britain*, lies in the ambiguity about the language of race and culture. The trans-Atlantic celebration of 'Anglo-Saxon' had different meaning in the New World from that of the Old World. 'WASP', the acronym for White Anglo-Saxon Protestant, is a twentieth-century American invention unknown to the Victorians.[14] For some scholars, the polygenesis of Knox and his followers and this construction of an Anglo-Saxon identity in the 1850s and 1860s signify that racism was an intellectual construct generated within Europe in the period of the absent-minded imperialism of free trade. Here both the chronology and the exclusion of the colonial encounter do less than justice to a substantial body of evidence attesting to the long-term influence of the colonial encounter and the specific internal and external transformations associated with the construction of a new democratic polity at home and an expansionary imperialism abroad.[15]

In the 1860s, leaders of the scientific community had little respect for the racial science of Hunt and Knox, and *The Roman and the Teuton* confirmed Charles Kingsley's reputation as a fine novelist and a poor historian. [16] More popularly based religious and humanitarian groups were outraged by the assault on the missionary movement and the anti-slavery cause. In 1873, in response to Francis Galton's suggestion that colonial development in east Africa would be best served by immigrants from China, the *Church Missionary Intelligencer* identified science and political economy as adversaries of Africans and the missionary movement.[17] Studies of juvenile literature, in identifying some correspondence between mid-Victorian racist thought and the racial stereotypes in boys' adventure tales in colonial settings, attribute an influence to the polygenists. If one looks closely at the citations of scientific racist ideas in juvenile literature, they are drawn not from the 1860s but from the 1880s, and especially from the 1890s onwards.[18] This chronology fits with the expansion in the market for juvenile magazines and fiction, and, as treated in Chapter 3, with the development of scientific racism as the new orthodoxy within professional science. Not only was the popularisation of scientific racism contemporaneous with the 'new imperialism' of the late nineteenth century, but in its popular form racial science incorporated the evident inequalities of the colonial world and made the endemic conflicts of colonial race relations part of its narrative.

Contemporaneous with the explosion in juvenile fiction, there was from 1870 onwards a great expansion in popular non-fiction aimed at both adult and juvenile readers. Publishers responded promptly to the new opportunities provided by the growth of mass literacy following the Education Act of 1870. This market received a further stimulus with the extension of education, especially at the secondary and post-secondary levels, from the 1890s onwards. School Boards purchased readers for classroom instruction, and some students and the growing ranks of teachers purchased general texts and educational magazines. The authors of these texts – by their own inclination and by the demands of the form – were drawn into making broad generalisations about racial groups. Improvements in printing technology reduced costs, and with the development of photography, these publications became much more lavishly illustrated.[19] Public displays at museums and exhibitions also played an important educational role. Along with the bones and artefacts collected by ethnographers from the remote parts of the empire, exhibits included photographs of racial types. In some cases, as at the Indian and Colonial Exhibition of 1886 and at missionary society and other exhibits, representative 'natives' were part of the displays, or painted plaster models of racial types added lifelike effects.[20]

Some commercial exhibitions included real specimen 'savages'. On 10 May 1887, twenty thousand spectators crowded into Earl's Court to see the opening of Buffalo Bill's Wild West Show. Queen Victoria herself attended a private performance and thereby gave the royal stamp of respectability to the encounter between American cowboys and, as the press reported, the 'Redskins'.[21] The APS occasionally received complaints about the treatment of people put on display. A Gujerati dwarf, anxious to return to India, received food but no pay for appearing in a Barnum and Bailey sideshow; a small group of Native Americans received no pay and insufficient food for appearing in an Earl's Court exhibition; and an enterprising showman had enticed a group of Bedouins complete with camels to put on exhibitions of scenes from the Bible, and had then abandoned them without pay at the Alexandra Palace in Muswell Hill. Familiar with the history of such exhibitions, in 1908 the APS received a commitment from the War Office that there would be 'no objectionable features in the performances of West African native troops in the forthcoming Military Tournament'.[22] More notoriously, the 'Savage South Africa' exhibit at Earl's Court in 1899 involved some two hundred 'Africans', including some who came from the West Indies and the United States as well as some specimen 'Kaffirs'. The exhibit displaying humans in chains and housed in cages offended moralists. They were particularly upset by its popularity among young women who paid to touch as well as see the savages. In the defence of public decency, the court upheld the closing of the kraal to women visitors. The APS was concerned about the keeping of people in cages, and about the possibility that they were slaves receiving no pay and compelled to participate in a humiliating exhibition.[23]

By the end of the nineteenth century, the growth of mass consumerism gave publishers and showmen the unprecedented means to disseminate representations of race to a public aware of racial conflict and subordination overseas. The adventure stories in juvenile magazines aimed to excite the reader's imagination through a realistic portrayal of encounters on the colonial frontier. Authors such as G. Henty prided themselves on the geographical and historical 'facts' they incorporated into their stories.[24] Popular writers of non-fiction sought to give their accounts credibility by claiming to present authoritative and objective science. While it may not be possible to distinguish between 'fact' and 'fiction' in these sources, this material provides some idea of what writers and publishers presented to the public as reliable geographic and anthropological knowledge.

Victorian professional science grew out of a long and distinguished tradition of amateur science. This amateur pursuit of science did not diminish in the second half of the nineteenth century when professional scientists eventually established their dominance in research and in employment in government agencies and in universities and colleges. In fact, the amateur and professional scientists lived in a rather uneasy relationship as rivals contesting possession of the field. With its interest in the Victorian countryside, as well as in exotic plants and animals outside of the British Isles, natural history was the branch of amateur science which attracted the largest number of participants drawn from the broadest range of social classes. Even though conventionally it dealt with 'Nature' exclusive of human beings, natural history grappled with the distinction between what was natural and what was distinctly human. The Reverend John G. Wood, the most popular Victorian writer and lecturer on natural history, provided anthropomorphic studies of animal life and animalistic studies of human beings in their natural or pre-civilised state.[25]

In addition to the traditions of amateur science represented by Wood, a variety of popular science periodicals appealed to a general interest in science and provided specific information about particular science hobbies. More important in conveying scientific constructions of race to a more popular readership were a variety of illustrated, geographical reference works. These weekly and monthly serials and encyclopaedias, which contemporaries called 'self-educators', gave synopses of travel literature with the aim of providing a global survey of the world's peoples. From the 1860s to the early twentieth century, these sources changed in form and substance, reaching a larger public and over time incorporating the theories of racial inequality advanced by professional science.[26]

Popular science magazines

Naturalists from a broad range of social ranks spent their leisure time observing and recording in minute detail the flora and fauna of the Victorian countryside. Amateur scientists of a more mechanical bent spent their time as inventors tinkering with the exciting possibilities of electricity in the hope of becoming another Michael Faraday, Thomas

Edison or Alexander Graham Bell. A number of popular magazines, for example *Hardwicke's Science Gossip* (1865–93), the *English Mechanic and World of Science* (established in 1865), *Science Monthly* (1883–85), and Richard Proctor's *Knowledge, an Illustrated Magazine of Science* (1881–1904), appealed to amateur scientists among the growing ranks of salaried professionals, office clerks and skilled artisans.[27] At the same time, with the recent establishment of a national schooling system and its captive readership among teachers and students, and in a culture that placed a great deal of emphasis on self-improvement and upward mobility, individuals from a broad segment of society found in science an outlet for their intellectual curiosity and a means to enhance their self-esteem and social respectability. In the columns of *Nature*, for example, advocates of science for the working classes proclaimed the social benefits of science hobbies.[28]

The promotion of government-financed, university-based research by leading professional scientists such as T. H. Huxley and Norman Lockyer, the editor of *Nature*, posed a threat to the hopes and ambitions of publicists for amateur science. Government-endowed science, like an endowed church, created the prospect of a scientific establishment with a privileged and exclusive professional clergy. In contrast to the gospel of self-help and the heroic engineers publicised by Samuel Smiles, professional, endowed science threatened the free market in ideas and inventions by which ingenious amateurs hoped to establish their fame and fortune.

Readers of *Hardwicke's Science Gossip*, *Science Monthly*, or *English Mechanic and World of Science* were active practitioners of amateur science, not passive observers who simply followed the activities of professional scientists at second hand. As field naturalists, backyard astronomers and independent inventors, they were more interested in communicating with one another than learning what the professional scientists had to offer. Consequently, science magazines for the amateur hobbyist made only a few isolated observations on the racial question. For example, *Hardwicke's Science Gossip*, a magazine for field naturalists and claiming to have the largest correspondence columns of all the science periodicals, defined the scope of natural history as the animal and plant world exclusive of human beings. Consequently, it contained no articles on developments in racial science. Similarly, the *English Mechanic and World of Science*, which dealt more with the physical sciences and appealed to mechanical inventors, contained only a few pieces on science and race. For example, in 1886, an elementary school teacher wrote in requesting information on how to conduct anthropometric measurements of his students, and quickly received two replies offering advice.[29]

One of the few articles on race in the *English Mechanic* was a lengthy extract from a rambling address by Sir George Campbell, MP and former Indian administrator, at the Anthropology Section of the British Association in 1886. A parliamentary supporter of the anti-slavery society and the APS, Campbell, who had recently visited the southern United States, observed that 'their knowledge of the subject [anthropology] was still very limited, and their progress slow'. He claimed to take a practical view of the subject, and after allusions to stock breeding and varieties in the animal world he noted that 'as regarded the mind, they had yet to learn that there were very wide differences of mental capacity between different races'.[30] The editor of the *English Mechanic*, who could have selected other commentaries at the British Association more confident in asserting the inequality of races and more in keeping with the direction of professional science, may have included this singular extract out of political sympathies with Campbell's rather old-fashioned liberal sentiment.

Some magazines attempted to satisfy the interests of both the amateur hobbyist and a broader general readership, and these more frequently included articles that dealt with the question of race. The main source of these observations, though, was not articles dealing with the developments in biological or anthropological science, but rather reviews of travel literature. These magazines also retained a measure of scepticism about the findings of anthropologists. In 1881, in *The Academy*, a review of science and literature aimed at a well-educated readership, F. W. Rudler began his otherwise favourable review of Tylor's *Anthropology* with the observation: 'Even now the aims of anthropology to take rank as a distinct science are not too freely conceded.' According to the reviewer, some viewed it as 'an incoherent assemblage of facts and fancies – amusing, in its own way, but of little or no educational value', while others thought it 'a useful study for medical men, but not a subject of any general interest'.[31] Similarly, in *The Science Monthly*, Coutts Trotter repeated Sir Henry Maine's observation that ethnology was the one subject in which 'the greatest amount of nonsense can be talked with the least corresponding effort'. Such scepticism did not serve to discipline the use of commonplace generalisations about race and culture. In his article, Coutts Trotter argued for the British annexation of New Guinea, claiming that the Papuans had little to lose, for they lacked both 'ambition and discontent – those twin virtues which form the basis of modern civilisation'.[32]

Other than *Nature*, the science magazine which most frequently dealt with the question of race, but at the same time retained a measure of scepticism about professional science, was Richard Proctor's *Knowledge: an Illustrated Magazine of Science*. Aiming at a wider and less

[116]

well educated readership than *Nature*'s, Proctor began the first number of *Knowledge* by attacking the smug superiority of professional scientists. He criticised their private technical language, and specifically pointed to the obscurantism of the racial scientists:

> The general public do not want Science to be presented to them as if they were of intelligence inferior to their teacher's. But they cannot be expected to take an interest in statements couched in abstruse or technical terms. Nor is Science degraded when plain untechnical language, such as we propose to use in KNOWLEDGE, is employed; when, for instance ... a race of men is not described as 'microscene and dolichocephalic', but as small-faced and long-headed.[33]

Knowledge also reprinted from the Globe a satirical attack on the Anthropological Institute. The article ridiculed the appearance of four specimen 'savages' at the Institute, and suggested that the visitors might conduct their own anthropology of the anthropologists by observing 'that the English are in many ways ... a peculiar race of men, and that the variety known as "anthropologists" are especially remarkable for their age, their fondness for palavers, and their inquisitiveness'.[34] Proctor's distrust of professional science led him into a long-standing rivalry with Norman Lockyer and his advocacy of government-sponsored, institutionalised research.

For Proctor, government funding of science would simply provide a new source of patronage reserved for a professional elite. Proctor held out the possibility of a career in science for talented individuals, claiming that a successful science publicist and lecturer might clear in profit £500–£1000 per year, as much as the salary of a university professor. With an eye for potential readers, and perhaps for potential self-improving scientists, *Knowledge* noted the rapid increase in the size of the 'professions', including school teachers and office clerks, in the 1870s.[35] Ironically, Proctor's own efforts to make his way as a science publicist did not prove as rewarding as he had promised his readers. He relied on financial support from his wife, a wealthy American widow, and consequently spent part of each year in the United States. While there, he collected material from the American press and scientific sources.

In *Knowledge*, he reprinted these American articles which questioned the benefits of emancipation, claimed that blacks were incapable of exercising the franchise, and made derogatory observations about Jewish and Catholic immigrants.[36] *Knowledge* also included largely descriptive reviews of travel literature. The review of J. A. Froude's *The English in the West Indies* approved of the author's claim that the black population was unsuited to representative government. In a brief article on the 'British race', the focus was not on the fixed typology of the 'Saxon'. Contrary to the anthropometry of Dr John Beddoe, the article celebrated the mixed ancestry of the British population, and this mixture made 'the British race' and gave it the qualities making it 'beyond all question predominant in the world'. [37] Such patriotic boasting of the qualities of a British 'race' did not depend on the new anthropometry with its fixed, measured types; its roots lay back in the eighteenth century and its vigour in the 1880s related to anxiety about Britain's leadership in an imperial world order.

Knowledge and other popular science magazines in the 1880s did not act as conduits for scientific racist theories developed by the professional scientists. Among amateur hobbyists and advocates of science for the populace there was some resistance to the pretensions and exclusiveness of the professional scientists. While this resistance to the authority of professional science may have limited the dissemination of their theoretical racism, it did not translate into opposition to biological determinist explanations. Racial stereotypes and assumptions of racial superiority were conveyed by periodicals aiming at a general readership –for example *Knowledge* or *The Academy* – not by a presentation of the racial theories of leading scientists but mainly by incidental reviews of travel literature. For a more sustained presentation of racial science in a popular form, one needs to look to popular writers on natural history and serialised, illustrated reference works produced for a respectable Victorian readership seeking self-improvement through the acquisition of knowledge.[38]

The Reverend John G. Wood

Of the nineteenth-century lecturers and authors on natural history, the Reverend John G. Wood (1827–89), had the largest following among general audiences and children. Wood graduated from Oxford in 1848 and was ordained in the Church of England in 1852. He began earning an income from his writing in 1851, and by the early 1860s devoted more and more of his energies to writing and lecturing. He established his reputation through a series of hugely successful anthropomorphic homilies on the domestic virtues of common animals. For example, his *Common Objects of the Country* (1858) sold 100,000 copies, and his *Homes without Hands* (1865), a 600-page study of the habitations of animals, proved even more successful in total sales. His success as a children's author won him the position of editor of *The Boy's Own Magazine* for 1865. Wood, who published more than seventy books, gained equal fame as a lecturer on natural history throughout England, and made two successful tours of the United States. As an admitted populariser, he aimed to keep natural history free from the technicalities of biological science, and to awaken and excite his public's curiosity in nature.[39]

Wood's main focus was on 'Nature' rather than 'Man'. He first dealt with the subject of race only briefly in *The Boy's Own Book of Natural History* (1861). In an introductory section of nine pages, Wood identified a distinct place for human beings in the order of creation, and stressed the unity and common origin of racial varieties. To emphasise this point he specifically rejected the claim of affinity between the ape and the Negro as argued by the polygenists.[40] Wood's science was Christian, pre-Darwinian, and on the racial question, monogenetic.

In spite of his Christian and monogenetic viewpoint, Wood's description of racial groups, in *The Boy's Own Book of Natural History*, followed the common format of mid-nineteenth century racial typologies. His scheme of classification was borrowed directly from Charles Pickering, *The Races of Man and their Geographic Distribution* (1850). Pickering, an American doctor and member of the United States Exploring Expedition, 1838–42, provided a racial typology that was similar to that of polygenetic defenders of slavery in the United States.[41] In borrowing uncritically from Pickering, Wood, despite his religious belief in monogenesis, showed little sensitivity to the ethical dimensions of his racial typology. In his correspondence and in his conversation, Wood showed no inhibition about making prejudicial remarks. Upon return from his tours to America, his son recalled how the clergyman entertained the family with anecdotes about black waiters and Chinese immigrants.[42]

In *The Boy's Own Book of Natural History*, Wood provided brief descriptions of the physical characteristics of Pickering's eleven 'races', and gave short imaginative descriptions of savage life. For example, his picture of Native Americans came straight from the cowboy and Indian thrillers so popular in the juvenile literature of the 1860s. Wood informs his juvenile readers that 'No blood hound ever followed his prey with more certainty than the American Indian when on his "war-path"', and 'when near them his approach is silent as the gliding of a serpent, his blow as deadly as its fangs'.' This conventional image of the savage hunter became a standard by which other peoples could be compared. Describing the Malays, Wood observes that 'As the American Indians are slayers and robbers by land, so are the Malays murderers and pirates by sea.'[43]

From the success of his *Illustrated Natural History*, Wood's publisher, George Routledge contracted with him to produce a lavishly illustrated 'Natural History of Man' as a 32-part serial. Routledge put up the considerable sum of £5,000 for its production, and in the initial contract with Wood based the author's royalties on a sale of

15,000 copies per issue. This estimate proved somewhat optimistic, and as the first few issues hit the news-stands, production runs were reduced, until after six months 6,000 copies became its normal run. That number of copies was about the same as that for the Christmas annuals Routledge published for the juvenile market, but not near the 20,000 copies of James Fennimore Cooper's *Last of the Mohicans* the publisher produced in 1867, or the 52,000 copies of *Uncle Tom's Cabin* produced in four editions between 1869 and 1878.[44] While not as great a success as some of Wood's other popular science works, *The Natural History of Man* reached a larger readership than works more frequently referred to in the history of scientific racism. At the price of a shilling an issue, however, the serial aimed at a middle-class readership. Subsequently published as a two volume set, it was favourably assessed in an illustrated review in *Nature*, and E. B. Tylor, despite his reservations about the distortions of its illustrations, recommended Wood as the most comprehensive and readily available compendium on the arts and culture of primitive man.[45]

Coming out of a natural history tradition which kept human beings apart from nature, Wood defined his subject as dealing with those peoples and cultures 'who have not as yet lost their individuality by modern civilisation'.[46] This conception of his work led to geographic and cultural imbalances. As a two-volume set, the first volume dealt with Africa, and the second volume dealt with the rest of the world, largely on the Americas and Australasia, very briefly on Japan, China and India, and only a few pages on ancient man in Europe. He included no discussion of comparative anatomy but rather relied on travel accounts, feverishly working in the British Museum Reading Room to extract forty-eight pages of text for each issue. Nor was Wood an evolutionist, for he refused to accept the application of Darwin's ideas to human beings.[47]

The absence of comparative anatomy and of evolutionary theory did not mean that Wood's text, and its accompanying engravings, were free of racial stereotyping. Wood, in common with many mid-Victorians, no longer believed in the 'noble savage'. He notes that the Samoans 'approach nearer to the "noble savage" of the poet than most races of men', but yet even they 'have many of the imperfections which necessarily accompany savage life'.[48] In his search for the pure unmitigated savage, Wood noted how the accoutrements of civilisation reduced significant differences. When Australian Aborigine cricketers toured England in 1868 and played in 'the cricketer's costume', he observed that 'there was nothing remarkable about them'. When dressed in native costume, including black ballet tights for Victorian decorum, the cricketers became Aborigines once again with their natural athleticism fully revealed.[49]

Wood drew a stark contrast between civilised Victorian standards and savage life, so that the two represented the extremes of virtue and vice. For Wood, as for many of his contemporaries, the stereotype of the 'Negro', a racial caricature firmly fixed and rich in association from the long history of slavery and the struggle for abolition, served as a standard by which other peoples could be measured. In part the colour symbolism of black against white, of evil versus good, made this representation the most dramatic contrast between civilised and savage life. Although important, the role of this colour symbolism should not be exaggerated. Wood did not rank races by complexion, placing the lighter-coloured nearer to civilisation and the darkest at the lowest level of savagery. Displaying a certain sophistication about colour distinctions, he emphasised, as did contemporary travel accounts, that Africans varied a great deal in physical appearance and were proud of the particular traits of their own group, including for some a pride in the darkness of their complexion.[50]

The peoples of east and southern Africa he treated more favourably, following received opinion that the Zulus were the aristocrats of the continent, and putting particular emphasis on their proximity to European standards of beauty. Relying on two of the more Negrophobic travellers in West Africa, Captain Richard Burton and Winwood Reade, the naturalist provided his readers with a distorted, contemptuous portrait of West Africans. Just in case the readers missed the point, J. B. Zwecker, his illustrator, provided engravings that made Wood's text visible.[51] The point of these distorted images was to build in the reader's mind a correlation between physical appearance and mental attributes.

Nonetheless, these attributes of the savage, including stupidity, indolence, superstition, cruelty and immorality, were not dependent upon skin colour; nor were they derived from a racial typology provided by science. When describing a particular group, Wood referred to them in the singular and generalised to all 'uncivilised' peoples. Relying on Francis Galton's *Travels in South Africa* (1853), Wood readily converted the traveller's negative comments on the Damara peoples of South West Africa into universal attributes of savage life:

> the savage is essentially cruel, not having the least regard for the sufferings of others, and inflicting the most frightful tortures with calm enjoyment. As for morality, as we understand the word, the true savage has no conception of it ... Honesty, in its right sense, is equally unknown, and so is truthfulness, a successful theft and an undetected falsehood being thought evidences of skill and ingenuity, and by no means a disgrace.[52]

In his two-volume survey of human varieties, Wood assigns these same attributes to all peoples he classifies as 'savages', finding similarities in the facial expressions of Africans and Polynesians, while the Maoris, whom some scientists classified as 'Caucasian', he characterises as a stereotypical savage 'whose ambition is murder, and whose reward is to eat the body of his victim, who never does a stroke of work that he can avoid, and who leads a life of dissipation as far as his capabilities go'.[53] Humanitarian agencies such the APS complained about descriptions of peoples as 'savages' and preferred the language of 'uncivilised' with the implicit promise of assimilation to civilised conditions. Eventually, as the racial discourse came to focus on race relations within multi-racial colonial societies, the language of specific racial types and the generic language of 'savage' declined in use to be replaced by new generic terms to describe a transformed and racialised world order, namely, the 'non-Europeans', the 'non-whites', and the 'coloured' races.[54]

In common with his travellers' accounts, Wood uses the status of women to demonstrate how savage life failed the test of Victorian civilisation. His standards, though, are those of a patriarch and not a feminist. As is extensively documented in studies of gender and imperialism, most notably in the abolition of sati in India earlier in the nineteenth century, accusations that women suffered abuse both justified imperial interventions and served to denigrate non-western cultures.[55] In southern Africa, Wood claims that women did almost all manual labour, and consequently worked twice as hard as English agricultural labourers. He explains that polygamy was a means to provide for the division of labour among the female population. For the amusement of his readers, he comments on the universal tensions within a household, for 'Domestic life has, of course, its drawbacks among savages as among civilised nations', and, he observes, 'there are, perhaps, times when the gallant soldier, who has been rewarded with a wife or two for his courage in the field, wishes himself once more engaged in a war march'.[56] As a result of the division of labour, Wood notes, men have retained their fine physical form, but on the other hand, the women are 'bowed by reason of the heavy weights which they have to carry, and they rapidly lose that wonderful symmetry of form which distinguished them in the bloom of their youth'.[57]

Victorian prudery did not restrain Wood from reporting on his travellers' comments on the sexual attractions of the women they encountered. Citing Winwood Reade, Wood comments on the 'soft dark eyes', 'sweet smiles' and 'graceful ways' of the women of Angola. He notes that the women can 'involuntarily win a kind of love', but 'though they can inspire a passion, they cannot retain the love of an intellectual man'. At times, the naturalist could be more specific, quoting Captain James Grant's remark on a Watusi woman: 'her small breasts were those of a crouching Venus'.[58] In contrast, in old age, in both Africa and Australia, Wood depicts women as grotesque old hags worn down by their labours.[59]

The clergyman paid special attention to violence against women. In Fiji, he claims that the practice of strangling widows on the death of their husbands, and the consequent neglect of children, as well as cannibalism, continual feuding and the strangling of the aged, have caused the population to decline, and, he observes, 'very few Fijians die from natural causes'.[60] He claims that African men used sticks and whips to discipline their wives. Once again for the amusement of his readers and in affirmation of male authority, Wood reports that in the Congo, 'women do not resent this treatment, and indeed, unless a woman is soundly flogged occasionally, she thinks that her husband is neglecting her, and feels offended accordingly'. The low status of African women, described as a state of virtual slavery, led them, according to Wood, to quarrel amongst themselves just like the 'querulous spirit' of English women 'in the most degraded neighbourhoods'.[61] As a popular author, Wood's task was not simply to provide a synopsis of travel literature; he had to make that material both interesting and meaningful to his readers. Accustomed to the dynamics of gender inequities at home, his readers, at Wood's invitation, engaged in an amusing parlour game of comparing and contrasting the familiar and the exotic in alien cultures.

Just as the status of women provided one test of savage morality, their response to white colonisers was an equally important test. For Wood, distrust and treachery characterised colonial relationships. He observed: 'In common with other savage races, the Australians are apt to behave treacherously to the white man when they find themselves able to so with impunity.'[62] Contrary to the views of abolitionists and supporters of the APS, Wood emphasised that the vices of savages were natural to them and not the result of corrupting European influence, for 'savages [were] not indebted to Europeans for all their vices'. According to Wood, many of 'the greatest evils of the world, such as drunkenness, cruelty, immorality, dishonesty, lying, slavery, and the like, are to be found in full vigour among savage nations, and existed among them long before they ever saw an European'.[63] As a clergyman, Wood focused on the sinful character of savage life, but gave no sign of the promise of conversion or liberation common in missionary and anti-slavery publications. Wood was first and foremost a practitioner of natural history, and his construction of savage life by implication reflected the natural endowment of peoples living in an uncivilised state.

Wood's descriptions of colonial encounters assumed an unequal contest with conflict as the invariable outcome. The power and wealth of Europeans, according to Wood, excited fear and envy among savage peoples such as Australian Aborigines:

> the people are very crafty: mild and complaisant when they think them-selves overmatched, insolent and menacing when they fancy themselves superior, and tolerably sure to commit murder if they think they can do so with impunity. The only mode of dealing with these people is the safe one to adopt with all savages: i.e., never trust them, and never cheat them.[64]

Not pausing to consider aboriginal entitlement to land, or its appro-priation by white settlers, Wood identified the adoption of European concepts of property as the source of proverbial thievery among colo-nised peoples. Having no property as natural savages, 'they are honest because there is no use in stealing', but once the idea of property is adopted, savages steal rather than work, and thus 'from being honest they become thieves'. In this tendency, Wood affirmed the familiar trope of his sources, for savages revealed their paradoxical nature com-bining together 'the strength and craft of man with the moral weakness of children'.[65]

Endowed with such flaws of character and faced with the advance of Europeans equipped with their superior technology and moral fibre, the uncivilised, he predicted, faced extinction. Wood gave the usual examples of this natural law that the higher must supplant the lower in citing the cases of the Tasmanians and the Australian Aborigines, but he also saw that the same fate awaited the Maoris, and citing Captain Speke, suggested that the African might be 'superseded by a being superior to himself'.[66] This conclusion was not necessarily an instance of 'social Darwinism', for Wood made no mention of natural selection or of Spencer's 'survival of the fittest'. In Wood's scheme, the process fulfilled a Biblical prophecy for, in the case of the Australian Aborigines, they failed 'to exercise dominion over the beasts and the birds', and 'although they inherited the earth, they did not subdue it, nor replenish it'. Consequently they were doomed to be replaced by whites who would perform 'their duties as men'.[67] Here Wood invoked not Darwin's law but God's law to explain the retreat of aboriginal peoples before the advance of European colonialism.

As a work of popular science, Wood's *Natural History of Man* con-veyed a racialist vision of savage life without explicit recourse to the racial typologies of the comparative anatomists. The work served as a compendium of observations drawn from an extensive range of travel literature; and its contents, especially in recounting the sins of savages but without the promise of conversion, often had closer links to missionary publications than to anatomical texts. The appeal and success of Wood's work should serve as a warning against drawing too hard a distinction between the influence of scientific and non-scientific sources in the Victorian racial discourse. Wood's popular science was pre-Darwinian, even Biblical, and on the racial question monogenetic. His whole effort to popularise natural history ran counter to the efforts of professional scientists who sought greater precision by measuring and defining an ever-increasing number of racial types. Their science depended upon the invention of a private language exclusive to experts. Wood's descriptive everyday language, derived from travel accounts, constructed a bipolar representation of the generic 'savage' characterised by the vices that were most sternly condemned by the standards of Victorian respectability. Just like the domestic homilies of his natural history, Wood told a moral tale. His narrative set out the ethical groundwork for British imperial interventions and for the subordination of colonised 'savages' unsuited by nature to Victorian civilisation.

Robert Brown

In the 1870s, the Reverend Wood's main rival as a populariser of scientific ideas about race was Robert Brown (1842–95), an Edinburgh-trained botanist and journalist, who made his reputation as the author of weekly and monthly illustrated serials on the world's countries and peoples. Whereas Wood approached his subject in the tradition of natural history, and with a special talent for writing for juveniles, Brown adopted the stance of the professional objective scientist. Like Wood in his natural histories, Brown made limited use of physical anthropology and relied mainly on travel literature supplemented by his own experiences in North and Central America, the West Indies and North Africa. He also shared with Wood an ability to generalise freely about the moral and psychological characteristics of various peoples, though Brown's descriptions were more secular in the sense that they owed less to conventional Christian morality than to the equally conventional ethics of political economy.

As an able student in biology at the University of Edinburgh, Brown first travelled to Greenland, and then after graduating, the British Columbia Botanical Association of Edinburgh sent him in 1863 to the Pacific Northwest to collect exotic seeds to be sent back to Scotland. Arriving in Victoria after visiting the West Indies, Central America and California, Brown impressed the local colonists with his talents as an explorer and scientist, and in 1864 they employed him as commander of the Vancouver Island Exploring Expedition. He published an account of the expedition and a number of articles relating to the botany and geography of British Columbia. He gave lectures in natural history at the School of Arts and at Heriot-Watt College in Edinburgh, and at the Mechanics Institute in Glasgow. He applied for university appointments but failed to gain the chair of botany at the Royal College of Science in Ireland in 1868, and failed once again in 1873 to win the chair of botany at the University of Edinburgh. Frustrated in his attempts to obtain an academic post, Brown, now married, sought to make his way as a journalist and popular author.[68]

In 1876, Brown and his wife moved to London where he took up a position with the *Echo*, and then in 1878 he joined the editorial board of the *Standard*. He remained with the *Standard* until his death in 1895, and gained recognition as an able professional journalist, serving as vice-president of the Institute of Journalists in 1890. In addition to his newspaper work, he contributed regularly to *All the Year Round* and the *Academy*, and wrote for *Chambers' Encyclopaedia* and other reference works, including editing *Science for All*, a five-volume popular science of everyday life published in 1877–82, and reissued in a variety of editions thereafter. He specialised in writing large, amply illustrated geographical works for Cassell. These works were issued in weekly or monthly parts and then sold as multi-volume sets. First printed in serial form at the cost of 6d per issue, *The Races of Mankind: Being a Popular Description of the Characteristics, Manners and Customs of the Principal Varieties of the Human Family* was then published as a four-volume set in 1873–76. An enlarged six-volume edition, retitled *The Peoples of the World*, was published in 1881–86 and reissued in 1890–94, and again in 1898–1900. A similar work, *The Countries of the World: Being a Popular Description of the Various Continents, Islands, Rivers, Seas, and Peoples of the Globe*, appeared as a six-volume set in 1876–81, and then as a new revised edition in 1884–89, with a reprint in 1894–99. His publisher, Cassell, viewed Brown not simply as a journalistic writer but as a specialist who brought scientific expertise to his subject.[69]

In contrast to Wood's descriptions of 'natural man' unaffected by western civilisation, Brown aimed to depict peoples as they existed in the present. Consequently, the Scottish journalist described both the culture of aboriginals and their status as colonised subjects. Like Wood, Brown made limited use of comparative anatomy. His first series, *The Races of Mankind*, began with a single page on racial classification, and in the revised version, *The Peoples of the World*, the thirteen-page introduction gave his most extended treatment of comparative anatomy. He borrowed his typology from R. G. Latham (1812–88), a

medical doctor and influential philologist who was director of ethnology at the Crystal Palace and a member of the Ethnological Society
in the 1850s.[70] While Brown, in common with many Victorian commentators, ranked his primary races hierarchically, he had little use
for the technicalities of comparative anatomy and derided the efforts of
those he termed 'closet naturalists' and 'untravelled anthropologists':

> They find in their museums a shelf of skulls labelled more or less accu-
> rately; they compile a few vocabularies from the travels of voyagers not
> much better informed, and even less scientific, than themselves; they
> separate off these word-lists into families, and attach some type of skull
> to each, and call the result an 'ethnological scheme', any objections to
> which are overwhelmed with a cloud of fragments of speech, mixed with
> the names of bits of bone.[71]

Affirming monogenesis as the orthodox scientific view, Brown claimed
that 'The best naturalists, even those whose faith is laid deep in Darwinian soil, are satisfied that whatever might have been the origin of
man, the diversified races … are all sprung from one stock.' He reviewed polygenist claims only to reject them and to point out that differences in physical features such as skin colour and hair texture were
biologically insignificant. More importantly, intermarriage between
families over time had intermixed physical and linguistic characteristics making 'hybrid' peoples. Rejecting Paul Broca's claims for the
infertility of racial crosses, Brown claimed that hybrid peoples were
fertile; this fact, he writes, 'goes far to prove that the different families
of men are "races" of the same species'.[72]

Rather than tracing origins, Brown focused on the migration of
peoples over time. He pointed to the distribution of populations in
the Oceanic islands, the first settlement of the Americas from Asia,
and the Central Asian origin of Europeans as evidence of the role of
migration in human history. He placed European colonialism since
1500 within this broad context, as white settlement advanced in the
Americas and Australasia, and aboriginal peoples retreated and declined. Although he affirmed human unity and the role of migration in
the distribution of the world's peoples, he nonetheless saw significant
differences between racial groups. These differences were a product of
human development over a great span of time. Quoting E. B. Tylor,
Brown remarked: 'the black, brown, yellow, and white men, who we
may examine on our quays, may be regarded as living records of the
remote past'.[73]

His limited use of comparative anatomy in no way inhibited Brown's
recourse to racial stereotypes. Even though Brown had travelled widely
in the Americas, Europe and North Africa, his travels seem to have
narrowed rather than broadened his mind. His observations consisted

of a series of binary contrasts of the virtues of the English as against the vices of all foreign peoples, both European and non-European. His description of English virtues, including 'truth, fidelity and sincerity', contrasted with his list of the vices of the Irish, Italians, French and Germans.[74] He followed the conventional distinction between 'semi-civilised' and 'savage' peoples, but dishonesty, treachery and cruelty were as much a characteristic of the peoples of India and China as of the indigenous inhabitants of the Americas, Australasia and Africa.[75]

Statements about racial and ethnic groups are invariably comparative statements, as the traveller contrasts the vices of the observed with the virtues of the observer. In *The Races of Mankind*, he had dealt briefly with 'the European stock', affirming European historical achievements and predominance in the world. In *The Peoples of the World* in 1881–86, Brown informed his readers that he deliberately avoided the term 'Anglo-Saxon', and chose the term 'English'. From the amalgamation of original inhabitants and successive waves of Celtic, Teutonic and Norman invaders, the English were 'a mongrel race'. Contrary to the racial types measured by anthropometry, Brown boasted, as Defoe had done before him, that this mix of peoples made the 'True Born Englishman'.[76]

Calling on his readers to reflect on the troubled world outside the British Isles, Brown concluded *The Peoples of the World* with a tribute to the 'conservatism' of the English.[77] As a leader writer for the *Standard*, a leading Conservative London daily, he was not exceptional in equating his own political principles with the nation's virtues. The pre-eminent English virtues of self-reliance and self-discipline, of thrift and industry, and of sincerity and integrity were the common touch-stone of Brown and his readers drawn from the ranks of respectability among the middle and upper-working classes. Beneath these ranks stood the residuum who not only failed to live up to respectable standards but indulged in a contrary set of vices. Externally, the failings of the residuum were also the failings of the 'lesser breeds without the law'. These 'Victorian values', not the abstractions of science, were the common foundation of the racialism of Wood, Brown, the professional scientists and their lay public.[78]

The most common charge that Brown levelled against alien races was that they were dishonest and lazy. Here one might see the psychology of projection at work, out of guilt over the theft of aboriginal lands and over idleness projected onto stereotyped colonised peoples. Brown's friends reported that he was manic about work and never at ease in leisure; even on vocation in North Africa he organised his time into productive use.[79] The danger of the psychology of projection or of the analysis of the binary opposites of constructed identities is twofold. First, they threaten to make racism internal to the mind of the coloniser; and second, they threaten to overlook the political and economic imperatives that not only transformed the lives of peoples subject to colonial rule but also created new institutional structures in the organisation of production and labour, in governance and the law, and in new patterns of everyday life that made racial difference, subordination and conflict meaningful and oppressive.[80]

In his representation of the world's peoples, Brown relied on his experience as a traveller in colonial and multi-racial societies where forms of institutionalised racism either were in place or were in the process of construction. When he travelled to British Columbia, the United States and the West Indies, Brown identified with the white community and shared their deep suspicion and hostility toward non-whites. In *The Races of Mankind*, Brown relied on his own encounters with Amerindian peoples, but the attributes he assigned to them he assigned with equal certainty to peoples he had never met. Like Wood, Brown called Native Americans thieves and liars for not respecting the property rights of the settlers who had dispossessed them of their land: 'They are, as nearly all savages are, very honest among themselves, but with the whites they are not at all backward in stealing.'[81] He reported that Native Americans had the intelligence to benefit from some education, and he had some hope for a settled life among the agriculturalists and 'half-breeds' of the eastern part of the continent. In contrast, he predicted that 'The prairie Indian must hunt the buffalo, *or die*; the salmon or fish-eating Indian must spear the salmon, *or die*; a nation of hunters must hunt, or become beggars on the bounty of the Government or their neighbours.'[82]

With some insight he observed that conflict, suspicion and treachery were endemic in colonial situations. In *The Races of Mankind*, advising readers of his own extensive travels in the Pacific Northwest, he denied that there was some abstract 'law of Nature' at work, for the decline of the 'wild races' had specific observable causes: disease, principally smallpox; drunkenness, which he attributed to an insatiable native demand and the greed of unscrupulous white traders; the increased violence from western firearms in warfare both with rival bands and with Europeans; dysentery from the adoption of white man's food; and respiratory ailments brought on by the adoption of European clothing and blankets.[83] For Native Americans, the relentless advance of the Europeans led, according to Brown, to 'feelings that, as an independent people, their years [were] numbered', and the state of mental depression weakened 'the power of throwing off disease'. This state of mind was 'shortening the days of the race', and, Brown affirmed, there was 'no maudlin sentimentality in this, but stern reality'.[84]

Despite his pessimistic conclusion, he had one test of the capacity of indigenous peoples to survive. Used throughout his several series, he measured the future prospects of colonised peoples by their capacity to perform settled labour, usually in agriculture, under European direction. Brown thought that, with few exceptions, aboriginal peoples could not meet this test and were doomed.[85] In the United States, even blacks, having survived over two centuries of slavery, declined under emancipation. Brown acknowledged that this view would offend 'many excellent and well-meaning philanthropic persons (for whom [he] entertain[ed] the greatest respect)'. In contrast to the advocates of humanitarian and missionary causes, who favoured intervention into the lives of alien peoples to convert them to the norms of Christian and Victorian respectability, Brown, in the 1870s, favoured letting well enough alone:

> if we look solely to the philanthropy of the subject, and the general happiness and prosperity of savage nations, we shall best consult their interests eventually by keeping away from them, and leaving them in that condition of human existence which they are best able to occupy; for where one is benefited and ameliorated by civilisation a thousand are ruined, morally, physically, and politically; resulting sooner or later in the utter extinction of their race, language, and traditions.[86]

Brown was not consistent in this stance. In the reissue of *The Races of Mankind* as *The Peoples of the World* in 1881–86, this discussion was omitted, and in other works written in the 1890s, especially on colonialism in Africa, he was a strong advocate of imperial intervention.[87]

A more important strategy for distancing himself from the human cost of his tale of human suffering and destruction, and the more effective means for disarming humanitarian critics was Brown's claim to be representing the realistic, value-free observation of objective science:

> We need not stop to inquire into the morality of all this, or whether mankind at large would be benefited or otherwise by the extinction of some races, or anent the rights of mankind involved. We, as men of science, are only concerned with the fact that these things are brought about, and their cause; but with the ethical side of the question we are, fortunately, not called upon to deal.[88]

Despite this claim, even on his own terms, he could not avoid 'the ethical side of the question'.

Brown recognised that the world he described was one of conflict which generated relations characterised by suspicion, deceit and violence. It was not simply that Brown's remarks were the product of prejudice, but rather that the polarities of good and evil, of white and black, reflected what Frantz Fanon called the Manichean world of colonialism.[89] Brown provided his own psychological explanation for that colonial reality. For example, with allusions to similar flaws among the Italians and the Irish, he explained that the long history of foreign rule in India created a population habituated to 'perjury and lying'. 'The defence of the weak has always been duplicity and flattery', he observed; and 'nations which have been frequently conquered', according to Brown's Lamarckian reasoning, 'in time become, by the transmission of the acquired instinct, a race of hereditary liars'.[90]

In confirmation of this vision stood Brown's contrasting case of an alien race of people who made model colonists. From his travels in California and British Columbia, he praised the industrious work of Chinese migrant labourers. He described the 130,000 Chinese colonists on the Pacific coast as the innocent victims of the 'most absurd unreasonable prejudice' of the white community. He admired them first because he saw them as passive victims in the face of maltreatment, secondly because they were industrious workers, and lastly because they were obedient subjects, who did 'not interfere in any way in politics', and gave 'little trouble to the law'. Brown hoped that by finding employment in railroad construction as non-union labourers, they might 'help to neutralise the effects of continual strikes'.[91] What Brown found puzzling was that Chinese labourers were exceptional and not typical colonial subjects.

The peoples with the longest history of labouring under coercive conditions for Europeans were Africans and their New World descendants, and yet for Brown and his sources, the history of the slave trade, slavery and abolition raised troubling issues in the past and in the present. In his observations on slavery and its aftermath, Brown presented a revised and widely endorsed view of the achievements of the anti-slavery movement and of philanthropists' engagement with the imperial project. Identifying slavery as an African institution and not a result of contact with European traders, he nonetheless followed abolitionist portrayals of the horrors of the middle passage. Confirming his own opposition to slavery, he claimed that the slave trade ended for economic reasons rather than as a result of the lobbying of humanitarians.[92] Furthermore, its end had unforeseen benefits in the European exploration of Africa, the introduction of legitimate commerce, and consequently, 'the natives became more industrious and less brutal than before'. Most of his commentary in his several series focused on the results of emancipation, reiterating what had become the common political assessment that abolition in the West Indies was a 'philanthropic act, but commercially, it was the ruin of most of the islands'. In assessing the results of abolition, Brown cited conversations with planters during his travels in the southern United States and in Jamaica during the late 1860s. Since the end of the slavery, blacks were 'relapsing into barbarism and misery'; and furthermore, 'unable to estimate the value of his newly-acquired freedom at its just value, or how to reap the truest advantages from it, the Negro [had] become a pest in the Southern States'.[93] At greater length in *The Countries of the World*, like Carlyle and J. A. Froude before him, Brown reiterated the claim that the natural fertility and abundance of the tropics created no incentive to labour so that in the West Indies the ex-slaves 'entirely relapsed into laziness and idleness'. In the midst of an abundant and idle supply of black labour, the hard-pressed planters were forced to import coolie labour from India and China. Demagogues had incited the blacks to rebel in 1865, and Jamaica wisely reverted to crown colony government. In Brown's fanciful political assessment, the Jamaica Assembly had been excessively democratic in that the black majority's interest was represented to the exclusion of 'the respectable white and coloured inhabitants'. In a revealing anecdote, he recounted, 'Wherever I have met the Negro in the British Colonies ... I have found him tolerably well-behaved, not pig-headed, and just a little too fond of putting himself forward, and apt, if a little civility were shown him, to get familiar and impertinent'.[94]

Although his views were representative of the trend in the 1870s and 1880s toward a more critical assessment of anti-slavery and missionary endeavours, Brown and his publisher had to be wary of offending potential readers. In so far as a market existed for these geographic compendia, the anti-slavery and missionary movements had been important agencies for cultivating that interest. Interjected along with his descriptions of peoples and places, Brown frequently reassured his readers that his heart was in the right place, or that he had sound reasons for dissenting from the views of respected philanthropists.[95] In support of this view, Brown relied on the accounts of Sir Samuel Baker, an African explorer and outspoken critic of the anti-slavery movement. Borrowing some four pages of text directly from Baker, Brown advised his readers that from his experience the African traveller was 'capable of giving a calm unbiased opinion'. From his family's interest in sugar plantations in the West Indies and Mauritius, and from his own experience as a planter in Ceylon, Baker had little use for abolitionist and philanthropic opinion. According to Baker,

So long as it is generally considered that the Negro and the white man are to be governed by the same laws and guided by the same management, so long will the former remain a thorn in the side of every community to which he may unhappily belong ... It is the grand error of equalising that which is unequal that has lowered the Negro character and made the black man a reproach.[96]

Just as English instincts included 'industry and energy', the African 'will assuredly lapse into an idle and savage state, unless specially governed and forced to industry'. Challenging his abolitionist opponents, Baker claimed this truth was 'contrary to public opinion in England, where the vox populi assumes the right of dictation upon matters and men in which it has had no experience'.[97]

Considering the response of some of his readers, Brown noted that Baker's opinions might 'gall the prejudices of certain well-meaning and kindly people', and observed that 'most of us have an utter hatred for slavery'. Nonetheless, Brown persisted in his hostility toward Africans and humanitarian causes, concluding his assessment of the 'African Freedman' by observing: 'The philanthropist has his work laid out for him before he can convert the African freedman into a civilised being, capable of conducting his affairs on anything but an African model. And the sooner he knows it the better.'[98] The heated debate over slavery had raised 'the disturbing elements of social and even theological acrimony', but as a scientist, Brown once again affirmed: 'with these questions we, as ethnologists, have nothing to do'.[99]

As interest grew in European colonialism in Africa, Brown, in his later writings such as *The Countries of the World* (1884–89) and more particularly in his four-volume survey, *The Story of Africa and its Explorers* (1892–95), paid greater attention to developments there, and more stridently defended the subordination of African land and labour to white colonial interests. In *The Story of Africa and its Explorers*, completed shortly before his death in 1895, he noted Africa's role in the origins of civilisation in Egypt and its place in the Roman Empire. For Brown, who had spent vacations in the Barbary States, this history was a link to Europe rather than to black Africa. From this perspective he described European contact from the fifteenth century as 'The Re-Opening of Africa', and made the extraordinary claim that this renewed contact marked the beginning of 'the re-settlement of Europeans in Africa as their home'.[100] Writing in the 1890s, he made the amused boast that where not long ago Grant, Speke and Stanley had made their intrepid journeys, now modern transportation by steamers and railways made it possible for English tourists to push their offspring in perambulators on the shore of Lake Nyassa.[101]

Surveying the recent history of colonisation in Africa, the British government, made wary by a cautious and parsimonious public, had prevaricated about its imperial role. Rather than this 'reluctant imperialism', Brown favoured a forward policy of expansion which, in establishing control under British law and administrative expertise, would benefit both Europeans and Africans. Unlike his earlier concern for the impact of colonialism on Native Americans, he showed little concern for African rights or interests. Brown retained his trust in the competence of British colonial administration and its agencies. Just as he had praised the Hudson's Bay Company for its judicious relations with the Native Canadians, so he gave a fulsome tribute to Sir George Goldie and to the Niger Company for its competent management of its dual role of administrative and commercial agency.[102]

The history of 'native wars' in South Africa had acted as a deterrent to white immigration, but the discovery of diamonds and gold excited new interest tarnished only by the inflated promises of colonial promoters. Brown looked forward to a 'confederation of South Africa' formed by the union of British and Dutch settlers. The only territories not in white control were those lands set aside for Africans 'as little monuments to our scruples – testimonials that,' he wrote, 'in eating up the Black Man's land, we had the utmost regard for his rights'. These scruples, he noted, were 'old-fashioned prejudices' and there was a 'danger of forgetting that they ever existed'.[103]

In the light of these sentiments, Brown defended Cecil Rhodes and the British South Africa Company, skirting around the issue of the Company's responsibility for war in Matabeleland. In his view, 'the inevitable law of the whites in South Africa finding elbow-room at the cost of the blacks would have held true – sooner or later'. Noting the gruesome toll inflicted by 'the deadly Maxim guns', he nonetheless vindicated imperial progress by contrasting Bulawayo as 'Lobengula's squalid kraal' with the modern town of 1895, which had a newspaper, hotels, electric light, telephones, a promised water-works, and Mr Rhodes' residence on site of Lobengula's kraal itself.[104]

As an accomplished journalist and populariser of science, Robert Brown provided his readers with a set of negative stereotypes of the world's peoples whose pre-eminent vices contrasted with the virtues of Victorian respectability. As an experienced traveller, he made little use of comparative anatomy in depicting racialised groups within a colonial context. Aware of racial conflict, Brown saw European colonial ascendancy as inevitable, and the subordination of non-Europeans was the price they paid for the advance of civilisation. Unlike the Reverend John Wood or the ethnologists in the Anthropological Institute, Brown did not search for 'natural man'. Consequently, scientific naturalism, or a generalised form of biological determinism, was implicit rather than explicit in his surveys. Scientific naturalism underlay his constructions of race in so far as he judged various peoples to be incapable of adjusting to modern colonial conditions as settled agriculturalists or as wage-labourers. Brown's bipolar constructions of a Manichean colonial order recognised neither the specific ethnic boundaries nor racial types constructed by the anthropologists. While claiming to respect the humanitarians of the past, he devalued their achievements and derided their role in moralising the project of empire. In the context of South Africa, he noted: 'the "native question" is ... one on which it is impossible to pronounce a decided opinion'; and having 'got into politics, the "facts" are manipulated to suit rival "views".'[105] He avoided these disputes by taking on the mantle of the objective scientist. Nonetheless, his commentaries, while presented as an extensive synopsis of scientific and geographic knowledge, mixed together race, culture and politics. When he addressed more recent developments in the empire, his science was barely distinguishable from the leaders he wrote for the *Standard*. It is this generic toxic mix, rather than the more systematic theories of evolutionary science or of racial types, that gave race-thinking its potency. When conditions existed for professional science to begin to have a popular influence – not before the 1880s and more evidently in the 1890s and after – constructions of race as presented by Wood and Brown were already commonplace and served as the foundation for the dissemination of a more authoritative and professional racial science.

Edward Clodd

Both Wood and Brown set out to describe the world's peoples rather than to offer an explanation of human physical and cultural varieties. Consequently, neither author found much need for comparative anatomy or evolutionary theory. Two other popular writers, Edward Clodd and Professor Augustus Keane, defined their task in a different fashion. They sought to present the ideas of professional science to both popular and juvenile readerships. Edward Clodd sought to inform his readers, and in particular juveniles, about evolution and how scientific findings related to Christian moral and religious teaching. Professor Keane's focus was less on evolution and more specifically on the question of race, as he became the most important populariser of racial typologies between the 1890s and 1914. From the standpoint of the history of scientific ideas, it may seem that comparative anatomy should be discussed before evolution, but in dealing with the chronology and logic of the popularisation of professional science, Clodd and evolution prepared the ground for Keane and racial types.

Edward Clodd (1840–1930), a banker from a Liberal Nonconformist background, was a popular science writer, and an activist in promoting secular education and a number of other progressive causes including votes for women. Assisting Richard Proctor in editing *Knowledge*, Clodd gave lectures on astronomy and on primitive man at Nonconformist chapels, and promoted education through the National

Sunday Schools Association. Clodd fit Proctor's model of a successful amateur scientist. He began work at fourteen as a bank clerk, and after some difficult financial years rose to be secretary of the Joint Stock Bank. Thereafter he combined his banking career with his popular science and various political, intellectual and philanthropic pursuits. Becoming more secular over time, Clodd's scientific interests turned to cultural anthropology and folklore. He was the president of the Folklore Society in 1895, and though by the 1880s he had become an agnostic, he retained his interest in education. He was chair of the Rational Press Association from 1906 to 1913, and a member of the founding council of the Secular Education League in 1907.[106]

Clodd, an indefatigable host and conversationalist, had a wide circle of friends within the literary and scientific intelligentsia. At his home in Tufnell Park, he spent evenings discussing the adventures of his neighbours – Joseph Thompson, an explorer in Masailand, Paul Du Chaillu, a writer of mixed African and European descent who had ventured into the central African rainforest, and H. W. Bates, who had travelled extensively in South America. Among his acquaintances he counted Samuel Butler, E. B. Tylor, T. H. Huxley, A. H. Keane, A. C. Haddon, Rider Haggard and Sir James Barrie. As a member of the Folklore Society he met Sir Richard Burton, Andrew Lang and Mary Kingsley. He also belonged to the Omar Khayyam Club, a dinner club for sceptics, which included among its members George Meredith, Thomas Hardy, H. W. Massington, George Gissing, James Bryce, Henry James, Holman Hunt, Frederic Harrison and Grant Allen. He entertained his friends on weekends at Aldburgh House, and was especially noted for his antics on his yacht. In addition to those listed above, his weekend guests included James Frazer, G. M. Trevelyan, Moncure Conway, Ray Lankester, Flinder Petrie, W. B. Yeats, H. G. Wells, J. B. Bury, and Leslie Stephen. He was a close friend of Grant Allen, who was most renowned for his novel *The Woman Who Did* (1895) but was also a writer and reviewer on human evolution and history.[107]

Clodd and his friends in no way constituted a common school of thought but rather represented the diversity of views among those who engaged in the discourse on race between the 1880s and 1914. The more strident advocates of empire and publicists of more overt forms of racism included Burton, Keane, Haddon, Haggard and Barrie. On the other hand, Du Chaillu, Thompson and Kingsley were three of the more sensitive travellers in Africa. Moncure Conway, a Unitarian preacher and free-thinker, had championed the abolition of slavery. In addition to his espousal of Positivism, Frederic Harrison was a critic of the excesses of imperialism and along with Conway supported Catherine Impey and the Society for the Recognition of the Brotherhood of

Man. Two prominent Liberals, G. M. Trevelyan and James Bryce, were 'Pro-Boers' opposed to the South African War. Just as his friends held diverse opinions, so too Edward Clodd himself struggled to reconcile his religion with evolution and his liberalism with colonial racial oppression.

Clodd suffered a crisis of religious faith in the 1860s, partly as a result of reading E. B. Tylor's *Primitive Culture*, and initially devoted his efforts to writing secular children's books that attempted to reconcile religion and evolution. *The Childhood of the World – A Simple Account of Man's Early Years* sold 20,000 copies within four years of its publication in 1873, and included among its readers the Prince of Wales who reportedly read it at bedtime to the royal grandchildren. To give his young readers a sense of human life in the earliest stone age, he invited them to imagine life 'Far across the wind-tossed seas, far away in such places as Australia, Borneo, and Ceylon', where lived 'at this day creatures so wild that if you saw them you could scarcely believe that they were human beings and not wild animals'.[108] Similarly, to demonstrate the progressive development of evolution, Clodd contrasted the savage and civilised stages of human existence: 'The savage, who has to make constant use of his bodily powers to secure food, is, by practice, fleeter of foot and quicker of sight than civilised men, who, using the power of his mind, excels the savage in getting knowledge and making good and also bad use of it.'[109] In paying little attention to the physical distinctions of race and more to the stages of cultural evolution, Clodd's popular accounts owed much more to E. B. Tylor and A. R. Wallace than to the racial typologists.

Clodd's rational and secular viewpoint, as well as his evolutionary perspective, gave his writings a cultural relativist slant. Nonetheless, the effect of his presentations was to stress the contrast between 'non-civilised' and 'civilised' cultures, and to emphasise the vast temporal distance between non-Europeans and his readers in an evolutionary time frame. For example, in *His Childhood of Religions*, first published in 1875, and according to his publisher reaching 11,000 copies in its edition of 1889, Clodd instructed his juvenile readers in how to read the Bible. The account of creation in Genesis was not unique to the Judeo-Christian tradition, but comparable to similar myths and legends in other religions. Furthermore, if read not as a literal account but as a metaphor, Genesis, with its seven stages of creation, was quite compatible with evolutionary science.[110]

In his comparative study of religions in the same work, he associated the major religions of south Asia with the eastern branch of the Aryan race, and identified Islam as a Semitic religion. He defended Mohammed as a great prophet and advised he readers: 'We must no more blame him for many of the sad errors and views mixed up with Islam than we should blame Jesus for the evils which have crept into Christianity.'[111] Despite this cautionary note, Clodd still offered a common, contradictory stereotype of Mohammed's Arab followers: these 'are to-day what they were hundreds of years ago; lovers of freedom, temperate, good-hearted; but withal crafty, revengeful, dishonest'.[112] Clodd's lessons on how to read the Bible, his cultural relativism and his evolutionary science alarmed some of his contemporaries. In a tract by the Catholic Truth Society, Catholicus advised parents 'to sweep this refuse of German scepticism out of our schools'.[113]

In *The Childhood of Religions*, Clodd briefly discussed what he termed 'ethnology', or the study of human races. He offered no detailed racial typology, affirmed the common origins of human beings, yet stressed the contrast between races which had evolved over long periods of time. 'Our present knowledge', he observed, 'strengthens the early belief that man first arose in one part of the earth'. Since those early origins, 'changes in climate, removal to new lands, different food, working through long ages', have created 'wide varieties in his descendants, such as we see between an Englishman and a Negro, and between a Hindu and a Chinaman'.[114] In this fashion, Clodd's secular and evolutionary accounts reinforced the racial differences made familiar in the Reverend Wood's natural history and Robert Brown's geographic science, as well as in the literature of travel and exploration, and in missionary publications.[115]

In identifying a savage stage and treating some non-western cultures as living fossils representing the early stages of human development, Clodd conveyed an implicit ranking of cultures into 'higher' and 'lower' races. In *The Story of Creation: A Plain Account of Evolution* (1888), a successful popular work for adults which sold 2,000 copies in its first week of publication and 5,000 copies in three months, Clodd discusses the evolution of the brain, noting the distance between apes and human beings, and between civilised and savage peoples. In its serialised version in *Knowledge*, he cites Darwin's observation of the people of Tierra del Fuego for the claim that 'Such races are much nearer to the ape than the Caucasian'. At the same time he acknowledges 'The fundamental likeness between the varieties of man', but explains the existence of human variation by the process of evolution.[116] Paying closer attention to Darwin and his theory of sexual selection, Clodd explains the origin of racial variations 'through the potent agency of natural and sexual selection acting upon variations induced by diverse conditions – conditions which have surrounded man in virtue of his migrations from pole to pole, and which have called his industry and resource into full play'.[117] A graph of the genealogy of human races presents seven generations of evolution. According to the graph, which Clodd does not discuss in his text, the black races – Papuans, Australians, Negroes, etc. – appear in the fourth generation and show no subsequent evolution, whereas Mongols, Native Americans, and Mediterraneans also appear in that fourth generation but do show further evolution. The Mongols evolve into a fifth generation of Chinese, Lapps, Tatars, Esquimaux, etc., and the Mediterraneans into Semitic and Aryan races. These latter two evolve in a sixth and a seventh generation into the modern European nationalities.[118]

Out of his own interests, Clodd paid more attention to cultural rather than biological evolution, and included an account of the 'evolution of society'. Incorporating the Malthusian logic of human fertility exceeding the means of subsistence, Clodd stressed the role of mortality in evolution, including 'the wholesale destruction of communities by wars, pestilences, famines, and catastrophes'. Affirming that 'Man's normal state is therefore one of conflict', Clodd advances the case that the strength of human emotions and 'savage instincts' led to a struggle for food and mates much fiercer than that in the animal world. Yet out of this fierce struggle, humans evolved 'curiosity, the mother of knowledge', the 'germ of the highest and purest love of man for women', and 'in the conflicts between tribes, patriotism, morals and the hardy virtues'. Out of this same struggle, the features of a modern social and political order evolved, as conflict dictated the rise of the ablest leaders and the rule of the wisest to develop the basis for law and order. With this evolution, communities grew in size and in their needs, and to satisfy these new demands work became divided, 'hence specialisation of peoples into classes, with all the complex duties of modern societies'.[119]

This evolution worked itself out not only internally but globally, as the higher civilisations, a product of the challenging environments of temperate climates, dominated over the less highly developed:

> The enterprise of the higher races has explored and utilised large tracts, and the pressure of population at the centres of civilisation has within quite recent periods vastly extended their radii, but whole empires, advancing to a certain stage, have through isolation and the tyranny of custom, or dread of change, stagnated, whilst the lowest races have remained unmodified, like the lowest organisms, and have more or less succumbed before the imported vices and the weapons of the white man.[120]

Noting that in nature and in human society the 'normal state is one of conflict', he observed that 'among advanced nations the military method may be more or less superseded by the industrial'. Under these modern conditions, 'men may be mercilessly starved instead of being mercifully slain, but, be it war of camps or markets, the ultimate appeal is to force, and the hardiest and craftiest win'. This brutal message rested uneasily with Clodd's Liberal Nonconformist conscience. He noted that 'In a barbaric society weaklings like Newton and hunchbacks like Pope would have been allowed to perish', but under civilised conditions they are protected, and 'humanity is enriched by their genius'.[121]

For his general readership, Clodd faithfully represented the theories of natural and cultural evolution advanced by Darwin Wallace, and Tylor. Like them he did not resort to racial typologies or to a rigid biological or anatomical determinism beyond the framework of scientific naturalism. The sharpest rejoinder to the claims of biological determinism occurred not over race but over gender. In 1881, *Knowledge* printed a provocative article entitled 'Are Women Inferior to Men', rejecting a French author's attempt to use craniology to prove the natural inferiority of women. A lively exchange followed in the correspondence columns in which a number of letter writers, including several women, took the advocates of comparative anatomy to task for reaching conclusions so far out of touch with the reality of everyday relations between men and women. The controversy and resultant correspondence may have been deliberately provoked by Clodd, who was sub-editor of the magazine and vice-president of the London National Society for Women's Suffrage.[122]

Edward Clodd's popular presentation of the evolution of races and cultures had little recourse to racial typologies or the technicalities of comparative anatomy, and no consideration of the unorthodox thesis of polygenesis, and yet his scientific naturalism and evolutionary framework stressed the distance in time between savage and civilised, and readily made competition in the market-place and conflict on the colonial frontier seem part of a natural process. The inequality of races in power, wealth and status was a natural condition, and change occurred by conflict and destruction. In this fashion, Clodd's science fused with his liberal banker's political economy sanctioned the existing order within both the metropolitan society and the emerging global hierarchy in the external colonial world.

Professor Augustus H. Keane

As a populariser, Edward Clodd's primary focus was on evolution. In this sense, his observations about race were implicit in his writings, but he did not set out to address the question of race directly. On the other hand, Professor A. H. Keane addressed the question of race directly, and as a linguist rather than a biologist advanced his own theories about the origin and distinctive character of human races.[123] Unlike Wood or Brown, Keane did not primarily aim to engage his readers' curiosity in nature or foreign peoples, but rather attempted to communicate the findings of professional science to a wider audience.

The enormous expansion of the size of the reading public, and the reduction of the prices of publications for middle-, lower middle-, and respectable working-class consumers, afforded Keane, Robert Brown, Edward Clodd and others opportunities that simply did not exist for the mid-Victorian racial determinists such as Knox and Hunt. When Sir Harry Johnston expressed his dismay at the public ignorance about the peoples and cultures of the empire, and called for government support for anthropological studies, he also recognised Keane's contribution: 'Popular anthropology – I mean anthropology popularised – owes much to the labours and researches of Professor A. H. Keane.' Despite the scorn of experts, Johnston praised newspapers and other publishing enterprises for their efforts 'to invigorate knowledge by hypnotising the British public into the purchase of encyclopaedias, histories, and self-educators.' He continued: 'In my own humble opinion, these agencies have by such means increased the general education of the upper and middle classes by at least one-fifth'.[124] Keane and other popular writers produced this ephemeral literature in response to this growing market. They were also innovators in applying the lessons of their racial science to political topics of the day and in using photographs to make colonised peoples visible as racial types.

Keane, described in one obituary as a 'hard working literary man', earned a reputation as a populariser rather than as an innovator in anthropology. Having established his credentials as an expert in the field, Keane specialised in writing for a student and adult readership interested in acquiring authoritative knowledge of the peoples of the empire and the wider world. In addition to his reviews for *Nature*, he wrote 110 articles for the *Academy*, and numerous entries on racial, ethnic, and linguistic groups for the *Encyclopaedia Britannica, Chambers' Encyclopaedia*, and 800 entries for *Cassell's Storehouse of General Information*. With a growing market for large, illustrated reference works and school texts, he found publishers ready to call upon his linguistic and ethnological expertise in translating foreign travel, scientific and ethnological works and in editing school geography books. For *Stanford's Compendium of Geography and Travel*, a frequently reissued reference work, he helped produce volumes on *Africa* (1878, 1884, 1895, 1904), *Asia* (1882, 1893, 1896, 1906), *Australasia* (1879, 1883, 1888, 1908), and *Central and South America* (1878, 1885, 1901, 1909–11). He wrote two texts on anthropology: *Ethnology* (1896) and *Man, Past and Present* (1899). He also contributed to *The Living*

Races of Mankind: A Popular Illustrated Account of the Customs, Habits, Pursuits, Feasts and Ceremonies of the Races of Mankind throughout the World (1905), which was a serialised magazine amply illustrated with photographs of exotic peoples. In 1908 he published another illustrated text, *The World's Peoples – A Popular Account of their Bodily and Mental Characters. Beliefs, Traditions, Political and Social Institutions*. For his contributions to ethnology, Keane received a civil list pension in 1897.[125]

Keane's books were largely descriptive, providing a catalogue of characteristics for each racial or ethnic group in turn. Not content with physical classification alone, Keane, as a linguist, thought that mental characteristics could also be classified and would reveal sharper differences of race. As a result he had no hesitation about drawing up psychological profiles for each racial group.[126] For example, in *Man: Past and Present*, a text published by Cambridge University Press, Keane headed each chapter with a brief racial taxonomy. Much like labels attached to exhibits at a zoo or in a museum, the taxonomy included a brief description under the following headings: Primeval Home; Present Range; Physical Characteristics – Hair, Colour, Skull, Nose, Eyes, Stature, Lips, Legs, Arms, Feet; Temperament; Speech; Religion; Culture. Under temperament, Keane provided a brief summary of mental attributes and abilities. For example, the Southern Mongols were, according to Keane, 'Somewhat sluggish, with little initiative, but great endurance, cunning rather than intelligent; generally thrifty and industrious, but most indolent in Siam and Burma; moral standards low, with slight sense of right and wrong.'[127] In contrast, the 'Caucasic Peoples' were 'All brave, imaginative, musical, and richly endowed intellectually'. Keane reserved his highest praise for the innate superiority and political leadership of the Saxons, whom he described as an identifiable racial type.[128] Keane justified these confident descriptions of mental as well as physical attributes by the claim that he depicted only 'ideal types' from which real individuals might vary. This philosophical nicety made little imprint on the general reader, for Keane's ideal type frequently appeared as a photograph of a real living person.[129]

In Keane's work, the form in which he presented his racial typologies was as important as their content. Wood, Brown and Clodd all aimed to inform their readers, but what distinguished Keane's work was that in the form of encyclopaedia entries or in the taxonomies of his textbooks, he intended his descriptions to be authoritative statements of scientific knowledge. These typologies, presented in a more succinct and systematic fashion than in Wood, Brown, or Clodd were intended to be learned by rote by captive student audiences, or more importantly by their teachers. A. C. Haddon, who held the first lectureship in anthropology at Cambridge, claimed that one of the skills to be learned from the subject was that of 'race discrimination'. In 1906, the examinations for the Diploma of Anthropology at Oxford required students to be proficient in the identification of racial types from representative photographs.[130]

The descriptions of these 'ideal types' appeared and reappeared in Keane's numerous articles and books. In 1894, in an article on 'The World: Population, Races, Languages, and Religions' for *The Church Missionary Intelligencer*, he described the 'Negritic Temperament' as 'sensuous, indolent and unintellectual, fitful, passionate and cruel, though often affectionate and faithful; little self-respect, hence easy acceptance of yoke of slavery; mental faculties generally arrested after puberty. Science and art undeveloped'.[131] This description was an abbreviated synopsis of his entry on 'The Negro' for *Cassell's Storehouse of General Information* (1890–4). The same description only slightly modified appeared as his characterisation of 'Sudanese Negroes' in *Man, Past and Present* (1899). It was used as description of 'the Negro type' by Richard Lydekker in his introduction to *The Living Races of Mankind* (1905), and Keane himself repeated it in a slightly extended form in his typology of the 'Negro or Black Division – Western (African) Section' (which included Africans and African-Americans) in *The World's Peoples* (1908).[132]

Convinced that politicians and the public were profoundly ignorant of the lessons of racial science, he sought to explain the profounder causes behind contemporary political developments. In January 1884, just when Gladstone had sent General Gordon to Khartoum, Keane provided *Nature*'s readers with an ethnological survey of the Sudan. Ignorance of ethnology contributed to the crisis, for the common description of the people as Arabs and Negroes was inaccurate. Keane pointed out the population's 'Hamitic' roots, a branch of the Caucasian type with historical links to Christianity and Islam. Khartoum had been a centre of European commerce and civilising influence since the early nineteenth century, and on this basis, he justified British intervention against the 'barbarism and villainous Arab slave-dealers of Central Africa'.[133]

Having always insisted on placing blacks in the lowest and whites in the highest category of human development, Keane persistently denied the achievements of African peoples. He used his knowledge of Asian and ancient languages to claim that the ruins of Great Zimbabwe were of Phoenician origin, and in *Man, Past and Present* he described the Benin bronzes as the work of Portuguese artisans.[134] He applied the same generalisations to peoples of African descent in the New World.

In a review for *Nature* in 1884, he used Haiti as proof of black incapacity for self-government, and then extended this assessment to the United States approving of white dominance in the South as the only means to prevent black reversion to savagery. Keane saw these examples as 'a crushing reply to those sentimental philanthropists who go about preaching the doctrine of the inherent equality of all mankind'.[135]

When he turned to assess the racial and historical roots of the war in South Africa in *The Boer States* (1900), Keane blamed the humanitarianism of the past as the source of the conflict. The root of Anglo-Boer hostility lay in the error of the philanthropists in destroying the Boers' labour supply with the abolition of slavery. Colonial policy under Lord Glenelg who, according to Keane, was 'unfortunately a member of the Aborigines Protection Society', was based upon the myth of the noble savage, and ignored the fact that the Africans were 'treacherous and cruel hordes, accustomed from old to raid, plunder and murder'.[136] Subsequent conflict, especially from 1880 to the outbreak of hostilities in 1899, he attributed to the duplicity and narrow nationalism of a new Boer race which had evolved from the inferior stock of the original Dutch settlers. Keane condemned critics of the war and defenders of African interests as latter-day Glenelgs, 'whose first thoughts are always for the alien, their last for their country-men; who were ever ready to champion the rights of others and neglect their own; who could smile, and smile, and smile away an empire'.[137]

Keane's importance lies not in the originality of his contribution to scientific racism, but in his prolific production of works for the general public. When he turned his attentions to writing popular works on anthropology in the 1890s, Keane was already an experienced author of school texts. In his early career as a language teacher he had produced a number of school grammars of English and foreign languages. In 1892, he produced a revised sixth edition of Keith Johnston's *School Physical and Descriptive Geography*, a text of the London School Board. The text informed students that countries with 'the greatest variety of climate and landscape ... [had] produced the most highly-developed races', a principle best exemplified by the people of the British Isles. On a global scale, according to the text, there was 'a general agreement' that the Aryan or Indo-European peoples were 'the most highly-developed nations of the world'. With their growth 'in civilisation and intellectual power from age to age', they had extended their rule, 'supplanting many inferior races, and re-peopling wide areas, as in America and Australia'.[138]

Keane's text, *Ethnology*, published in the Cambridge geographical series in 1896 for the educated adult or post-secondary student, was welcomed by Grant Allen as 'the first systematic treatise on Ethnology as a whole that has appeared since the general acceptance of the evolutionary theory'. In his review in the *Academy*, Allen noted that the text, 'designed rather for instruction than amusement', demonstrated the author's 'grasp, acuteness, delicacy, logical faculty', and showed that the author was 'tolerably free from bias of any sort'. Although he could be 'at times just a little dogmatic', and given to a 'somewhat aggressive tone towards orthodox theology', Allen stressed that Keane was 'a firm and reasoned monogenist', and claimed that he left 'the polygenists (if there are any) without a leg to stand upon'. Nonetheless, Allen, who had once taught in a government college in Jamaica, queried the 'somewhat undue importance', Keane assigned, 'to the essential mental differences between races', and suggested that his poor opinion of African-Americans came from prejudicial American sources.[139]

It was a measure of Keane's reputation that, despite his ambivalent defence of monogenesis, his impatience with theology, and his criticism of humanitarian causes, the Church Missionary Society commissioned him to contribute to a new edition of the Church Missionary Atlas. The essay, reprinted in *The Church Missionary Intelligencer* in 1894, made some concessions to its sponsors. Keane affirmed, citing Professor W. H. Flower, that there were three main racial groups – black, yellow and white – and all three originated from 'a common prototype'.

> This doctrine, in which Science and Revelation are in complete harmony, rests on the strong grounds that all human groups, from the highest to the lowest, have an instinctive sense of their common humanity, are fruitful among themselves, and in other respects present such close physical and mental qualities as are best explained by their common descent from a common ancestry.[140]

These common mental traits, Keane assured his missionary readers, were seen in human capacity to reason, best evidenced in the universal possession of complex patterns of language even among 'the most degraded races, such as the Fuegians, the Hottentots, and the Australians'. Despite these reassuring remarks, Keane then concluded with his familiar racial taxonomy which provided a brief derogatory description of Negritic and Mongolic temperament, and a contrasting complimentary one of the Caucasic group which alone was responsible for 'all great names in philosophy and poetry'. He also classified his three races by forms of religious belief, with the black category being 'non-theistic', the yellow 'polytheistic', and the white 'monotheistic'.[141] Keane was not the only populariser of scientific racism for missionary societies. In a seven-part series in 1896, Leonard T. Horne informed Sunday School readers of *News from Afar*, published by the London Missionary Society, of the scientific facts about 'Race Types'.[142] Science and religion, and especially anthropology and the missionary movement, had once been antagonists. By the end of the nineteenth century, the new racial orthodoxy of professional science had gained respectability and found acceptance within the missionary movement itself.

Keane's most ambitious enterprise in popular anthropology involved the production of extensively illustrated works for the publishing firm of Hutchinson. In 1905, *The Living Races of Mankind*, a fortnightly serial with 800 photographs as well as 25 coloured plates and maps, marked a new venture in the use of photographs to present anthropology and racial science to the lay public. As early as the 1850s, ethnographers had realised the potential of photography to conserve a record of 'disappearing races' (either by extermination or cultural assimilation). They also thought that specimen racial types photographed in the field or in England (largely of individuals on display at touring exhibitions) would provide data for the measurement of racial differences. In practice, photographs did not prove useful for such measurements, but the camera proved a useful aid in fieldwork and by the end of the nineteenth century, the Anthropological Institute as well as ethnographic museums had extensive photographic archives.[143]

Improvements in photography and printing technology made it possible to reproduce these photographs in magazines with large circulations at a low cost. *The Living Races of Mankind* cost seven pence per issue, whereas an issue of Wood's *Natural History of Man* of 1870 cost one shilling. Under the editorship of Keane and Richard Lydekker, from the Zoology Department of the British Museum, the serial brought together, as its covers announced, a team of 'eminent specialists'. Keane produced about half of the issues including those on Japan, Korea, Southeast Asia, India, Ceylon, Central Asia, East, Central and Southern Europe, and the British Isles. Keane collaborated with Sir Harry Johnston on the issues on Africa, and Lydekker produced those on North and South America. In 1908, Keane produced for Hutchinson *The World's Peoples* with 270 photographs, many the same as those in the *Living Races of Mankind*, and some of which were borrowed from the Anthropological Institute's collection.[144]

As popularisers, Keane and Lydekker recognised they had to cultivate their readers' interest in their esoteric subject. In his introduction to the *Living Races of Mankind*, Lydekker noted that anthropology had 'the reputation of being a dry and difficult – not to say repellent – science, mainly concerned with measuring and comparing the relative proportions of skulls and bones'. He promised his readers that these dull details were no longer necessary, as 'a large amount of information with regard to the leading characteristics of the different living races of mankind' could be presented 'in the most popular and interesting manner possible – namely, by actual photographs of the races themselves'. The editor also promised to make the prose interesting by paying attention to customs including 'those connected with birth, marriage, and death; their modes of thought and mental characteristics; not omitting their games, sports, and pastimes'.[145] In the preface to *The World's Peoples*, Keane similarly distinguished between the specialists' interest in 'such abstruse matters as, for instance the origins of exogamy', and the needs of 'the general reader who wants a broad and intelligible view of tribal, national, and social relations'. He promised to deal with 'established facts' and matters of public interest after the fashion of *The Living Races of Mankind*.[146] Despite these promises, both Lydekker and Keane began these works with an account of the nature and the origin of racial groups. In contrast to his article for the Church Missionary Society, Keane reiterated more emphatically his theory of 'unorthodox monogenesis', which stressed that the primary racial groups diverged at an early stage of human evolution. Both authors discussed racial types, included descriptions of racial temperament, and used photographs to illustrate the contrasting features of these types in support of a text which stressed an ascending hierarchy of black, yellow and white races.[147]

On the whole, reviewers welcomed these productions, but worried about the distorting process by which the knowledge of experts was conveyed to the general public. In *Man*, the Anthropological Institute's new popular journal, the reviewer of *The World's Peoples* notes: 'no where else can such a large and varied series of ethnological portraits be found in so small a compass'. Commenting on the problems of popularisation, the reviewer fears there is a tendency to be too certain and even 'dogmatic' over matters still under dispute. He cautions the reader about Keane's certainties about the prehistoric period, but concludes by acknowledging 'the many obligations which anthropology already owes him', and hopes that Keane will continue 'to apply his unrivalled knowledge to the popularisation of a science of such great practical import to our world-wide Empire'.[148]

The photograph offered a powerful means for the presentation of images of race. In a friendly fashion, Sir Harry Johnston mocked the use of photographs in ethnographic exhibits. He was especially harsh on illustrations of British physical types by 'one or two picture-postcards of fishermen or Welsh cottagers, wearing stage costumes, together with some monstrously faked sickly-sweet "types of English beauty" (in some cases amiable ladies of the stage whose birthplace was on the Continent of Europe)'.[149] His real complaint, though, was not with the use of photographs but that there were an insufficient number of them. The photograph gave the illusion of an objective presentation of reality, free of the distortions and ambiguities of either the written text or, as in earlier productions, of an artist's engraving. While ethnographers and popularisers like Keane and Lyddeker celebrated the realism of the photograph, the pictures did not 'speak for themselves', nor were they 'worth a thousand words'. The authors not only selected the photographs but through the accompanying text instructed the reader on how to identify the traits belonging to each racial type.

With its focus on exotic peoples and cultures, ethnography excited an erotic interest which the photograph made public and potentially pornographic. Whether in the form of travel accounts, more formal ethnographic surveys or social evolutionary theory, Victorian travellers and anthropologists, some of whom like Sir Richard Burton had reputations as notorious libertines, had long taken an interest in human sexuality as depicted in the eroticised bodies of the colonial other, and as constructed in cultural practices such as religious ritual, rites of passage to adulthood, and courtship and marriage.[150]

The photograph transformed the cultural context of this fascination, by taking an image photographed in one context and reproducing it in a different context which transformed its meaning and use. For example, advertising directed at 'native' consumers became seditious pornography in the view of white settlers. In an infamous case in Bulawayo in 1911, Sam Lewis, an English settler, shot an African youth on the report that he had made sexual advances to Lewis' two daughters. The defence argued that the homicide was justified because the youth's intent was proven by the discovery of a photograph of a nude white woman among his personal belongings. In his report in the *Star*, a London daily, Sir Harry Johnston thought that the photograph may have been planted by the police, but he also remarked that many Africans possessed pictures of naked or semi-naked white women. European sellers of alcohol, tobacco and matches advertised and wrapped their products with these pictures, or simply carried on a trade in pornography.[151] In Rhodesia, African males with photos of white women possessed pornography; in London, English consumers who bought illustrated magazines with photographs of 'natives' purchased ethnography.

Ethnographic photographs may have had a scientific purpose when taken in the field, but that purpose was transformed by the publisher's market-place. When the covers of *The Living Races of Mankind* displayed bare-breasted African and Polynesian women on Edwardian news stands, English readers purchased more than ethnography. Science made such objectification acceptable. Anthropology and the photograph provided a licence to deviate from the taboos of respectability. Out of the conjunction of race, gender and sexuality, popular anthropology made visible through the photograph a long-standing racial boundary between the sexual propriety of the civilised metro-pole and the disordered sexual licence of non-European cultures.[152]

The ethnographic photograph, constructed to depict human beings in 'nature', had the effect of freezing these peoples in time. These 'natural' humans were without civilisation or history, and consequently their human capacities and potential were defined by their biological inheritance. This objectification of exotic peoples and cultures by the photograph reinforced typological thinking about race. At the very time that science, both professional and popular, imposed this reinvig-orated rigidity on their constructed identities of non-European peoples, colonialism confronted indigenous cultures and prompted adjustments to western economic, social, cultural and political institutions. The scientific lesson, popularised by Professor Keane and the photographs, was that colonised people were by nature different and unsuited to civilised western practices. Science and photography sanctioned a path of separate development in which new regulatory and coercive practices were required for new kinds of colonial multi-racial societies within a global hierarchy based on differences of race.

If we shift our focus away from the origins of Victorian scientific racism in the 1850s and 1860s to its popularisation in the 1880s and after, the imperial context in which scientific racism reached a broader public becomes more evident. Magazines aimed at the science hobbyist were at most limited and ineffectual vehicles for the dissemination of this scientific racism, and even showed some resistance to the preten-sions of the professional scientists. Ephemeral publications aiming to inform the general public about exotic peoples and cultures were more important in the representations of race in popular science. The works of the Reverend John Wood, Robert Brown, Edward Clodd and Professor Augustus Keane supplied an expanding market, and presented towards the end of the nineteenth century a more secular and authoritative message incorporating the ideas of professional scientists and applying the lessons of their science to colonial racial conflicts.

Like most late Victorian professional scientists, all four of the popularisers thought that all humans in their various forms by race and culture had a common origin. As a naturalist seeking humans in a 'state of nature', the Reverend John Wood, relying on travel literature, conveyed derogatory stereotypes not through comparative anatomy or Darwinian evolution but through descriptions of savage life as sinful and degraded. Just as he had done with anthropomorphic homilies of animal life, Wood told a moral tale based on representations of savage life well-established within the common culture, derived from travel literature and informed in part by missionary publicity, and not de-pendent on the controversial racial science of the 1850s and 1860s.

Robert Brown's works from the 1870s and 1890s presented similarly derogatory stereotypes, though he was less concerned with sin than the work ethic. Deriving his impressions from his own travels and from works of geography and exploration, Brown, a professional journalist, focused on peoples as colonised subjects in the present. He constructed a Manichean world deeply suspicious of foreigners in general and persons of colour in particular. Critical of past philanthropic engagements with empire, he supported colonial interventions including war and other coercive means to establish European dominance as the inevitable route to progress and civilisation. Edward Clodd, a secularist and a supporter of liberal causes such as education and votes for women, popularised theories of biological and cultural evolution for adults and juveniles. With an interest in folklore and cultural anthropology, he adopted a more cultural relativist stance toward world religions and was not as prone as the others to presenting negative stereotypes. Nonetheless, Clodd's evolutionary perspective separated people in time and provided for a ranking of lower and higher races and cultures. Professor Augustus Keane, writing his popular works in the 1890s and after, and with an established reputation as a professional expert, combined technical anatomical and linguistic data together with psychological profiles of racial types. Keane's descriptions did not challenge the negative stereotypes evident in Wood, Brown, travel literature or other popular sources. If anything, Keane's confident succinct typologies were excessive even by the standards of the 1880s, and yet stood unrevised as authoritative statements for two or more decades.

The technical details of the classification of races, of the craniologists' indices of head size and shape, or of Keane's theory of racial origins, were less important than the knowledge that leading scientific experts found the long-standing impressions of travellers and the casual observations of journalists quite compatible with the latest findings of science. In this way the scientists failed to live up to their promise to provide a more accurate, 'objective' view of the world. This failure can best be explained by the power of their own ideology rooted in their class and gender, in their creed of professionalism, and in their links with colonising interests. The new authority gained by science in the late nineteenth century can best be explained by going beyond the particulars of what individual scientists thought and wrote about race to look at the culture of science, and the domestic and imperial context that informed late Victorian racial discourse.[153]

In contrast to the reforming enthusiasms of the early nineteenth century, which included the liberating message and crusading cultural imperialism of the missionary and anti-slavery movements, a more pessimistic outlook emerged in the later nineteenth century. In the constructions of racial difference, this transition may have begun not in the metropolis but in the colonial locale. Here the experience of the colonial encounter – the failure of missionaries to meet expectations for the conversion of the heathen; the failure of slave emancipation to fulfil either abolitionist hopes or the predictions for free labour forecast by a liberal political economy; the hostility of planters and white settlers toward imperial visions rooted in humanitarian rhetoric; and the exercise of imperial authority resorting to coercion and violence against indigenous peoples and racialised subjects – worked to set in motion a longer-term process of erosion and eventual collapse of the optimism and promise of the liberating visions of the early nineteenth century.[154]

In the period after 1870, the 'Great Depression' and the emergence of industrial competitors, chiefly France, Germany and the United States, aggravated social tensions at home and intensified foreign rivalry abroad. The renewed interest in imperial adventures was partly a defensive reaction against increased foreign competition and a diversion away from domestic social problems. The impetus behind imperial interventions was also a response to a crisis in the periphery where colonial rule and capitalist development transformed indigenous economies and cultures, and produced instability, conflict and wars of resistance. Domestically, the working out of the new politics of democracy together with a more organised and militant trade unionism, nationalist agitation in Ireland, new demands by women questioning the gender prescriptions of domesticity, and the emergence of an urban consumer culture all signified changes to the established order. By the 1880s, the long-term continuities of the rule of state and empire through a patrician elite and locally through the dynamics of paternalism and deference within communities were, in the language of Richard Price, a system of social relations in decay.[155]

In a world where the uncertain prosperity of the metropole seemed to be more and more closely linked to the vitality of the empire, there was a search for a new understanding of stability and order in the heartland of empire and in the multi-racial creations of the imperial project. Scientific naturalism by its method and by its understanding of the processes of continuity and change in nature promised new authoritative answers. This promise was so attractive that the new social sciences modelled their methods and theories on its achievements. In this context, 'race', a product of nature and not a construction derived from the history of human cultural encounters, became a building-block in the quest for a new hierarchical world order. Among the most articulate advocates of this vision were leaders of scientific community – for example Francis Galton and the supporters of eugenics – who used biological determinism to portray inequalities of class, gender and race as part of the natural order. This view neatly reconciled the promise of improvement for appropriately endowed, talented and industrious individuals with the permanence of a hierarchy as the less gifted majority remained trapped in its biologically determined and historically inherited or imposed social status.[156] Imperialist success abroad and widespread acceptance of the propriety of inequalities at home generated a climate conducive to scientific naturalism's affirmation that familiar hierarchies were in accordance with the dictates of nature.

By the 1880s the professionalisation of science and the fragmented specialisation of intellectual endeavour permitted the scientific community to speak with greater authority freer from the criticism of amateur moralists, philanthropists and humanitarians. At the same time, the reform and expansion of educational institutions allowed the science of race to reach a broader readership through the texts, encyclopaedias and other reference works sold to captive students and self-improving volunteers. In this context, the ideology of scientific racism was less a powerful rationale for the expansion of empire than was the liberal imperial mission which sought to convert the world to the norms of Victorian commerce, Christianity and civilisation. If scientific racism only developed the institutional framework to propagate its message in the 1890s and after, then the ideology may have served a rather different function than sanctioning the expansion of empire.

By the 1880s and 1890s there was a far greater willingness to admit a double standard by which colonised peoples by race and culture were designated as fundamentally different. Consequently, the institutions and norms of British society were seen as inappropriate, and colonial regimes needed new strategies of separate development. As the assertion of this double standard became more pronounced, the older liberal vision seemed an unrealistic, sentimental survivor from the early nineteenth century. Nonetheless, the new realism, supported by the claims of 'objective' science, whether professional or popular, never had the field to itself. On the one hand, new strategies were needed to administer and exploit the human resources of a multi-racial empire; on the other hand, imperial ideology still proclaimed the benevolence of British rule and the universal veracity of political and legal practices rooted in the British historical experience. Racism was an imperfect instrument for the reconciliation of these contradictions. The complex transformations that were occurring within colonial societies constructing an historically unprecedented, modernised, hierarchical, multi-racial order confounded the scientists' unreal world of nature. In developing a new language of race relations, the Victorians attempted to come to grips with this complex, contradictory and unnatural world.

Notes

1 John M. MacKenzie, *Propaganda and Empire: The Manipulation of British Public Opinion, 1880–1960* (Manchester: Manchester University Press, 1984); Penny Summerfield, 'Patriotism and empire: Music-hall entertainment, 1870–1914', and other essays in John M. MacKenzie (ed.), *Imperialism and Popular Culture* (Manchester: Manchester University Press, 1986); David Cannadine, 'The context, performance and meaning of ritual: The British monarchy and the "Invention of Tradition", c.1820–1977', in E. Hobsbawm and T. Ranger (eds), *The Invention of Tradition* (Cambridge: Cambridge University Press, 1983), pp. 120–38, and *Ornamentalism: How the British Saw their Empire* (Oxford: Oxford University Press, 2001); Geoff Eley, 'Beneath the skin. Or: How to forget about the empire without really trying', *Journal of Colonialism and Colonial History*, 3 (2002); J. A. Mangan, *The Games Ethic and Imperialism: Aspects of the Diffusion of an Ideal* (New York: Viking, 1986); Jeffrey Richards (ed.), *Imperialism and Juvenile Literature* (Manchester: Manchester University, 1989); Anne McClintock, *Imperial Leather: Race, Gender, and Sexuality in the Colonial Contest* (London: Routledge, 1995), pp. 207–31.
2 Bernard Porter, *The Absent-Minded Imperialists*; John M. MacKenzie, '"Comfort" and conviction: A response to Bernard Porter', *Journal of Imperial and Commonwealth History*, 36 (2008), 659–68; Richard Price, 'One big thing: Britain, its empire and their imperial culture', *Journal of British Studies*, 45 (2006), 602–27; Stuart Ward, 'Echoes of empire', *History Workshop Journal*, 62 (2006), 264–78; Thompson, *Empire Strikes Back*.
3 For examples, see the account of West Indian bandsmen at the Colonial and Indian Exhibition in *Pall Mall Gazette* (20 May 1886), 4; or the Indian dignitaries bowing before the Queen at the opening of the same exhibition in *The Graphic* (15 May 1886), 492. At George V's coronation a mixed group of coloured subjects in London were photographed shouting out 'All Hail to the Chief', in *The Daily News* (5 June 1911), 5, 8. On advertising, picture postcards and other ephemera of empire, see MacKenzie, *Propaganda and Empire*, pp. 21–30. On minstrel shows and advertising, see Lorimer, *Colour, Class*, pp. 86–90. Dr Beecham, posing as John Bull, even cured the dyspepsia of the grateful, subservient subjects of the empire in *The Graphic* (15 May 1886), 547.
4 M. D. Blanch, 'British society and the war', in P. Warwick (ed.), *The South African War: the Anglo-Boer War, 1899–1902* (London: Longman, 1980), pp. 210–38; cf. the earlier study by Richard Price, *An Imperial War and the British Working Class* (London: Routledge, Kegan Paul, 1972); Bill Nasson, *The War for South Africa: The Anglo-Boer War, 1899–1902* (Cape Town: Tafelberg, 2010); Kenneth O. Morgan, 'Lloyd George, Keir Hardie and the importance of the 'Pro-Boers', in G. Cuthbertson and A. Jeeves (eds), *South African War, 1899–1902: Centennial Perspectives*, issue of *South African Historical Journal*, 41 (1999), 290–311.
5 Adam Hochschild, *King Leopold's Ghost: A Story of Greed, Terror and Heroism in Colonial Africa* (New York: Houghton Mifflin, 1998); Cline, *Morel*; Grant, *A Civilised Savagery*; Jonathan Hyslop, 'The imperial working class makes itself "white": White labourism in Britain, Australia, and South Africa before the First World War', *Journal of Historical Sociology*, 12 (1999), 398–421. See also Chapter 7.
6 Laura Tabili, 'A homogeneous society?', pp. 53–76; Peter Fryer, *Staying Power*; Colin Holmes, *John Bull's Island: Immigration and British Society, 1871–1971* (London: Macmillan, 1988); Colin Holmes (ed.), *Immigrants and Minorities in British Society* (London: Allen and Unwin, 1978); Kenneth Lunn (ed.), *Hosts, Immigrants and Minorities: Historical Responses to Newcomers in British Society, 1870–1914* (Folkstone: Dawson, 1980); P. Kennedy and A. Nicholls (eds), *Nationalist and Racialist Movements in Britain and Germany before 1914* (London: Macmillan, 1981); on the history of minorities in Britain, see the journal *Immigrants and Minorities*.

7 R. J. Halliday, 'Social Darwinism', 389–405; G. Himmelfarb, *Victorian Minds*, pp. 314–32; Paul Crook, '"Historical monkey business": The myth of Darwinized British imperial discourse', *History*, 84 (1999), 633–57; Jones, *Social Darwinism*, pp. viii–xiv.

8 J. W. Burrow, 'Introduction', in Charles Darwin, *The Origin of Species* (Harmondsworth: Penguin, 1968), p. 33; R. M. Young, *Darwin's Metaphor*; Michael Ruse, *The Darwinian Revolution: Science Red in Tooth and Claw* (Chicago, IL: University of Chicago Press, 1979); Desmond and Moore, *Darwin's Sacred Cause*. See also Chapters 2 and 3.

9 David Davies, *The Last of the Tasmanians* (New York: Barnes and Noble, 1974), pp. 235–6; Vivienne Rae-Ellis, 'The Representation of Trucanini', in Elizabeth Edwards (ed.), *Anthropology and Photography* (New Haven: Yale University Press, 1992), pp. 230–3.

10 Susan Thorne, 'Religion and empire at home', in Hall and Rose (eds), *At Home with the Empire*, pp. 143–65, and Thorne, *Congregational Mission*; Thompson, *Empire Strikes Back*, pp. 101–18; Andrew Porter, *Religion Versus Empire*; Hall, *Civilising Subjects*.

11 Lorimer, *Colour, Class*, pp. 81–6; on abolitionist narratives in children's literature, see Kathryn Castle, 'The representation of Africa in mid-Victorian children's magazines', in G. Gerzina (ed.), *Black Victorians/Black Victoriana*, (New Brunswick, NJ: Rutgers University Press, 2003), pp. 145–58.

12 Darwin's great cause in defence of a common humanity and opposition to slavery did not deter him from relying on common ethnic stereotypes, Desmond and Moore, *Darwin's Sacred Cause*, pp. 366–9; British missionaries in Africa celebrated western science and technology but not the science of race, John MacKenzie, 'Missionaries, science and the environment in nineteenth-century Africa', in A. Porter (ed.), *The Imperial Horizons of British Protestant Missions, 1880–1914* (Cambridge: William B. Eerdmans, 2003), pp. 106–30; Lorimer, 'Science and secularization', pp. 212–35.

13 Bolt, *Victorian Attitudes*, pp. 1–28; Michael Banton, *The Idea of Race*, pp. 13–62; Reginald Horsman, 'Origins of racial Anglo-Saxonism in Great Britain before 1850', *Journal of the History of Ideas*, 37 (1976), 381–410.

14 On Dilke, see Chapter 2; Paul A. Kramer, 'Empire, exceptions, and Anglo-Saxons: Race and rule between the British and United States empires, 1880–1910', *Journal of American History*, 88 (2002), 1315–53; *NOED* [www.oed.com]; Mandler, *English National Character*; Robert Colls, 'Englishness and the political culture', in Robert Colls and Philip Dodd (eds), *Englishness: Politics and Culture, 1880–1920* (London: Croom Helm, 1986), pp. 43–54; Raphael Samuel (ed.), *Patriotism: The Making and Unmaking of British National Identity, vol. I: History and Politics* (London: Routledge, 1989).

15 Banton, *Idea*, pp. 60–1; Michael Banton, 'The internal and external conditions of racial thought', *Ethnic and Racial Studies*, 6 (1983), 246–5; Hall, *Civilising Subjects*; Hall, McClelland and Rendall, *Defining the Victorian Nation*.

16 Lorimer, *Colour, Class*, pp. 137–61; R. B. Martin, *The Dust of Combat: A Life of Charles Kingsley* (London: Faber and Faber, 1956), pp. 264–8; J. W. Burrow, *A Liberal Descent: Victorian Historians and the English Past* (Cambridge: Cambridge University Press, 1981), pp. 98, 157–8.

17 'The Negro', *Church Missionary Intelligencer*, new ser., 9 (1873), 225–50, responding to a report in *The Times* (5 June 1873).

18 Brian V. Street, *The Savage in Literature: Representations of 'Primitive' Society in English Fiction, 1858–1920* (London: Routledge Kegan Paul, 1975), pp. 5–7, 49–77, 96–8; Patrick Dunae, 'Boys' literature and the idea of race', *Wascana Review*, 12 (1977), 84–107; Dunae, 'Boys' literature and the idea of empire', *Victorian Studies*, 24 (1980), 105–21; Dunae, 'New Grub Streets for boys', pp. 12–33, Stuart Hannabuss, 'Ballantyne's message for empire', pp. 53–71, and Jeffrey Richards, 'With Henty to Africa', pp. 72–106, in Richards (ed.), *Imperialism and Juvenile Literature*; Castle, 'Representation of Africa', pp. 145–58.

19 G. R. Searle, *A New England? Peace and War, 1886–1918* (Oxford: Oxford Univer-

sity Press, 2004), pp. 109–11, 542–3, 571–6; Stephen Heathorn, *For Home, Country and Race: Constructing Gender, Class, and Englishness in the Elementary School, 1880–1914* (Toronto: University of Toronto Press, 2000); R. D. Atlick, *The English Common Reader: A Social History of the Mass Reading Public, 1800–1900* (Chicago, IL: University of Chicago Press, 1957).

20 *The Graphic* (8 May 1886), 495 and (15 May 1886), 535–6. On the Indian and Colonial Exhibition and other such events, see MacKenzie, *Propaganda and Empire*; Claire Wintle, 'Model subjects: Representations of the Andaman Islands at the Colonial and Indian Exhibition, 1886', *History Workshop Journal*, 67 (2009), 194–207. On museum displays, see Johnston, 'The empire and anthropology', 140–2; Annie E. Coombs, *Reinventing Africa: Museums, Material Culture and Popular Imagination in Late Victorian and Edwardian England* (New Haven, CT: Yale University Press, 1994); Richard D. Altick, *The Shows of London* (Harvard: Belknap, 1978); D. K. Van Keuren, 'Museums and ideology', 171–8; Stocking, *Victorian Anthropology*, pp. 263–5.

21 *The Times* (10 May 1887), 10a, and (12 May 1887) 6f; *Standard* (10 May 1887), 3d, and (12 May 1887), 5g; *Pall Mall Gazette* (10 May 1887), 11; *Penny Illustrated Paper* (14 May 1887), 317–18; *Evening News* (10 May 1887), 2e, and (12 May 1887), 2f.

22 RH, Anti-Slavery Papers, Brit. Emp. S18 Correspondence C150/246, Clayton Drake to H. R. Fox Bourne, 3 April 1899; C151/85, Henry Gurney to H. R. Fox Bourne, 9 June 1894; C150/89. S. Boyd to H. R. Fox Bourne, 16 July 1909; RH, Brit. Emp. S20, E5/10 APS Minute Book, 7 May 1908.

23 RH, Anti-Slavery Papers, Brit. Emp. S18 Correspondence C151/139, J. Hinscliff to H. R. Fox Bourne, 11 September 1899; *AF*, new ser., 5 (June 1899), 436–9, and (April 1900), 526; *The Times* (9 September 1899), 13a–b; Fernando Henriques, *Children of Conflict: A Study of Inter-Racial Sex and Marriage* (New York, E. P. Dutton, 1975), pp. 140–1; Ben Shepard, 'Showbiz imperialism', in MacKenzie (ed.), *Imperialism and Popular Culture*, pp. 97–103; MacKenzie, *Propaganda and Empire*, p. 104.

24 Richards, 'With Henty to Africa', pp. 72–106.

25 Bernard Lightman, 'Introduction', pp. 1–12, and '"The voices of nature": Popularizing Victorian science', pp. 187–211, Barbara T. Gates, 'Ordering nature: Revisioning Victorian science culture', pp. 179–86, in Lightman (ed.), *Victorian Science*; Keith Thomas, *Man and the Natural World* (Harmondsworth: Penguin, 1984), pp. 30–50, 187–8; John MacKenzie, 'Introduction', in MacKenzie (ed.), *Imperialism and the Natural World*, pp. 1–14.

26 Peter Broks, 'Science, the press and empire', in MacKenzie (ed.), *Imperialism and the Natural World*, pp. 141–63; Lorimer, '*Nature*, racism', 369–85.

27 The number of males employed in professional occupations and subordinate services grew from 204,000 in 1871 to 348,000 in 1901, and those employed as clerks in commercial occupations grew from 212,000 in 1871 to 597,000 in 1901 (B. R. Mitchell and Deane, *Abstract of British Historical Statistics* (Cambridge: Cambridge University Press, 1962).

28 'Natural history for the working man', *Nature*, 29 (7 February 1884), 344. On the periodical *Nature*, see Chapter 3; Thompson, *Empire Strikes*, pp. 98, 112–18.

29 *English Mechanic and World of Science*, 42 (26 February 1886), 547, and 43 (5 March 1886), 20.

30 *English Mechanic and World of Science*, 44 (10 September 1886), 31; on Campbell, see Chapter 5.

31 *The Academy*, 19 (14 May 1881), 356–7.

32 Coutts Trotter, 'Some account of New Guinea', *Science Monthly*, 1 (1883–4), 69, 70–2.

33 *Knowledge* (4 November 1881), 3.

34 'Savage and anthropologist', *Knowledge*, 4 (6 July 1883), 7.

35 Richard A. Proctor, *Wages and Wants of Science-Workers* (London: Smith and Elder, 1876), pp. 7–8, 35–6; Percy Russell, 'The occupations of the people of England and Wales in 1881', *Knowledge* (30 November 1883), 330–1, noted an increase in male clerks from 89,630 in 1871 to 175,468 in 1881.

36 'The Civil War in America', *Knowledge* (1 September 1887), 246–7; *Knowledge* (15

September 1882), 255; E. S. Morse, 'The kinship of men and apes', *Knowledge* (2 April 1888), 121–2.

37 'The British Race Today', *Knowledge* (1 November 1885), 21.

38 The following treatment of four popular science authors – Wood, Brown, Clodd and Keane – is revised and extended from an earlier essay, Lorimer, 'Science and secularization', pp. 218–28.

39 Theodore Wood, *Rev. J. G. Wood. His Life and Work* (London: Cassell, 1890); F. A. Mumby, *The House of Routledge, 1834–1934* (London: G. Routledge and Sons, 1934), pp. 75–9; *The Times* (5 March 1889), 9; B. B. Woodward, 'Wood, John George (1827–1889)' rev. P. Osborne, *NODNB* (2004).

40 Rev. John G. Wood, *The Boy's Own Book of Natural History* (London: Routledge, Warne, and Routledge, 1861), pp. 1–9.

41 Charles Pickering, *The Races of Man; and their Geographical Distribution with an Analytical Synopsis of the Natural History of Man by John Charles Hall*, new edn, (London: H. G. Bohn, 1850). For the British edition, the introduction by Dr John Charles Hall of the Royal College of Physicians, Edinburgh, argued for monogenesis within a Biblical time frame.

42 T. Wood, *Rev. J. G. Wood*, pp. 205–6, 210–13.

43 Wood, *The Boy's Own Natural History*, p. 8.

44 BL, British Publishers Archive, George Routledge and Co., 1853–1902, mic. reel 2, Contracts, vol. 3: R–Z, fol. 355, Contract between George Routledge and Sons and Rev. John G. Wood for *The Natural History of Man* (1867), and Addendum to the Wood Contract, 1 October 1869; and reel 4, Publication Books, vol. 1, January 1867 – January 1870 (Chadwyck-Healey, 1973); see also reel 4, Publication Books, vols 1 and 4; J. G. Wood, *The Natural History of Man, being an Account of the Manners and Customs of the Uncivilised Races of Man* (London: Routledge), vol. 1 (1868) and vol. 2 (1870); T. Wood, *Rev. J. G. Wood*, pp. 76–9; F. A. Mumby, *House of Routledge* (London: Routledge, 1934), p. 78.

45 H. Power, *Nature*, 3 (3 November 1870), 10; E. B. Tylor, *Nature*, 9 (12 February 1874), 279, and (27 April 1874), 479, 482; Tylor, 'Selected Books', *Anthropology*, n.p.

46 Wood, *Man*, vol. 1, p. v.

47 T. Wood, *Rev. J. G. Wood*, pp. 113–14.

48 Wood, *Man*, vol. 2, p. 343.

49 Wood, *Man*, vol. 2, p. 3.

50 Wood, *Man*, vol. 2, pp. 1–4; W. H. Flower, 'Comparative anatomy of man', 79, advised against this familiar comparison; Bolt, *Victorian Attitudes*, pp. 130–4; H. A. C. Cairns, *Prelude to Imperialism*, pp. 75–6; Lorimer, *Colour, Class*, pp. 75–81.

51 Wood, *Man*, vol. 1, pp. 1–4, see also pp. 91–2, 659; cf illustrations of 'Negro' (vol. 1, pp. 656, 661) with those of the 'nobler Kaffir' (vol. 1, pp. 3, 35, 53, 82); see also vol. 1, frontispiece and p. vi.

52 Wood, *Man*, vol. 1, p. 338; Francis Galton, *The Narrative of an Explorer in Tropical South Africa* (London: John Murray, 1853), pp. 72, 132–5, 187–94, 231–4.

53 Wood, *Man*, vol. 1, p. 4, and vol. 2, p. 195.

54 On the language of 'savage', see Report of the Select Committee on Aborigines (British Settlements) [1837], *British Parliamentary Papers* (Shannon: Irish University Press, 1968), pp. 3–6; on language of 'race' and 'race relations' see Chapters 5 and 6.

55 Catherine Hall, 'Of gender and empire', pp. 46–76; Lata Mani, *Contentious Traditions: The Debate on Sati in Colonial India* (Berkeley, CA: University of California Press, 1998); Himani Bannerji, 'Age of consent and hegemonic social reform', in Clare Midgley (ed.), *Gender and Imperialism* (Manchester: Manchester University Press, 1998), pp. 21–44; Philippa Levine, 'Sexuality and Empire', in Hall and Rose (eds), *At Home with the Empire*, pp. 122–42.

56 Wood, *Man*, vol. 1, p. 234 and p. 73.

57 Wood, *Man*, vol. 1, pp. 91–2.

58 Wood, *Man*, vol. 1, pp. 422, 453; see also his comments on Tahitian women, *Man*, vol. 2, p. 399.

59 Wood, *Man*, vol. 1, p. 92, and vol. 2, p. 5.

60 Wood, *Man*, vol. 2, pp. 294–7.

61 Wood, *Man*, vol. 1, p. 688, and p. 235; see also p. 458.
62 Wood, *Man*, vol. 2, p. 6.
63 Wood, *Man*, vol. 1, p. 338.
64 Wood, *Man*, vol. 2, p. 47.
65 Wood, *Man*, vol. 1, p. 376.
66 Wood, *Man*, vol. 1, p. 466, and vol. 2, pp. 69, 105, 187, 202.
67 Wood, *Man*, vol. 2, p. 105.
68 Thomas Seccombe, 'Brown, Robert (1842–1895)', rev. Elizabeth Baigent, *NODNB* (2004); *The Times* (29 October 1895), 8c; John Hayman, 'Introduction', *Robert Brown and the Vancouver Island Exploring Expedition* (Vancouver: University of British Columbia Press, 1989), pp. 3–28, and 'Appendix I: Published writings by Robert Brown relating to the Northwest Coast', pp. 198–201.
69 Simon Nowell-Smith, *The House of Cassell, 1848–1958* (London: Cassell, 1958), p. 104; *The Times* (29 October 1895), 8c.
70 Robert Brown, *The Races of Mankind: Being a Popular Description of the Characteristics, Manners and Customs of the Principal Varieties of the Human Family* (London: Cassell, Petter and Galpin, 1873–6), vol. 1, p. 1; *The Peoples of the World* (London: Cassell, Petter and Galpin, 1881–6), vol. 1, pp. 1–13; *The Countries of the World: Being a Popular Description of the Various Continents, Islands, Rivers, Seas, and Peoples of the Globe* (London: Cassell, 1884–9), vol. 1, p. 1; R. G. Latham's ethnological works include *The Natural History of the Varieties of Man* (London: 1850), *The Ethnology of the British Colonies and Dependencies* (London: 1851) and *Varieties of the Human Race* (Orr's Circle of the Sciences), vol. 1 (London: 1854); Curtin, *Image of Africa*, pp. 336–7, 369–70, 398; Stocking, *Victorian Anthropology*, pp. 53, 103–4.
71 Brown, *Peoples*, vol. 1, p. 7.
72 Brown, *Peoples*, vol. 1, pp. 1, 3; *Races*, vol. 3, p. 206; neither Brown nor other popular science publications, or the prevailing view of professional scientists (Chapter 3), support Robert J. C. Young's reliance on Broca and his theory of the infertility of racial crosses in *Colonial Desire: Hybridity in Theory, Culture and Race* (London: Routledge, 1995).
73 Brown, *Peoples*, vol. 1, p. 6; see pp. 3–6.
74 Brown, *Peoples*, vol. 6, pp. 309–10, 319–20, and pp. 15, 264; vol. 5, pp. 178–9, 269.
75 Brown, *Races*, vol. 1, pp. 24–38, 229–30; vol. 2, pp. 112–14, 123, 234–7; vol. 3, pp. 4–10, 103, 161; vol. 4, pp. 110–15, 173; *Countries*, vol. 5, pp. 44–5.
76 Brown, *Races*, vol. 4, p. 290; *Peoples*, vol. 6, pp. 309–10.
77 Brown, *Peoples*, vol. 6, p. 320.
78 F. M. L. Thompson, *The Rise of Respectable Society* (London: Fontana, 1988); James Walvin, *Victorian Values* (London: Sphere, 1987); Lorimer, 'From Victorian values to white virtues', pp.109–34; see also Lorimer, *Colour, Class*, pp. 108–30.
79 [A. J. Wilson], 'In Memory', in Robert Brown (ed.), *The Adventures of John Jewet*, (London: Clement Wilson, 1896), pp. 5–7; Hayman, *Robert Brown*, pp. 22–3.
80 For an effort to balance psychoanalytical and historical approaches, see Joel Kovel, *White Racism: A Psychohistory* (London: Free Association, 1988); for an example of post-modern literary determinism, see Robert Young, *White Mythologies: Writing History and the West* (London: Routledge, 1990); for reflections on historical approaches to the culture of empire, Richard Price, 'One big thing: Britain', 602–27; Cooper, *Colonialism in Question*.
81 Brown, *Races*, vol. 1, p. 27.
82 Brown, *Races*, vol. 1, pp. 31, 229–30; see also Hayman, *Robert Brown*, pp. 21–2.
83 Brown, *Races*, vol. 3, pp. 199–216; cf. a more recent analysis, Eric Wolf, *Europe and the People without History* (Los Angeles, CA: University of California, 1982), pp. 158–94.
84 Brown, *Races*, vol. 3, p. 215.
85 Brown, *Races*, vol. 1, pp. 229–30, vol. 2, pp. 85, 113; *Countries*, vol. 6, pp. 152, 159.
86 Brown, *Races*, vol. 3, pp. 220–1.
87 Brown, *The Story of Africa and its Explorers* (London: Cassell, 1892–95), vol. 4, pp. 132–5, 148–51.

88 Brown, *Races*, vol. 3, p. 221.
89 Frantz Fanon, *The Wretched of the Earth* (Harmondsworth: Penguin, 1967), pp. 29–34.
90 Brown, *Races*, vol. 4, p. 116.
91 Brown, *Races*, vol. 4, pp. 212, and 21; see also pp. 172, 208–15.
92 Brown, 'The Slave Trade', *Races*, vol. 3, pp. 177–98; this chapter was omitted in the revised edition, *Peoples of the World*.
93 Brown, *Races*, vol. 3, pp. 186–7, 195–6; see also *Countries*, vol. 2, pp. 167–73, 183–90.
94 Brown, *Races*, vol. 3, p. 196; *Countries*, vol. 2, pp. 312, 314.
95 Brown, *Races*, vol. 3, p. 196n, and *Countries*, vol. 2, p. 312; even in his youthful travels in British Columbia in the 1860s, Brown took a dim view of missionary efforts, Brown, 'Mission work in British Columbia', *Mission Life* (1 September 1870), 532–41; Susan Thorne, 'Religion and empire at home', pp. 143–65. See also Chapter 7.
96 Brown, *Races*, vol. 2, p. 302; Robert O. Collins, 'Samuel White Baker: Prospero in Purgatory', in R. I. Rotberg (ed.), *Africa and its Explorers: Motives, Methods, and Impact* (Cambridge, MA: Harvard University Press, 1973), pp. 141–8.
97 Brown, *Races*, vol. 2, p. 303.
98 Brown, *Races*, vol. 3, p. 198.
99 Brown, *Races*, vol. 2, p. 306.
100 Brown, *Africa*, vol. 1, pp. 2–4.
101 Brown, *Africa*, vol. 1, pp. 6–7.
102 Brown, *Africa*, vol. 4, p. 191; and *Races*, vol. 3, pp. 212–14.
103 Brown, *Africa*, vol. 4, p. 158.
104 Brown, *Africa*, vol. 4, pp. 256–8.
105 Brown, *Countries*, vol. 6, pp. 155–6
106 E. P. Haynes, 'Clodd, Edward (1840–1930)', rev. J. F. M. Clark, *NODNB* (2006); Joseph McCabe, *Edward Clodd* (London: Bodley Head, 1932).
107 McCabe, *Clodd*, pp. 39, 55, 90, 99–100.
108 Edward Clodd, *The Childhood of the World. A Simple Account of Man's Early Years* (London: Macmillan, 1873), p. 5; McCabe, *Clodd*, pp. 29–32.
109 Clodd, *World*, pp. 11–12.
110 Edward Clodd, *The Childhood of Religions: Embracing a Simple Account of the Birth and Growth of Myths and Legends* (1875) (London: Kegan Paul Trench, 1889), pp. 10–44, 230–40.
111 Clodd, *Religions*, p. 222.
112 Clodd, *Religions*, p. 210.
113 Catholicus, *A Caution against the Educational Writings of Edward Clodd* (London: John F. Shaw, 1880), p. 3.
114 Clodd, *Religions*, pp. 78–9.
115 Susan Thorne, *Congregational Mission*, pp. 89–123; Gareth Griffiths, '"Trained to tell the truth": Missions, converts, and narration', pp. 158–72, and Patrick Harries, 'Anthropology', pp. 238–60, in Norman Etherington (ed.), *Missions and Empire*, OHBE Companion Series (Oxford: Oxford University Press, 2005); Andrew C. Ross, 'Christian missions and mid-nineteenth century change in attitudes to race: The African experience', in Porter (ed.), *The Imperial Horizons*, pp. 85–105; Lorimer, *Colour, Class*, pp. 75–82.
116 As extracted from *The Story of Creation* in Edward Clodd, 'Social evolution', *Knowledge* (1 August 1887), p. 221.
117 Edward Clodd, *The Story of Creation: a Plain Account of Evolution* (London: Longmans, 1888), p. 203.
118 Clodd, *Creation*, p. 132.
119 Clodd, *Creation*, pp. 211–14.
120 Clodd, 'Social evolution', p. 221.
121 Clodd, 'Social evolution', p. 221.
122 'Are women inferior to men?' *Knowledge* (4 November 1881), 6–8, and (18 Novem-

ber 1881), 47–8; readers' responses (11 November 1881), 35, (25 November 1881), 77–8, (2 December 1881), 95; Miss A. W. Buckland, 'The Wyandotte Indians' (23 December 1881), 158–9; revived debate in *Knowledge* (20 February 1885), 157, (6 March 1885), 203, (17 April 1885), 332, (1 May 1885), 379; McCabe, *Clodd*, p. 32.

123 On Keane's racial theories, see Chapter 3.

124 Johnston, 'The empire and anthropology', 143–4.

125 *Who Was Who, 1897–1915*; Sir Edward Brabrook, 'A. H. Keane', *Man*, 12 (1912), 53; E. A. Parkyn, *Man*, 8 (1908), 190–1; *The Times* (5 February 1912), 11d; A. H. Keane, *Anthropological, Philological, Geographical, Historical and Other Writings Original and Translated by A. H. Keane* (London: privately printed, [1897]).

126 Keane, *Ethnology*, p. 171; for example, 'Wales – the Welsh', *Cassell's General Storehouse of Information* (1894) vol. 4, pt 2, p. 353.

127 Keane, *Man, Past and Present*, p. 170; the description of Southern Mongols above Keane adapted from his earlier entry in *Cassell's General Storehouse of Information* (1890–94), p. 367.

128 Keane, *Man, Past and Present*, pp. 442, 532.

129 Keane, *Ethnology*, pp. 223–9, and *The World's Peoples* (London: Hutchinson, 1908), pp. 11–12. See also Chapter 3.

130 Haddon, *History of Anthropology*, pp. 13, 47–8; C. H. Read, 'Anthropology at the universities', *Man* 6:38 (1906), 56–9.

131 A. H. Keane, 'The world: Population, races, languages, and religions', *The Church Missionary Intelligencer*, 45 [n.s. 19] (1894), p. 729.

132 Keane, *Man, Past and Present*, p. 36; 'Negro', *Cassell's Storehouse*, 43–4; R. Lydekker, 'Introduction', in A. H. Keane, R. Lydekker *et al.* (eds), *The Living Races of Mankind* (London: Hutchinson, 1905), p. vi; Keane, *The World's Peoples*, p. 16.

133 A. H. Keane, 'Egyptian Sudan and its inhabitants', *Nature*, 24 (24 January 1884), 294; see also his discussion of the Hamitic peoples in 'Who was Prince Alumayu?', *Nature*, 21 (20 November 1879), 61–2; [A. H. Keane], 'The Hamitic Race', *Cassell's General Storehouse of Information*, p. 220–1; *Man, Past and Present*, pp. 87–94. Edith R. Saunders, 'The Hamitic hypothesis: Its origins and functions in time perspective', *Journal of African History*, 10 (1969), 521–32; Andrew P. Lyons, 'Hamites, cattle and kingship: An episode in the history of diffusionist anthropology', *Canadian Journal of Anthropology/Revue Canadienne d'Atrhopologie*, 4 (1984), 57–64.

134 A. H. Keane, *The Gold of Ophir: Whence Brought and by Whom?* (London: Edward Stanford, 1901); Keane, 'Introduction', in R. N. Hall, *Great Zimbabwe, Mashonaland, Rhodesia* (London: Methuen, 1905); Keane, *Man, Past and Present*, pp. 58–9, 102–3.

135 A. H. Keane, 'The Haitian Negroes', *Nature*, 31 (4 December 1884), 99.

136 A. H. Keane, *The Boer States: Land and People* (London: Methuen, 1900), pp. 194–202.

137 Keane, *Boer States*, p. 201.

138 Keith Johnston, *School Physical and Descriptive Geography*, London Geography Series, 6th edn revised by A. H. Keane (London, 1892), pp. 66–7.

139 *Academy*, 49 (22 February 1896), 159–60; E. Clodd, *Grant Allen: A Memoir* (London: Grant Richards, 1900), pp. 37, 40–3.

140 Keane, *Church Missionary Intelligencer*, 722; reprinted in *Church Missionary Atlas* (London: Church Missionary Society, 1896), pp. 3–10.

141 Keane, *Church Missionary Intelligencer*, 722, 729.

142 *News from Afar*, new series, 2 (1896), 41–2, 56–7, 86–7, 121–2, 138–9, 152–3, 184–5.

143 Elizabeth Edwards, 'Introduction', pp. 3–17; Roslyn Poignant, 'Surveying the field of view: The making of the RAI photographic collection', pp. 42–73; Brian Street, 'British popular anthropology: Flexibility and photographing the Others', pp. 122–31; and other essays in Edwards (ed.), *Anthropology and Photography*. Also David Green, 'Photography and anthropology: the technology of power, *Ten.8*, 14 (1984), 30–7.

144 Lydekker (ed.) *The Living Races of Mankind*, cover and title page; Keane, *The World's Peoples*, title page.

145 Lydekker, *Living Races*, p. i.

146 Keane, *World's Peoples*, pp. vii–viii.
147 Keane, *World's Peoples*, pp. 1–12; Lydekker, *Living Races*, pp. i–vii.
148 E. A. Parkyn, *Man*, 8 (1908), pp. 190–1.
149 Johnston, 'The empire and anthropology', 141–2.
150 Fawn M. Brodie, *The Devil Drives: A Life of Sir Richard Burton* (New York: Ballantine, 1969); on Victorian domestic sexual attitudes and anthropology, see Stocking, *Victorian Anthropology*, pp. 197–208, 216–19; Kuklick, *The Savage Within*, p. 13.
151 'The Bulawayo Case – by Sir Harry Johnston', *Star* (26 August 1911), 4(d).
152 Philippa Levine, 'Sexuality and empire', pp. 122–44, and 'Sexuality, gender and empire', in Levine (ed.), *Gender and Empire*, pp. 134–55; Anna Stoler, *Carnal Knowledge*, pp. 41–78.
153 Robert Young, 'The historiographic and ideological contexts of the nineteenth-century debate on man's place in nature', in M. Teich and R. Young (eds), *Changing Perspectives in the History of Science* (London: Heinemann Educational, 1973), pp. 344–478.
154 Richard Price, *Making Empire*; Alan Lester, 'Humanitarians and White Settlers in the Nineteenth Century', in N. Etherington (ed.), *Missions and Empire*, pp. 64–85; Thorne, *Congregational Mission*; Hall, *Civilising Subjects*. See also Chapter 5.
155 Freda Harcourt, 'Disraeli's imperialism, 1866–1868: A question of timing', *Historical Journal*, 23 (1980), 87–109; R. Robinson, 'Non-European Foundations of European Imperialism', pp. 117–42; Richard Price, *British Society, 1680–1880: Dynamism, Containment and Change* (Cambridge: Cambridge University Press, 1999), pp. 329–35, 339–42. See also Chapter 2.
156 Jones, *Social Darwinism*, pp. 140–59; Searle, *Eugenics*, pp. 39–66, and Searle, 'Eugenics and class', in Charles Webster (ed.), *Biology, Medicine, and Society, 1840–1940* (Cambridge: Cambridge University Press, 1981), pp. 217–42.

PART III

The language of race relations

CHAPTER FIVE

From colour prejudice to race relations

Even though scientific racism, whether professional or popular, argued for the natural inequality of racial groups, it was surprisingly deficient in describing how that natural inequality should be given form in the political, legal and social institutions and conventions of multi-racial colonial societies. Beyond the claim that the whites should be dominant and persons of colour should be in a subordinate position, the scientists had little to say about the political, legal and social relationships of groups defined as 'races'. Unfortunately, our historical and literary studies of racism have followed the lead of the scientists. Consequently, we know much more about the construction of identities of 'race' than we know about Victorian thought on relationships between groups designated as races.[1]

The scholarly focus on identities and stereotypes of 'race' rather than on the language of 'race relations' gives a distorted view of the Victorians. It allows the scientific advocates of racial inequality to define the discussion in terms of an imagined, ordered world of nature, whereas a focus on ideas about race relations provides a better sense of how the Victorians dealt with a disordered colonial world of racial subordination and conflict. Furthermore, as the Victorians thought about race relations, they confronted the glaring contradiction between forms of political and social subordination in the multi-racial colonial world and the legitimised forms of political and social inequality of the metropolitan society of the United Kingdom. Faced with these manifest contradictions, Victorian commentators both disagreed with one another and, over time, invented a new vocabulary of race relations.

The social history of language has concentrated mainly on the languages of class and gender. In comparison, the language of race, and especially the language of race relations, is an underdeveloped area of study. Although often overlooked, the nineteenth-century literature on race relations is sufficient in range and interest to deserve its own full-length treatment. Here, one can only begin an outline sketch of the direction of Victorian thought on race relations. This chapter describes the competing strands of thought about race relations as they developed in the course of the nineteenth century. Chapter 6 will look at the Edwardian discourse on the 'colour question' which informed the immediate context for the invention of race relations.

The Victorian language of race relations originated with the anti-slavery movement and associated humanitarian agencies such as the APS. Through these humanitarian agencies and through sympathetic officials at the colonial office – for instance under-secretary James Stephen and colonial secretaries such as Lord Glenelg – it was incorporated into the ideology of the civilising mission. Operating under the presumption that British interests and those of subject colonial peoples were compatible, exponents of this mission believed that Her Majesty's Government had a special responsibility for the protection of indigenous peoples and subject persons of colour. The readiest means to offer that protection was through the conventions of the rule of law. Peoples who came within British jurisdiction were to be treated as subjects of the crown, and protected by the conventions of equality under the law and rights to due process. Of course, the idea of equality before the law is itself problematic, and is more significant as part of the ideology of British governance than as a description of the law, jurisprudence and legal administration in practice. In colonial jurisdictions, not only were the legal niceties between indentured servitude, slavery and free labour tested, but master and servant law and vagrancy laws originating in England were subject to additional arbitrary and harsh practices.[2]

The humanitarians' language of race relations enshrined its own cultural imperialism, which innocently presumed that the way to progress and virtue lay with assimilation to the conventions of metropolitan Britain. The nineteenth-century language of race relations matured and diversified as colonial racialism confounded this confident promise of assimilation. Multi-racial colonial societies appeared to be differently constituted from British society, and consequently a lexicon of race relations developed to describe those differences and to articulate not a doctrine of assimilation but one of separate development. In the early nineteenth century, when the anti-slavery movement was at its height, the voices for assimilation were loudest; by the end of the nineteenth century, the voices for separate development predominated. Neither point of view established exclusive control of the field.

In wrestling with these issues, the Victorians invented a new language of race relations. That language encompassed the changes taking place in relations between groups designated as races and the divisions within nineteenth-century thought on the question. Consequently, it not only defined and justified new forms of racial subordination but also retained remnants of the older assimilating imperialism, and gave expression to the newer voices of radical and Asian and African protest against colonialism and racialism. As historians of class have observed, this language did more than express consciousness of social differences, or describe changing patterns of subordination; it was itself an 'intervention' giving definition to that consciousness and legitimacy to forms of subordination. Like the language of class, the language of race relations was also disputed territory in which competing visions contested for authority and legitimacy. Like most contests, this struggle ranged unequal forces against one another. Within the context of late nineteenth-century imperialism and the concurrent orthodoxy of racial inequality given authority by professional and popular science, a new and vigorous racialism prevailed; it is often overlooked that a minority of dissidents also enriched the vocabulary of existing forms of resistance to racism.

The Victorians had an enormously rich, varied and flexible vocabulary to describe differences in cultures defined by the ethnocentric norm of the metropolitan society placed at the pinnacle of human progress and achievement. From this standard a rich and variable set of binary opposites contrasted the 'savage' with the 'civilised', the 'higher' and 'lower', and the 'superior' and 'inferior' races. In contrast to the comparative anatomists' efforts to define fixed racial types, this language had even greater ambiguity about whether characteristics were biologically or culturally determined.

As we have seen in Part II, the science of race rested upon building a correlation of physical traits with the looser and more flexible vocabulary of cultural or psychological characteristics. There were efforts to give this latter language greater precision. Herbert Spencer applied his powers of deduction to developing binary profiles of 'savage' and 'civilised' mentalities. More significantly, the evolutionary anthropology of E. B. Tylor and others attempted to use the established classifications of 'savage', 'barbarian' and 'civilised' to describe stages of human development. In seeking naturalistic rather than historical explanations for changes over time, the evolutionists searched, with limited success, for cultures untouched by the West, and consequently their chosen objects of study and their schemes of classification gave an artificial precision to their stages of development.[3]

In practice, the usage of terms such as 'savage' and 'civilised', including their various analogues, to describe the unequal relationships between European colonisers and what were termed 'subject races' remained far more flexible than the language of the scientists would suggest. In part, that flexibility stemmed from the fact that colonial relationships were in a state of flux, and the language changed to suit those changes and to suit the political dynamics of the disputed territory of racial discourse. As observant and informed witnesses, commentators recognised that economic and social relationships between British imperial interests, including white settlers as well as commercial, missionary and administrative functionaries, and indigenous and migrant populations, who came to be identified as 'non-Europeans', were not fixed by nature but subject to the contingent circumstances of the particular locale and to the negotiated outcome of coercion and consent between the colonisers and the colonised. They realised that a new world order was coming into being. The imperial agencies effecting this transformation created conflict and even destruction. The task was not simply to assess the sources of this conflict but to identify the social conditions and institutional framework under which racial subordination, political stability and economic development could co-exist.

Their working model of a more or less successful example was, of course, the metropolitan society of the British Isles in which subordination on the basis of class and gender, political stability and advanced economic development had taken place. The question was whether this model could work in societies in which the population was not simply divided along the lines of colour, but differentiated by culture. These cultural differences, which co-existed with the visible distinctions of colour, were an outcome of differing histories, stretching back to periods prior to contact with the West and including a more recent past of racial conflict and subordination. The issues addressed were complex and difficult, and we continue to struggle with them in the present. Needless to say, the Victorians gave a variety of answers: some of their ideas are offensive to the values of the twentieth-first century; most were confused, especially on the relationship of race and culture; many were as imperfect as our answers; and a few were perceptive in identifying the direction of change and sources of conflict.

Abolitionist origins

The term 'colour prejudice' had the longest historical ancestry originating in the last half of the eighteenth century with the challenge to the introduction of racial slavery into England and with the campaign against the slave trade. In its origins the language of prejudice was diffident and uncertain in its use. In his life-long labours in support of blacks in England and his extensive writings on slavery, Granville Sharp confronted the question of racial inequality but did not use the term prejudice to describe the attitudes of his slaveholding opponents. In 1769, he referred to blacks and mulattoes born in England as 'Eng-

lishmen born', and asserted that the common law, unlike the law of colonial slave societies, did not distinguish between the colour of either
natural born subjects or resident aliens. He warned his readers that, in
his terms, 'the distinction of colour' prevalent in the colonies might be
introduced into England. He advised that these distinctions applied not
simply to Africans but also to mulattoes and American Indians, and
suggested that there were 'many honest weather-beaten Englishmen'
who had 'as little reason to boast of their complexion as the Indians'.[4]
In 1788, a report of the Committee for the Abolition of the Slave Trade,
signed by Sharp, derided the pro-slavers' claims about the inferiority of
blacks, affirming 'the absurdity of the notion that their understandings
are not equally susceptible of cultivation with those of white people'.[5]
Anxious to head off a rumoured parliamentary initiative by the West
India interest, Sharp wrote to the Archbishop of Canterbury in 1786,
warning against any effort 'to set up uncharitable and unchristian
distinctions of complexion in this kingdom'.[6] Using similar language,
John Stuart, or Ottobah Cugano, an emancipated African slave and
abolitionist living in England, wrote to Sharp explaining why the black
poor refused to settle in New Brunswick. In addition to the coldness of
the winters, Stuart observes that the 'inhuman Distinction of Colour,
has in every point, and every view, spread its Predominant Power
over all the northern Climes'.[7] To Granville Sharp and his abolitionist
friends, and to the black victims of racial oppression, the 'distinction of
colour' was clearly unreasonable, and one of the many evils associated
with slavery.

On occasion, the word 'prejudice' was used to describe attitudes
and behaviour toward persons of a different skin colour. In 1788, the
Reverend John Newton, the former slave trader converted to the cause
of abolition, and author of the hymn 'Amazing Grace', when describing the fearful response of Africans to enslavement by Europeans, suggested that Africans had 'probably, the same natural prejudice against
a white man, as we have against a black'.[8] The idea of prejudice, and
its projection onto the responses of Africans, implied that such feelings were unjustified or unwarranted. In this instance, Newton also
described such feelings as natural, but more commonly such attitudes were identified as a product of slavery. From his experience in
Barbados, William Dickson, another abolitionist, wrote, in 1789, that
slavery produced 'an irresistable tendency to fix monstrous *prejudices*
(I say nothing here of *vices*) in the minds of the mere, ignorant vulgar.
The poor whites in Barbados have no idea that the blacks are, any way,
intitled to the same treatment as white men' [*sic*].[9] This link between
the origins of racial prejudice and the history of slavery would be a
persistent theme in nineteenth-century racial discourse.

In 1820, after reviewing Granville Sharp's papers and pamphlets in preparation of a memoir of the famous abolitionist, Prince Hoare expressed surprise that Sharp and his friends had to contest the claims of the natural inferiority of Africans advanced by David Hume and by more notorious defenders of the planting interest such as Edward Long and Samuel Estwick. Writing for an abolitionist readership and in a time when the abolitionist cause was in the ascendant, Hoare thought: 'It is surprising, and to posterity will appear hardly credible, that the force of prejudice was so great in the enlightened nations of Europe.'[10] By the early nineteenth century, the abolitionists had adopted the term 'prejudice' to describe both the belief in the inferiority of Africans and the denial of the legal rights of subjects based upon distinctions of colour.

In the language of the abolitionists and their supporters, such discriminatory attitudes and practices were referred to as instances of 'prejudice against colour', or more specifically as 'colour prejudice'.[11] They presumed that such prejudice was a creation of race slavery, and they hoped that with emancipation its force would diminish over time. Nonetheless, they anticipated it might well prove to be one of the enduring legacies of slavery. From the 1840s through to the 1860s much of the abolitionist discussion of colour prejudice focused on the United States, recognising that it affected white behaviour and institutions both in the slave South and in the free North. This critique of racial oppression in the United States, encouraged by leading American and African-American abolitionists, rested in part on a presumption that British opinion and behaviour were relatively free of such prejudice.[12] Nonetheless, anti-slavery activists and other advocates of the rights of persons of colour recognised that similar attitudes were engendered by colonial relationships within the British Empire. Both the BFASS and the APS identified prejudice as a root cause and potential legacy of the Mutiny in India in 1857. British officials applied the hateful epithet 'nigger' to Indians, and the humanitarian agencies feared that the spread of such racial contempt would be destructive of Britain's imperial and civilising role in India.[13]

While it would be mistaken to presume that the abolitionists and others were free of a sense of racial consciousness and even superiority, it is nonetheless significant that a vocabulary developed which identified colour prejudice as an evil engendered by slavery and colonialism. In 1860, L. A. Chamerovzow, the Secretary of the BFASS, in a letter to Lord Brougham, an elderly radical Whig and long-time supporter of the abolitionist cause, observed: 'The prejudice against colour I have always regarded as the terrible legacy Slavery has bequested to Freedom, & many generations must die out before it is itself obliterated.' In assessing attitudes in Britain, Chamerovzow added, 'I am quite of your view that we ought to endeavour to prevent the contamination from affecting our own people here in England.'[14] The abolitionists thought that the oppression stemming from such prejudice required redress, and presumed that persons within the United Kingdom were at least less prone to such prejudices than those individuals living within the racially oppressive cultures of slave and colonial regimes.

This presumption was to a degree politicised by the victims of racial oppression for their own purposes. Within the United Kingdom, African-American refugees from slavery and racism in their own country took a leading role in exposing forms of discrimination and in building a contrast between American and British attitudes. This campaign by fugitive slaves and black abolitionists reached its height during the crisis years prior to and during the American Civil War, but even after 1865 prominent African-Americans continued to see British sympathisers as a source of support.[15] Most notably, the Freedmen's Aid campaign, involving forty to fifty British organisations, assisted recently emancipated slaves by sending donations in cash and goods estimated in value at £120,000. Similarly, the Jubilee Singers raised £30,000 for Fisk University from three British tours in 1873, 1875 and 1884.[16] On occasion, international organisations with British head-quarters and American affiliates experienced significant ruptures due to the practice of racial segregation in American branches. In 1876–78, through the advocacy of Catherine Impey, the Good Templars, a tem-perance organisation supported by members of the Society of Friends, became embroiled in a controversy between its British and American branches. The Ancient Order of Foresters, a largely working-class Friendly Society, experienced a more significant split in 1888, when over five hundred members of the English High Court of the Order voted to cancel the charter of the American Subsidiary High Court due to the provision of a colour bar in American lodges. In the 1890s, when Ida B. Wells, an outspoken African-American advocate, campaigned in Britain against lynching in the United States, she too became em-broiled in controversies between British and American temperance and feminist organisations over the practice of racial segregation.[17]

While the language of colour prejudice had its origins among early and mid-Victorian abolitionists, and even though it persisted through the late nineteenth century and into the early twentieth, claims that such prejudices were part of American and colonial cultures and not part of the metropolitan culture need to be treated with a fair degree of scepticism. The Victorians generalised freely about the character of racial groups, and as we have seen in the discourse about race in professional and popular science, exhibited few inhibitions about incorporating commonplace prejudices into their science. All that one can establish with any certainty is that the language of colour prejudice played a part in the Victorians' discourse about race relations. It fostered a sense of contrast between the metropolitan culture and those multi-racial societies with a legacy of slavery, such as the United States, or within the British Empire of multi-racial colonial societies with or without a past history of race slavery.

This sense of contrast was important for two reasons. First, for the champions of the imperial ideology of the civilising mission among some colonial office administrators and among advocates of humanitarian agencies such as the missionary societies, the anti-slavery movement, and the APS, the idea that the law and its administration should be colour blind created a standard against which colonial variations could to be tested. For example, Sir Charles Lucas at the colonial office thought that British public opinion offered some check on the excesses of colonial racialism. Similarly, Ramsay MacDonald, attempting to define imperial policy for the new Labour Party, struggled unsuccessfully to define an 'imperial standard' free of colour prejudice yet compatible with the demands of white labour in the self-governing dominions.[18] Secondly, this sense of conflicting standards created opportunities for educated West Indians and Africans, as well as Indian nationalists and migrants, to contest discriminatory laws and practices in conflict with the ideological pretences of the metropolitan culture.[19] Finally, the contrast between metropolitan claims to be free of colour prejudice and the colonial practice of discrimination informed Victorian efforts to identify and explain the distinguishing features of social relations of multi-racial colonial societies.

The sense of contrast between colonial or American attitudes and British opinion created a need to explain the variance from the presumed norm of the metropolitan culture. The enslavement of Africans in the New World, and the analogous forms of conflict and oppression in the struggle between white settlers and aboriginal peoples over land, or the imposition of British rule upon the people of India, seemed to offer self-evident explanations for the development of colour prejudice.[20] In addition to these historical explanations, newer psychological explanations appeared with greater frequency during the second half of the nineteenth century. In this view, colour prejudice was a question of 'instinct', as peoples of differing physical appearance distrusted, feared or were repulsed by one another. For example, in Parliament in the 1860s, questions were asked as to why qualified Indian medical doctors were limited to service in the Indian Army under inferior pay and conditions of service, and debarred from writing competitive examinations for service in the British Army. One of several answers given was that British soldiers, despite the accepted competence of the Indian doctors, would not trust and would not tolerate treatment from a physician of an alien race.[21] The abolitionists were aware that the argument of instinct also served to defend the subordination and exploitation of blacks both slave and free. In 1856, the *Anti-Slavery Advocate*, a British Garrisonian publication, affirmed: 'we do not believe in the instinct of race', and forcefully proclaimed: 'the American prejudice against colour is so intense, and the antagonism produced by the institution of slavery so vehement, that the white race has succeeded in persuading themselves that their dislike of the black is no fault of their own, but is naturally implanted in them'.[22] The *Anti-Slavery Advocate* rooted its opposition to slavery and its critique of colour prejudice in its optimistic creed of Victorian liberalism committed to the rule of law and the equality of all subjects before the law. Over time, as the language of race relations developed and matured within the context of the racial conflict endemic to late nineteenth-century colonialism, the language of the abolitionists seemed naive, sentimental and even archaic.

In origin and development, the language of colour prejudice applied to white attitudes to blacks, both slave and free, in the slave societies of the Americas. By the 1850s and 1860s, humanitarian advocates applied the term to the attitudes of British officials, residents and travellers towards the peoples of India and towards indigenous peoples in colonies of settlement. For the humanitarian lobbyists, slavery and colonisation were twin evils by which lust for conquest and greed for land and profit overwhelmed standards of justice or feelings of Christian brotherhood, and inflicted suffering, oppression and even death on African slaves, their free descendants and aboriginal peoples throughout the British Empire.[23] Flushed with their victory over the West Indian planters in 1833, and feeling that British national honour was sullied by the conduct of colonisers toward indigenous peoples, the abolitionists headed a Select Parliamentary Committee into the status of aboriginal peoples in 1835–37. With the momentum mounted by this parliamentary enquiry, Dr Thomas Hodgkin (1798–1866) and other leading abolitionists founded the APS.[24] In his dedication to the advocacy of the rights of indigenous peoples, Hodgkin has been compared to his better-known friend, Thomas Clarkson, who with equal dedication performed a similar role as researcher and publicist for the anti-slavery movement. Under Hodgkin's direction as secretary from 1837 to 1866, the APS aimed to collect information about aboriginal peoples and to act as a lobby for coloured subjects of the crown in accordance with the recommendations laid down in the Parliamentary Report. Hodgkin found that the political work of publicity and lobbying dominated the activities of the APS, and in 1844, he founded the Ethnological Society of London to carry on the work of gathering information about the peoples and cultures of the empire. Ironically, Hodgkin, who died in 1866, saw his vision of humanitarianism and science working in harmony disrupted by the contentious birth of the new science of anthropology, and the assault on humanitarian advocacy by a younger generation of scientific racists.[25]

Rather than the language of 'race', the Parliamentary Report of 1837 and the early publications of the APS more commonly used the older language of 'nation' and 'native'. These reports referred to conflicts between British settlers and aboriginal peoples as conflicts between nations, and identified indigenes as 'native' inhabitants of their country or simply as 'natives'. The Parliamentary Report specifically advised against the universal application of the term 'savage' to aboriginal peoples, and in its construction of differing and unequal relations described the British as 'civilised' in contrast with the 'uncivilised' or 'semi-civilised' or 'barbarous' peoples of the empire.[26] Forthright in its condemnation of the destructive impact of colonisation on aboriginal populations, the recommendations of the Parliamentary Committee sought to bring relations between British settlers and aboriginal peoples under the rule of law. The committee recognised that an unequal power relationship existed in the conflicts over land and domicile, and distrusted colonial legislatures dominated by settler interests. Identifying aboriginal peoples as needing protection, the report looked to the executive branch of the government, the crown and its officers as the most capable of administering the law in a just and impartial fashion. While still early in the historical development of the language of natural rights within racial discourse, the report addressed the 'natural' entitlements of aboriginal peoples. Although not altogether consistent in the application of the language of rights, the report did recognise aboriginal entitlements to land. Presuming aboriginal ownership of land, it nonetheless advised against the signing of treaties. In some cases, it proposed compensation in the form of government-provided schools for land acquired by colonisers through force or deception. It also assumed that, in contrast to Europe with its surplus population, the lands of the periphery were under-populated. Consequently, even when aboriginal entitlement to land was recognised, the report assumed vacant lands were plentiful, and European settlers had a right to occupy those lands.[27] While the report attempted to set out some principles for policy and administrative practice in governing relations with aboriginal peoples, the magnitude of this task and the ambiguities surrounding aboriginal rights and entitlements meant that the recommendations did not offer remedies for existing injustices but rather attempted to provide a framework for dealing with future conflicts.

In its trust in the rule of law, the report, citing precedents going back to Charles II and legislation as recent as 1834, claimed that it was not pronouncing new principles, but simply seeking ways for existing principles to be made effective. Claiming that British rule rested on principles of justice and humanity for 'native inhabitants' including 'affording them protection in the enjoyment of their civil rights', the report and its evidence described the colonial encounter as a tale of oppression, desolation and even extermination as evil as the slave trade and slavery. The committee members, some of whom were Quakers or belonged to other Nonconformist sects, were no doubt still enthused by the prospect of a more equal playing field in regard to civil liberties; these had been established by the recent end of religious disabilities in the Repeal of the Test and Corporation Acts (1828) and the Catholic Emancipation Act (1829), by the extension of the franchise in the Reform Act of 1832, and by the abolition of slavery (1833). They believed in equality before the law as a principle, but in practice that belief was at best an ideal to be attained, and at worst a legal fiction. Even after 1832, the property-based franchise imposed restrictions by class and gender. Marriage and property law discriminated against women; vagrancy laws criminalised the poor; and master and servant law and its jurisprudence favoured employers and made the contractual obligations and the conduct of employees subject to criminal prosecution and penalties.[28] Aware of abuses under slavery and apprenticeship in the West Indies, and as evidenced by interviews they conducted, the commissioners warned against the abuse of vagrancy laws by white planters and settlers seeking to coerce and exploit coloured labour.[29]

Though claiming to follow the principles laid down in the 1837 report, the APS, from the outset, more directly championed the principle of equality before the law. In contrast to the missionary societies, the APS took on a more political role, concerning itself directly with the 'civil and political condition of the natives'. Asserting that aboriginal peoples had 'a right to the protection of British laws', the APS, in the buoyant mood of its foundation, declared: 'The distinctions which have been drawn between the privileges and immunities of the settler and the native must be removed.' In its memorial to Lord Durham in 1838, the society observed that Native Canadians should have 'the fullest and most complete participation in the rights of British subjects'. In the same year, it recommended to the colonial secretary Lord Glenelg that indigenous peoples under British jurisdiction in South Africa should enjoy equal status as British subjects. By 1850, in a memorial to Lord John Russell on the Government of Australia Bill, the society provided a fuller elaboration of equal status under the law for Australian Aborigines as British subjects.[30] Nonetheless, what the claim of equality before the law meant in 1838 or in 1850, especially when applied to colonial jurisdictions, is problematic. What can be ascertained is that the mantra of equality before the law regardless of race or colour became a standard by which humanitarian advocates would judge colonial practice, and a central concept in the disputed terrain of Victorian racial discourse.

From its foundation the APS acted as a watchdog on colonial administrators always ready to demand reform of abusive practices in accordance with the recommendations of the Parliamentary Report of 1837. This Select Committee's inquiry and report, the founding of the APS, and the establishment of the BFASS shortly thereafter in 1839, were inspired by an enormous optimism about the advance of liberty and reform witnessed within the lifetime of this generation of philanthropists. To an even greater extent than the anti-slavery activists, who had little anticipation of the 'problem of freedom' that would follow the ending of slavery, the advocates of the rights and interests of aboriginal peoples and of colonised persons of colour in general had little appreciation of the magnitude of their reforming agenda or of the unintended consequences of their philanthropy. In its annual report for 1846, the APS reviewed its first decade and found that the catalogue of abuses in colonial jurisdictions had not diminished. Among some settlers, the advocacy of the APS had excited criticism, but such opposition only vindicated the society's efforts to provide justice under the rule of law and to advance the 'uncivilised' along the path to civilised conditions.[31]

Victorian liberalism – assimilation and inequality

Other observers of colonial developments, including those with experience in colonial administration, were equally aware that the humanitarian-inspired reforms had not achieved adequate protections under the law for colonised peoples. Herman Merivale (1806–74), a brilliant student who became professor of political economy at Oxford and then served as an under-secretary in the colonial office from 1847 to 1859, provided one of the most comprehensive and influential treatments of colonial developments. Merivale's *Lectures on Colonization and Colonies*, originally delivered at Oxford in 1839–41 and republished with revisions in the form of appendices in 1861, provided an assessment of colonial policy and experience at a point in time when significant changes were occurring in relations with peoples differentiated both by culture and by the visible distinctions of race. On the one hand, there was the issue of the relations with aboriginal peoples in colonies of white settlement, and on the other hand, there were questions of the uses of land and labour in tropical dependencies, some of which until recently had depended on slave labour. Out of his interest in history and ethnography, Merivale was concerned with differences of culture rather than race. A sceptic about the biological determinism of the new anthropology, he offered more complex reasons for the failure of colonial policy to resolve racial conflicts.[32] His lectures informed the thinking of colonial officials into the early twentieth century, and his form of reasoning has a more central place in Victorian racial discourse than that of his eccentric contemporaries Robert Knox and James Hunt.

Merivale addressed the question of relations between white settlers and what he termed 'native tribes', by which he meant aboriginal peoples principally in Australia, New Zealand, British North America, and southern Africa. He also dealt with 'the labour of subjected native races', which included the former slave populations in the West Indies and migrant labourers. Within his chosen theme of colonisation, in his 1861 revisions, he excluded from his study 'what we usually call "inferior" not merely "savage", races, in subjugated dependencies'. Here he distinguished between colonies of British settlement in conflict with 'savage' races from more 'populous and semi-civilised regions' where the British came as rulers and not as settlers. In the latter category he presumably had India in mind. While he determined that this latter subject did not belong in his lectures on colonisation, he saw that problems were similar to those in colonies of settlement and that relations with his so-called 'inferior' races were becoming more significant.[33]

He identified three possible outcomes of contact between white colonisers and native races – extermination, insulation and amalgamation. Only the last option was a practical basis for policy. Extermination was not really a question of policy at all, but too often the shameful result of white settlers' assault on aboriginal land and peoples. Merivale rejected the idea that such extermination was the working of some natural law, which in an 1861 appendix he identified with Darwin. Rather, he identified specific causes attributable to the actions of white intruders – warfare, disease, hunger and despair – worked to destroy indigenous peoples and cultures.[34]

The second option of insulation, equally unworkable in his view, created reserve lands under the supervision of white administrators. The aim of such a policy was not so much to preserve aboriginal custom and autonomy but to facilitate the civilising process. This policy of 'retaining them as insulated bodies of men, carefully removed, during the civilising process, from the injury of European contact', had proved unworkable in the United States. There white settlers had dispossessed Native Americans of reserve lands and resettled them on new lands subsequently subject to further encroachment.[35] This process, in Merivale's view, was destructive both of aboriginal populations and of the civilising objective of the policy. It also rested on the mistaken view that aboriginal peoples had not yet come under destructive European influences of disease, drink, and greed:

> Desolation goes before us, and civilisation lags slowly and lamely behind. We hand over to the care of the missionary and the magistrate, not the savage with his natural tendencies and capacities, and his ancestral habits, but a degraded, craving, timid, and artful creature, familiarized with the powers and vices of the whites, rendered abject or sullen by ill-treatment, and with all his remaining faculties engrossed by the increasing difficulty of obtaining subsistence in his contracted hunting grounds.[36]

Merivale's critique of the destructive impact of colonialism freed him from the need to assess the value and integrity of aboriginal cultures and the means to provide for their protection and cultivation. It also gave freer scope for the presumptions of his political economy to argue for an aggressive policy of 'amalgamation', or, in our language, of modernisation. Whether we use his language or our language, Merivale advocated a strident cultural imperialism resting on firm mid-Victorian liberal foundations.

He chose the terminology for his third and preferred option deliberately. By 'amalgamation' he meant more than the assimilation of aboriginal peoples to the culture and society of white colonists: 'By amalgamation, I mean the union of natives with settlers in the same community, as master and servant, as fellow-labourers, as fellow-citizens, and, if possible, as connected by intermarriage.' While admitting that such a proposal might seem 'somewhat wild and chimerical', he pointed to the example of the Metis population of the Red River settlement in the Canadian West. He thought that the 'prejudices of colour' were an irrational legacy of slavery, and that intermarriage would overcome such animosities.[37] Even though he applied the language of 'inferiority' to non-Europeans in general, this assessment was cultural rather than biological. In his original remarks of 1841, he defended the capacity of non-Europeans for improvement and assimilation through education. He confidently observed: 'even the lowest of them are capable of acquiring settled habits, and susceptible of spiritual and intellectual training, I do not think any dispassionate inquirer can possibly doubt'.[38] In looking to education to achieve assimilation, Merivale thought in terms of religious instruction and industrial training, but by 1861 he had become more cautious about the success of missionaries and about the pace of anticipated change.[39]

In advancing a liberal vision of amalgamation, Merivale presumed that social inequalities would nonetheless exist, and non-whites would

[176]

serve primarily as servants or as wage-labourers. He objected that such a servile status was too readily identified as a form of slavery. In reminding his readers that modern class relationships within western European society were of both a recent and unusual character, he observed: 'Service without dependence, and dependence without control, are ideas foreign to the savage or the half-reclaimed.' His defence of assimilation through education was quite consistent with the subordination of native races, for, he observed, 'there is surely no reason in this why they may not enter by degrees into the sphere of civilization, although remaining always a subordinate race to the Whites'.[40]

Merivale's views on the social relationships between racial groups were most evident in his discussion of the labour of his 'subjugated native races', and of the question of status before the law. He addressed the question of labour in his commentary on the much-debated status of free labour in the British West Indies. From his political economy, he defined the issue as a question of the relationships between land, capital and labour, and differences of race or culture played at most a subordinate part in his calculations. Just as Wakefield had argued against the creation of a yeomanry of small-holders in Australia, Merivale warned against the ex-slaves becoming a self-sufficient peasantry in the West Indies. Under such a development they would regress into indolence and savagery, and impede the creation of a modern agricultural system producing export commodities, principally sugar, on large estates using wage labour. He claimed that the abolition of the slave trade and of slavery had led to the stagnation of the West Indian economy, and while defending free trade, he recognised that economic difficulties were compounded by the need to compete with slave-grown Cuban sugar. Consequently, though he rejected the planters' complaints about blacks as labourers, he admitted that employers faced problems in recruiting workers for plantations without the inducement of better wages.[41]

The variety of circumstances within the West Indian islands provided a ready test of his political economy. On Barbados, control of the ownership of land and the density of the population created conditions for the conversion of slave labour into effective wage labour. In Jamaica, fertile land was in short supply, yet the availability of unworked land gave the ex-slave population the option of working the land and marketing their own produce, and made it difficult to recruit plantation workers on terms desired by the planters. In Trinidad and Guiana, the limited supply of labour hindered the development of new plantations. Merivale's answer to the labour needs of Trinidad and Guiana was immigration. He looked to free blacks from the United States as one potential source, and to coolie labourers from India as another.

He warned against a system of indentured labour, for in Mauritius a new form of slavery had come into existence. He also thought that the transportation of Indian indentured labour to the West Indies would be costly, and feared that an indentured system would bring a host of new problems. Beyond the conditions of labour under the indenture system itself, there was the status of migrants who decided to become permanent residents. There were also shorter-term and longer-term social problems associated with the imbalanced sex-ratio of a largely male indentured labour force.[42]

Treating persons of colour largely as a potential wage-labour force, Merivale envisaged a social hierarchy in which divisions of class and race coincided. In this context, he did not address the question of the legal and political status of his black and brown proletariat, though he did see the emergence of a coloured middle class as a sign of progress. Although he never addressed the question directly, there was no impediment in his analysis to the replication of the class, legal and political inequalities of the metropolitan society in the West Indies.

He addressed the question of status under the law directly when he treated the situation of aboriginal peoples in colonies of white settlement. He warned against the call of philanthropists for the extension of the principle of equality under the law, as productive of more harm than good. He supported Sir George Grey's objection to the assumption that British law should not apply to aboriginal customs, and argued for the application of the law to practices which violated established moral principles, including cannibalism, human sacrifice, infanticide and male abuse of women. Drawing on the experience of New Zealand in his first edition of 1841, he also thought that questions of property should be dealt with under British law. He defended the right of settlers to possess land on which aboriginal peoples had not established effective occupation. He realised that conflicts over land often led to bloodshed and the decimation of aboriginal peoples, but here he criticised philanthropists for defending aboriginal title to lands for which they were incapable of establishing possession.[43]

In his 1861 revisions, Merivale extends this idea, making the astute observation that the demand for equality under the law requires the capacity of those subject to the law to enforce their entitlement. The philanthropists err in thinking 'that by proclaiming that all fellow-subjects of whatever race are equal in the eye of the law, we really make them so'. He offers the prospect that the African or Maori 'may be rendered equal in legal rights with the settler, but he is not really equal in the power of enjoying or enforcing those rights'. Despite this insight, Merivale fails to address the question of what are the conditions needed to make equality under the law a social reality and not a legal fiction. Instead, he uses the 'uncivilised' condition of aboriginal peoples to advance the case for a special protected but unequal status under the law, claiming that 'a state of fictitious equality is far worse than one of acknowledged inferiority, with its correlative protection'.[44] Merivale's advocacy of what he terms 'amalgamation', including his rejection of colour prejudice, and his defence of the capacity of all peoples to assimilate to western norms, is quite consistent with a vision of institutionalised inequality under the law. He considers that 'they [the natives] can only meet with the whites in the same field of hopeful industry on the footing of inferiors, and that, if such subordinate position is not recognized by law, and compensated by legal protection, it will be enforced, at a heavy disadvantage to them, by the prevailing sentiment of the conquering race'.[45] This protected status would persist until such time as missionaries and other educators had provided the requisite training in the ideas, conventions and habits of Christian and western culture.

In his 1861 revisions, he omitted Australia altogether and observed that frontier conditions, involving hostilities and even warfare with indigenous peoples, only existed in South Africa, New Zealand and the Pacific Northwest. Furthermore, the development of self-government in colonies of white settlement effectively removed the status of indigenes from the imperial jurisdiction, and he had little confidence in the capacity of colonial legislatures to deal with native rights. Like other colonial office administrators, he thought that the imperial government played a useful if increasingly obsolete role of intermediary between conflicting settler and aboriginal interests.[46] In this context, Merivale's promise of amalgamation, even his idea of protected if unequal status under the law, offered little defence against the relentless advance of what he termed the 'conquering race' of white colonisers.

The issue of the history and status of aboriginal peoples, including the case for amalgamation advanced by Merivale, were taken up and reviewed by James Ward in his Le Bas Prize essay of 1873. Like Merivale before him, and as Benjamin Kidd and others would continue to argue for the remainder of the century, Ward claimed that Europeans, with their superior social and economic organisation and advanced technology, had a right to settle and bring into productive use those lands not effectively occupied by aboriginal peoples. Though he addressed the status of aboriginal people in general, making occasional references to New Zealand and southern Africa, his principal interest was in the colonisation of the Americas. Still attached to the romantic idea of North American Natives as noble savages living in a state of natural freedom, Ward defended the policy of setting aside reserved lands for aboriginal populations.[47] Ward's essay was not particularly influential, for specific policies evolved directly out of administrative experience largely under the jurisdiction of the self-governing colonies. Apart from the continuing activities of agencies such as the APS, Ward's essay reflected the state of informed opinion in the 1870s and 1880s. The idea of a transition to civilised or modern conditions managed in stages, with separation on reserves as a temporary means to facilitate assimilation, created a powerful rationale for special and unequal status under the law.

Nonetheless, established humanitarian agencies, such as the APS, persisted in their call for equality before the law regardless of race or colour. They did so despite the informed analysis of the colonial situation by experienced administrators such as Merivale. More significantly, the humanitarian agencies persisted in their message despite their loss of political credibility. For a generation which witnessed the global dimensions of racial conflict – the Indian Mutiny in 1857, the wars in New Zealand between settlers and Maoris in the 1860s, the ending of slavery by civil war in the United States, and the controversy surrounding the Jamaica Insurrection and its bloody suppression by Governor Eyre – abolitionist and humanitarian assertions of the universal value of individual liberty protected by equality before the law seemed naively and even dangerously detached from the political realities of colonial life. In 1873, in its thirty-sixth annual report, the APS warns that the slave-holding mentality is still alive but has now transformed into institutions that 'continue to be animated by the same principle of oppression'. At home in the United Kingdom, 'A legal code, slowly built up and often reformed, secures to the English people generally equality before the law, and to every individual what is known as "liberty of the subject".' In contrast, in the colonies, for individuals freed from the restraints of law, 'the temptation to oppress the weaker race becomes irresistible'. Consequently, to maintain national self-respect and to fulfil the responsibilities of empire, Great Britain cannot 'permit her own subjects to treat human beings as property, or to establish institutions which degrade or oppress men of a different race'.[48] In its annual report for 1876, the APS defended its role as watchdog over colonial abuses, and claimed that its policies offered the best way to secure the well-being of both colonists and indigenous peoples. This goal could only be achieved 'by placing the weaker party under the effectual protection of the law, by scrupulously respecting their personal liberty, and by endeavouring so to bring them under the influence of education and Christianity as to qualify them for the exercise of the various rights and duties of citizenship'.[49] The APS's monthly journal, the *Colonial Intelligencer and Aborigines' Friend*, claims it 'is no enemy to colonists', but warns that 'the worst enemies' of the colonists 'are those of their own household, who endeavour to aggravate the differences of race, and whose vicious theories as to the natural subordination or inferiority of people of colour have borne fruit in many evil deeds'.[50] In its publications, the APS seldom mentioned theories of racial inequality, offered virtually no commentary on the literature of travel and exploration, and simply ignored both the physical anthropologists' racial typologies, and the cultural anthropologists' evolutionary schemes for human development.

The focus of the APS was on the immediate political question of how to address reported abuses inflicted upon colonised peoples. For the APS, this challenge was not so much a question of race as a question of culture. On the one hand, there was the culture of the settlers and the colonisers committed to the defence and advancement of white control and privilege. The remedy here was the controlling hand of imperial authority in London kept mindful of its humanitarian responsibilities by the vigilance of the APS. On the other hand, there was the culture of indigenous and colonised peoples of colour. For the APS and its supporters, the exercise of legal entitlements and liberties presumed that individuals lived under 'civilised' conditions. The 'uncivilised' or 'weaker races' that the APS considered its duty to protect had only one historical destiny – assimilation to the norms of western culture. The most difficult challenge, and the one the APS never successfully resolved, was how to manage this transition to 'civilised' or modern conditions.

In an early and rare use of the term in 1876, the APS condemned the policy of 'segregation' developed by Sir Theophilus Shepstone in Natal. In criticising these practices, the *Colonial Intelligencer* reported that Africans had their livestock confiscated, and migrant labourers from outside the colony faced six months compulsory labour on railway construction. In contrast, following the recommendations of Bishop Colenso, its principal correspondent on South Africa, the APS had urged Lord Carnarvon, the colonial secretary, to adopt a policy of 'gradually modifying the tribal system'. According to the APS, the colonial office should codify native law and subject it to interpretation not by the colonial government, but by the courts, maintain a separation between military and civilian administration, put in place extensive facilities for education in native districts, discourage brutal punishments, and enable individuals to buy land and acquire 'the status of citizens'.[51] In this fashion, under the direction of F. W. Chesson, its executive secretary from 1866 to 1888, the APS adopted a policy of assimilation. It offered a limited toleration to indigenous cultures in the short term, and expected within two or three generations a transition to civilised conditions defined by Victorian middle-class respectability.[52]

The instrument for this assimilation was education. In a paper on 'The Education of Native Races in the British Colonies', presented before the Liverpool Social Science Congress in 1876, Chesson drew a parallel between the recent introduction of state education in England in 1870 and the need for schools for the colonised children of the empire. In his view, primary education in England was an instrument for the civilisation of the children of residuum. Chesson advocated that the colonial state replace the missionary societies as the provider of schools for native children. The schools could be legitimately funded from the taxes on parents. This schooling would provide instruction in the English language and would focus especially on industrial training to prepare students for a productive life as labourers in a modern economy. Laden with frequent asides describing the barbarous nature of various indigenous cultures from Australia to West Africa, Chesson emphasised in his conclusion: 'one of our chief objects should be to secure control over the children at the most impressionable age, and to retain that control long enough to make a relapse into barbarism difficult, if not impossible'.[53]

Upon the achievement of respectable standing, signified by the ownership of private property and conformity to western Christian standards of family life, aboriginal peoples and persons of colour more generally would attain equal standing in the law, including an entitlement to the vote. In his view of reports from mission schools as far afield as Australia, the South Pacific, Canada and southern Africa, Chesson reported that children of colour responded well to instruction, and that these students and their parents wanted such schooling to be made more available. The problem was not the ability of the children but that the demand for schooling exceeded the resources of the missionary societies. In addition, Chesson argued that the schools needed a secular, practical curriculum beyond the scope of a missionary education. Consistent with its principled opposition to race prejudice, the APS, in 1876, protested against the exclusion of non-white children from the government school in Durban.[54]

While the APS persisted in its call for equality before the law, its construction of 'uncivilised' and 'civilised' categories imposed significant restrictions upon its advocacy for colonised peoples. Having at best a limited toleration for customs that varied from a westernised norm, the APS, not unlike human rights advocates in more recent times, faced difficult ethical and political choices. While prepared to recognise a limited autonomy for aboriginal peoples and their leaders, colonial administration involved codifying traditional practices into law, and disputes would be subject to interpretation by jurists schooled in English legal conventions. In Natal, a controversy arose out of the treatment of Christian Zulu women. Upon the death of their husbands, these widows returned to their families to be placed into arranged marriages, possibly with non-Christian husbands. To the APS and to Florence Nightingale, who corresponded on the subject, these forced marriages were a form of slavery sanctioned by British colonial authorities and imposed upon these widows and their children.[55]

On the civilised side of the equation, the APS proudly reminded its supporters of its past role in securing the coloured franchise at the Cape in 1853. In 1877, the APS sponsored a memorial to Lord Carnarvon on 'Native Rights in South Africa'. The signatories to the memorial included thirty-eight MPs, twelve members of the legal profession ranging from a judge of the high court to a justice of the peace, other notables among the clergy and, from science, no less a figure than Charles Darwin. The list of MPs included regular supporters of the APS such as Charles Dilke, Thomas Bazley, W. McArthur, Leonard Courtney and T. B. Potter, but also a future colonial secretary, Joseph Chamberlain. The memorialists claimed that they had 'no desire to see masses of uncivilised men invested with political rights', but affirmed that 'native Africans who [had] acquired both education and property should not be excluded from the elective franchise'. The APS and their supporters tried to reassure their critics that qualified Africans were a minority among their uncivilised brethren, and that there was no danger of swamping the votes of the white minority. With this significant limitation on eligibility for full political rights, the APS and their supporters nonetheless envisaged a future South Africa in which 'the organic law of the State should embody the principle of an equality of rights without regard to colour or race'.[56]

In its assimilating creed of equality before the law, the APS expressed a limited tolerance, even at times an outright contempt, for non-western cultures, and its recommendations of how equality of rights and liberties might be implemented in practice were full of Victorian liberal compromises. Nonetheless, the APS kept the older vision of a colour-blind empire alive, and consequently, any deviation from the metropolitan norms regarding status before the law and the rights of citizens still needed to be explained and justified as consistent with the imperial mission of serving the interests of both the colonisers and the colonised. By the 1880s, the survival of a vision of a colour-blind empire faced greater challenges under the new imperialism. The focus of attention had shifted to Africa and other tropical dependencies. In so far as commentators drew on relevant historical experience, they relied not so much on the record of 'native' policy in the self-governing colonies of white settlement, nor upon the post-abolition experience of the West Indies, as upon the jurisprudence and administrative practice in India and on the experiment in post-emancipation reconstruction in the United States.

In 1879, Sir George Campbell (1824–92), a former Indian administrator with a reputation as an energetic and independent innovator, a Liberal MP for Kirkaldy, and a supporter of the BFASS and the APS, drew on his Indian experience and his recent visit to the southern United States to offer advice on what he termed 'the management of coloured races'. Ready to admit that British rule in India was 'avowedly absolute and despotic', Campbell claimed that the Raj was blameless of 'any habitual subordination of the rights and interests of the coloured races to those of the whites'. He was nonetheless critical of white oligarchies in crown colonies and protectorates for their treatment of coloured labourers, either ex-slaves of African descent or migrant and indentured labour from Asia.[57] Looking to the United States as an alternative experiment in post-emancipation political and social relations, Campbell was unusual among British travellers in that he not only reported the views of white Southerners but also sought out the opinions of black politicians, clergymen and other leaders of the African-American community. While with some minor reservations he accepted the white South's view of Reconstruction as a record of the incompetence and corruption of black politicians and Northern carpetbaggers, he also observed that the reassertion of white political dominance and the dispossession of blacks of their legal and political rights were equally a story of illegality, fraud and intimidation.[58]

Contrary to those American and British observers who remained nostalgic for the slavery, Campbell was impressed by the abilities and progress of African-Americans since emancipation. He thought they were better off than the poor of India – admittedly not the highest standard of comparison – and observed that landowning blacks displayed the virtues of hard labour, and 'thrift, carefulness, and family affection'. He thought that they, as an independent peasantry, had the potential to become 'a comfortable, well-to-do population' which he claimed 'may compare very favourably not only with the Indian ryot, the Russian serf, or the Irish tenant-farmer, but also with the Dorsetshire labourer'.[59] He was also impressed by the fact that a people from a variety of African cultures had developed into a common African-American, English-speaking culture, adhering to Christianity, desirous of education and capable of further advance. In fact, on the question of education and intelligence, Campbell thought that 'the intellectual gulf between the two races [did] not seem to be very wide and evident'.[60]

Despite these signs of improvement, the evidence of the ex-slaves' cultural assimilation, and the admitted inter-dependence of the white and black communities, Campbell observed a growing separation between the races in the South. In what he termed 'The Caste Question', he saw this separation was primarily due to white prejudice, but he also noted, partly in response, that blacks also preferred to have their own schools and churches. Writing prior to the implementation of 'Jim Crow' segregation, he observed little in the way of 'incivility', and identifying himself as a British Radical, expressed surprise at the equality between whites and blacks on tram cars. Noting that 'like separate Hindu castes, they [did] not intermarry, or worship or eat together', he reported the horror of all sectors of white opinion about miscegenation.[61] Such views, in his opinion, were contrary to Christian teaching and to the founding principles of the republic, but nonetheless, he saw that separation was not necessarily an obstacle to continued progress within the African-American community.

As a Victorian liberal, the Scottish MP looked to the emergence of a black middle class as the engine of progress. While claiming to understand their sense of grievance, he also thought that such professionals over-reacted to racial discrimination, displaying a degree of resentment that even a sympathetic liberal such as Campbell thought too assertive. Through the development of an African-American middle class, fostered through serving the needs of its own community, rather than confronting the racial exclusiveness of the whites, Campbell predicted a positive future for African-Americans.[62] The progress evident in the African-American community had, in Campbell's mind, lessons for British colonial rule in Africa. While still trusting in administrative authority as in India, he thought that the goal in Africa, unlike in Inda, should be a more thorough assimilation where colonial law and administration should not try to accommodate indigenous customs.[63]

In his survey, *The British Empire*, published in 1887, Campbell returned to his theme of the management of the coloured races, and once again his Indian experience and his American travels shaped his views. Frankly admitting that the British ruled India as a 'paternal despotism', Campbell again claimed that the Raj was free of corruption and nepotism. Even though appointments to the civil service were made in London not India, the process, he claimed, was free of considerations of colour or race. Those few Indians who travelled to Britain to write the examinations were, in his words, 'Europeanised' in culture.[64] While he expressed his dismay over the Ilbert Bill (1883) which to his mind set a precedent giving Europeans a privileged status under the law, he still maintained that the Raj protected the interests of Indians. Ruling independently of considerations of race or colour, and allowing for freedom of expression, including, in his view, an excessively critical press, British authority depended on the respect and even awe of the Indian population. While he claimed that his colleagues in India were uncertain if the ultimate aim of British policy was Indian self-government, he favoured greater Indian involvement in local self-government to strengthen consent for British rule.[65]

Administrative rule in India avoided, so Campbell thought, the forms of unjust or unequal treatment which were so prevalent elsewhere in the empire, including the self-governing colonies of white settlement, and the crown colonies and protectorates. In the latter jurisdictions, colonial administrators, in collusion with tiny white oligarchies, implemented policies in regard to land, immigration, labour and taxation which favoured the narrow class interests of whites. Assessing the issue of Chinese and Indian immigration and the traffic in South Sea Islanders in Queensland, he thought that either such immigrants should be barred altogether or they should be accorded equal treatment under the law. After serving an indenture, they should have rights of permanent domicile and the status of free and equal citizens. He specifically demanded that Indian immigrants not be 'treated as an inferior or servile race'.[66] The political status of the crown colonies, he recognised, was largely determined by the fear of representative government where a coloured majority might rule over a white minority:

> The coloured majority not being deemed fitted for free institutions, or, at any rate, not fitted for a power which might make them dominant over the whites, the power of the Crown has been introduced in various forms, and more or less completely.[67]

In this context, he once again preferred the Indian solution recommending nominated rather than elected councils to act as advisory board to colonial governors.[68]

Just as Campbell defended the record of British administration in India, so he advocated the British government serve as the protector of the interests of 'coloured' populations against white class interests. He thought that the southern United States had made a better adjustment to emancipation than had the British West Indies, but nowhere in America did blacks constitute a majority. The prospect of black and brown majorities in crown colonies and in Africa necessitated other options. He remained attached to a policy of assimilation in Africa, and was most critical of white minorities manipulating the law and electoral qualifications to secure control. He criticised the legislative inventions of Natal, which after 1883 used a language test, not required of Europeans, to exclude all but a few of an Indian minority equal to the whites in number, and even more completely denying representation from the African majority. To his mind, it would be better to limit the vote to whites, then at least the need for the colonial office as mediator between whites and the brown and black majority would be more evident.[69]

By 1887, Campbell's administrative solutions through mediation by the imperial government exemplified an increasingly outmoded mid-Victorian liberalism. He claimed there were two options of 'real self-government or a paternal government', and there was no half-way station between the two. Given his knowledge of the American experiment with multi-racial democracy, the history of white oligarchies in crown colonies, and the recent policies on immigration and indentured labour of the dominions, he was sceptical of self-government in the hands of whites:

> Where there are large native or coloured populations, I wholly distrust self-government in the hands of planters, and much misdoubt government by modern speculative and commercial Joint Stock companies, the memory of the East India Company notwithstanding. I think that in all these cases, either you must really and truly give the coloured people a large share of representation in any elective system, or if that cannot be, you must come to paternal government after all.[70]

Blind to the political problems of the Raj, Campbell's chosen preference for a 'paternal' solution had as much political credibility as his concluding recommendations of his survey of the British Empire. Writing in 1887, after the debacle with Gordon in Khartoum and after the discovery of gold on the Rand, he advised against further financial and military commitments in Egypt and the Sudan, and suggested that Britain not expand its political obligations in southern Africa. In the House of Commons, Campbell had the unenviable reputation as one of the MPs most likely to be shouted down by his colleagues. His speeches on behalf of humanitarian agencies such as the APS, and his defence of Indian interests under the despotic rule of the Raj, met with little respect from younger politicians whose enthusiasm for a new 'realism' in the conduct of colonial policy recast the discourse on 'race' and 'race relations' under the new imperialism.[71]

From the colour question to race relations

From the 1890s to 1914, a number of administrators, journalists and commentators reassessed what came to be known as the 'Native Question', or the 'Colour Question'. Relations between the metropolitan industrialised world and the periphery were entering into a new stage necessitating a reassessment of social and political relationships. Neither Merivale's vision of amalgamation nor Campbell's faith in paternal administration seemed adequate in this new context. Elements of this perceived crisis, particularly the sources of racial conflict and the issue of colour prejudice as evidenced by developments in the self-governing dominions, India, South Africa and the United States, stimulated extensive commentary in books, periodicals and newspapers, and gave rise to a new and modern language of race relations.

Old-style colonisation, as had been addressed by Merivale, in the view of commentators such as Benjamin Kidd and James Bryce, had come to an end with white settlers' occupation and control of the temperate zones of the world. Under the new imperialism, European powers and the United States had extended their control in the tropics, and there they faced fundamentally new conditions. As a commonplace observation most clearly advanced by Kidd, the development of the tropics was essential for continued global economic growth, but these areas were occupied by non-European populations acclimatised to an environment unsuited, it was assumed, to white settlement. In this view, the resources of the tropics could only be developed with the use of coloured labour.[72] A past record of slavery and other forms of coerced labour in the tropics, and a troubled present of atrocities in the Congo, of abuses against African workers as well as Indian indentured labourers in South Africa, and of lynchings in the United States, to name only the most sensational examples catching the attention of the press, prompted at best a critique of such exploitation and at worst an explanation for and justification of such conduct.

The occupation of lands and the efforts to mobilise indigenous and migrant labour on mines, plantations, farms and large-scale projects such as railway construction raised profound political questions about the status of indigenous and migrant populations under the law, and their role within the new polity of colonial regimes. For example, the existing language of 'civilised' and 'uncivilised', as used by the APS or the colonial office, described both the characteristics of peoples and the social conditions under which they lived. This cultural distinction, in the analysis of Mahood Mamdani, was more significant than race, and had long-term consequences in South Africa and throughout colonial Africa.[73] 'Uncivilised' conditions included, among other elements, communal ownership of land, retention of an indigenous language, heathen religious and cultural practices in contravention of Christian norms, non-western forms of governance and law usually described as 'tribal' or 'traditional', and non-capitalist forms of production and labour. 'Civilised' conditions included private ownership of property, the adoption of the English language and the Christian religion, including in particular western practices in regard to marriage and family life, and cash income as educated professionals, as independent or tenant farmers, as traders or shopkeepers, or as wage-labourers.[74]

The issue of the status of peoples of non-European origin living under 'uncivilised' conditions, or in non-western societies assigned 'civilised' or 'semi-civilised' status, or under 'civilised' conditions in the United States or self-governing colonies of white settlement, or in some state of transition between these categories, was variously called the 'Native Question', or the 'Colour' or 'Race Problem', or, in the context of the United States, the 'Negro Question'.[75] In *Through Afro-America* (1910), William Archer, a journalist and drama critic who had visited the American South, attempted a more formal definition of the 'race problem'. Presuming a state of inequality between racial groups, Archer observed, 'The race problem means ... the problem of adjustment between two very dissimilar populations, locally intermingled in such proportions that the one feels its racial identity potentially threatened, while the other knows itself in constant danger of economic exploitation.'[76] The language of the 'race problem' or 'colour question' could be applied generically to any situation involving contact or conflict between peoples designated as belonging to different races. In most instances, these terms applied to colonial or former colonial societies with ethnically or racially mixed populations, with market economies, and with some form of democratic or more limited representative government. Prior to the First World War these novel creations of the modern period of history, with its readier means of communication and transport for the voluntary or forced migration of peoples, had few historical precedents for guiding policy-makers. Although not by any means a comprehensive list even in 1914 (notable omissions were Brazil and South America more generally), the United States, the West Indies, South Africa, India, and the self-governing dominions with white majorities (Canada, Australia and New Zealand) dominated British discourse on the subject.

Commentators anticipated that these historical examples set a trend that would become more common in the course of the new twentieth century. The distinguishing feature of these new societies was that whites, whether a majority or a minority, were in a dominant, privileged position, and peoples of colour, whether a majority or a minority, were in a subordinate, disadvantaged position. Inequalities based on race were institutionalised in law, politics and the customary practices of everyday life. This institutionalised inequality fostered a climate of antagonism and even violence. Nonetheless, the future anticipated by analysts of this new order projected changes in the culture of non-European populations, but entertained no fundamental alteration to the privileged political and social status of dominant whites. The racial discourse developed, not exclusively but for the most part, as a way to understand the dynamics of these societies, and as an effort to manage racial inequalities so as to avoid violence and instability.

Consequently, the development of a new language of what eventually would be termed 'race relations' became a potent instrument in support of racial inequality.

By the beginning of the twentieth century, the scale and pace if not the form of these transformations seemed unprecedented, and these changes took place, at least in the British case, within a political context which was equally without precedent. A viable colonial order resting on institutionalised racial inequality required legitimacy both in the perspective of the metropolitan culture and, if possible, in the respect for the law and its agents among the subject colonised peoples. This legitimacy had to be reconstructed under the newly embraced framework of 'democracy', but the forces of democracy worked in contrary directions. From the standpoint of the norms of metropolitan society, subjects of the crown, unless exceptional circumstances existed, had, it was claimed, equal status and due process under the law. In light of the broadening of the franchise in the United Kingdom, by the end of the nineteenth century there also existed an expectation of some degree of elected representation in government. Once again, exceptions were recognised, but the contentious question was whether differences of class, gender or race constituted legitimate grounds for making an exception to equal status under the law or the right to vote.

Whites males in the self-governing colonies had the vote, and there elected governments, most notably in Australia with a labour government, were supposedly at the vanguard of democracy. These same democratic states implemented exclusionary immigration policies. In so far as 'non-white' migrant and indentured labourers were admitted at all, as in Queensland or British Columbia, or as necessitated by the imperatives of the South African economy, restrictive legislation proscribed an unequal, inferior status in terms of employment, domicile and other entitlements under the law, and with a few notable exceptions such as the Cape, explicitly or practically excluded persons of colour from the vote.[77] In addition to this evidence of the racial discrimination and exclusion under the law in the self-governing dominions, developments in the United States, principally the implementation of segregation under 'Jim Crow' legislation and the extensively reported incidents of lynching, made the exercise of democracy for whites seem incompatible with just and equal treatment for persons of colour.

On the other hand, in India and in crown colonies in which white oligarchies or administrators ruled Asian or African populations, or descendants of these peoples, the forces of democracy presented a different challenge. Recognising that colonial rule could not depend on force alone but relied on a mix of coercion and consent, colonial administrators faced a new political reality. Regardless of the hierarchy of racial types described by the scientists and of the commonplace affirmation of the natural inequality of races, the living representatives of those types refused to accept their designated condition. Asian and African nationalists demanded equal status under the law, equal opportunities for employment, especially for qualified professionals in government service, greater participation in elected or nominated councils, and ultimately self-government.[78]

These demands were not unrelated to the conduct of the white dominions. Their immigration policies as well as the systemic racism institutionalised in the new Union of South Africa broke the last pretence of a colour-blind empire in which all subjects were equal in the eyes of the monarch and the law. Perceptive colonial administrators recognised that adjustments would have to be made in light of these changing circumstances and of the demands of politically engaged brown and black activists for legal equality, the franchise, and self-government for the empire's subject peoples of colour. On the global scale, this new reality, best signified by Japan's defeat of Russia in 1905, meant that the new twentieth century would have to address the question of colour and invent new ways to deal with the contrasting challenges of the exclusionary and discriminating practices of white democracies, and the democratic demands of Asian and African nationalists.

In the light of this new context, the language of 'race' displayed an inventiveness and a flexibility quite in contrast to the efforts of science to fix the characteristics of racial types. The term 'race' itself retained its malleable character. It was never restricted to visible physical and biologically determined traits, and incorporated cultural attributes belonging to nations and ethnicities in Europe whose derivation linguists and historians established in the remote past and whose essence persisted as mysterious traits of personality in the present. For example, the *Spectator* in 1890 considered the tortuous efforts to find a political balance between Czechs and Germans in the new Bohemian constitution. Describing relations between the two groups as an instance of 'race-hatred', the weekly observed that divisions, beyond their separate languages, were not that apparent, but nonetheless ran deep, being made up of 'the indefinable aggregate of inherent differences which we call "race"'.[79] The Bohemian conflict was only one instance of such conflicts, as the *Spectator* identified differences of 'race' at the root of the national animosities so prevalent in European politics in 1890.

The ambiguity and political consequences of this ill-defined essence of 'race', more potent as a psychological force than as a distinctive physical trait, led some observers to reconsider its presumed significance. Out of the crisis over Home Rule for Ireland, several commentators criticised what they termed the 'race theory' which identified distinct Teutonic and Celtic traits within the English and Irish populations. Among both supporters and opponents of Home Rule, some challenged the equation between 'races' and 'nationalities' in general and took specific exception to the derogatory description of Irish Celts as wanting either the capacity for self-government or the qualities of other ethnicities making up the United Kingdom.[80]

In addition to this criticism of 'race theory' as it applied to European nations, a few commentators challenged the presumption of European racial superiority that accompanied the exercise of imperial authority in Asia and Africa. Catherine Impey, editor of the *Anti-Caste* and founder of the Society of the Brotherhood of Man, rejected all forms of discrimination based upon differences of skin colour or gender or nationality. In 1892, the *Anti-Caste* affirmed: 'It is an error fraught with gravest results to humanity to suppose that colour is any evidence whatever of inferiority.' Familiar with examples outside of the British Empire and the United States, Impey observed, 'Where equal opportunity has been afforded, as it has in Brazil and some other countries, the evidences of natural inferiority are *not to be found*', and concluded, 'what is lacked by the so-called "inferior races" is not natural capacity, but opportunity of developing and exercising it'.[81] Writing in 1905 in the aftermath of the South African War, John Godard equated imperialism with the doctrine of racial supremacy, and argued that both were destructive of democracy in Britain and antithetical to its cultivation in the colonies. Jean Finot, a French journalist and editor of *Revues des Revues*, similarly rejected discrimination rooted in racial prejudice and claimed that doctrines of racial supremacy had no scientific foundation. His works, *Race Prejudice* (1906) and *The Death-Agony of the 'Science' of Race* (1911), were made available to English readers through the assistance of his friend W. T. Stead. Gustav Spiller, a German immigrant, a member of the Ethical Society and organiser of the Universal Races Congress of 1911, also refuted scientific racist theories. In his studies of race relations in the United States and South Africa, Sydney Olivier saw that the emergence of racial segregation was based on ideas of racial superiority and what he termed the 'race-barrier' theory or the 'colour-line and race-differentiation theory'.[82]

The ill-defined meaning assigned to 'race' was the key to its political utility. The most mysterious and most telling essence of 'race' which British commentators, especially imperial advocates, assigned to themselves were those masculine attributes of energy, innovation and purposefulness associated with the gentry and upper middle class, and required both of political leaders and of colonial administrators. These were the qualities Sir George Campbell found most wanting among the peoples of India and among African-Americans. They were the distinguishing marks of what Lord Rosebery called an 'imperial race', which he hoped to find among the young male students at Glasgow and other British universities.[83]

Late Victorian and Edwardian observers retained much of the existing language to describe the presumed inequality of races, but added their own innovations which were less in keeping with the typologies of the anthropologists and more in line with the description of colonial political, economic and social relations. The older language of 'savage and civilised' or 'uncivilised and civilised' or 'lower and higher' or 'inferior and superior' persisted. In addition, Benjamin Kidd, in his *Social Evolution* (1894), introduced the language of 'less developed races' and of 'unprogressive and progressive races'.[84] Kidd's new categories rest upon his construction of the exceptionalism of the history of western civilisation, and its greater 'social efficiency'. He questions what 'constitutes superiority and inferiority of race', and, as a critic of anthropology and of biological determinism, argues for a new set of criteria for comparing differences of race:

> We shall probably have to set aside many of our old ideas on the subject. Neither in respect alone of colour, nor of descent, nor even of the possession of high intellectual capacity, can science give us any warrant for speaking of one race as superior to another ... It is only the race possessing in the highest degree the qualities contributing to social efficiency that can be recognised as having any claim to superiority.[85]

On the basis of the greater social efficiency of developed, western societies, Kidd argued that imperial control of the tropics were both necessary for the modern global economy and justifiable as a trust in which Europeans acted as the guardians of social evolution for the rest of humanity. Just as Kidd shifted the discourse on global inequality from considerations of the racial types to the comparative study of economic and social development, other observers moved from the characteristics of 'races' to the psychology of race relations.

In his Romanes Lectures for 1902, James Bryce entitled his study as *The Relations of the Advanced and the Backward Races of Mankind*. With the eye of a constitutional expert, and familiar with India, the United States and South Africa, Bryce was convinced that the increased contact between racial groups in recent years represented a 'crisis in the history of the world' as momentous as the new age initiated by Columbus. In his prescription for sound policies by which to manage racial subordination and conflict, his originality lay in the attention he paid to the social and psychological animosities which characterised relations between his 'advanced and backward races'.[86]

Bryce's language was taken up by Leonard Alston in 1907. In *The White Man's Work in Asia and Africa*, Alston argued that two distinct and unequal races could not live together on terms of equality, but in a modern world economy non-whites would become 'proletarian races'. In this role, they needed the paternal protection of an imperial authority against the self-interested politics of white capitalists and settlers. On the other hand, G. K. Chesterton, addressing a conference on Nationalities and Subject Races in London in 1910, asked with a fair measure of sarcasm how one distinguished between the advanced and the backward races. For his part, he confessed, he preferred the latter group, for 'what we call the backward peoples of the world are the peoples who are keeping the secrets of humanity'.[87] The innovations and the flexibility of the language of race reflected, as Bryce recognised, important changes in political and social relationships. As will be explored in Chapter 6, Bryce and others developed a new vocabulary to describe what would come to be known as 'race relations'. The new language was also an intervention providing new legitimacy for forms of racial separation and subordination. Its exponents articulated a more sophisticated, and to the twenty-first century, a more familiar defence of racial inequality.

The language of race relations arising from the need to codify the practice of racial exclusion and discrimination in the law had a more direct and measurable impact than the professional scientists' efforts to establish a racial typology. In the human world of political power and social conflict, in contrast to the natural world of the scientists, there were only two races: whites and non-whites. The self-governing colonies and their member states and provinces – namely Australia, Canada, New Zealand and South Africa – led the way in defining the world's peoples in this stark manner, and in doing so created an embarrassment for the British government.[88] The foreign, colonial and India offices had to contend with the warnings of the government of India, sensitive to nationalist criticism of its failure to protect Indians overseas. Similarly, they received protests from the governments of China and Japan anxious to defend their status in the community of nations. In addition, from India and South Africa, as well as from sympathetic voices elsewhere, the protests of Asian and African nationalists exposed the hypocrisy of an empire pretending to provide just and equal treatment under the law.

To be effective, the law had to provide precise, workable definitions, and consequently colonial law-makers and the colonial office wrestled with the difficult task of giving racial categories legal standing. In 1896, an Inter-Colonial Conference in Australia considered the definition of the 'coloured races' under New South Wales legislation:

all persons belonging to any coloured race inhabiting the Continent of Asia or the Continent of Africa, or any island adjacent thereto, or any island in the Pacific Ocean or the Indian Ocean, not being persons duly accredited on any special mission to Her Majesty by the Government or rule of any country, state, or territory, or to this Colony under the authority of the Imperial Government.[89]

This Australian effort at a definition suitable for an exclusionary immigration policy grew out of fifty years of innovation in designating the Chinese, South Sea Islanders and, more recently, Indians and Japanese, as undesirable races to be excluded, or to be subject to discriminatory legislation in regard to conditions of residence, trade or labour. This provision conformed to the recommendations of the colonial office that such exclusions apply to immigrant labourers but not to ministers of religion, missionaries, teachers, tourists, merchants, scientists and students. Nonetheless, the act did apply to all labourers designated as 'coloured', including those who were British subjects, and consequently failed to pass the scrutiny of the colonial office.[90]

In the light of its need to maintain good relations with the governments of China and Japan, and of the political necessity to avoid, if possible, further alienation of subjects of the crown in India and elsewhere, the colonial office favoured language which gave less direct offence. At the Colonial Conference of 1897, Joseph Chamberlain supported the desire to exclude non-whites, but pressed colonial premiers to follow the lead of Natal, which had developed a literacy test in a European language to be administered at the discretion of local officials. The test, along with its discretionary and even arbitrary administration, achieved the goal of exclusion and yet avoided the offending language of race. Australia and New Zealand adopted the 'Natal formula', and Canada devised its own similar strategy by demanding that immigrants travel directly from their homeland to a Canadian port. Since such trans-Pacific transport was not readily available, the policy provided a significant barrier to Asian immigrants.[91]

In South Africa, language analogous to the Natal formula was adopted for determining the political status of residents of colour. Ever inventive, the legislators of Natal bowed reluctantly to colonial office preferences, and found criteria that were not of race but of political tradition to exclude Indians and Africans from the franchise. The excluded persons included those 'who (not being of European origin) [were] natives or descendants in the male line of natives of countries which [had] not hitherto possessed elective representative institutions founded on the Parliamentary franchise'.[92] Nonetheless, the legislators of Natal preferred more direct language, and when applying the parliamentary exclusions of 1896 to local elections in the Municipal

Corporations Act of 1905, simply designated Africans and Indians under the definition of 'uncivilised races'. Such a blatant statement of racial inferiority within the law antagonised opinion in India and failed to meet the colonial office requirement that discriminatory laws avoid the language of race or colour.[93]

Having a special responsibility for relations with the Dominions, including the writing of memoranda on the troubled history of immigration and other restrictive legislation, Sir Charles Lucas, for the benefit of his colonial office colleagues, devised in 1907 a working definition of the 'native'. According to Lucas, the term 'native' described 'the coloured man in his own home, either having lived there from all time or having immigrated, forcibly or otherwise, so as to have in past times formed or now to form the bulk of or a dominant element in the population'.[94] By making 'native' and 'coloured' equivalent, the negative attributes of 'native' were strengthened, and ironically its one positive attribute was weakened. The 'native' lost the attachment to a particular place with the entitlements inherent in the status of aboriginal settlement. Now the 'native' had become simply a member of the coloured races subject to the legislative proclamations and administrative discretion of white politicians and officials.

Even the efforts of the colonial office to act as a protector of the interests of native or coloured races further entrenched this sense of two all-encompassing categories of Europeans and the others. In 1905, after the protests of dominion governments, the colonial office withdrew a confidential circular defining the kinds of legislation which might be reserved due to offending language having wider imperial implications. Consequently, this power of reservation applied only in Natal, the Transvaal and the Orange River Colony to 'Any Bill whereby persons not of European birth or descent may be subjected or made liable to any disabilities or restrictions to which persons of European birth or descent [were] not also subjected or made liable'.[95] In practice, governors of other self-governing colonies were not obliged to reserve such legislation, but they could do so at their discretion. Lord Elgin, as colonial secretary, continued to correspond with governors on the question of withholding approval of such legislation.

The political dance to find an acceptable language for implementing the exclusionary and discriminating policies of the self-governing dominions thinly disguised the obvious political clout of white racism. The ambiguity of the language of 'native' and 'coloured' was no insignificant quibble. It had direct implications for the exercise of the franchise under the new South African Union. In 1906, the APS and Sir Charles Dilke corresponded with the colonial office on behalf of Dr Abdurahman, president of the African Political Organisation (Coloured

People) Association, and forwarded the Association's petition regarding the franchise. The issue was over the provision of clause 8 of the Treaty of Vereeniging stating that the question of self-government would be resolved prior to the question of the 'native franchise'. Two matters were in contention. First, would those Africans, coloureds and Indians who already had the vote, as in Cape Province and elsewhere, have a vote for the new Union parliament? Second, did the word 'native' in the treaty apply to Indians and coloureds, or simply to those whom Botha and Kitchener had crudely referred to as 'Kafirs', or as an official at the colonial office more discreetly referred to as 'aboriginal Africans'? Officials at the colonial office disagreed among themselves about the meaning of 'coloureds' and 'natives'. They were certain that, in the Afrikaans version of the treaty, the Boers intended to include all non-whites in the term 'native', and they also recognised that for white South Africans, regardless of ethnic origin, the terms 'native' and 'coloured' (meaning non-white) were synonymous.[96]

The political imperatives shaping the legalese of legislation and colonial office memoranda also transformed the common language of commentary, particularly in the perplexing context of South Africa. These new terms described the reality of a new and more intense racial consciousness. The language of 'coloured races' itself and its equation with the older usage of 'native' presumed its binary opposite. The converse of 'coloured' was not 'non-coloured', but the more evocative 'white' with its associations of cleanliness, purity and virtue. Whites in contrast to 'natives' were also 'civilised', as against the 'uncivilised' or 'semi-civilised' labels attached to 'coloureds'. Occasionally, commentators recognised the imprecision and even inaccuracy of these labels, but nonetheless conformed to common usage. Dr Ferguson-Davie, the Bishop of Singapore, offering pastoral advice against inter-marriage between Europeans and 'natives', advised his readers: 'I use the term *natives* in inverted commas as the easiest means of designating the inhabitants of various countries outside of Europe in which Europeans settle temporarily. I have no intention of implying any inferiority in the use of the term.'[97] Similarly, Latimer Fuller, attempting to explain the practice of segregation in the Church of England in South Africa, commented: 'The expressions 'black and white', 'native and European' are employed, not because we Westerners are either white or necessarily European, nor because the Bantu are either black or especially native, but because they are the common expressions and convey to ordinary people the intended sense.'[98] Despite these reservations, both the common usage and the intent to justify these distinctions meant that this vocabulary not only persisted but proliferated.

Another and increasingly common innovation was the contrast

drawn between 'non-European' and 'European' peoples. In the mid-nineteenth century, philologists coined the term 'non-European' as a means to classify languages into a 'European' and catch-all 'other' category. By the end of the nineteenth century, 'non-European' became not simply a linguistic term but a racial designation for all peoples not of European descent.[99] In keeping with his division of the world between the developed West and the less developed periphery, between the temperate zones and the tropics, and between the progressive and unprogressive races, Benjamin Kidd in his *Social Evolution* (1894) found the term 'non-European' a convenient and comprehensive designation for his global comparison. 'The contrast already to be distinguished between the advancing and the unprogressive races of European race is more noticeable', he observed, 'when the former are compared with non-European peoples'.[100] Even the advocates of anthropology adopted the new universal designation. In 1914, Sir Richard Temple, as reported in *Man*, the Royal Anthropological Institute's popular journal, promoted the practical application of the science of man to 'non-European races' in the colonies.[101]

This terminology also became commonplace in the language of colonial office administrators. In his memorandum on coloured immigration in 1908, Sir Charles Lucas used the phrase 'non-Europeans' to clarify the application of the Natal formula. 'The principle of the Natal Act, which Mr. Chamberlain accepted and recommended, is not to specify any particular race, but to exclude all who cannot write a European language, *i.e.*, not to distinguish in any way among non-Europeans between those who are and those who are not British subjects.'[102] In discussing Transvaal legislation directed against Indian migrants and residents in general, and against Indian traders in particular, Lucas cited Lord Milner's reference to 'the principle of uniformity of legislation with regard to non-European persons which had been approved by the Colonial Conference at Bloemfontein'.[103]

This new short-hand classification of 'non-European' not only facilitated the construction of racial barriers in law and policy but also exposed the contradictions and inconsistencies in institutionalised inequality to those more critical of these developments. Some colonial administrators found troublesome this lumping together of great varieties of peoples into the one 'non-European' designation. In his discussion of 'The Coloured Races', Sir Charles Bruce, a former governor of Guiana and Mauritius, warns against too easy an assumption of European superiority, for 'those who, reasoning on the false analogy of the relations between whites and negroes in America, infer an inherent inferiority of all coloured races and hold that there can be no equality between the races of European and non-European descent'. For those making this assumption, Bruce suggests, 'the example of Japan ought to convince of their error'.[104]

From a perspective more critical of imperialism and concerned with new democratic trends in politics both within states and internationally, Graham Wallas also used and extended the new vocabulary in his comments on the 'growing urgency of the problem of race'.[105] In his exploration of the limits of democracy in *Human Nature in Politics* (1908), Graham Wallas shifted from the traditional focus on political theory to probe questions of political behaviour. Addressing the question of citizens' participation in representative institutions, he noted that the extension of democracy since 1870 had occurred at the same time as improvements in communications had brought races into closer contact, and the expansion of empire had brought diverse peoples under imperial jurisdiction. As a critic of imperialism, Wallas was unwilling to 'draw any intelligible and consistent conclusion from the practice of democratic States in giving or refusing the vote to their non-European subjects'. In addition to 'non-European', Wallas used the less-common phrase 'non-white'. Looking at British colonial experience, he addressed 'the political questions raised both by the migration of non-white races and by the acquisition of tropical dependencies'. He asked whether principle of 'no taxation without representation' should apply to Asiatic populations.[106] Turning to British possessions in Africa, he used the term 'non-European' to describe the diversity of peoples having various forms of political relationships within colonial jurisdictions. He observed that 'the non-European majority of Kaffirs, Negroes, Hindoos, Copts, or Arabs is regulated on entirely different lines in Natal, Basutoland, Egypt, or East Africa'. This diversity was simply a matter of 'historical accident', and created conditions for racial strife, 'either from aggression of the Europeans upon the right reserved by the Home Government to the non-Europeans, or from a revolt of the non-Europeans themselves'. According to Wallas, 'Blacks and whites are equally irritated by the knowledge that there is one law in Nairobi and another in Durban.'[107] While recognising that the inconsistencies and even contradictions evident in law and policy might be a product of accident, he nonetheless thought that empires were built on power not sentiment.

Aware of the emotive power of popular jingoism, Wallas, nonetheless, had little patience with appeals to 'the white man's burden'. In the first half of the nineteenth century, he observed that European colonists in contact with 'non-European races' were in 'their impulses and knowledge alike revolted from the optimistic ethnology of Exeter Hall'. Recognising the beginnings of nationalism among the peoples of Asia and Africa, he also was certain that 'the non-white races within the Empire show[ed] no signs of enthusiastic contentment at the prospect of existing, like the English "poor" of the eighteenth century, as the mere material of other men's virtues'.[108] Foreseeing a global struggle with imperial rivals, where Germany or Russia were Britain's most likely opponents, Wallas sees two contrary tendencies at work. On the one hand, an imperial war is the likely outcome 'If the white inhabitants of the Empire are encouraged to think of themselves as a "dominant race", that is to say as both a homogeneous nation and a natural aristocracy.' On the other hand, 'the non-white inhabitants of the Empire' will be employed in this imperial war, and 'we must discover and drill those races who like the Gurkhas and the Soudanese, may be expected to fight for us and to hate our enemies without asking for political rights'. This imperial conflict, he predicts, will result in the conquest of territories with 'white and yellow and brown and black men hating each other across a wavering line on the map of the world'.[109]

Wallas was unusual in his use of 'non-European' and 'non-white' as equivalents. The more common usage was still the generic 'coloured races' contrasted with 'whites'. Like Wallas, other authors who used the notion of 'non-white' did so in the context of an anticipated rise of Asian and African nationalism. Writing from Beijing in 1910, anxious about Japan's new status and aware of political developments in China and India, B. L. Putnam Weale in his *Conflict of Colour* (1910) points out that whites constituted a minority of the world's population, and that Europe divided by national and imperial rivalries, faces the prospect of the larger numbers and greater solidarity of the peoples of Asia, Africa and the Americas. Consequently, he warns that conditions of the new century are unlike those of the nineteenth, and 'Inevitably must it follow that the world of non-whites will make the position of white races beyond their boundaries more and more precarious.'[110] While anxious about the future of relations between what he termed the 'white' and the 'coloured world', Weale was not a crude racial supremacist. He wished to preserve western ascendency, but like Wallas, he saw the need for a change in European and American presumptions about race, and for a rethinking of international and imperial relationships.

Out of the extensive Edwardian commentaries on the 'race problem' or the 'colour question', the term 'race relations' came to describe the social and political dimensions of 'race' both within multi-racial societies, such as the United States and South Africa, and in its international dimension of relations between states, and especially of transnational, multi-racial entities such as the British and other empires. In *Human Nature and Politics*, when Graham Wallas turned from his analysis of the nation-state to examine 'Nationality and Humanity', he introduced his chapter as a discussion of 'international and inter-racial relations'.[111] Pointing out the inadequacy of the nationalists' presumption of the homogeneous character of the citizenry, as exemplified by Mazzini and Bismarck, he ridiculed 'modern English imperialists' who similarly envisaged the empire like a nation-state with a homogeneous white population. He probed the likely consequences of what he called 'political "Darwinism"' which saw that empires, like species, were in a struggle for survival.[112] Even if an imperial war resulted from such illusions, the victor would 'be compelled to consider the problems of race'. He saw no escape from 'humanitarianism' in considering the ethical and political status of diverse peoples, and what he called 'the practical problem of race relationship'.[113]

The phrase 'inter-racial relations' gained currency from the reports of the Universal Races Congress which met in London in July 1911. In his article in anticipation of the Congress in *Review of Reviews*, W. T. Stead welcomed the Congress for bringing together those few 'who recognise[d] the necessity of applying ethical considerations to inter-racial relations'.[114] The term 'race relations' may have had an American origin. *The Oxford English Dictionary* cites the title of an article in the *Political Science Quarterly* for 1911.[115] The earliest use of the term which I have encountered in British sources is a review of a biography of an African-American ex-slave in the *Anti-Slavery Reporter* in 1896, but subsequently in its articles on the United States and South Africa the abolitionist journal did not use the term.[116] In his conclusion to *White Capital and Coloured Labour*, published by the Independent Labour Party in 1906, Sydney Olivier explains his title and the contents of his pamphlet as 'discursive in regard to race-relations'.[117] In 1910, William Archer, from a less critical perspective on racial inequality and oppression, states that he has undertaken his exploratory travels through 'Afro-America', because 'a great deal of what passes in England as advanced thought on the subject of race-relations is very superficial and remote from the realities of the case'.[118] Even though tentative in its origin, the invention of race relations marked a significant turning point. Though not yet liberated from biological determinism, the focus had begun to shift from the construction of the characteristics of specific racial types to political and social relationships with both a local and international dimension.

The Victorians invented a new language of race relations. This language enabled the construction of institutionalised racial inequality in the law and its administration, and sanctioned the practice of racial subordination and separation in the new kind of multi-racial societies engineered by colonialism. Historical transformations of this magnitude, involving profound political questions about the rights and entitlements of individuals and groups subject to British authority, engendered a variety of responses within the metropolitan culture. Rather than engage in a futile search for a typical or representative voice, the historical task is to gauge the range of responses and to assess which voices were dominant and which ones were dissenting in this discourse. The new language of race relations had transformed the scope of this discourse by the end of the nineteenth century. The old-style liberalism of the humanitarian movement preaching the possibility of a colour-blind empire seemed archaic, and the new style jingoism celebrating the majesty and success of imperial domination seemed equally unsuited to the governance of a global empire in which colonised subjects of colour far outnumbered the white kith and kin of the United Kingdom and the self-governing dominions. There was a widespread anticipation that nineteenth-century practices would no longer prevail in the new twentieth century. When the Pan-African Conference met in London in 1900 and issued its address to the world, it began with W. E. B. Du Bois' famous prediction: 'the problem of the twentieth century is the problem of the colour line'. The dimensions of this colour line soon became apparent in the metropolitan responses to the reconstruction of the new Union of South Africa. The new language of race relations matured and diversified in the first decade of the twentieth century, as the Edwardians explored the unprecedented dynamics of multi-racial societies created by empire within the equally untried terrain of an emerging democratic culture.

Notes

1 For an earlier exploration of this theme, see Lorimer, 'From natural science to social science', pp. 181–212.
2 Douglas Hay and Paul Craven (eds), *Masters, Servants, and Magistrates in Britain and the Empire, 1562–1955* (Chapel Hill, NC: University of North Carolina Press, 2004); Robert J. Steinfeld, *Coercion, Contract and Free Labor in the Nineteenth Century* (Cambridge: Cambridge University Press, 2001).
3 See Chapter 3.
4 Granville Sharp, *A Representation of the Injustice of Slavery* (1769), pp. 91, 109, 152–9.
5 BL, Add MS 21,254 fol. 29. Report of the Committee for the Abolition of the Slave Trade, 15 January 1788.
6 Granville Sharp to the Archbishop of Canterbury, 1 August 1786, in Prince Hoare, *Memoirs of Granville Sharp* (London: 1820), pp. 263–4.
7 Gloucester Record Office. Granville Sharp Papers, D3549 drawer 13. John Stuart (Ottobah Cugano) to Granville Sharp, n.d.; on Cugano see D. Dabydeen, J. Gilmore and C. Jones (eds), *The Oxford Companion to Black British History* (Oxford: Oxford University Press, 2007), pp. 123–5; Lorimer, 'Black slaves and English liberty', 136–9.
8 John Newton, *Thoughts on the African Slave Trade* (London: 1788), in *The Journal of a Slave Trader*, ed. Bernard Martin and Mark Spurrell (London: Epworth, 1962), p. 103.

9 William Dickson, *Letters on Slavery* (1789), p. 57.
10 Hoare, *Memoirs*, p. 94.
11 Wilson Armistead, 'Colour prejudice', in *Tribute for the Negro* (London: 1848), pp. 81–91; 'Prejudice against colour', *ASR*, new ser., 1 (June 1853), 121–3; see also Lorimer, *Colour, Class*, pp. 33–7, 51–6; Christine Bolt, 'Some notes on abolitionist attitudes to race', *Victorian Attitudes*, pp. 225–9.
12 Glasgow Emancipation Society, *Report of Speeches and Reception of American Delegates* (Glasgow, 1840), pp. 12–13, 19–20; *Chambers's Journal*, 3 (January–June 1855), 185–8, and 7 (January–June 1857), 211–14; commentary on the American Embassy's denial of a passport to Sarah Remond, an African-American anti-slavery lecturer in the United Kingdom, *Morning Star* (10 December 1859), 4d–e; *Anti-Slavery Advocate*, 2 (2 January 1860), 294.
13 *Colonial Intelligencer and Aborigines' Friend*, new ser., 1 (1857–8), 345–64, 392–4, 486–90, and 2 (1859–60), 67–74; *ASR*, 3rd ser., 6 (1858), 263–4; [W. H. Russell], 'The Sahib and the nigger', *The Times* (20 October 1858), 10a–b, and leader 8c–d.
14 University College, London. Brougham Papers 143. L. A. Chamerovzow to Lord Brougham, 3 October 1860.
15 Blackett, *Building the Anti-Slavery Wall*; Fiona Spiers, 'Black Americans in Britain and the struggle for black freedom in the United States', in J. S. Gundara and I. Duffield (eds), *Essays on the History of Blacks in Britain* (Aldershot: Avebury, 1992), pp. 81–98; Lorimer, *Colour, Class*, pp. 45–56; Vanessa D. Dickerson, *Dark Victorians* (Urbana and Chicago, IL: University of Illinois Press, 2008).
16 Howard Temperley, *British Anti-Slavery, 1833–1870* (London: Longman, 1972), pp. 258–61; Christine Bolt, *The Anti-Slavery Movement and Reconstruction, 1833–77* (Oxford: Oxford University Press, 1969); Fryer, *Staying Power*, pp. 440–41; Doug Seroff, 'The Fisk Jubilee Singers in Britain', in Rainer Lotz and Ian Pegg (eds), *Under the Imperial Carpet: Essays in Black History, 1780–1950* (Crawley: Rabbit, 1986), pp. 43–54.
17 *ASR*, 3rd ser., 20 (1877), 21, and 21 (1878), 74–5, 148; *AF*, new ser., 1 (Feb. 1879), 89–91; on the Foresters, see *Anti-Caste*, 1 (April 1888), 1, and 1 (Sept. 1888), 4; Vron Ware, *Beyond the Pale: White Women, Racism and History* (London: Verso, 1992), pp. 169–224; David A. Fahey, *Temperance and Racism: John Bull, Johnny Reb, and the Good Templars* (Lexington, KY: University Press of Kentucky, 1996). See also Chapter 7.
18 TNA, CO885/19 Miscellaneous No. 217 Confidential. *Native Races in the British Empire* [C.P.L] (31 December 1907), p. 8; Ramsay MacDonald, *Labour and Empire*, pp. 49–68; Huttenback, *Racism and Empire*. See also Chapters 2 and 6.
19 See Chapter 7.
20 Charles Saville Roundell, 'What is the duty of the mother country as regards the protection of inferior races in her colonies and dependencies?', *Transactions of the National Association for the Promotion of Social Science* (1866), 126–40.
21 *Parl. Debates*, 3rd ser., 158 (21 June 1861) H/L, 1391–1407, and 170 (28 April 1863), 857–8.
22 *Anti-Slavery Advocate* (2 June 1856), 367.
23 Society of Friends, *Information respecting Aborigines in British Colonies* (London, 1838), pp. iv–vi; APS, *Regulations of the Society and Address* (London, 1838), pp. 3–7 and 'Preface', *Report of the Parliamentary Committee on Aboriginal Tribes reprinted with comments by the Society* (London, 1837), pp. v–xi; *The Colonial Intelligencer and Aborigines Friend*, 1 (Dec. 1847), 170–1.
24 H. R. Fox Bourne, *The Aborigines Protection Society: Chapters in its History* (London, 1895), pp. 3–13; James Heartfield, *The Aborigines' Protection Society: Humanitarian Imperialism in Australia, New Zealand, Fiji, Canada, South Africa, and the Congo, 1836–1909* (New York: Columbia University Press, 2011), pp. 9–41.
25 Fox Bourne, *Chapters*, pp. 14–25; Michael Rose, *Curator of the Dead: Thomas Hodgkin (1798–1866)* (London: Peter Owen, 1981), pp. 104–17; Zoë Laidlaw, 'Heathens, slaves and aborigines: Thomas Hodgkin's critique of missions and anti-slavery', *History Workshop Journal*, 64 (2007), 133–61; Louis Rosenfeld, *Thomas Hodgkin:*

Morbid Anatomist and Social Activist (New York: Madison, 1993); A. M. Kass and E. H. Kass, *Perfecting the World: The Life and Times of Dr. Thomas Hodgkin, 1798–1866* (Boston: Harcourt Brace Jovanovich, 1988). See also Chapter 7.

26 *Report on the Select Committee on Aborigines (British Settlements)* [1837], British Parliamentary Papers, pp. 3–6.

27 *Report of the Select Committee*, pp. 3–6, 75–80; Julie Evans *et al.*, *Equal Subjects, Unequal Rights*, pp. 27–34.

28 Lee Holcombe, *Wives and Property: Reform of Married Women's Property Law in Nineteenth-Century England* (Toronto: University of Toronto Press, 1983); Douglas Hay and Paul Craven (eds), *Masters, Servants and Magistrates*; Evans *et al.*, *Equal Subjects, Unequal Rights*.

29 *Report of the Select Committee*, p. 78.

30 Fox Bourne, *Chapters*, pp. 15–16, 18, 21–3; see also APS, *Extracts from Proceedings of the Society*, (London, 1841), vol. 3, pp. 87–8.

31 APS, *Ninth Annual Report* (London, 1846), pp. 10–13, 26–8; on the West Indies after emancipation, Holt, *Problem of Freedom*. See also Chapter 7.

32 Herman Merivale, *Lectures on Colonization and Colonies* [1861] Reprints of Economic Classics (New York: Augustus Kelly, 1967); David McNab, 'Herman Merivale and the Native Question, 1837–61', *Albion*, 9 (1977), 359–84; Leslie Stephen, 'Merivale, Herman (1806–1874)', rev. Donovan Williams, *NODNB* (2004).

33 Merivale, *Lectures*, pp. 513–14.

34 Merivale, *Lectures*, pp. 509–10; 544–7.

35 Merivale, *Lectures*, pp. 509–10; see also pp. 506–9.

36 Merivale, *Lectures*, p. 489.

37 Merivale, *Lectures*, pp. 511, 538.

38 Merivale, *Lectures*, p. 549.

39 Merivale, *Lectures*, pp. 549–53; (1861), pp. 554–63.

40 Merivale, *Lectures*, pp. 537, 549.

41 Merivale, *Lectures*, pp. 314–23, 329–32; (1860), pp. 336–9; on Wakefield and Australia see p. 385; Stanley Engerman, 'Comparative Approaches to Ending Slavery,' in H. Temperley (ed.), *After Slavery: Emancipation and its Discontents* (London: Frank Cass, 2000), pp. 281–300.

42 Merivale, *Lectures*, pp. 336–48.

43 Merivale, *Lectures*, pp. 487–98.

44 Merivale, *Lectures*, p. 522.

45 Merivale, *Lectures*, p. 523.

46 Merivale, *Lectures*, pp. 514–21.

47 James L. Ward, *Colonization and its bearing on the extinction of the Aboriginal Races* (Leek: 1874), pp. 4–7, 10–21, 70–99, 114–33; Evans *et al.*, *Equal Subjects, Unequal Rights*.

48 'The annual report, 1873–74', *Colonial Intelligencer* (1874–78), 122–3.

49 'The annual report, 1875–76', *Colonial Intelligencer* (August 1876), 329.

50 *Colonial Intelligencer* (August 1876), 336.

51 *Colonial Intelligencer* (August 1876), 330–1; 'The Cape and Natal', *Colonial Intelligencer* (November 1875), 260–4.

52 H. C. Swaisland, 'Chesson, Frederick William (1833–88)', *NODNB* (2005) [www.oxfoddnb.com]; Fox Bourne, *Chapters*, pp. 25–43. See also Chapter 7.

53 'The education of native races in British colonies', *Colonial Intelligencer* (January 1877), 345–53. After the First World War in Canada and Australia, a policy of forced assimilation, or what some critics see as cultural genocide, involved the separation of children from families and communities to live at state-sponsored residential schools run by mission churches. It is not clear that Chesson had in mind such a strategy, for he, like his predecessor Hodgkin and his successor Fox Bourne, was sceptical about missionaries' emphasis on religious conversion rather than the 'natural rights' of indigenous peoples.

54 Twenty-six children, the offspring mainly of English soldiers and African or creole women, had attended school in St Helena, but upon arrival in Natal were excluded on grounds of their colour. 'Coloured children in Natal', *Colonial Intelligencer* (Febru-

ary 1876), 284–6.
55 'Native law in Natal', *AF*, new ser., 1 (1878), 1–5; 'Woman slavery in Natal', *AF*, new ser., 1 (April 1880), 222–3.
56 'Native rights in South Africa', *Colonial Intelligencer* (September 1877), 413–17.
57 Sir George Campbell, *Black and White: The Outcome of a Visit to the United States* (New York: R. Worthington, 1879), pp. 111–13; several chapters appeared originally in *The Fortnightly Review*, 31 (1879), 449–68, 588–607; G. Le G. Norgate, 'Campbell, Sir George (1824–1892)', rev. David Steele, *NODNB* (2004).
58 Campbell, *Black*, pp. 162–94.
59 Campbell, *Black*, pp. 160–1, see also 128–31, 144, 157.
60 Campbell, *Black*, pp. 136, 129.
61 Campbell, *Black*, pp. 194–7.
62 Campbell, *Black*, pp. 161, 198–9.
63 Campbell, *Black*, pp. 120–4.
64 Sir George Campbell, *The British Empire* (London: Cassell, 1887), pp. 7–8, 71–4, 84–6.
65 Campbell, *Empire*, pp. 71–8, 84–6, 97–8.
66 Campbell, *Empire*, p. 156, and pp. 31–3, 102–13, 131–5, 150–60.
67 Campbell, *Empire*, p. 102.
68 Campbell, *Empire*, pp. 111–13.
69 Campbell, *Empire*, pp. 105–13, 131–3, 173.
70 Campbell, *Empire*, p. 166.
71 'Campbell, Sir George (1824–1892)', *NODNB*.
72 Benjamin Kidd, *Control of the Tropics*; see also J. W. Fortesque, 'The influence of climate on race', *Nineteenth Century*, 33 (1893), 862–73; Sir Charles Bruce, *The Broad Stone of Empire: Problems of Crown Colony Administration, with Records of Personal Experience* (London: Macmillan, 1910), vol. 1, pp. 306–69; L. W. Lyde, 'White colonisation of the tropics', *United Empire*, new ser., 1 (1910), 763–72.
73 Mamdani, *Citizen and Subject*.
74 [H. R. Fox Bourne], 'The duty of civilised states to weaker races', *AF*, new ser., 4 (April 1891), 169–76; 'The claims of uncivilised races', *AF*, new ser., 5 (December 1900), appendix; 'The claims of uncivilised communities', *AF*, new ser., 8 (October 1907), 82–8; APS, *The Native Question in South Africa* (London: P. S. King, 1900); H. R. Fox Bourne, *Blacks and Whites in South Africa: An Account of the Past Treatment and Present Conditions of South African Natives under British and Boer Control* (London: P. S. King, 1900) 2nd edn, pp. 89–93; TNA, CO885/19 Miscellaneous No. 217 Confidential. [C. P. L.], *Native Races in the British Empire* (31 December 1907) [cited hereafter as Lucas, *Native Races*]; Evans *et al.*, *Equal Subjects, Unequal Rights*. See also Chapter 7.
75 For example: APS, *The Native Question in South Africa*; Alexander Davis, *The Native Problem in South Africa* (London: Chapman Hall, 1903); Sir Harry Johnston, 'The "native" problem and sane imperialism', *Nineteenth Century*, 66 (July–December 1909), 234–44; Anon, *A Question of Colour: A Study of South Africa* (London: Blackwood, 1906); Roderick Jones, 'South African Union and the colour question', *Nineteenth Century*, 66 (July–December 1909), 245–56; William Archer, *Through Afro-America: An English Reading of the Race Problem* (London: Chapman Hall, 1910) (reprint Westport, CT: Negro Universities Press, 1970); Charles F. Aked, 'The race problem in America', *Contemporary Review*, 65 (1894), 818–27; 'The negro problem in America', *Spectator*, 26 October 1901, 595–6; J. A. Hobson, 'The negro problem in the United States', *Nineteenth Century*, 54 (October 1903), 581–94; for a more complete list, see Lorimer, 'From natural science to social science', p. 196 n45.
76 Archer, *Through Afro-America*, p. xii.
77 Huttenback, *Racism and Empire*.
78 See Chapter 7.
79 'The Bohemian "Settlement"', *Spectator* (25 January 1890), 109; cited as a common definition of 'race' by the *Oxford English Dictionary* (1933).
80 William Dalton Babington, *Fallacies of Race Theories as Applied to National Characteristics* (London: Longmans Green, 1895); John Mackinnon Robertson, *The Saxon and the Celt: A Study in Sociology* (London: University Press, 1897).

81 *Anti-Caste* (November 1892), 3–4.
82 John G. Godard, *Racial Supremacy: Being Studies in Imperialism* (London: Simpkin, Marshall, 1905); Jean Finot, *Race Prejudice* (London: Archibald Constable, 1906) and *The Death-Agony of the 'Science' of Race* (London: Stead Publishing, 1911) with preface by W. T. Stead; Gustav Spiller, *Science and Race Prejudice* (London: Sherratt and Hughes, 1912, reprinted from *The Sociological Review* (October, 1912); Sidney Olivier, *White Capital and Coloured Labour* (London: Independent Labour Party, 1910; Westport, CT: Negro Universities Press, 1970), pp. 50–1, and 'The Transplanted African', An Address to the Church Congress, Southampton, 3 October 1913, printed in his *Letters and Selected Writings* (ed.) with memoir by Margaret Olivier (London: George Allen and Unwin, 1948), p. 195; on the Universal Races Congress of 1911, see Chapter 8.
83 Campbell, *Black*, pp. 138–9, and *Empire*, pp. 74–5, 84–6; Lord Rosebery, 'Questions of empire' [Address delivered as Lord Rector to students of the University of Glasgow, 16 November 1900] in *Miscellanies: Literary and Historical* (London: Hodder and Stoughton, 1921), vol. 2, pp. 229–63, see p. 237.
84 Benjamin Kidd, *Social Evolution*, pp. 48–52, 59–60.
85 Kidd, *Social Evolution*, p. 348; see also pp. 283–6; 305–8.
86 James Bryce, *The Relations of the Advanced and the Backward Races of Mankind* (Oxford: Clarendon Press, 1902) The Romanes Lecture 1902 [facsimile University Microfilms International, Ann Arbor, MI, 1979], pp. 6–8. See also Chapter 6.
87 Leonard Alston, *The White Man's Work in Asia and Africa: A Discussion of the Main Difficulties of the Colour Question* (London: Longmans Green, 1907) pp. 80–92, 102–17, 121–5; G. K. Chesterton, remarks at the Fifth Session, in N. F. Dryhurst (ed.), *Nationalities and Subject Races* (London: P. S. King, 1911), pp. 127–8.
88 Lake and Reynolds, *Drawing the Global*.
89 Quoted in Huttenback, *Racism and Empire*, p. 161.
90 TNA, CO886/1 Dominions No. 2.Very Confidential. Suggestions as to Coloured Immigration into the Self-Governing Dominions [CPL] July 1908, pp. 6–7; Huttenback, *Racism and Empire*, pp. 160–1.
91 Huttenback, *Racism and Empire*, pp. 21–2, 140–94.
92 TNA, CO886/1 Dominions No. 1. Confidential. The Self-Governing Dominions and Coloured Immigration [C.P.L] July 1908, p. 28; Huttenback, *Racism and Empire*, pp. 200–3.
93 TNA, CO886/1 Dominions No. 1, July 1908, p. 46.
94 Lucas, *Native Races*, p. 1; for the attributes commonly associated with 'natives', J. C. Furnas, *Anatomy of Paradise: Hawaii and the Islands of the South Seas* (New York: William Sloane, 1948), pp. 23–31. See also Chapter 6.
95 Cited in TNA, CO886/1 Dominions No. 1, July 1908, p. 30, see also pp. 47–51 for examples of Transvaal legislation denied approval.
96 TNA, CO417/434 APS to the Colonial Secretary, 13 July 1906; 'South African Natives and the Transvaal Constitution', *AF*, new ser., 7 (April 1906), 602–15.
97 C. J. Singapore, 'Inter-Marriage between Europeans and 'Natives', *The East and the West*, 11 (1913), 13.
98 Latimer Fuller, 'The separation of black and white in church', *The East and the West*, 10 (1912), 382.
99 'Non-European', *NOED* [www.oed.com].
100 Kidd, *Social Evolution*, p. 60.
101 *Man*, 14 (1914), p. 58.
102 TNA, CO886/1 Dominions No. 1, July 1908, p. 53.
103 TNA, CO886/1 Dominions No. 1, July 1908, p. 48.
104 Bruce, *Broad Stone*, vol. 1, p. 382.
105 Graham Wallas, *Human Nature in Politics* (1908) (London: Constable, 4th edn, 1948), p. 6.
106 Wallas, *Human Nature*, pp. 6–8; the earliest usage of 'non-white' cited in the *NOED* [www.oed.com] (2006) is from 1910.
107 Wallas, *Human Nature*, p. 9.

108 Wallas, *Human Nature*, pp. 288, 282–3.
109 Wallas, *Human Nature*, pp. 283–4, 288.
110 Weale, *Conflict of Colour*, p. 101. See also Chapter 2.
111 Wallas, *Human Nature*, p. 269.
112 Wallas, *Human Nature*, pp. 274–82, 287–94; on imperial federalists and political liability of their 'white' empire, Green, 'Political economy of empire, 1880–1914', pp. 356–7, 365–7; Bell, *Greater Britain*.
113 Wallas, *Human Nature*, pp. 283–4, 288.
114 [W. T. Stead], 'An open sore of the world', *Review of Reviews*, 42 (July–December 1910), 335; G. Spiller (ed.), *Papers on Inter-Racial Problems Communicated to the First Universal Races Congress* (London: P. S. King, 1911); Lord Avebury, 'Inter-racial problems', *Fortnightly Review*, n.s., 90 (July–December 1911), 581–9; H. H. Johnston, 'Racial problems', *Views and Reviews: from the Outlook of an Anthropologist* (London: Williams and Norgate, 1912), pp. 237–42.
115 R. P. Brooks, 'A local study of the race problem – race relations in the eastern Piedmont Region of Georgia', *Political Science Quarterly*, 26 (June 1911), 193–221; *NOED* [www.oed.com] (2006).
116 *ASR*, 4th ser., 16 (1896), 307.
117 Sydney Olivier, *White Capital*, p. 172.
118 Archer, *Through Afro-America*, p. x.

CHAPTER SIX

The colour question: 'The greatest difficulty in the British Empire' (1900–14)

The construction of institutionalised racial inequality, facilitated by the new language of race relations, was first and foremost a political exercise. Born out of the intense political rivalries of the 1860s, and wearing a cloak of scientific objectivity, the inventors of the science of race, principally the anthropologists, were ready to offer their expert advice to colonial officials, but largely avoided public political commentary on the legal status and political rights of the non-European objects of their study. Consequently, the authors who had the most interesting and influential observations to make about the unequal status of racial groups were those who understood the political arena and were ready to engage in it. Their deliberations on the politics of race relations, as distinct from the science of race, deployed the new language of race relations. Through this language, participants spoke not with one but with various voices on the subject. Some even dissented from the hegemonic racism of the age.

In contrast to the rich historiography on South Africa, our histories of racism as an ideology within the metropolitan culture have not paid sufficiently close attention to the ways racial inequality was constructed and justified, as it was instituted in the political practices, in the law and its administration, and in the emerging social conventions of multi-racial colonial societies.[1] As Michael Adas has ably shown, the confidence, even arrogance, of nineteenth-century Europeans who believed in the moral legitimacy of their colonial interventions and in their political capacity to effect this modernising transformation, did not come in the first instance from theories of racial superiority. Developments in western science and technology, most evident in the emergence of industrial economies and the growth of western-dominated world trade, provided the readiest measure of the comparative status of the world's peoples, and the best test of the presumed superiority of western civilisation. Although Adas sees racist ideology, which he defines in terms of biological determinism, as a secondary theme in the construction of western imperial ideology, its civilising mission and its secularised goal of modernisation, the power of the ideology of race grew out of the ambiguity of race and culture.[2] Although he puts more weight on technology as a Victorian measure of development, in cultural terms Adas' assessment is not dissimilar from Peter Mandler's 'civilisational perspective'. Victorian liberal elite culture had confidence both in its sense of superiority and its belief in progress of the barbarian and the savage toward a civilised ideal over time. Here the evolutionary paradigm provided a vastly longer period of historical time, and defined stages of development in economics, society and politics as well as in biology and culture. The many applications of the evolutionary stages of development, with their ambiguities about race and culture, fuelled the colonisers' confidence that both the coloniser and the colonised would benefit from the conversion to conditions of modernity.[3]

Discussions of the 'Native Question' or the 'Colour Question' presumed that persons of colour lived and laboured within a modernising colonial society in a status subordinate to white officials, employers and settlers. In this discourse, the racial typologies of the physical anthropologists, whose categories became more finely defined by fixing each ethnic group as a distinct race in its natural habitat, had at best a marginal role. Colonialism in its transformation of societies and cultures acted as an enormous engine for the voluntary and forced migration of the world's peoples. In contrast, the anthropologists' scientific naturalism situated its chosen subjects within their 'natural' habitats theoretically untouched by the colonial encounter. The scientists of race had little interest in peoples and cultures subject to the transforming power of empire, and pursued those so-called original or primitive peoples on the margins of the newly constructed modernising multi-racial colonial order.

Within these colonial societies racial conflicts seemed endemic both from the colour prejudices of dominant whites and from the assertions from persons of colour seeking to protect their autonomy or improve their status. Such conflicts threatened the construction of viable political and social entities in the multi-racial colonial world. Trained in the classics, and drawn to make comparisons between the British Empire and its Roman predecessor, colonial officials recognised that modern racial tensions and colour prejudices were unknown in the Roman world.[4] Pessimistic about the future of empire, they forecast that racial conflict would lead to the decline of the British Empire in the new twentieth century. Those commentators who looked more to the future than to the past were equally certain that the twentieth century would be unlike the nineteenth. It was widely anticipated that the peoples of Asia and Africa would assert their rights in an emerging international order. From the perspective of the colonial office, Sir Charles Lucas, anxious about the future of empire, observed that 'The greatest difficulty in the British Empire is probably the colour question.'[5]

Modern imperialism and racial conflict

Like an earlier generation of abolitionists, enthusiasts for colonial development greatly underestimated the immensity of their modernising project. They faced one evident political reality – the colonial subjects of colour who were to be the instruments of this transformation did not behave in accordance with the stereotypical attributes ascribed to them by the scientific experts. Therefore, social, political and legal relationships had to be constructed out of a mixture of coercion and consent that defined the negotiated outcomes between the colonisers and their colonial subjects of colour. In the task of constructing colonial race relations, policy makers and political commentators had in mind the norms of the metropolitan culture. These norms were enshrined in an 'invented tradition' of recent creation and designed to give historical legitimacy to the accommodations of an aristocratic elite to the new practices of a deferential Victorian democracy.[6] The discourse on race served the purpose of defining multi-racial colonial societies as fundamentally different from the metropole, and thus the emerging conventions about 'democracy' in terms both of the rights of citizens as political participants and of the rights of subjects under the law need not apply.

In the late Victorian and Edwardian period, the imperial metropole of London informed the creative ferment of new thinkers and new ideas about politics, society and culture. The rich mix of Positivist, Progressive, New Liberal, Ethical, Fabian, Labour, Socialist and other clubs and organisations established a circle of friendship and acquaintance for discussion of the challenging issues of race, empire and democracy. The leading and most influential participants – for example the members and associates of the Rainbow Circle, including J. Ramsay MacDonald, J. A. Hobson, Sydney Olivier, John M. Robertson, William Pember Reeves, Graham Wallas, L. T. Hobhouse – moved between the worlds of political advocacy, journalism, and the academy (many as lecturers in university extension programs). For some – J. A. Hobson for example – their unorthodox opinions were an impediment to academic positions, but others benefited from the expansion of the universities and from the establishment of new chairs and departments in the social sciences. Here the lead was taken by the newly founded London School of Economics, but London, Oxford, Cambridge and the new civic universities recruited established authors, many with experience as journalists, to staff these new academic ventures. Just as the natural sciences had led the way in the change from gentlemen amateurs to research professionals, so too the creation of new social science disciplines meant that the production of knowledge was increasingly, though never completely, in the hands of professional academics.[7]

In these formative years of the new social sciences, the contentious matters of race and empire played a significant role in the social and political theories of leading authors. In large part, these considerations imposed themselves through external events, principally the South African War of 1899–1902, and the post-war reconstruction of the new union.[8] For this new kind of multi-racial society, historical precedents or contemporary examples were few in number. As constructed by the late Victorians, the history of the West Indies since emancipation, including the use of indentured labour from India, pointed to the need for some form of compulsion to produce a reliable, disciplined labour force. India was often cited as a successful model of benevolent bureaucratic rule by a small British elite over a much larger population alien in race and religion. The recent history of the southern States in America, with its legalised segregation under Jim Crow legislation and widely reported vigilante terrorism of the lynch mobs, proved more troubling and contentious. Some authors – for example L. T. Hobhouse and Graham Wallas – while influenced by this discussion on race and empire, probed a broader theoretical concern that biological differences of race, like differences of gender, imposed limits on those natural and civic rights accompanying democratic forms of government.[9]

The commentaries on this perceived global crisis of increased racial contact and conflict, as evidenced by developments in the self-governing dominions, India, South Africa and the United States, gave rise to a new and modern language of race relations. This language had a rich vocabulary to describe conditions of racial inequality. Its richness and utility depended not on its biological determinism but on the ambiguous meanings of race and culture. Out of a sense of contrast between the past and the present, Edwardian commentators identified colour prejudice and associated racial antipathies as a distinctly modern phenomenon.

From their classical education and out of interest in comparing imperialism in the ancient and modern worlds, several colonial administrators observed that the question of colour perplexed the British Empire but not its Roman forerunner. Familiar with the universal claims of Roman citizenship, and with the multi-racial and multiethnic character of slavery in ancient Greece and Rome, Lord Cromer, in his *Ancient and Modern Imperialism* (1910), observed that Roman citizens belonged to a variety of races and colours, and that intermarriage existed and faced no legal or other prohibitions. As a result of his searches, Cromer reported: 'I have been unable to discover any distinct indication that colour antipathy existed to any marked extent in the ancient world'.[10] One reason of this difference from the experience of the modern world, according to Cromer, who had consulted with classical scholars, was that there was no association between skin colour and servile status. The 'moderns' and the 'ancients' differed, he observed, as 'the former ... only enslaved the coloured races, whereas the latter doomed all conquered people indiscriminately to slavery'. The enslavement of Africans since the fifteenth century identified slavery with 'difference of colour' and, in Cromer's opinion, 'must have helped bring into prominence the idea of white superiority, and thus to foster a race antipathy which, by a very comprehensible association of ideas, was not altogether confined to those coloured races who were enslaved'.[11]

Sir Charles Lucas, who published his own study of *Greater Rome and Greater Britain* in 1912, and who had a distinguished record in classics as an undergraduate at Oxford, affirmed that eminent scholars concurred in Cromer's judgement. The experience of Rome, according to Lucas, offered little or no guidance. Like Cromer, the colonial office civil servant also associated the origins of modern colour prejudices with the enslavement of Africans in the New World, and similarly argued that this colour consciousness extended to other peoples within the modern colonial empires.[12] Quite independently and from the history of Australia which had little direct link to the enslavement of Africans, Sir Samuel Griffith, Premier and Lieutenant-Governor of Queensland, wrote in 1894: 'The strong feeling of antipathy to Asiatic races that is now so marked a feature of the British speaking people in America and Australia seems to be a modern phenomenon. History records no instance of similar race hatred.'[13] This association of colour prejudice with the modern historical period was commonplace, but at the same time other explanations linked prejudice not with history but with human nature.

Even though colour prejudice seemed to be a product of modern historical conditions, Cromer also thought that racial antipathy derived from deep-seated instincts. Despite the well-intentioned commitment to the civilising mission and the goal of assimilation under British law, subject colonial peoples and their British governors were growing farther and farther apart:

The foundations on which the barrier wall of separation is built may be, and, without doubt, to a certain extent are, the result of prejudice rather than of reason; but however little we may like to recognise the fact, they are of so solid a character, they appeal so strongly to instincts and sentiments which lie deep down in the hearts of men and women, that for generations to come they will probably defy whatever puny, albeit well-intentioned, efforts may be made to undermine them.[14]

Seeing little hope for resolving these conflicts, Cromer sought to manage them through his preferred option of the autocratic rule of colonial administrators like himself. Equally distrusting of democracy and colonial nationalism, he observed that, unlike in the Roman Empire, a common language served not as an agency of assimilation but of disaffection: 'Language is not, and never can be, as in the case of Ancient Rome, an important factor in the execution of a policy of fusion. Indeed, in some ways, it rather tends to disruption, inasmuch as it furnishes the subject races with a very powerful arm against their alien rulers.'[15] Equipped with the English language, Cromer realised, from his own experience, that Indian and Egyptian nationalists became more effective opponents of colonial administrators.

Sharing the commonplace view that racial antipathies were a product of the modern era, Sir Charles Lucas more specifically claimed that racial conflicts intensified as modern political and social institutions developed. Having long experience of the disputes between the self-governing dominions and the imperial government over restrictive immigration policies, he had no illusions about the relationship between democracy and racism. If anything, he was nostalgic for an older mid-Victorian liberalism in which the status of a British subject, regardless of creed or colour, had some meaning. He faced, though, new political realities in which an emerging, and implicitly racial, distinction was drawn between a British subject under the Crown and a British citizen, born or domiciled within the British Isles with specific entitlements to political rights and privileges. The Imperial Conference of 1911 made it evident that each dominion defined its own criteria for citizenship, at times not including British subjects, and often specifically excluding persons of colour.[16] Both Cromer and Lucas defended their own special interests. Cromer placed his trust in the authority of the administrator in the locality; Lucas thought that the colonial office served as a mediating influence between white colonists and the so-called 'native' interest. Their reflections drew largely on their own administrative experience and constituted informed, even expert, commentary on what contemporaries termed the 'colour question'.

The association of colour prejudice or racial antipathy with the modern period of history, as a legacy of race slavery and as a feature of multi-racial societies created by colonialism, led to a rather unsystematic but nonetheless informative quest to identify the sources of racial conflict. In the course of this commentary, given prominence by developments in South Africa, the older language of colour prejudice diversified into our modern lexicon of race relations. Apart from an exceptional few dissenters, most participants in this discourse on race relations presumed a generalised inequality between whites and all persons of colour. Beyond this presumption of racial inequality, the specific racial types imagined by biologists and anthropologists had little role in this discussion. The scientists of race placed their racial types and their evolved distinctive characteristics within the natural habitat of their imagined origins, whereas the discourse of race relations dealt with new multi-racial societies, invariably colonies or former colonies, created by the encounter of indigenous peoples and migratory or transitory populations. These migrants included not only European settlers and transients, such as colonial officials and military personnel, but also the descendants of Africans transported as slaves, the more recent migration of indentured workers, and voluntary migrants in Asia and Africa drawn to the opportunities in developing market economies.

This mix of peoples and cultures, brought together by the conquests and migrations of their ancestors, or more recently by voluntary or coerced migration, formed the constituent elements of a new social order with a modernising economy linked to world markets. Beyond the production and export of agricultural crops, there were in some notable cases, such as South Africa, where a significant industrial sector in mining demanded new labourers engaged in new kinds of work under new forms of relations with employers. Just as the New Liberalism and the new social sciences addressed the role of the state in urban-industrial conditions, so too these modernising multi-racial societies experiencing rapid change required new thinking about how to provide for peace, order and good government. Within the British Empire, colonial jurisdictions had long experience in adapting political institutions, administrative practice and the law to address the task of governance. By the end of the nineteenth century metropolitan accommodations to a new deferential democracy seemed ill-suited to the requirements of good governance in a colonial setting. The task of adaptation and reform was not made easier by the varied and unanticipated responses of the colonised to the colonial encounter. By the late nineteenth and early twentieth centuries, some of the Queen's subjects in her African, Asian and Caribbean possessions, much to the disquiet of white colonial elites and officials, demanded the new entitlements of British citizens.[17] Outside and within the universities, the practitioners of the

[214]

new social sciences were ready to tackle this pressing concern about the political and social dimensions of racial inequality, and about the signs of disquiet and even resistance among the colonised subjects, the so-called 'natives', of the empire.

The psychology of race relations

Of the new social sciences, psychology had the closest links to the established natural sciences, especially biology. As such, it promised new and better insights into the colour question. Beyond probing reasons for the presumed inequality between races and for white superiority, late Victorian and Edwardian observers sought explanations for the conflicts between peoples identified as belonging to different races, for the global dimensions of such conflicts, and for their peculiar, even irrational, intensity. The new language of race relations dealt less with the stereotyped attributes of racial groups, and instead addressed the behaviour of these groups toward one another. Consequently, the language of race relations more specifically described the social and political dimensions of racial conflict, and looked to psychology rather than comparative anatomy to find the source of these antagonistic behaviours. In the longer term, the new language of race relations served as the medium for the construction of what we now identify as institutional or systemic racism, which originated before and survived after the retreat of the older biological determinism of race science between the 1930s and 1950s.

James Bryce (1838–1922), an Ulster Scots Presbyterian, a radical Liberal and supporter of the North during the American Civil War, a constitutional expert best known for his *American Commonwealth* (1888), and a global traveller and mountaineer in Europe, Central Asia and North America, provided a pioneering and influential study of the political dimensions of ethnic and race relations. Bryce's influence derived in part from his expertise in the comparative study of constitutions, and from his political orthodoxy as a Gladstonian Liberal sympathetic to nationalist causes and oppressed minorities. As a Liberal MP, he supported Gladstone and Home Rule for Ireland, and had supported and helped organise lobby groups defending oppressed minorities in the Ottoman Empire, including Bulgarian Christians and Armenians. A frequent and sympathetic visitor to the United States, he largely adopted the views of those of his American academic and political friends who were critical of Reconstruction and supportive of segregation. Having recently visited South Africa in 1897, Bryce brought his political expertise and informed global perspective to the delivery of the Romanes Lectures on the emerging pattern of race relations and the psychological sources of racial conflict. His lectures, *The Relations of the Advanced and the Backward Races of Mankind*, published in 1902 just as attentions turned to the post-war reconstruction of South Africa, had a formative influence, at least until the First World War.[18]

For Bryce, racial antipathies included conflicts between European ethnicities – for example the British and the Boers – as well as between peoples differing in skin colour. He identified four forms of race relations, and only two of these were relevant to the new modern conditions of increased contact between races within capitalist, industrial societies governed by democratic political institutions. In earlier forms of colonisation, such contact had resulted in the extermination of conquered peoples, or in the absorption of aboriginals within the new dominant settler populations. Under modern conditions, Bryce speculated that the only two outcomes were the intermingling of racial groups to produce a new variety, as in the white populations of the United States, or the coexistence of two or more races as separate entities within one society, as with blacks and whites in American democracy, or as he thought was materialising in South Africa and other colonial societies.[19]

Adopting an evolutionary or developmentalist perspective by distinguishing between 'advanced' and 'backward' races, Bryce was particularly concerned with the state of coexistence and its implications for social relationships and their institutional expression in politics and the law. Where two races were dissimilar, especially in skin colour, Bryce used the phrase 'physical repulsion' rather than 'colour prejudice' to describe the principal obstacle to intermarriage. The greatest repugnance to colour existed among the 'Teutons', and consequently, he wrote, 'Where Americans, Englishmen, and Germans rule, there is not intermarriage with the coloured races, and consequently no prospect of ultimate race-fusion.'[20] Bryce depicts inter-racial unions in terms of white male dominance and subordinate female passivity, for 'the higher race has more to give, and that the lower race wishes to receive. The idea and habits of the white men tell upon and permeate the offspring of mixed marriages with all the greater force because that offspring seek to resemble its higher rather than its inferior progenitor.' As examples of positive mixtures from the past, he cites the European experience of Teutons and Celts, and Teutons and Slavs, but draws the conventional conclusion that the offspring of whites and blacks or of whites and South Asians result in inferior progeny.

Bryce counsels against a policy of encouraging racial inter-marriage and fusion, for in his view the benefits derived from the improvement of inferior races would not outweigh the loss to the superior. Appealing to the contemporary concerns with national or social efficiency, and implicitly treating white female fertility as a national resource, Bryce warns that 'nothing is more vital than that some races should be maintained at the highest level of efficiency, because the work they can do for thought and art and letters, for scientific discovery, and for raising the standard of conduct, will determine the general progress of humanity'.[21] In theory, Bryce claimed, a fusion of races was the answer to 'Race-antagonism, an evil more dangerous, because rooted in nature', but he recognised that the more common situation was one of contact without fusion of racial groups.[22]

This situation, derived from repulsion due to differences of colour or religion, he classified into three forms. In India and in tropical colonies, an 'advanced' European minority, who were temporary residents and not settlers, ruled over a 'backward' coloured majority. In areas of white settlement, employers brought voluntary and indentured immigrants from India and China to meet specific needs for manual labour. Finally, there were situations where two races existed side by side within the same community, as in the American South which, he estimated, had a population of 7 million blacks and 14 million whites.[23]

Where two races lived in the same communities, racial 'antagonism' was the inevitable outcome. For Bryce, this antagonism stemmed first from the fact of inequality. He defined this inequality not in terms of wealth or social status, but in terms of 'intelligence and will' which encouraged the stronger race to ill-treat the weaker. Antagonism also grew out of 'dissimilarity of character' of the races, and the resultant mutual incapacity of understanding. Finally, the races lived in an atmosphere of 'distrust' growing out of the fact that the 'backward race' attempts 'to protect itself by guile'. In contrast, 'the more advanced race relies upon the prestige of its knowledge, the force of its will, and its ingrained habit of dominance'. In this fashion, Bryce incorporated the presumed inequality of races by their biological inheritance and by their innate psychology into the explanation of racial conflict. These conflicts, Bryce thought, led to widespread and intense violence, both from the barrier which race created to sympathy across racial lines, and because of the solidarity of racial groups in conflict with others.[24]

Having established both the inequality of races living within communities and the sources of racial antagonism and violence, Bryce then dealt with the political consequences of such relationships. In the situation where a superior race also had a privileged political status, it would abuse its political power to the disadvantage of the backward race. On the other hand, if both races shared a common political status, including the franchise and the right to hold public office, then the races tended to create their own political parties, and two separate nations could emerge. As political institutions became more democratic in form, the danger of nationalism intensified. On the one hand, the denial of political privileges contradicted principles of universal rights, but on the other hand, the extension of the franchise to the 'backward' created opportunities for the corruption and intimidation of these voters. This problem, Bryce observed, grew worse as the lower race advanced in 'intelligence and knowledge'. In the past, serfs and slaves accepted their condition, whereas with greater independence African-Americans, Filipinos, and Egyptian fellahin displayed greater discontent.[25]

With increased contact between races in the modern world, and with the antagonism, violence and political conflict endemic in race relations, Bryce concluded his discussion with some recommendations about policy. Despite the offence given by the efforts of the white dominions to restrict immigration, he defended such a policy as the best means to avoid even graver political difficulties. These problems were a consequence not of the actions of responsible human agents but of the dictates of human nature beyond the control of political idealists or of more realistic makers of policy. Bryce affirmed: 'Nature may be supposed to know better than we do; and the efforts of man to check her have been often foolish and most ineffective.' Consequently, 'the Californian and the Australian, crudely selfish as some of their arguments may appear, seem to be right in believing that a large influx of Chinese labour would mean the reduction of the standard of life, and with that the standard of leisure and mental cultivation, among their artisan class'. Beyond the dictates of nature, Bryce also reaffirmed the danger which 'the presence of an alien and politically untrained element breeds in a democratic community' and observes, 'we may pause before condemning the policy the Americans and Australians have adopted'.[26]

While accepting policies of racial subordination and exclusion, Bryce, nonetheless, thought that certain political and legal guarantees should be made to 'backward' races. These included protection of persons and property, entrance into the professions and other occupations based on merit and not race, and equal access with whites to due process before the courts. Citing the experience of the southern United States, he counselled against the extension of the franchise to a 'backward race'. Using the term 'discrimination', a relatively new word in the lexicon of race relations, he also affirmed that 'race and blood should not be made the ground of discrimination'. On the vote, he preferred an education or property qualification rather than a racial one, and thought it better to exclude some poor whites than to alienate all persons of colour.[27]

In his concluding remarks, he reiterated his sense that world developments had reached a new stage. Advances in science and medicine would enable whites to live in the tropics, and increased economic productivity and trade would lead to increased contact and conflict between racial groups. He noted the increase in the 'sentiment of race-pride, the keenness of race-rivalry', but ended optimistically by pointing to the evidence of human progress since the commencement of European colonisation some 400 years earlier.[28] By shifting the focus away from the stereotyped traits of 'race' to the nature of race relations, Bryce and his contemporaries laid the foundations for a much more substantial and tenacious defence of racial inequality.

Even though he presumed that peoples could be classified into 'advanced' and 'backward' races, his analysis of racial inequality and conflict rested more on psychology than biology or physical anthropology. He admitted that various races might receive an education and be improved by it, and that the indelible character of race rested less upon intelligence than upon psychological traits such strength of will and tenacity of purpose. Similarly, racial antagonism and conflict were psychological in origin. In comparison to Cromer or Lucas, for example, Bryce offered an ahistorical and unchanging view of race relations. Racial prejudice was not rooted in a history of slavery and colonialism, nor was it a product of rational conflicts over economic or other self-interested motivations, but rather it found its source in human nature. White prejudice was a natural instinct, and as such social relationships, the law and political institutions had to conform to this 'reality'. Consequently, bureaucratic rule by colonial administrators, exclusionary immigration policies, and the construction of unequal and segregated communities in the American South and in South Africa were justified despite their denial of the universality of human rights under the law, and despite the pressure to extend democratic citizenship to all adults. Bryce's shift from a biological to a psychological defence of racial inequality rested upon a circular but nonetheless powerful logic. The mounting evidence of a pervasive racialism became a justification for institutionalising racial inequality as the natural and inevitable condition of multi-racial societies created by the human agency of western colonialism. In this way, the new language of race relations departed from the optimism of Victorian liberalism with its promise of progress and assimilation within a hierarchically ordered but colour-blind empire.

In 1900, in the midst of the South African War and its fractious impact on the Liberal Party, a collection of essays, entitled *Liberalism and Empire*, edited by F. W. Hirst, Gilbert Murray, and J. L. Hammond, considered how the tenets of Gladstonian liberalism needed to be revised in light of the new realities of empire, democracy and white racism. Espousing what came to be known as the 'new liberalism', the contributors were critical of the South African War, viewing it as a capitalist conspiracy. Nevertheless, they recognised the need to reconsider the economic, political and social development of the empire, including the future of its most troubling possession, South Africa.

Gilbert Murray, an Australian and a professor of classics at Glasgow University, addressed the issue of colonial labour and race relations in his essay, 'The Exploitation of Inferior Races in Ancient and Modern Times'. Claiming to examine the question in 'a purely scientific spirit' and 'without sentiment', Murray began by observing that the recruitment of labour was a necessary element of the productive system of any society. He then developed a comparison between slavery in the ancient world and forms of labour under modern colonialism, cautioning that it was an error to define ancient forms of slavery too narrowly in light of the law or of the practices of modern chattel slavery. In his view, ancient slavery was comparable to a variety of forms of colonial coerced and indentured labour, except that the ancients recruited labour by force, whereas in the modern world, economic necessity worked to compel a variety of destitute aliens into manual labour under cruel and oppressive conditions.[29] Citing James Bryce's *Impressions of South Africa* and his own knowledge of conditions in Queensland, Murray attributed the exploitation of coloured labour to the extraordinary intensity of racial hostility among whites. He observed: 'This curious feeling, a compound in which physical repulsion, race-hatred, and pride of birth seem to be accentuated by actual shame and remorse, appears to be even stronger in South Africa than in most similar societies'.[30] Arguing that the need to exploit cheap alien labour created both ancient slavery and modern colonial systems of labour, Murray claimed the effects on the labouring population were also similar. Free men, like white men, despised the work done by slaves and aliens; the labourers themselves lapsed into a 'state of extreme degradation and immorality'; and eventually they lost hope and died of despair.[31]

Using his analogy to ancient slavery to build a critique of the abuses of colonial labour, especially in South Africa, Murray does not appeal to the old pieties of anti-slavery sentiment, and advances an innovative case for unequal but protected status under the law. He predicts that colonial empires will make increased use of unskilled alien labour in spite of white workers' fears of competition. Just as Australians and Americans are hostile to Chinese immigrants, he observes that 'English democracy will never allow coloured labourers to be imported in any large numbers into this country'. Despite their fears, he claims white workers would benefit from 'the freer exploitation of coloured labour' much in the way that they have benefited from free trade and the introduction of machinery. In his view, 'a few old-fashioned ideal-ists' may raise the question of preparing the inferior races for freedom and self-government, but 'the question is a distasteful one to a modern politician', and 'no political party with the prospect of holding office seems to have the faintest hope of achieving that end or even much desire of working towards it'.[32]

In light of these political realities, Murray argued for imperial regu-lation of coloured labour by systems of special legislation under the jurisdiction of colonial administrators and not white settlers. He called for a fundamental change in the law: 'Let us frankly abandon for the present the ideal of one universal British law – we have never really acted upon it. Let us recognise the dependent condition of the natives, help towards liberty those that can be helped, and defend the rest by every possible means from masters who are sure, at the best, to exploit them harshly.' Murray's advocacy of a special status under the law and of the paternal role of imperial administration rested upon a belief in racial inequality:

> There is in the world a hierarchy of races. The bounds of it are not, of course, absolute and rigid, as the negro judges in America and the many eminent natives of India show; but, on the whole, it seems that those nations which eat more, claim more, and get higher wages, will direct and rule others, and the lower work of the world will tend in the long-run to be done by the lower breeds of men.[33]

In articulating what he claimed was a more realistic vision of racial subordination and conflict, Murray redefined liberal policy as a paternalistic obligation to subject races no longer to be assimilated to metropolitan norms, but to be provided for under a separate and inferior status.

Other commentators, citing Bryce's Romanes Lectures directly or adopting his language, attempted, like Murray, to justify racial subordination and segregation as a paternalistic protection against white prejudices. In a similar fashion to Bryce, they focused on the psychological and sociological character of race relations, and they confirmed their belief in the inequality of racial groups, and sanctioned the institutional expression of that inequality in social practice, in politics and in the law. Borrowing Bryce's terminology of 'advanced and backward races', Leonard Alston, in *The White Man's Work in Asia and Africa* (1907), identified two approaches to race relations: the more pessimistic view that the character of the lower types was fixed by their biological inheritance, or the more optimistic position that the character of races was attributable to differing environments, and that the 'backward' races were capable of improvement over time.

Speaking as someone who had lived in Australia and had served as an educator in India, Alston claimed to be a 'realist' but nonetheless adopted the optimistic view.[34] His optimism, though, was of a very measured kind. He reminded his readers of the shock at confronting the objects of their 'philanthropic fancies' in the East End of London, in China or, as he described, in Port Said, 'the poverty-stricken black races – perhaps a swarm of chattering men, women, and boys, dressed indistinguishably', and 'smothered in dirt from head to foot, shrieking, laughing, sky-larking, like half-human children, chattering interminably, thoroughly contended with the life of the moment and utterly neglectful of the morrow'. In this view, he agreed with 'the closet optimist' affirming that the salvation of the lower races could only come through contact with the 'guiding and restraining' influence of higher races over a lengthy period of time.[35]

This long-term perspective ran up against the real world of the politicians who by necessity took a short-term view. Citing and quoting from Bryce's *Impressions of South Africa*, Alston stressed that whites combined a contempt for manual labour and a 'tyrannical' attitude with an 'aversion for men of different colour, unreasoning but not unreasonable, which [was] one of the most deep-seated instincts of human nature'.[36] To check the potential abuse of persons of colour, Alston argued for imperial control over local legislatures. He compared this external regulation to the factory legislation of the industrial revolution, as the 'native' was equally vulnerable if not so attractive as the child labourer. Even though the whites' tendency toward brutal treatment of the coloured needed to be controlled, this antipathy functioned as the 'unformulated dictates of an instinct for the good of humanity'. It led whites to exclude Indians and Chinese from America and Australia, and thus preserved those lands for a 'European stock' capable of fully developing them for the benefit of human civilisation.[37]

Another proponent of white colonial nationalism, Richard Jebb, while advocating a civic nationalism and fearing what he termed a 'tribal nationalism', similarly defended the dominions' policies of racial exclusion. Having toured the white dominions after graduation from Oxford, Jebb, a journalist and Shropshire country gentleman, sympathised with the dominion's nationalist aspirations. In advance of most imperial advocates, he envisaged the empire as an association of independent nations, and redefined imperial citizenship so as to make it subject to the authority of individual member states, and compatible with the dominions' exclusionary immigration policies.[38] In 1908, in a paper on 'The Imperial Problem of Asiatic Immigration', delivered before the Royal Society of Arts, Jebb put his emphasis on the dominions' aspiration to establish 'an indigenous democracy of the British type' within the Pacific zone, including Australia, New Zealand and Canada, especially British Columbia. He claimed that coloured immigration in general, and Asiatic immigration in particular, would frustrate this noble end because, using Bryce's terminology, 'fusion' was either impossible or only productive of 'a racial and social type inferior to the Anglo-Saxon'. Consequently, the only outcome of such immigration would be to 'create a "helot" class, for which no place can be found in a pure democracy.'[39] In an earlier visit to South Africa in 1906, Jebb did not express concern about the 'helot' class of the African majority excluded from citizenship, but rather in a series of articles in the *Morning Post*, assessed the prospects for overcoming Boer and British antagonisms to build not only a unified state but a common white South African nationalism.[40]

While much of the commentary on the future of the empire focused on the empire of white settlers to the exclusion of colonial dependencies with non-European populations, especially among imperial federalist advocates, some observers extended their horizons and envisaged a global order bifurcated like the empire itself by an international colour line.[41] Like Bryce before him, Alston foresaw greater racial contact with the expansion of international trade and modern industry. Envisioning a coloured proletariat, he called the peoples from the Arabian Gulf to the Sea of Japan 'the world's slum population', and identified two hereditary classes, 'the thrifty' and 'the unthrifty'. The latter included most of the peoples of Asia and Africa, as well as the black population of the southern United States. Like Gilbert Murray, he thought that white labour's opposition to cheap coloured labour was short-sighted, for all would benefit from increased trade and productivity. Nonetheless, he supported exclusionary immigration policies, for Asians and Africans could be hosts of disease, or sources of the moral degeneration of whites.[42] Alston foresaw that the extension of democracy to 'half-civilised territories' was probably inevitable, but he had little faith in its outcome. Ultimately, he appealed to a vague Christian paternalism in which over time the 'lower' races would come to accept or be compelled to adopt the wisdom of white Christian ways.[43]

In 1910, in an essay on 'Empires and Races' in the *Contemporary Review*, Newton H. Marshall similarly appealed to Christianity as the only hope against a growing sense of racial antagonism. Like Kidd, Bryce, Alston and others, Marshall observed that the old-style imperialism was over, and a new era of global relations had commenced. With modern transport and communications, this new era was characterised by increased contact between the races and by greater 'racial cleavage and repugnance'. He thought that the growing intensity of national rivalry, most evident in the arms race, would coalesce nationalities into antagonistic 'racial empires'. Even socialism, the international movement most opposed to the arms race, sanctioned greater racial exclusion. Socialists and labour groups in the United States, Australia and New Zealand opposed Asiatic immigration. In the United States along with their fellow white citizens, socialists were prejudiced against blacks and abhorred inter-racial marriage.[44] In the United States and South Africa, Marshall, citing Bryce, noted 'a repugnance physical, aesthetic and intellectual', led whites to deny the humanity of blacks. In Marshall's opinion, similar attitudes were evident in India, and elsewhere whites were in contact with persons of colour. Summing up his survey of global relations, Marshall observed: 'In all this we have stumbled upon little that could be regarded as very hopeful. We have been driven to anticipate the building up of a group of world-empires separated by radical racial repugnance.'[45]

This focus on 'racial repugnance' or 'racial instinct' led some commentators to speculate on the origins of such feelings. While many identified the association of persons of colour with low social status and with manual, servile and even degrading forms of labour as the principal source of antipathy, others speculated that such deep-seated attitudes resided in the complex psychology of sexual attraction and repulsion. Late Victorian and Edwardian writers, in comparison to their mid-Victorian predecessors, were both more open in their discussion of race and sex, and more willing to justify racial subordination and segregation on the basis of what they claimed were the natural or instinctive reactions to racial differences. This form of commentary was most evident in the discussion of relations between whites and blacks in the United States and in southern Africa. These reports recited the familiar litany of the former slaves' relapse into African savagery, the potency of African sexuality and fecundity, and the need for a political and legal separation and subordination of blacks within white-dominated democracies.[46] Occasionally, the growing separation of the races invited comparisons to India, and commentators described race relations as a form of 'caste' relationship.[47] Most notably, in the *Anti-Caste*, the magazine that she founded in 1888, Catherine Impey dedicated herself to opposing what she termed 'colour caste', or 'caste prejudice', meaning 'the evils of Caste as it prevails in countries where our white race habitually ostracises those who are even partly descended from darker races'.[48] Eventually, not only the American example but also the American language of 'segregation' came more frequently into use. As the political settlement of the new South African Union took shape, commentators applied the language of 'segregation' to the emerging pattern of race relations there.[49]

These issues received their most sensational treatment in press coverage of the 'Black Peril' in South Africa. In 1911, a series of sensational reports of alleged black assaults on white women led the press to draw obvious parallels to the well-publicised reports of lynching in the United States.[50] The fears of a 'Black Peril' were given further currency by South African and English suffragists who pressed for the vote for white women. In an article in *Englishwoman*, Francis Bancroft (Frances Charlotte Slater) accepted African male aggression against white women as a reality, but attributed its cause to the past and present sexual exploitation of African women by white males. The absence of the franchise and its possession by a minority of black men signified the inferior status of white women, and encouraged black sexual aggression. Bancroft argued that African men considered white women suitable objects of exploitation just as white men had abused their black sisters. These fears of the 'Black Peril' led Bancroft and others to discourage English women from emigrating to South Africa as domestics or in other capacities. Votes for white women in South Africa, in this view, would enlarge the white constituency and control the sexual conduct of both white and black males.[51]

Beyond the sensational press coverage of the 'Black Peril', these ideas had some influence on sources that were usually critical of racial prejudice. W. T. Stead, the editor of *The Review of Reviews*, who declared himself to be an imperialist and yet publicised the evils of racial prejudice and the political demands of Asian and African nationalists, observed that black women were in far graver danger than white women. He sarcastically suggested that the APS should solicit funds to supply African women with revolvers to fend off white attackers. In reporting Bancroft's article, he thought that she exaggerated the danger of the 'Black Peril', but nonetheless, his commentary and his headline, 'Nemesis in South Africa – White Women Reaping what White Men have Sown', gave some credence to white phobias.[52] Similarly, Annie Besant, a leading English champion of Indian nationalism, accepted the idea of the 'Black Peril', while criticising the excesses of white colonialism. In a lecture on 'Coloured Races in the Empire', given at Letchworth Garden City Summer School, in 1913, she drew a distinction between 'colour' and 'race'. Judging people by the colour of their skin, she claimed, was simply 'prejudice', whereas there remained more profound differences of race. In this way, she defended her friends in the Indian nationalist movement and their opposition to discrimination in South Africa, while retaining a very negative view of Africans whom she termed 'Kaffirs'. She both accepted the reality of the 'Black Peril' and attributed its source to white male exploitation of women of colour.[53]

As a journalist, drama critic and translator of Ibsen, William Archer

(1856–1924) provided the most specific treatment of the instinctive and sexual origin of racial attitudes. His account of his travels, *Through Afro-America* (1910), parts of which first appeared in *Westminster Gazette*, gave the appearance of a more dispassionate treatment of race relations. He recounted his conversations with both whites and blacks. For example, he much preferred Booker T. Washington to W. E. B. Du Bois, whom, despite his cosmopolitan intelligence, Archer found to be an idealist and a fanatic. Archer had little use for the excesses of scientific racism, expressed interest in black education, and found 'Jim Crow' discrimination defensible, but unjust in its administration, and unworkable in the long run.[54]

Nonetheless, at the root of the 'race problem' he identified an instinctive prejudice. He invited his English readers to imagine Nottingham – a city of a quarter of a million and comparable in size to Washington, D.C. – as having eighty to a hundred thousand black residents. In his imaginary Nottingham, its citizens would experience a daily encounter with physical differences which 'our deepest instincts, inherited through a thousand generations, compel us to regard as ugliness – an ugliness often grotesque and simian'. He warned against trivialising this antipathy as mere 'prejudice', and stressed that such 'race-instincts' were implanted by nature, and thus were 'an unalterable fact of white psychology'.[55]

The 'crux of the problem', according to Archer, rested in sexual relations between the races. In the American South, white males were subjected to the 'altogether unfair and unwholesome ordeal' of living in the presence of black women who were both 'physically well-developed' and unconstrained by conventional sexual morality. Archer thought that blacks, both males and females, were subconsciously attracted to whites as a means to improve the quality of their offspring. The 'degrading casual commerce' between white men and black women, as much as the reported sexual aggression of black males against white females, lay at the root of the white Southerners' attitudes, for 'much of the injustice and cruelty to which the negro [was] subjected in the South [was] a revenge, not so much for sexual crime on the negro's part, as for an uneasy conscience or consciousness on the part of whites'.[56] Archer combined this psychologism with a firm belief in black inferiority to white. This 'huge historic gap' was not a consequence of slavery, but had deeper roots in African savagery, and would require, in his estimation, as many as ten to fifteen generations to overcome. In his defence of white superiority, Archer rejected the claims of recent critics such as Jean Finot on race prejudice, J. A. Hobson and H. G. Wells on racial oppression in the United States, and Sydney Olivier on racial intermixture in the West Indies. Archer was so convinced of the inequality of the races and the power of 'race-instinct', that he recommended segregating African-Americans into a separate black state kept under the watchful surveillance of Washington.[57]

By 1914, the language of 'race-instinct' had come to rival and even replace the language of 'colour prejudice', but it never established exclusive jurisdiction in the field. The psychology of instinct had clear implications for what was now called 'race relations', but in prescribing a new social order the new language had to contest established conventions about the social, political, and legal expression of racial inequality. For example, William Archer's remedy for Afro-America in the creation of a separate, if subordinate, black state had little practical merit in 1914. The same remedy applied on the global scale of the British Empire had no merit whatsoever. As Benjamin Kidd, James Bryce and others realised, the European control of the tropics depended on the political subordination and mobilisation of indigenous or migrant populations of colour and their labour.

In fact, both critics of imperialism and the defenders of the older ethos of the civilising mission found that the new language of 'race-instinct', the evidence of the exclusionary racism of the white dominions, and the racial arrogance of officialdom in India and elsewhere threatened the moral purpose and therefore the legitimacy of the imperial enterprise. In attempting to define an 'imperial standard' for the Labour Party, Ramsay MacDonald noted that 'men on the spot' frequently claimed that differences of race and 'what are called "instinctive"' repulsions between black, white and yellow' meant that principles such as laws resting on the consent of the governed and the right to due process were inapplicable in colonial situations. Following examples using language expressive of white racist attitudes toward groups he identified as 'natives' and 'niggers' in the Congo, South Africa and the United States, MacDonald affirmed: 'the plea that the circumstances of a Colony in which the European population is only as 1 to 10 of the native justify a suspension of the ordinary methods of justice and the ordinary methods of regarding humanity, cannot be entertained for an instant'.[58] In a less obviously imperial context, Graham Wallas, probing the limits of reason in the political behaviour of democratic citizens in *Human Nature in Politics* (1908), also commented on racial instinct. Citing the behaviour of children of different races toward one another, the affection of white children toward their non-European nurses, and examples of what he termed 'sex love' between partners of different races, he concluded that 'intellectual association is a larger factor than instinct in the causation of racial affection and hatred'. American workers' hostility to Chinese immigrants, in his opinion, was simply a matter of lower wages. Even racial stereotypes underwent dramatic

[227]

changes, as the Japanese who were depicted as sinister in 1859 were treated with new respect, he claimed, after their victory over Russia.[59]

At the same time as these reservations were made about the new language of 'race-instinct', the older language of 'colour prejudice' experienced a revival. Concerned observers worried that the new intensity of racial consciousness and exclusiveness threatened the traditional claims of a colour-blind empire.[60] Sir Harry Johnston, looking to Christian religion to redress the rising intensity of colour prejudice and its threat to the moral sanction of imperialism, reported that at the coronation of George V in 1910, white South African troops refused to sit at the same table as Maori soldiers from New Zealand. For Johnston this display of racial arrogance did not reflect the spirit of empire; in his opinion, 'Here we see the real "little England" spirit!'[61]

In addition to this discussion of colour prejudice, a new word, 'racialism', coined in a different context, came to describe the practice of racial exclusion and discrimination. As one might expect, the inventors of the new term were victims of such practices, but ironically those victims were white and British. In January 1907, the *Daily Chronicle* reported that the manifesto of the new Constitutional Party of the Orange River Colony included 'opposition to all racialism'. The new party expressed the dissatisfaction of British immigrants with Boer nationalism, affirming, 'The party programme includes equal rights for all whites; the treatment of natives with justice and fairness, as in the past, but with the provision that the natives should be under local control'.[62] Those more critical of white settler politics recognised that past conduct toward Africans and Indians had been neither fair nor just, and thought that imperial not local control best protected the interests and rights of persons of colour.

While the new term 'racialism' as it appeared in the British press applied to Boer nationalism and attitudes toward white British residents in South Africa, it was a term which could not help but cross the colour line. In 1909, A. B. C. Merriman-Labor, a Sierra Leonean student and writer, created an imaginary parliamentary debate on a new constitution for 'Disunited West Africa'. His fictional Irish MP, Harry Hardbone, applied his home rule principles and declared: 'Any imperialism which does not take cognisance of the claims and rights of the black and yellow races, is selfish racialism, yea less – it is foolish nationalism.'[63] Merriman-Labor's political fiction, while original in 1909, pointed toward the future of 'racialism'. Invented two or more decades before the more common equivalent, 'racism', it would serve after the First World War as a critical term in the analysis of practices of subordination, discrimination and exclusion.

Prior to 1914, the term 'racialism', as far as the British press indicates, had a more limited use in describing tensions between British and Boers. By 1910, as the new Union came into being, a headline in the *Westminster Gazette* pronounced, somewhat prematurely, 'The Death of Racialism' in South Africa. Quoting from a letter from a British officer, the report claimed that one of the achievements of the Botha–Smuts Government was 'the abolition of Racialism'.[64] In an article on 'Racialism in South Africa' in the *Empire Review* in 1911, a 'Transvaal Correspondent' was less optimistic. Despite the fact that General Botha had 'deprecated and disclaimed racialism', the author doubted if Uitlanders could advance the cause of 'anti-racialism' in the Union Parliament. Concerned about the teaching of the English and history in the schools, the author observed that teachers were 'young Boers, the product of that hotbed of racialism, Stellenbosch Training College'. Practices of 'racial favouritism' in elections and in government appointments and expenditures confirmed that what the Boers had lost on the battlefield, they had gained by the premature granting of responsible government.[65]

Originating in South Africa, 'racialism' and the more novel 'anti-racialism' had, prior to 1914, a limited application. Nonetheless, the evident increase in hostilities as a feature of what had now come to be known as 'race relations', and the invention of 'racialism' to describe as illegitimate forms of preference or discrimination based on group identity reflected that such assertions, whether constructed as a product of 'instinct' or of narrow self-interest, presented a disturbing political problem. Old imperial visions of an assimilating civilising mission now seemed naive and archaic, but the newer resolutions of the colour question through exclusion and separate development threatened the health and viability of an empire spanning the globe and instituting new forms of inequality among its diverse peoples. Among those who had to deal with this political challenge were colonial office civil servants and administrators. Though largely unsuccessful in finding policies to resolve the contradictory pressures at work, they nonetheless offered some perceptive observations on how the dynamics of race relations would reshape the empire in the new twentieth century.

Colonial administration and race relations

Faced with the unprecedented and perplexing challenge of race relations in the new South Africa, the evidence of a more virulent white racism in the self-governing dominions and the United States, and the need to develop new policies for the administration and development of tropical dependencies with non-European populations, some colonial administrators attempted to sketch out the basis for what they considered to be new and peculiarly modern conditions of political and social relations. In these reflections the typologies of the anthropologists were largely irrelevant, and the new psychology of instinct provided not a guide but a problem requiring astute political management. The task was to construct a polity in which the legitimate inequalities of social class existed and were parallel to the divisions of race without creating a discriminatory political and legal framework which unsettled the delicate balance of coercion and consent that made for a viable colonial order. This task was made more difficult by the challenge Asian and African nationalists were now advancing against colonialism. It should come as no surprise that this delicate balancing act proved impossible; what is surprising is the perceptive way experienced colonial administrators conceptualised the problem, and their application of the language of race relations to this end.

One of the best informed and most revealing surveys of race relations within the British Empire at the beginning of the twentieth century was provided by Sir Charles Prestwood Lucas (1853–1931) who prepared such a report for the colonial office in 1907. Educated at Winchester and a first-class classics scholar at Balliol College, Oxford, Lucas, through competitive examination, gained a position in the colonial office in 1877. He subsequently was called to the bar at Lincoln's Inn in 1885. Serving under both Conservative and Liberal colonial secretaries, he rose to the position of assistant undersecretary by 1897. Lucas headed the dominion division in 1907, and was register of the order of St Michael and St George, a Victorian knightly order for distinguished service to the state which, by historical accident, was administered out of the colonial office. As the author of a multi-volume *Historical Geography of British Colonies* (1888–1901) and in *Greater Rome and Greater Britain* (1912), he made his own contribution to the comparative history of empires by colonial officials and others with an interest in classical history.[66] For Lucas, slavery, compulsory labour and racial conflict were potential causes of decline, and comparisons with Rome were not always flattering to recent developments within the British Empire.

By his education, his political and social connections and his interests, Lucas fit the mould of the gentlemanly class which Cain and Hopkins describe as 'the backbone of the Colonial Office'.[67] In his survey of race relations, Lucas' gentlemanly values conveyed a nostalgia for the kindlier liberal certainties of the mid-Victorian empire. He put his trust in the disinterested and paternalistic authority of the gentlemen of the colonial office, but was uncomfortable with the crasser commercialism of more recent colonial developments. He distrusted the forces of democracy and expressed alarm about the increased intensity and brutality of racial conflict.

In September of 1907, in anticipation of the need to address troubling questions in parliament, Lord Elgin, the colonial secretary, suggested that the office conduct some form of discussion or review of 'native policy'. Elgin expressed particular concern about South African developments, including the status of Africans in the Transvaal and the Zulu uprising in Natal, but also saw troubles ahead in West and East Africa.[68] At the end of December 1907, Lucas had prepared a confidential memorandum on 'The Native Races of the British Empire' for private circulation within the colonial office. Despite his thirty years' service in the office, Lucas disavowed any particular expertise on local conditions, invited his colleagues to offer criticisms, and stated that his objective was only to stimulate discussion, with the possible result of formulating some general policy directives or at least creating a forum which might monitor developments.

Lucas had an ongoing responsibility for the contentious issue of the white dominions' restrictive immigration policies, and in 1907, he, in common with many others, saw that developments in South Africa threatened to transform the historical role of the imperial government as the arbitrator of conflicts between white settlers and indigenous peoples.[69] As events in South Africa unfolded and Elgin departed from the colonial office in April 1908, Lucas' review did not advance beyond the discussion stage. Nonetheless, his memorandum provides an assessment of current difficulties and future prospects from a long-serving, informed colonial office administrator. In comparison to his Liberal political masters, including Elgin, Churchill, the parliamentary undersecretary, and Asquith the prime minister, Lucas remained more attached to mid-Victorian ideas of assimilation.[70]

Lucas began his memorandum with a definition of the 'native races' which, he claimed, conformed to the ordinary usage of the term. This definition of 'native races' comprised all persons of colour, inclusive both of indigenous peoples and of peoples and their descendants who in origin had voluntarily or involuntarily migrated to the colony or dominion. Lucas' definition rested not on a racial typology derived from science but on a sociological, or even more exactly a political, identity of race conforming to the common usages of colonial administrators and white settlers. His native races included all persons of colour, or in the newly coined language of his time, all non-Europeans or non-whites. The identity of 'native', with its own powerful connotations of being 'natural' rather than 'civilised', was a matter of the individual's or the group's skin colour, and not derived from the place of one's birth or the birthplace of one's ancestors. Thus native races included aboriginal peoples, the ex-slave populations of African descent in the New World, and the populations of Asia and the islands of the Indian and Pacific Oceans including migrants from these regions who, largely as indentured labourers, had settled in the Americas, Africa, southeast Asia, the islands of the Indian and Pacific oceans, and Australia.[71] Lucas then discussed these populations in terms of their status as citizens under the law and in accordance with their political rights and privileges including the franchise. For this discussion, he separated the self-governing dominions from the crown colonies and protectorates.

In the dominions with their politically predominant white populations, the citizenship status of indigenes and persons of colour varied, though usually full citizenship rights were accorded only to whites. Native Canadians had the vote in Ontario but not in British Columbia. In Australia, Aborigines were excluded from the franchise everywhere, and some states, using the ordinary definition of 'native races', as did Lucas, also excluded peoples from Asia and Africa, and peoples of mixed descent. Maoris in New Zealand were 'in theory and practice' citizens but voted for their own separate four representatives in a legislature of eighty members. For South Africa, Lucas reviewed the Cape coloured franchise resting on a property qualification, the exclusive adult white male franchise in the Transvaal and Orange River Colony, and the special qualifications but practical exclusion of Africans in Natal. He further noted that in Rhodesia the law followed that of the Cape, but in a population with a tiny white minority, in 1903, white voters outnumbered black voters 5,200 to 51.[72]

Lucas contrasted these political inequalities in the dominions with the greater equality that prevailed in the crown colonies, observing that in general 'in the Crown Colonies, the natives [were] in principle, and to a large extent in practice, as much or as little citizens as the white men'. Where elected legislatures existed, he claimed there were no restrictions based on race, but did admit that in the British West Indies, for example, while blacks were not excluded, property qualifications favoured whites. Where there was no elected assembly, Lucas contrasted 'the more highly developed Eastern colonies' with the 'less organised communities' in Africa. In the former case, where legislative councils existed, there was no colour bar. Sinhalese, Tamil and Moormen sat on the council in Ceylon, and Chinese representatives served on the council in Hong Kong and the Straits Settlement. In West Africa, a mixed situation existed, with some Africans serving on legislative councils, but also a special legal status and provisions existed, 'arising out of and improving upon such tribal organisation and authority of native Kings and Chiefs as existed prior to the introduction of British rule or protection'. In Papua New Guinea under Australian jurisdiction, the exclusion of Papuans followed Australian practice, but contradicted the imperial convention of not limiting legislative councils exclusively to white members.[73]

In Lucas' judgement, the most complex question, and the one most directly faced at that time in Africa, was the link between rights of citizenship and land tenure. Contrasting European practice of private ownership of land with communal forms of land-holding, he applied the historical British practice of linking the franchise to property, observing: 'ordinary citizenship and tribal tenure are incompatible'. Observing that the Glen Grey Act (1894) of the Cape was exceptional in encouraging individual land tenure, but expressly not extending the rights of citizenship, Lucas concluded: 'The general principle, however, is, I take it, that parliamentary privileges, such as white men enjoy, apply in the case of natives in inverse proportion to the extent to which the tribal system holds.'[74] Lucas' dislike for specific colour-bar provisions in the law and his tying of the franchise with property or other qualifications reflected his attachment to mid-Victorian principles. While he recognised that universal suffrage might exist as a right in some jurisdictions, Lucas preferred a qualified franchise. In 1907, the franchise in the United Kingdom was restrictive both by gender and by property. The household franchise with a twelve-month residency requirement excluded women altogether, and made roughly forty per cent of the adult male population ineligible for the vote.[75]

As a colonial office administrator, Lucas was anxious to see a role both for the imperial government and for British public opinion. Consequently, he thought that the 'native races' fared better in the crown colonies than in the dominions. In the latter, he identified responsible government with 'party' government in which whites ruled in their own self-interest. In contrast in the crown colonies, white officials, not elected representatives, provided a more personal administration and were subject to the authority of the imperial government which itself came under the scrutiny of British public opinion. He cited the West Indies, Mauritius and the Seychelles as possible exceptions, for there a long-standing and more numerous creole white population persisted in its slave-holding legacy, but to Lucas' thinking, crown colony government to some degree balanced white and 'native' interests.[76]

In most instances, Lucas observed, whites went to the tropics 'to rule and trade' but not to settle. They constituted a smaller and temporary minority subject at times 'to panic and consequent cruelty'. Nonetheless, the 'native' populations were primarily in contact with officials and had greater confidence in their impartiality. With longer residence and larger numbers, whites would be less subject to panic, although, he admitted, familiarity from long association 'hardly seem[ed] to diminish the colour prejudice'. The real check on these tendencies lay in the influence of public opinion in England: 'The fate of the natives in a Crown Colony rests with a power in England influenced by a public opinion which has no colour prejudice and only English traditions and views of political equality and justice'.[77] He readily admitted that these metropolitan views existed in ignorance of colonial realities, but nonetheless they provided a needed counter-weight to the racialism engendered in the colonial setting.

Having described conditions under the dominions and crown colonies, Lucas then identified problems that both forms of government faced in dealing with 'native races', and proposed some considerations for the development of imperial policy. He foresaw two alternatives: a policy of assimilation with the aim of creating a common citizenship regardless of race, or a policy of separate development. With the important exception of a people having 'an old civilisation of its own', such as in India or China, the policy of keeping a 'native race' separate and its institutions unchanged within a European-dominated polity was simply unrealistic and undesirable. His preference for assimilation expressed an unmitigated cultural imperialism which recognised little if any value in non-western cultures. To Lucas, 'The ordinary savage system of tribal chiefs is and must be unprogressive; it must break down sooner or later as this and that coloured man meets with new ideas, which it is impossible, even if it were desirable, to keep out.'[78] Under these circumstances and using an analogy to British parliamentary and legal practice, Lucas thought that policy should aim to create

> ordinary citizenship for all colours alike under whatever is the government of the country, and the making of laws for the benefit of natives by a Colonial Legislature in which they are represented, just as one class and another in this country is legislated for by a Parliament representing all classes. In other words, that the natives should be an integral part of the community, and that they should be legislated for rather as a class than as a race.[79]

Mindful, no doubt, of the objections likely to be raised by his colleagues in the colonial office, Lucas immediately pointed to potential difficulties with his treatment of race as comparable to class. Equality of citizenship created the prospect of a black majority in South Africa able 'to swamp the whites'. Furthermore, recent experience in the United States suggested there were enormous difficulties in creating equal citizenship. In support of his case, Lucas used the example of the Cape franchise and pointed with a measure of pride to the intervention of the Duke of Newcastle and the colonial office in 1853 to protect the coloured vote.[80]

Even if assimilation to equality of citizenship was the long-term goal, the policy of separate development was more practicable in the short term. For Lucas, separate development was at best a transitional policy preparing the way for assimilation. Lucas identified three possible ways to deal with this short-term separate system, and clearly he had in mind the situation in South Africa. Consequently, his reflections lost sight of the West Indies or other situations where voluntary or indentured immigrant labourers constituted part of the 'native races'. His three options were the system of native reserves, the employment of European residents as with some Indian princes and in the Malay states, and the use of native chiefs as government officers, which he identified with Lord Lugard's innovations in Northern Nigeria. A system of native reserves created the greatest degree of separateness by excluding whites from reserve lands. Lucas thought that protection from white appropriation of land was the primary purpose of reserve policy. The problem of the reserve was that its very separateness created an obstacle to assimilation, and consequently it was at best a temporary measure.[81]

In Lucas' view, the reserves were a training ground for citizenship, and to facilitate this end, he looked to the system of a European resident. Such an arrangement existed in Basutoland, 'where there [was] a well-organised tribal system with chiefs guided by white officers, and now possessing an advisory Council'. He thought that 'such a reserve may well be made a good training ground for ordinary citizenship'.[82] The 'personal element' of the resident, in his opinion, would best overcome the 'evils of a separate native organisation'. The main difficulty in South Africa was an insufficient number of suitably trained officials to fulfil that role. He differed with the Report of the Natal Native Affairs Commission which saw the purpose of these officials as being to break down the authority of the chiefs and the tribal system. In contrast, Lucas looked with favour upon Lugard's administration through district and village headmen in Northern Nigeria. This form of indirect rule, for Lucas at least, served not so much to preserve indigenous institutions but to facilitate a transition to western practices. The chiefs, he wrote, 'have become or are becoming regular salaried officers of an organised government working under European supervision; and, simultaneously, a fixed quantity, the district, is taking place of a moveable quantity, the clan, as a unit of the system'. Lucas recommended that greater recognition be given to the role of 'natives' in administration, even possibly establishing an order of merit, or even in addition to legal penalties, forms of demerit or stigma for a chief or tribe which violated civilised conventions.[83]

The aim of policy would be the eventual creation of equality of citizenship by building mechanisms for a transition through intermediate stages. Lucas admitted there was a risk that separate institutions would serve as obstacles to the process, but the policy also offered the attraction of maintaining for the present white political control: 'The ultimate goal being the same standard for coloured and white, there can yet be intermediate stages of citizenship, which will give the natives some standing and voice in the State but not equality with the white men.' The difficulty was to come up with a means to put the 'native races' on the road to citizenship without weakening the political position of whites. The West Indian solution of no official colour bar, but a property qualification for the vote which favoured whites was no longer feasible because it was 'not palatable with democracy'. Separate constituencies for a designated number of native representatives as in New Zealand provided for 'representation without equality'. Though a similar arrangement was recommended by the South African Native Affairs Commission, Lucas thought it was at best an intermediate stage and feared that, as the Commission intended, it would be a fixed settlement which would permanently under-represent the African population.[84]

For Africans to obtain a legal equality of citizenship, Lucas imposed a rigid test of assimilation. He thought that some form of educational test was essential, and proposed a variety of suitable requirements. Should enfranchisement apply to a whole clan or tribe, he suggested that three-quarters of the group be professing Christians with the ability to speak, read and write English, and a similar proportion be ready to abandon communal land-holding in favour of each family having lots of a size sufficient to confer the franchise. In the case of conferring the franchise on individuals, Lucas recommended a knowledge of English as a testimony to loyalty to the empire, and the profession of Christianity, except in the case of adherents to other 'civilised' religions such as Islam and Buddhism. In Lucas' scheme, provisions for training and education would be provided, and as the transition toward a western norm advanced, the special status of laws governing communal land-holding, of laws and courts, and of special taxes would be eliminated.[85]

The most difficult problem, to his mind, was how to handle this transition. He put his trust not in legislatures subject to the whims of elected party interests but in the personal element of the independent, trained resident working under the control a governor or permanent board. Lucas presumed that the subjects of this process, his so-called native races, would be willing participants in these changes. It was a measure of his ethnocentric and strident commitment to assimilation that at no point did he consider that a sense of ethnic identity defending traditional practices, or even a sense of nationalism seeking a different form of political settlement, might exist or emerge to push developments in an unanticipated direction.

Before turning in his memorandum to the immediate and most pressing concerns of South Africa, Lucas suggested a variety of means through which the colonial office could monitor developments and exert an influence. His suggestions ranged from an advisory board which could issue model laws or rules to a more modest information-gathering service. This information ranged from agricultural and in-dustrial training manuals to labour codes regulating the truck system, apprenticeship, labour services for rent, and uses of compulsory labour on roads and public works. Although none of these proposals had any immediate result, Lucas hoped that certain general principles would be enunciated which would then both influence colonial practice and be influenced by that experience in turn. 'There are certain principles which hold all the world over', he asserted; 'I should like as far as pos-sible to keep them in our shop window, to add to them from time to time, and to keep ourselves and the public, including the colonial public, informed where and how and when this or that principle is being put into practice.'[86] Such principles provided a justification for the intervention of the imperial government into internal colonial af-fairs, and it was this intervention that dominion governments most particularly resented. The elimination of this imperial factor was at the heart of the emerging compromise between contending British and Boer interests seeking to exclude Africans and other persons of colour from political rights and privileges in the new Union of South Africa.

In the concluding section of his memorandum, Lucas applied the principles in his review to South Africa. He listed the complications of the South African situation: the numerical superiority of Africans and the conflicting political interests and histories of the British and Boer populations. In addition, there existed other minorities, principally the 'coloured' – a largely Afrikaans-speaking people of mixed ancestry – and the Indian community, including indentured labourers in Natal. Lucas also accepted the commonplace geographic determinism of the age with its racialist implications. In his view South Africa had a cli-mate that in some regions bore similarity to parts of Australia and to the southern United States, where experience had shown that manual labour was better performed by blacks than whites. His gravest fear was that the system of native reserves would create a form of apartheid institutionalising permanent inequality along racial lines.

> The whole of South Africa is and must be for white and coloured men alike and interspersed. It is impossible to divide it up and assign one part to white and another to coloured. Moreover, there might be, as I infer, a tendency, having further developed and emphasised the system

of native reserves, to try and make a bargain with the Imperial Government on the basis that certain classes of natives might be transplanted to the reserves, leaving the remainder, even more than at present, a permanently subordinate non-citizen element to do unskilled labour under a dominant white community. Thus, instead of levelling up, of very gradually working towards general citizenship not based on colour, we should have more separation than ever, and be further removed than ever from a final solution of something like equality of races.[87]

Lucas recognised that the political task in South Africa was to work out a compromise, but he feared that his rather old-fashioned, and what some of his contemporaries would call 'sentimental', views would not form part of the settlement.

Consistent with his earlier observations, he recommended that native policy be kept independent of elected legislatures, and be handled administratively through a professional service under the high commissioner and paid for out of the civil list. To assist with the training of both European officials and salaried African agents with their administrative functions, he recommended a special colonial office standing committee and the annual publication of information and reports. In support of his recommendations, he appended the resolutions on federation and the native franchise from the recent conference of African and coloured delegates meeting at Queenstown, Cape Province, on 28 and 29 November 1907.[88]

Although Lucas' memorandum only had a short life as a discussion paper, it does provide some insight into the tensions between the mid-nineteenth-century belief in assimilation and the newer prescriptions of separate development. His commitment to the values of self-help and self-improvement involved him in support for the Working Men's College in Great Ormond Street. Lucas became president of the college, founded by Thomas Hughes and F. D. Maurice, after his retirement from the colonial office in 1911. His interest in improvement of the working class did not make him into an unreserved admirer of the labour movement. In a colonial office minute in 1907, he even suggested that the narrow self-interest of whites in the dominions was the gravest threat to the empire. In *Greater Rome and Greater Britain* (1912), he identified the forces of democracy in general and the labour interest in particular with greater racial exclusiveness.[89]

From his experience of dealing with immigration regulations, Lucas associated the growth of exclusionary racialism with the advance of democracy, and feared it might damage the mystique of imperial rule by creating new classifications of citizenship based starkly on differences of race and colour. He recognised that new ambiguities, not to say exclusions, affecting the status of British citizens and subjects made the mid-Victorian ideal of a colour-blind empire largely illusionary. The entitlements of British citizenship attached most clearly to those Lucas described as 'natives of British soil', whereas the status of British subjects living within various colonial dependencies and protectorates remained uncertain. This confused picture was further complicated by the process of 'naturalisation' under which foreigners or aliens became British subjects. At the Imperial Conference of 1911, each dominion asserted the right to define citizenship on its own terms, including the authority to exclude persons of colour regardless of their status as British subjects. In exceptional instances, under the jurisdiction of His Majesty's Government itself, specific racial exclusions existed, and in Lucas' opinion, 'it may be presumed that some of the highest posts in the Empire would in fact be reserved for white men'.[90]

Even though Lucas thought that colour prejudice was a legacy of the enslavement of Africans in the Americas, he drew a distinction between such prejudice and discrimination on the basis of colour. For Lucas, 'colour discrimination' is based on 'practical experience' and has a rational basis. He assumes that colour prejudice is the usual condition and is shared by different races, for 'The white man may be, and usually is, prejudiced against the coloured man, because he himself is white, while the other is coloured; and the prejudice is probably mutual.' Nonetheless, discrimination rests upon the firmer basis of the presumed middle and upper class attributes and character of the 'Englishman'. 'But the white man, or at any rate the English-man', he comments, 'finds more rational ground for discrimination, in that the qualities, character and upbringing of most coloured men are not those which are in demand for a ruling race, and are not, except in rare individual cases, eliminated by education on the white man's lines.' He claimed that this view was confirmed by the fact that within a multi-racial empire, non-Europeans would prefer to be ruled by an Englishman than by either one of their own people or by 'a person of another coloured race'.[91]

In Lucas' opinion, distinctions of race had been accentuated as the distance between peoples had lessened, and as the forces of democracy, especially in the self-governing dominions, had advanced. Leading the way in pressing for these distinctions, he considered, were labour parties, trade unions and associated working-class organisations, most evident in South Africa and Australia. These agencies of democracy attempted to protect or advance the interests of the white working class out of fear of competition from cheaper coloured immigrant labourers. In contrast to this modern labour movement, Lucas pointed to the preceding advance of liberal reform since 1832, which, in his view, attempted to diminish class interests and to advance a 'common citizenship and equality of chances'. With the advance of democracy organised through labour parties, the politics of class re-emerged. A new conjunction between class and race or colour arose from the working-class majority identifying itself as part of a white race, and seeking protection against the competition of non-European labour. 'We have then', Lucas observed, 'as against the great fundamental class distinction in the Roman Empire between freemen and slaves, which was not based on race, a great fundamental distinction in the British Empire which is based on race, and which class interest has adopted and accentuated.'[92] Lucas worried that within white populations an identity of class pitted labour against capital. He hoped that the sense of common nationality and citizenship, even 'the natural instinct of race', would prove stronger than the identity of class. According to Lucas, 'It may be conjectured and hoped that the race instinct in the British Empire, more natural, less associated with material gains than the bond of class, will in the end prove the stronger force among the white citizens of the Empire.'[93]

Out of the identity of race and nation, Lucas foresaw the possibility of retaining a sense of affinity between the peoples of Great Britain and the dominions. He also thought that this connection would prove stronger than the ties of friendship with the United States, where the influx of immigrants of neither British nor even 'Teutonic' stock weakened a sense of 'race affinity'. In addition, the United States faced its own host of difficulties connected with the question of colour, and would not welcome a closer affiliation with an empire equally 'full of race and colour problems'.[94]

The reflections of Sir Charles Lucas on the 'colour question' suggest that there was more to late Victorian and Edwardian racialism than the derogatory attributes encapsulated in the commonplace stereotypes of racial groups. He feared, yet perceptively anticipated, that inequalities based on race would be entrenched in the political and legal fabric of South Africa and elsewhere in the empire. This form of institution-alised racism was a modern innovation constructed to address new kinds of multi-racial societies created out of the history of colonial conquest of aboriginal land and peoples, the enslavement of Africans, the accelerating migration of European settlers, and the global move-ment of non-European peoples as voluntary migrants or indentured labourers. As an experienced and informed administrator, Lucas looked for historical precedents but found few to guide him. Wrestling with visions of assimilation rooted in mid-Victorian certainties now contested by the new exclusionary racialism of separate development, he attempted to sketch guidelines for future developments. Given that the new landscape of race relations was unmapped, he offered a tentative survey. Other colonial office civil servants and administrators also attempted to address the 'colour question', and while they shared Lucas's concerns they offered a different kind of analysis.

Sydney Olivier (1859–1943), another colonial office civil servant who had also served in Jamaica as a colonial secretary and then acting governor, focused his commentaries on labour and development in colonies with substantial non-European populations, largely of African descent. Compared to Lucas, Olivier, a member of the Fabian Society, offered a different perspective on the dynamics of class and race, and yet conventional racial stereotypes still informed his opinions. In *White Capital and Coloured Labour*, first published by the Independent Labour Party in 1906, he identified the recruitment, motivation and discipline of black labourers as a significant problem in the economic development of the West Indies and Africa. He defended the existing restricted franchise in Jamaica, while encouraging the education of the black peasantry as the means to eventual citizenship.[95] Nonetheless, his socialist politics and criticism of colonial policy subjected him to the scrutiny of colonial office colleagues and colonial secretaries such as Joseph Chamberlain. Among his political friends, he was equally outspoken, leading dissident Fabians against the South African War, and against imperialist policies advocated in *Fabianism and Empire*. Adopting G. B. Shaw's labelling of the Fabians as the Tories of the socialist movement, Francis Lee has identified Olivier as a Tory paternalist inspired by a secular vision of the civilising mission in which improving reforms flowed from the top downward.[96]

The combination of his experience as a colonial administrator and his socialism gave Olivier an unusual perspective. Concerned with questions of colonial development, and especially the problem of recruitment of waged workers, he recognised that patterns of labour in non-industrial societies conformed to traditional practices, whereas forms of regular, disciplined, intensive labour were a recent product of industrialisation. The creation of a landless proletariat, dependent on wage income and peculiarly vulnerable to capital's extraction of surplus value, were, in Olivier's political economy, recent historical creations peculiar to western industrial societies. Consequently, the problem of colonial labour was not one of dealing with the 'lazy native' but one of replicating the unusual regularity and intensity of industrial labour in a non-industrial colonial context.[97]

In *White Capital and Coloured Labour*, Olivier addressed conditions in what he described as 'mixed communities' having the 'difficulties that arise out of inter-racial relations in the industrial category'.[98] Using his Jamaican experience, his analysis was original in its language and in its comparative approach. He contrasted patterns of institutionalised segregation and virulent racism in the United States with his knowledge of the West Indies. While admitting that colour prejudice was evident in the British Caribbean, he claimed that neither formalised segregation nor such violent racial antagonisms existed. Furthermore, he saw that South African labour and social relations seemed to be closer to the pattern in the United States, and from there he feared the infection would spread to the rest of colonial Africa and globally to wherever there existed a conflict between white capital and coloured labour.

Olivier accepted that inequalities in social status between racial groups rested upon differences in class and culture, but he rejected crude biological claims of racial superiority, which he identified as the 'race-barrier theory', or the 'race-differentiation formula', or more simply as 'racial discrimination'.[99] In *White Capital and Coloured Labour*, he attempted to shift the focus away from considerations of the nature of race as an inherited biological category to considerations of the nature of social relationships within multi-racial communities.

> If we carefully compare the essentials of the situation as between a modern industrial community and a tropical dependency, where white enterprise is exploiting native resources, we shall, I believe, be forced to recognise that inhuman social conditions arise in them much more out of the opposition in the categories of Capital and Labour than out of the opposition in the category of race or colour.[100]

Olivier's thesis was an innovative yet early statement of the view that racial inequality and conflict were analogous to the social inequities and conflicts of class. Even though his thesis represented a departure for its time in its view both of race and of class, one needs to exercise care not to exaggerate Olivier's radicalism. As a son of an Anglican clergyman with a gentleman's school and university education, as a colonial civil servant, and as a Fabian socialist, Olivier accepted the legitimacy of the inequalities of social class, while seeing a need for state intervention to remedy grosser forms of inequity.

While he thought that racial conflict was rooted in the economic and social conflicts, he also accepted that there were substantial differences attributable to 'race'. In some measure, like Mary Kingsley whom he admired, Olivier offered a cultural relativist perspective. This view accorded a greater degree of respect and autonomy to Africans and their New World descendants, but also incorporated aspects of conventional racial stereotypes. In keeping with fashionable Edwardian interest in psychology, including the subconscious, psychic phenomena, and sex, Olivier generalised about distinctly African attributes defined as the binary opposite of distinctly European characteristics. Within this convention, he stressed black primitive affinities for the subconscious, emotional, spiritual and sexual aspects of life in contrast to white civilised focus on the conscious, rational, scientific and intellectual. He recognised that the complete human personality needed to encompass all these attributes, and to some degree African strengths matched European deficiencies. Despite his sophistication in attempting to be free of Victorian moral conventions and to develop a more relativistic stance, Olivier simply reinvented the old polarity of black and white, observing: 'The subconscious, subliminal part of the influences and powers that we discern in the human mind bears a much greater proportion to the conscious and rationalised part in the African than in the civilised European.'[101] Olivier then turned these attributes of the African personality into an explanation for black resistance to the allurements of capitalist wage-labour:

> Take into account with this fluid mass of temperament the great bodily strength of the African, his efficient nutrition, his reproductive vitality, and his comparative intractability to anything except physical force in the attempt of the white man to make him work for his profit, and it must, I think, appear difficult to imagine that he is not likely to have a good deal of his own way in his future social and industrial development.[102]

Reviewing efforts to compel black labour to conform to the expectations of white capital either by the creation of a monopoly of white landownership or by taxation, Olivier compared African resistance to poll taxes to John Hampden's protests against ship-money. In this regard, black labourers showed less servility than the white industrial proletariat. In Olivier's opinion, colonial developers could not rely on compulsion alone but would need to come to terms with Africans' understanding of relations of capital and labour, and expectations of productivity and reward.

While Olivier's treatment of relations between white capital and black labour conveyed a measure of respect for African resistance and expectations, his treatment of race relations was not free from the commonplace presumptions of his fellow Edwardians. In accepting the stereotype of black sexuality, Olivier's effort at moral relativism, including a tolerant attitude toward West Indian sexual and marital relations, still rested upon a sense of his own racial and class superiority. Before his first visit to the West Indies, Olivier had viewed the offspring of sexual unions between differing races as degenerate, but changed his mind once in Jamaica. There he was impressed by the capacity and advance of a coloured bourgeoisie. In his discussion of race relations, he viewed mixed marriages as a means to both elevate blacks and alleviate racial misunderstanding. In assessing such inter-racial unions, he adopted the conventional wisdom of white creole society and of his own Edwardian set. Unions between white males and black or coloured females were acceptable, but unions between white females and males of any degree of non-European descent were not. Using language similar to James Bryce, yet more specific about the relationship of white female fertility to national efficiency and eugenics, Olivier explained that in the case of white women, whose number of potential offspring was limited, 'their maternity should be economised to the utmost'.[103] Consequently, the instinct against unions of white females and non-white males opposed what he termed 'backwards' breeding. Later, Olivier, identified as a 'Negrophilist', would find his ideas about miscegenation used against his analysis of the class origins of racism and racial conflict.

While it would be quite ahistorical to expect Olivier to be entirely free of the hegemonic racism of his age, it would be equally myopic to overlook the sophistication and originality of his analysis of racial conflict. He recognised that white colonists in the tropics took the 'short-term view' in their narrow self-interest in maintaining their dominance over the non-white majority. Nonetheless, Olivier recognised that the self-interest of the dominant class, in multi-racial as in industrial societies, needed to be expressed in a longer-term perspective that equated this narrow self-interest with the greater good of the society as a whole. Consequently, he commented, 'In industrial relations everywhere this altruistic projection and immediate self-interest takes form in the class-opposition of capital and labour: in communities of mixed colours it takes form in race-opposition and colour prejudice.'[104] Contrary to the healthier state of race relations which he observed in Jamaica, Olivier feared, with South African developments in mind, that whites would exclude themselves from manual labour altogether, employers would be entirely white, and persons of colour would be the working class. In these circumstances, 'the division in industrial relations does really come to correspond with the racial division, [and] the class prejudices and class illusions that arise between the capitalist and proletarian section of civilised societies energetically reinforce the race prejudices and race illusions that dominate all barbarous peoples'. These prejudices and illusions develop into what Olivier termed a community or 'corporate consciousness'. His most immediate example of this false consciousness was 'the recently prevalent absurdity of the myth of the "Anglo-Saxon" Race'.[105]

Equally distressed by developments in South Africa and the growth in racial exclusiveness, Sir Charles Bruce (1836–1920), who originally was a professor of Sanskrit and an educator in Ceylon and Mauritius before entering the colonial service, saw present-day conditions as uniquely 'modern', and required a reconsideration of the role of whites and persons of colour within the empire at large, and within multiracial colonial jurisdictions.[106] In *The Broad Stone of Empire* (1910) and in *True Temper of the Times* (1912), written shortly after the creation of the new South African Union, Bruce drew on his own experience as Lieutenant Governor of British Guiana and then Governor of Mauritius. Having served in tropical dependencies with non-European peoples including Amerindians, the descendants of African slaves, and indentured Indian and Chinese labourers, he recognised that the economic development in these colonies had to rely on coloured not white labour. Unlike Olivier, Bruce did not rely on an analysis of capital and labour, but like Lucas he realised the danger presented by the growth of a more assertive racial exclusiveness. From his experience in Guiana, he attempted to draw a balanced picture of the contributions of Amerindian, African and Indian labourers, but on the whole he held disparaging views of Africans and African culture. He defended the system of Asian indentured labour claiming that the migrants benefited from the system, and that after serving their indentures the immigrants had the right to residency and citizenship.[107]

Bruce's remarks incorporated a racial hierarchy of Europeans and non-Europeans which also differentiated between peoples of Asian and African origin. He painted a largely benign picture of race relations under British colonial administration. This defence of past practices made him resist the innovations of a more exclusionary racism and led him to a more perceptive vision of the requisite basis of a stable colonial order. Citing John Stuart Mill, Bruce identified two possible strategies – a constructive policy or one of repression. The former he identified with the principles enunciated in Queen Victoria's proclamation in 1858 following the Indian Mutiny, which stated: 'No native shall, by reason only of his religion, place of birth, descent, colour, or any of these things, be disabled from any place, office, or employment under the Government.' The repressive policy he identified with South African laws prescribing both the separation and the inequality of the races.[108] To serve the imperial policy of development, Bruce thought that the only option was a constructive policy. In his review of the history of colonialism, he cited and adapted Herman Merivale's stages, identifying extermination, servitude and amalgamation as three alternatives. Extermination through conquest, and servitude through slavery or other forms of forced labour belonged to past forms of colonialism, whereas 'amalgamation' was the only policy appropriate to modern conditions. 'Servitude' involved 'exclusion from civic rights', whereas 'amalgamation', following Merivale, viewed 'the native as potential citizen'.[109] Using Merivale's framework, and contrasting it with the handling of ethnic divisions within white populations, such as the British and Boers, or the French and English in Canada, Bruce defined the 'colour question' as one of the most pressing issues facing the makers of imperial policy:

> The question that concerns us is whether the modern conscience, which, in the relations between white races divided by differences of race and creed has substituted a constructive policy of amalgamation for a policy of extermination or servitude, is to prolong its activity into territories where social groups are divided by differences of race, creed, and colour, or whether in such territories the policy of an earlier conscience is to be revived.[110]

For Bruce, 'amalgamation' was the only realistic option.

In Bruce's opinion, 'the struggle for the control of the tropics is a struggle for the control of the only agency by which they can be made of value, – a coloured population.' Asking the rhetorical question of whether such control could be exercised 'by force or by consent', Bruce argued that a policy of consent involving the identity of the population with the colonial regime through participation in the political process as citizens was the only viable long-term policy.[111] Under the modern conditions of the early twentieth century, he observes that two principles have to be recognised: 'first, that labour and freedom are indivisible, and secondly, that the social class that develops the material resources of a territory cannot permanently be excluded from a share in the administration of the developed area'.[112] Writing in 1910 and again in 1912, this affirmation was not simply a matter of liberal principle, for Bruce considered it part of the new political reality exemplified by Japan's defeat of Russia in 1904–5.

As a consequence of this victory, Bruce claimed, 'the theory of a monopoly of capacity inherent in the trinity of race, creed, and colour peculiar to the West was destroyed'.[113] While not ready to accommodate Asian and African nationalist demands for political or cultural autonomy, Bruce affirmed that in the long term an oppressive racism would only engender conflict and disaffection. In support of these claims, and despite his negative remarks about Africans and their descendants, he cited William Archer on the advance of African-Americans since emancipation, and from his own knowledge of the West Indies, he praised the abilities and contribution of what he termed the 'Afro-European' population of mixed ancestry as middle-class professionals. For Bruce, the emergence of Japan was only a beginning of the transformation of relations between Europeans and non-Europeans, and he rejected 'as a fallacy the claim of Western civilisation to a monopoly of the capacity of self-government based on an indivisible interrelation between European descent, Christianity, and the so-called white colour'.[114]

Although not optimistic that the 'colour question' had an easy resolution, he affirmed that the only realistic and ethical policy was one resting on established liberal doctrines that 'the principle of freedom [be] interpreted as liberty of person and conscience and equality of opportunity for all, without distinction of race, creed, or colour, under a settled government'.[115] This conclusion, originally presented in a paper entitled, 'The modern conscience in relation to the treatment of dependent peoples and communities' at the Universal Races Congress in London in 1911, challenged the logic of what Bruce termed the 'colour bar', which he identified with the United States and South Africa. Nonetheless, his description of 'modern conditions' and his liberal conscience accommodated the hierarchy of social class. Bruce presumed that, with the exception of the meritorious able to take advantage of equality of opportunity, a correlation would still exist between colour, labour and inferior social status.

Despite their awareness of the novelty of modern conditions giving rise to new patterns of subordination, now identified as 'race relations', and their prescriptions for a viable colonial future, colonial administrators such as Lucas, Olivier and Bruce were on the losing side of the Edwardian discourse of race and race relations. Each of them looked at developments in South Africa with apprehension, and what they feared became a twentieth-century reality. The new lexicon of race relations, sanctifying white prejudice as natural instinct, did more than represent an intervention designed for the subordination of persons of colour. The language of race relations sanctioned forms of segregation and oppression which in the long term undermined the imperial project itself.

The two decades before the First World War, from an external context informed by developments in the colonial periphery – principally the reconstruction of the new South Africa – and within an internal metropolitan context shaped by the new politics of democracy and the birth of the modern social sciences, witnessed the invention of a new language of race relations. This language originated out of the need to manage new institutional forms of racial inequality and separation associated with multi-racial creations of empire – the self-governing dominions and the colonial dependencies. This new discourse on race relations focused not on the imagined natural habitats of the biologists and anthropologists but on a new multi-racial colonial order designed by the human agencies of colonial developers, soldiers and administrators, by white settlers, and by the indigenous and migrant populations of colour subject to these imperial interventions.

One common theme, regardless of the viewpoint of various authors, was the anticipation that the new twentieth century would be unlike its nineteenth-century predecessor. Consequently, there were few lessons available from the past of either the British Empire itself or its classical Roman forerunner. This historical novelty arose from an awareness of the global dimension of world trade and the necessity for the development of the tropics through the mobilisation of the labour of persons of colour. In the metropolitan culture and its replicated forms in the self-governing dominions of white settlers, emerging forms of democratic governance, with the historical experience of the American Republic as an ominous precedent, suggested that democracy for whites demanded the institutional subordination, separation or exclusion of subjects of colour.

Aware of the political dimensions of what they termed the 'colour question', commentators searched for a viable political order in which racial inequality institutionalised in law was compatible with social stability in the present and in an anticipated future in which differences in culture between groups designated as races would diminish, and the demand for equality by those assigned a subordinate position would intensify over time. By and large, observers recognised that a policy of coercion, in the form of the recruitment of labour or through the law and its enforcers, would be of doubtful success in the long term. A minority drew broader conclusions from the emerging activism of Asian and African nationalists and from the military victory of Japan over Russia. For these observers, resistance to the enforced inequality of race and non-European demands for participation in democratic politics required a substantial rethinking about the colour question, and especially in regard to the coercive policy of institutionalised racialism most evident in South Africa.

While there is no doubt that the dominant voices in the new language of race relations argued that institutionalised racial inequality was required to control racial conflict and to keep persons of colour in a subordinate status, it would be equally misleading to ignore the dissenting voices engaged in resistance to these regressive changes.

Notes

1 Rich, *Race and Empire*, is a notable exception here.
2 Adas, *Machines*, p. 12, 199–21, 327–42.
3 Peter Mandler, '"Race" and "nation" in mid-Victorian thought', in S. Collini, R. Whatmore and B. Young (eds), *History, Religion and Culture: British Intellectual History* (Cambridge: Cambridge University Press, 2000), pp. 224–44; Stocking, *Victorian Anthropology*; Burrow, *Evolution and Society*; Lorimer, 'Victorian Values', pp. 115–17.
4 [Baring, Earl of] Cromer, *Ancient and Modern Imperialism*; Lucas, *Greater Rome*; Bell, *Greater Britain*, pp. 207–26.

5 Lucas, *Greater Rome*, p. 97.
6 Cannadine, *Ornamentalism*; Hobsbawm and Ranger (eds), *Invention of Tradition*.
7 Heyck, *Transformation*, pp. 155–89; Porter, *Critics of Empire*; Peter Clarke, *Liberals and Social Democrats* (Cambridge: Cambridge University Press, 1978); Michael Freeden, *The New Liberalism: An Ideology of Social Reform* (Oxford: Clarendon, 1978); Michael Freeden, 'Hobson, John Atkinson (1858–1940) social theorist and economist', *NODNB*, [www.oed.com], 2006; Michael Freeden, 'Rainbow Circle (act. 1894–1931)', *NODNB*, [www.oed.com], 2006; Schneer, *London 1900*.
8 Ronald Hyam, 'The British Empire in the Edwardian Era', *OHBE*, vol. 4, pp. 47–63; John Eddy and Derek Schroeder, *The Rise of Colonial Nationalism: Australia, New Zealand, Canada and South Africa First Assert their Nationalities, 1880–1914* (Sydney: Allen and Unwin, 1988).
9 Hobhouse, *Democracy and Reaction*, pp. 84–96, 101–18; Wallas, *Human Nature*, pp. 6–10, 136–7, 286–90.
10 Cromer, *Ancient and Modern Imperialism*, p. 140; see also pp. 95–7.
11 Cromer, *Ancient and Modern Imperialism*, pp. 140–1, 142–3.
12 Lucas, *Greater Rome*, pp. 97–8.
13 Sir Samuel Griffith, 'Australia and the coloured races', *Review of Reviews*, 9 (May 1894), 577–78 cited in Huttenback, *Racism and Empire*, p. 157.
14 Cromer, *Ancient and Modern Imperialism*, p. 88.
15 Cromer, *Ancient and Modern Imperialism*, p. 107.
16 Lucas, *Greater Rome*, pp. 92–7.
17 H. H. Johnston, '"The rise of the native"', *Quarterly Review* 212 (January 1910), 121–51, reprinted in *Views and Reviews*, pp. 243–83; Shaw (ed.), *Fabianism and Empire*, pp. 20–1; Susan Bayly, 'The evolution of colonial cultures: nineteenth-century Asia', in Porter (ed.), *OHBE*, vol. 3, pp. 447–69; McCaskie, 'Cultural encounters', pp. 166–93, and Bickford-Smith, '"Creole elites", pp. 194–227, in Hawkins and Morgan (eds), *Black Experience*. See also Chapter 7.
18 Christopher Harvie, 'Bryce, James, Viscount Bryce (1838–1922)', *NODNB* (2004); Marilyn Lake and Henry Reynolds, *Drawing the Global*, pp. 49–74; John Stone, 'James Bryce and the comparative sociology of race relations', *Race*, 13 (1972), 315–28; Bryce, *Advanced*; Bryce, *Impressions of South Africa* (London: Macmillan, 1897).
19 Bryce, *Advanced*, pp. 9–15; and *Impressions*, pp. 433–63, 568–600.
20 Bryce, *Advanced*, pp. 18–20.
21 Bryce, *Advanced*, p. 36; Stoler, *Carnal Knowledge*, pp, 61–6.
22 Bryce, *Advanced*, pp. 23, 25–7.
23 Bryce, *Advanced*, pp. 27–9.
24 Bryce, *Advanced*, pp. 29–30.
25 Bryce, *Advanced*, pp. 30–2.
26 Bryce, *Advanced*, pp. 33–4.
27 Bryce, *Advanced*, pp. 39–43.
28 Bryce, *Advanced*, pp. 44–6.
29 Gilbert Murray, 'The exploitation of inferior races in ancient and modern times', in Francis W. Hirst, G. Murray, J. L. Hammond (eds), *Liberalism and Empire* (London: 1900), pp. 118–23, 136–8.
30 Murray, 'Exploitation', pp. 142–3; see Bryce, *Impressions of South Africa*, p. 441.
31 Murray, 'Exploitation', pp. 143–8.
32 Murray, 'Exploitation', pp. 150–1, see also p. 141.
33 Murray, 'Exploitation', p. 156.
34 Leonard Alston, *The White Man's Work*, pp. 4–8, 16–18; Alston was educated in Australia, taught for sixteen months at Elphinstone College, Bombay, and then served in an administrative post for non-collegiate students at Cambridge. See his *Education and Citizenship in India* (London: Longmans Green, 1910), title page and preface.
35 Alston, *White Man's Work*, pp. 80–1.
36 Alston, *White Man's Work*, pp. 83–5.
37 Alston, *White Man's Work*, pp. 91–2.
38 Richard Jebb, 'The imperial problem of Asiatic immigration', *Journal of the Royal*

Society of Arts, 56 (24 April 1908), 595.

39 Jebb, 'Imperial problem', 587–8.

40 Eddy and Schroeder, *Rise of Colonial Nationalism*, pp. 209–21.

41 Green, 'Political 'economy'', pp. 356–7, 365–7.

42 Alston, *White Man's Work*, pp. 103–7.

43 Alston, *White Man's Work*, pp. 125–36.

44 Newton H. Marshall, 'Empires and races', *The Contemporary Review*, 96 (September 1906), 304–13.

45 Marshall, 'Empires', 314–15.

46 Clowes' articles in *The Times*, reprinted in *Black America*; 'The relapse of the negro', *Standard* (20 September 1889), 3a; 'The negro problem in America', *Spectator* (26 October 1901), 595–6; 'The yellow and black difficulty', *Daily Telegraph* (29 August 1902), 6g. See also Chapter 2.

47 Campbell, *Black*, pp. 194–9; *ASR*, 4th ser., 13 (1893), 155; *Spectator* (26 October 1901), 595–6; TNA, CO886/1 Dominions No. 1. Confidential. The Self-Governing Dominions and Coloured Immigration. CPL July 1908, p. 15, refers to 'slave caste' citing blacks in the United States, or potentially Hindus in Australia.

48 *Anti-Caste*, 1 (March 1888), 1; see also 3 (February 1890), 1; 3 (July–August 1890), 1; 4 (April 1891), 2; on Impey and *Anti-Caste*, see Chapter 7.

49 *ASR*, 4th ser., 11 (1891), 31 in this early reference opposed segregation; *Spectator* (26 October 1901), 595–6; Archer, *Afro-America*, pp. 233–5; P. A. Silburn, a member of Legislative Assembly of Natal, *The Governance of Empire* [1910] (Port Washington, NY: Kennikat, 1971), p. 220; Fuller, 'Separation of black and white in church', 382; Cell, *Highest Stage of White Supremacy*, pp. 211–12, notes that as late as 1905 'segregation' had not yet become a formal term to describe a policy of racial separation in South Africa.

50 *Standard* (25 May1911); *Daily Telegraph* (6 June 1911); *Daily Express* (30 June 1911); *Star* (26 August 1911).

51 Francis Bancroft, 'White women in South Africa', *Englishwoman* (March 1911), 262–9. Francis Bancroft was the *nom-de-plume* of Frances Charlotte Slater (1862–1947), a South African novelist then living in England.

52 'Nemesis in South Africa – white women reaping what white men have sown', *Review of Reviews*, 43 (January–June 1911), 249; *Review of Reviews*, 44 (July–December 1911), 227; see also 331, 385–7, 494.

53 Annie Besant, 'Coloured races in the Empire', *The Indian Review*, 14 (April 1913), 288–94.

54 Archer, *Afro-America*, pp. 45–58, 62, 128–30, 170–74, 234–5; J. P. Wearing, 'Archer, William (1856–1924)', *NODNB* (2004).

55 Archer, *Afro-America*, pp. 7–9, 71.

56 Archer, *Afro-America*, pp. 213–16.

57 Archer, *Afro-America*, pp. 222–3, 225–44. See also Chapter 7.

58 Ramsay MacDonald, *Labour and Empire*, p. 58; see also 50–7.

59 Wallas, *Human Nature*, pp. 55–8.

60 Jean Finot, *Race Prejudice*; John G. Godard, *Racial Supremacy* (1905); Hilda M. Howsin, 'Race and colour prejudice', *Journal of East India Association*, new ser., 2 (1911), 61–90; Bacillus, 'Colour prejudice', *East & West*, 11 (July–December 1912), 657–66; Spiller, *Science and Race Prejudice*; Annie Besant, 'Coloured races', 288–94.

61 Johnston, 'Racial Problems', p. 241.

62 *Daily Chronicle* (2 January 1907), 6e.

63 A. B. C. Merriman-Labor, *Britons through Negro Spectacles* (London, 1909), p. 161.

64 'South Africa's future – problems to be solved – the death of racialism', *Westminster Gazette* (11 April 1910), 6c.

65 A Transvaal Correspondent, 'Racialism in South Africa', *Empire Review*, 20 (January 1911), 400–5.

66 R. A. Butlin, 'Lucas, Sir Charles Prestcott (1853–1931)', *NODNB* (2004); W. H. Mercer and A. E. Collins, *Colonial Office List for 1906* (London: 1906).

67 Cain and Hopkins, *British Imperialism*, pp. 124–5.

68 Hyam, *Elgin and Churchill*, p. 367–8.
69 TNA, CO885/19 Miscellaneous No. 217 Confidential. *Native Races in the British Empire* [CPL] (31 December 1907), pp. 23–6 (hereinafter cited as [Lucas], *Native Races*; Hyam, *Elgin and Churchill*, pp. 316, 367–8.
70 Hyam, *Elgin and Churchill*, pp. 370–8.
71 [Lucas], *Native Races*, pp. 1–2; Lucas provided the following population estimates: in Tasmania and Newfoundland no Aborigines survived; in Canada, 100,000 Natives in a total population of seven million; in Australia with no accurate census, he estimated 100,000 Aborigines in a population of over four million; in New Zealand, 48,000 Maoris in a population of 900,000 whites; in South Africa, he listed 4,652,000 Africans and 1,135,000 whites distributed as follows: in Orange Colony, whites numbered one-third of the population; in Cape Colony and Transvaal, whites were one-quarter of the population; in Natal, whites were 1 in 10 or 11; in Southern Rhodesia, 1 in 46; in Swaziland, 1 in 100; in Bechuanaland Protectorate 1 in 120; and in Basutoland, 1 in 350.
72 [Lucas], *Native Races*, pp. 2–3.
73 [Lucas], *Native Races*, pp. 3–4.
74 [Lucas], *Native Races*, p. 6.
75 Martin Pugh, *The Making of Modern British Politics, 1867–1939* (Oxford: Basil Blackwell, 1982), pp. 3–9.
76 [Lucas], *Native Races*, pp. 6–7.
77 [Lucas], *Native Races*, p. 8.
78 [Lucas], *Native Races*, p. 9.
79 [Lucas], *Native Races*, p. 10.
80 [Lucas], *Native Races*, pp. 10–11.
81 [Lucas], *Native Races*, p. 12.
82 [Lucas], *Native Races*, p. 12.
83 [Lucas], *Native Races*, pp. 15–17.
84 [Lucas], *Native Races*, p. 17; Lucas criticised Natal for its restrictive qualifications for African voters and opposed specific 'race representation' such as in Natal where the three African representatives had to be Europeans.
85 [Lucas], *Native Races*, pp. 18–20.
86 [Lucas], *Native Races*, p. 23.
87 [Lucas], *Native Races*, p. 26; see also pp. 23–6.
88 [Lucas], *Native Races*, p. 33.
89 TNA, CO194/271, no. 197, 4 January 1907 cited in Hyam, 'The British Empire in the Edwardian Era', p. 57; Lucas, *Greater Rome*, pp. 102–7; Butlin, 'Lucas', *NODNB*; Jonathan Hyslop, 'White labourism', 398–421.
90 Lucas, *Greater Rome*, pp. 96–7.
91 Lucas, *Greater Rome*, pp. 99–100.
92 Lucas, *Greater Rome*, pp. 102–7; Lake and Reynolds, *Drawing the Global*, pp. 219–22; Hyslop, 'White labourism'.
93 Lucas, *Greater Rome*, pp. 107–8.
94 Lucas, *Greater Rome*, pp. 110–11.
95 Olivier, *White Capital*; see also 'The Transplanted African', an address to the Church Congress, Southampton, 3 October 1913, printed in *Sydney Olivier, Letters and Selected Writings*, ed. with memoir by Margaret Olivier (London: George Allen and Unwin, 1948), pp. 189–95.
96 Francis Lee, *Fabianism and Colonialism: The Life and Political Thought of Lord Sydney Olivier* (London: Defiant, 1988); George Bernard Shaw, 'Some Impressions', in Olivier, *Letters and Selected Writings*, pp. 13–18; Norman and Jeanne MacKenzie, *The First Fabians* (London: Quartet, 1979), pp. 58–60, 268–74; R. V. Kubicek, *The Administration of Imperialism: Joseph Chamberlain at the Colonial Office* (Durham, NC: Duke University Press, 1969), p. 19.
97 Olivier, *White Capital*, pp. 72–84, 126–31.
98 Olivier, *White Capital*, pp. 172–3.
99 Olivier, *White Capital*, pp. 51, 57, 59; see also 'The transplanted African', pp. 194–5.

100 Olivier, *White Capital*, p. 122.
101 Olivier, *White Capital*, p. 47.
102 Olivier, *White Capital*, p. 49.
103 Olivier, *White Capital*, p. 37.
104 Olivier, *White Capital*, p. 161.
105 Olivier, *White Capital*, pp. 161–2.
106 *The Times* (14 December 1920), 14c; Bruce, *Broad Stone of Empire*, vol. 1, chs 10 and 11; Charles Bruce, *True Temper of the Times* (London: Macmillan, 1912), pp. 55–76.
107 Bruce, *Broad Stone of Empire*, vol. 1, pp. 306–16, 324–9, 344–7, 350–2, 380–2, 386–96; and *True Temper*, pp. 70–5.
108 Bruce, *True Temper*, p. 66; see also *Broad Stone of Empire*, vol. 1, pp. 393–4.
109 Bruce, *True Temper*, p. 57; *Broad Stone of Empire*, vol. 1, p. 379.
110 Bruce, *True Temper*, p. 64.
111 Bruce, *Broad Stone of Empire*, vol. 1, p. 393.
112 Bruce, *Broad Stone of Empire*, vol. 1, p. 373.
113 Bruce, *True Temper*, p. 68.
114 Bruce, *True Temper*, p. 75.
115 Bruce, *True Temper*, p. 75.

PART IV

Resistance

CHAPTER SEVEN

Resistance: initiatives and obstacles, 1870–1914

Even in the metropolitan culture inhabited by 'absent-minded imperialists', race and empire occasionally provoked ugly confrontations. In 1887, under the headline, 'A Negro Charged with Assault', the *News of the World* reported that 'William Roberts, 50, a negro', was charged with assaulting Robert Bateman who was knocked unconscious and suffered a concussion. At the Hoop and Toy, according to two witnesses, 'the accused went into the public-house bar and begged for drink and tobacco. When refused he used offensive language about Englishmen'. Bateman, 'an old soldier, asked him (Roberts) what he was, and the negro became very excited', and assaulted Bateman.[1]

May be this incident was just another pub brawl and a sign that drink and politics don't mix. Nevertheless, conflicts over empire, race and identity constituted the explosive powder set alight by this confrontation. William Roberts was not alone. In a less dramatic fashion but in a more sustained critique, educated West Africans and West Indians reported from the colonies an increase in discrimination on the grounds of colour. In 1883, James Renner Maxwell, a West African barrister educated in England, wrote to the Earl of Derby, the colonial secretary, complaining about the new Gold Coast Native Jurisdiction Ordinance. The Ordinance provided for a new and broader definition of 'native' which, according to Maxwell, would include 'Eurasians, Mulattoes, Hindoos, Sierra Leonites, West Indians, Liberians; graduates of Oxford, Cambridge, London, Dublin or Durham; doctors of medicine and members of the Royal College of Surgeons, clergymen, merchants, and other respectable people'. He complained that educated West Africans under the Ordinance would become 'natives' and be under the jurisdiction of native chiefs whom he described as 'illiterate and uncivilized'. For Maxwell, who reported that there had been little in the way of race discrimination previously, the ordinance was an unprecedented innovation introducing 'American distinctions into a British settlement'. Two decades before James Bryce delivered his influential lectures on racial antipathy, Maxwell had forecast: 'Such laws are the natural harbinger of race-feeling and race-animosity.'[2]

The practice of racial discrimination had significant implications for the advocacy of those humanitarian agencies which claimed to defend the interests of British subjects of colour. In 1882, D. G. Garraway, identified as a West Indian coloured man educated in England, wrote from Grenada to the BFASS, asking for support in his application for promotion in government service. Charles Allen had responded by denying the request as being outside the scope of the society's activity. Garraway, evidently certain that an Englishman would be given the appointment, wrote sharply in response to Allen, with the comment: 'you are mistaken in thinking that your Society would lose influence in going out of the Anti-Slavery department'. While recognising the role of the society's predecessors in the abolition of slavery, he observed: 'under altered circumstances its policy might properly be extended to the recognition and protection of the coloured race which directly suffer from the class prejudices engendered by the abominable system'. The correspondent suggested that the anti-slavery society would find new support 'If [it] identified [it]self more closely with the interests of the coloured people in the West Indies'. He had some doubts about this support, for he noted: 'whilst the majority of Englishmen loudly denunciate the slavery of the "blacks" they cannot help showing their prejudice against "colour"'. Citing an example of a London bank which had substantial business in the West Indies yet refused to employ persons of colour, Garraway identified the political problem persons like himself and the anti-slavery society faced. Repeating Allen's commitment that the abolitionists were 'always ready to work for the cause of the coloured races', Garraway commented: 'We ask for no more than this. But how to secure it. That is the question.' Despite their shared objective, the West Indian correspondent concluded: 'we differ as to the means to be adopted in attaining that object'.[3] In his appeal for assistance, Garraway was unusually direct and Allen offered a less than sympathetic response. While the West Indian's concluding remarks were more diplomatic in tone, they were misleading on two counts. The BFASS, despite its past record, was not ready to take up the challenge, and Garraway and others confronting intensified racialism in this period had not yet developed the political analysis to advance their cause.

The task of addressing the emerging forms of racism in the late nineteenth century presented a formidable intellectual and political challenge. Unfortunately, our narratives of racism and of colonial discourse do not take into account the unprecedented historical circumstances faced by critics of the hegemonic racism of the age. Some by their silence or by their construction of a form of linguistic determinism even ignore or deny the historical possibility of dissent. The unprecedented circumstances of modern forms of racism included a more fully articulated racial ideology sanctioned by science, but scientific racism was not the primary focus of dissenting activists. Critics focused upon recent developments in what came to be known as race relations, including forms of discrimination, segregation and exclusion in colonial states, and in modernising multi-racial societies such as the United States, and in that centre of attention in the British Empire at the beginning of the twentieth century – South Africa.

The focus on the institutionalised expression of racism in law, government, the economy and patterns of everyday life came in the first instance from persons of colour confronting racist practices. Resistance to racism did not flow directly as legacy from enlightenment thought, or from the political radicalism of the early nineteenth century, but developed out of the experience of those who directly confronted racist practices. Resistance to slavery began with the actions of black slaves. When Jonathan Strong and James Somerset fled from slavery in England in the 1760s, they inspired Granville Sharp to initiate the legal and moral challenge to slavery in England and in the colonies.[4] So too sustained opposition to the unprecedented patterns of racial exclusion, subordination and segregation in the last half of the nineteenth century began with persons of colour. Out of their resistance, the injustice of racial oppression was made visible. Even white British participants in the development of forms of resistance had, in most instances, some personal encounter with a family member, friend or acquaintance which exposed them to the injustice of racial prejudice and discrimination. The history of the nineteenth-century critique of racist ideology and of the political analysis sustaining resistance has yet to be written. What will be attempted here is a sketch of the historical sources of resistance in the late Victorian and Edwardian periods, and of the obstacles which served to marginalise and even silence the voices of dissent in this period.

The practices of racial oppression were the site of the political encounter because it was against those practices that racialised persons sought relief, and it was those practices of subordination, discrimination and exclusion which exposed the contradictions in the ideology of empire. Contrary to the constructions of the scientists, the victims of racial oppression did not live in a state of nature. They also knew down to their bones that the constructions of their intelligence, aptitudes, values and behaviours made by the whites they encountered as administrators, soldiers, traders, settlers and missionaries – let alone by the arm-chair anthropologists back in London – were not simply false, but a lie and an insult.[5] Racism as institutionalised in colonial jurisdictions or in white settler democracies alienated subjects of colour and exposed the hypocrisy of the imperial mission. These were the vulnerabilities upon which critics of racism could open a space for a dissenting discourse.

Just as colonial administrators educated in the classics looked to the Roman Empire for historical precedents for the British Empire, so too the critics of racism looked to the more recent past of the anti-slavery movement for lessons on how to address the new challenges presented by modern race relations. Out of its historic claim to lead the national conscience in opposition to slavery and related forms of racial oppression, the anti-slavery movement contained within it the potential for resistance to the more exclusionary racism of the later nineteenth and early twentieth centuries. The seed of this resistance existed in the alliance between the more radical branches of British abolitionism and African-American fugitive slaves and abolitionists. Their advocacy constructed a contrast between American slavery and race prejudice and British opposition to slavery and freedom from prejudice. Frederick Douglass became the symbolic representative of this alliance, and through his influence, even after 1865, this alliance was kept alive. As late as 1900, the Address of the Pan-African Conference to the Peoples of the World appealed to the memory of this alliance to resurrect an international movement against racial oppression.[6]

There was a brief attempt between 1893 and 1895 to resurrect such an alliance in the Society for the Recognition of the Brotherhood of Man (SRBM). Although there were some continuities between these efforts and H. Sylvester Williams' Pan-African initiatives of 1897 and after, the principal British humanitarian agencies did not have the political capacity to be part of such an alliance. Nonetheless, critiques of the ideology of race and its political application in new forms of racial exclusion and subordination were part of the ferment of ideas incubating in Edwardian London. The severest test of resistance to racism was South Africa. The humanitarian lobbyists and supportive MP's failed in their efforts, for the imperial parliament held its collective nose and approved the race-based constitution of the new South African Union. This failure had consequences of long-term duration outside of South Africa. After 1909, these dissenting voices became fragmented and marginalised within the politics and culture of the metropole.

Roots of resistance – the humanitarian lobby

While there was a historical potential for resistance to racism out of the British abolitionist and humanitarian movement prior to 1914, this potential was never realised. Even after the victory over slavery in 1833, and over apprenticeship in 1838, abolitionists struggled with 'the problem of freedom'. Historically, they and their contemporaries appropriately identified their movement as an 'anti-slavery' movement committed to ending chattel slavery, and not so readily as an 'emancipation' movement seeking to enable the slaves to create conditions of work and life that would give substantive meaning to their new freedom. The abolitionists understood that their task did not end in 1833 with the act abolishing slavery or in 1838 with the end to apprenticeship, for they realised that more than 200 years of race slavery could not be obliterated by acts of parliament. Their problem was that their political ideology, including their political economy, gave them a limited vision of what emancipation might mean for the ex-slaves' future. This limitation was seriously compounded as the nineteenth century progressed.[7]

The historic achievement of Britain's ending of its participation in the slave trade in 1807, the royal navy's suppression of the trade thereafter, the abolition of slavery itself in British colonies in 1834, and the subsequent ending of apprenticeship in 1838 created a potent legacy for the ideology of British imperialism. In the historical consciousness that informed justifications of empire, abolitionist achievements were celebrated as altruistic interventions over narrow, economic self-interest. Here was one of the first instances of a national campaign mobilising popular support to persuade parliament to end an intolerable evil. There were more petitions and more petitioners for the abolition of slavery in the early 1830s than there were petitions and petitioners demanding the reform of parliament. Quite appropriately, during its first session in 1833, the reformed parliament passed the act abolishing slavery in British colonial possessions, but not India. This legislation was both an historic advance in the liberation of peoples from racial oppression and an act of cultural imperialism. The established system of colonial slavery, most clearly identified with Africans and persons of African descent working on the sugar plantations of the West Indies, had lost its moral legitimacy. The insurrection of free blacks and slaves in Jamaica in 1831–2 exposed the moral bankruptcy of the planters; and parliament, prompted by the intensified campaign of the abolitionists, determined that colonial regimes would have to conform to the norms of the metropolitan culture.[8]

Having achieved such a remarkable victory over slavery in British domains, the abolitionists took on the world. To address slavery in the Americas – principally in the United States, Brazil and the Spanish colony of Cuba, the surviving trans-Atlantic slave trade, and the internal trade within Africa – the abolitionists founded the BFASS in 1839.[9] Their victory over slavery also inspired leading Quakers and other abolitionists to persuade parliament to conduct an enquiry into the destructive impact of European colonial settlement on aboriginal peoples. With the parliamentary report of 1837, philanthropists founded the APS to keep a watching brief on colonial administrators and white settlers, and to ensure adherence to the commission's recommendations.[10] As philanthropic agencies seeking to arouse public support and lobby governments to address publicised wrongs, both societies exposed abuses associated with slavery and colonialism. Yet neither society was anti-imperialist in sentiment. If anything, these philanthropists were the true believers in the civilising mission. They supported British intervention in foreign parts and the transformation of alien, heathen and uncivilised cultures. Committed by their religion to the belief in the common origin and common nature of all humans, and to the assimilation over time of colonised subjects regardless of race, the humanitarian lobbyists saw their special task as ensuring that British imperial interventions adhered to the goal of the civilising mission. In the process, they became informed critics of forms of racial oppression that colonialism imposed on aboriginal peoples and emancipated slaves.

The humanitarians' engagement with the project of empire and the political conditions requisite for success in lobbying Her Majesty's Government meant that they necessarily made accommodations to the hegemonic racism of the new imperialism. They also had a hand in the construction of the thinking about race relations which, by the early twentieth century, had institutionalised and made legitimate the subordination of racialised subjects within the empire. Both the BFASS and the APS, the principal organisations still active after 1865, were precursors of what today we term non-governmental organisations or NGOs. Like their present-day counterparts, these Victorian forerunners share a history full of moral and political ambiguities. On the one hand they were critics of European rule over subject colonised peoples, but on the other hand they promoted an assimilationist and modernist vision of human rights, and sanctioned western intervention in the non-western world. They criticised the conduct and administration of foreign and colonial policies, yet had to work with cabinet ministers and leading civil servants. From their foundation in the 1830s through the remainder of the nineteenth century, they pursued their reforms within a changing metropolitan political context. Having successfully developed the techniques of a single-issue lobby combining influence within parliament with the mobilisation of external public support, the humanitarian agencies proved unable to repeat the successes of 1807 and 1833. After 1867, they found that their earlier tactics carried less weight in a parliament based on enlarged urban constituencies and the organisation and electioneering of modern political parties.

At the same time, transformations in the external colonial world redefined the humanitarians' agenda. What they saw as the abuse of aboriginal subjects and colonial labourers took on new forms with the expansion of the colonial empires and the extension of the global economy and its new patterns of trade, production and dependency. In the colonies of white settlement, the development of self-government, especially in relations with aboriginal peoples, reduced the role of the colonial office and the effectiveness of humanitarian lobbyists pressing for intervention on behalf of indigenous peoples.[11] In the longer term, self-government for colonies of white settlement and the diminished role of the imperial factor in southern Africa meant that in 1909, the imperial parliament sanctioned the constitution for the new Union of South Africa, which incorporated rule by race. In the same year, the APS, the principal agency championing native rights, ceased to exist, and amalgamated with the BFASS. Trapped within their own history of earlier successes against the slave trade and slavery, and recognising that their influence came by working with ministers and civil servants, the humanitarians' new Anti-Slavery and Aborigines Protection Society continued its international campaign in the declining field of abolitionist philanthropy, but in place of a discourse about native rights the society placed its faith in the imperial rhetoric of trusteeship.

The initial abolitionist victories held the promise that humanitarian agencies could transform the colonial world by assimilation to the norms of the Victorian metropole. Through the experience of engaging with this enormous and in some sense arrogantly naive project, humanitarian reformers lost credibility with their larger public and with the political elite. An ambiguous and toxic mix of essentialised differences by race and culture articulated by travellers, scientists, settlers and colonial administrators questioned the sentimental, moralised vision of assimilation advanced by the philanthropists. In its place, the realists as champions of the new imperialism advanced a doctrine of racial exclusion and separate development for non-white colonised populations.[12] The philanthropists were fully aware of their reduced standing in public esteem. According to a sympathetic article in the *Westminster Gazette* in 1895, the proverbial 'man in the street does not think much of the British and Foreign Anti-Slavery Society ... it is a pottering, grandmotherly kind of body, which is always meddling with the business of friendly Powers and making trouble for Downing Street – that if anything, indeed, it is a degree more mischievous in its operation than the contemned A.P.S'.[13] The humanitarian reformers tried to keep alive their older sentimental vision, but they too were supporters of empire, and piece by piece they made accommodations to the dominant discourse of racial exclusion and subordination. By this accommodation, the reformers gave some sanction to new forms of colonial oppression and weakened their own capacity and the capacity of their allies among colonised peoples of colour to resist the advance of the hegemonic racism of this imperial age.

In 1908, Exeter Hall, located off the Strand in London and the symbolic centre of the humanitarian and missionary movements, was torn down. In an address about his recent trip to Uganda at the National Liberal Club, Winston Churchill reassured his audience with a refrain from the Battle Hymn of the Republic and the memory of John Brown. Even though it now lay as a pile of bricks and mortar, Churchill confidently observed that despite the 'many cheap sneers' of its critics, Exeter Hall 'lay mouldering in its grave but its soul went marching on'.[14] Picking up on Churchill's remark, Sir Thomas Fowell Buxton, the president of the BFASS, was far less confident. The 'soul of Exeter Hall', he remarked, 'was never so emaciated, never in so poor a state of health as at the present time, for it required all the efforts of this and kindred societies to excite interest in the welfare of the weaker races'.[15] By 1908, there were fewer people ready to sing the hymn of emancipation, and many of those were too old to march.

Cast in this light, as precursors of modern non-government organisations advocating intervention in non-western cultures or seeking reforms in western colonial regimes in defence of human rights that were deemed to be of universal value, the history of both the BFASS and the APS needs to be reconsidered. Even though the slave trade had virtually ended by 1914, and slavery in Africa, the Middle East and Asia would, with the exception of notable abuses of child labour that still survive, come to an end during the first three decades of the twentieth century, this considerable achievement came with the heavy price of the partition of Africa. British humanitarian agencies, by pressing intervention against slavery in Africa, became advocates for the colonial occupation of the continent. The history of the enslavement of Africans, of the ending of the trans-Atlantic slave trade, of the emancipation of persons of African descent in the Americas, and of the humanitarian impulse which justified western interventions in the non-western world had a profound impact on the origins and intensification of European racism. This history has implications far broader than the creation of racist stereotypes, for it shaped the new lexicon of race relations, including those universal designations defining the colonial Other – the natives, the coloured races, the non-whites and the non-Europeans.

While the abolitionist movement helped to build the claim that British imperialism was inspired by, and even uniquely inspired by, humanitarian motives, these philanthropic agencies, the true believers in the civilising mission, were also among the principal critics of Britain's failure to live up to its humanitarian claims. Consequently, the humanitarian agencies were at the same time exponents of cultural imperialism and critics of exclusionary racism. This Victorian critique of racism is largely ignored in our scholarship, and yet it is the historical root from which modern anti-racism developed. Now it would be historically naive to expect a fully articulated anti-racism to exist in the nineteenth century, any more than we expect a comprehensive doctrine of human rights to spring forth from the eighteenth-century enlightenment, or a contemporary feminism to be articulated by Victorian feminists both contending with and acculturated within an ideology of domesticity. If such a thing as a Victorian critique of racism existed, we need to understand it in its imperfections, its incompleteness, and its ambiguities and compromises with the hegemonic racism of its time.

The two principal organisations still active into the twentieth century, the BFASS and the APS, out of their initial successes in pressing for the emancipation of slaves and protection of aboriginal peoples in the 1830s, were committed to the common humanity of all peoples regardless of race, and provided an institutional foundation for resistance to the new ideology of racism evident from the 1850s onwards. While there were several attempts to initiate campaigns against forms of racialism in the later nineteenth century, the institutional base of such resistance within established humanitarian agencies collapsed in the first decade of the twentieth century. The BFASS was the larger, more prestigious, and politically influential body. It was also more directly involved with the advocacy of British intervention in Africa, and made less of a contribution to the discourse on race relations. On the other hand, the APS, slightly senior in its foundation but smaller and less influential, advanced a more sustained critique of colonial administration and practice, including racism and racial discrimination. It also advocated a more interventionist role for the colonial office, especially in protection of native rights against colonial adventurers, merchants, white settlers and their legislative assemblies.[16] In articulating a doctrine of aboriginal entitlement and in the defence of the rights of persons of colour as British subjects, the APS had a larger political agenda than the anti-slavery society. It had to contend with the dramatic transformations colonialism imposed upon subject peoples, most notably in South Africa, and a public, including politicians and civil servants, that was less and less responsive to its message. In its advocacy and in its failure, the APS attempted to reinvent a doctrine of native rights to address the complex new dimensions of the coexistence of differences in culture together with a common entitlement to civil rights.

With the emancipation of American slaves, the BFASS was the principal surviving abolitionist organisation in the United Kingdom after 1865. In the twenty years or more of British efforts to assist American abolitionists in their struggle against slavery, the BFASS represented the more moderate branch of abolitionist philanthropy. From its foundation in 1839, it also took an interest in the slave trade and slavery in Africa, and sought to influence the foreign office to press for diplomatic agreements with European, North African and Middle Eastern states to prohibit the import of slaves.[17] As the principal anti-slavery organisation post-1865, its opposition to slavery did not develop into a sustained critique of new forms of racial oppression that were a legacy of slavery, or that accompanied the new imperialism. With the colonisation of Africa, the society supported British interventions, which were often justified as initiatives against the slave trade.[18] It proved reluctant to expand its agenda to address newer forms of coerced labour, provided a limited response to racist practices pioneered in the United States, and took a secondary role in opposition to institutionalised racism as it developed most dramatically in South Africa.

With the ending of apprenticeship in 1838, and the economic difficulties of the sugar trade, the abolitionist organisation largely accepted the dictum that the 'mighty experiment' in emancipation had not fulfilled expectations. In hindsight, abolitionists saw the £20 million compensation for the planters as a deal with the devil required to get abolition passed through parliament. In addressing slavery in Africa, they looked not to the West Indies but to India. In 1843, slavery in India and Ceylon was declared illegal, but it was left up to individual slaves, in their various circumstances of dependency, to assert their freedom from their masters' control. When applied to Africa, this path to abolition appeared more likely to provide for an orderly transition. It satisfied the abolitionists' desire for moral reform while serving the political requirements of the foreign and colonial officers negotiating with the African elites of slave-holding societies.[19]

After 1865, the BFASS reached the high point of its visibility in the years between the Golden Jubilee of the abolition of slavery in 1884 and the Brussels Conference of 1889–90. At the Guildhall in London on 1 August 1884, under the sponsorship of Sir Robert Fowler – a London banker, Lord Mayor, Tory MP, committee member of the APS

and treasurer of the BFASS – some prominent politicians and the surviving stalwarts of the anti-slavery movement gathered to celebrate
the fiftieth anniversary of the Emancipation Act. Along with the dignitaries on the platform sat Thomas L. Johnson, a former Virginian
slave and missionary then resident in England, and an African slave
boy personifying the objective of their philanthropy. The boy, who had
been freed by General Gordon, was presented to the Prince of Wales
who, following his mother's lead, agreed to become a patron of the
society. Speaker after speaker identified the abolition of slavery and
the £20 million pounds compensation to slave-owners as an altruistic,
humanitarian act inspiring Britain's imperial mission. They linked
this message to their own personal involvement with the abolitionist
cause. The fifteenth Earl of Derby, recently appointed colonial secretary in Gladstone's cabinet, recollected his father's delight at the passage of the Emancipation Act when he had served as colonial secretary
in 1833. William Forster, Liberal MP, best known for the Education
Act of 1870, remembered his father, a Quaker abolitionist, who had
died prematurely while investigating the abuses of apprenticeship in
Jamaica.[20] Scarcely a month after this rededication to the anti-slavery
cause, Gladstone, after much procrastination, agreed to send an expedition to Khartoum to relieve General Gordon, a celebrated anti-slavery
hero.

The crisis in the Sudan made the public freshly aware of the slave
trade and slavery and of abolitionist objectives connected with British
imperialism in Africa. As European diplomats gathered for the Berlin
Conference, and Bismarck sought agreement on an orderly partition
of Africa, early in February 1885, news arrived that the Mahdi's forces
had taken Khartoum and Gordon had been killed. In the shock at this
news from the Sudan, the BFASS memorialised Gordon by making him
an abolitionist martyr. It persuaded Gordon's three sisters to support a
drive for a Lord George Gordon Memorial Fund, initiated by a generous
donation of £500 from Sir Robert Fowler.[21]

Later that same month, the Berlin Conference concluded with an
agreement on the European occupation of central African territories.
At Berlin, King Leopold II of the Belgians gained recognition of his
International Association in the Congo basin by declaring his support
for free trade and by promising that under his direction legitimate
commerce would replace the slave trade and slavery. For the BFASS,
despite its reservations about the conduct of Henry Stanley, Leopold's
explorer-agent in the Congo, the king's initiative offered the possibility
of giving the anti-slavery movement a new international dimension.[22]
From a European perspective, abolitionist philanthropy was suspect
as a peculiarly British and Protestant charity. Under the leadership of

Cardinal Lavigerie, continental Catholic anti-slavery organisations supported Leopold's initiatives in the Congo and offered the BFASS a new international alliance. On 31 July 1888, at a large public meeting chaired by Lord Granville, with many dignitaries including Cardinal Manning and even, so it was rumoured, King Leopold himself in attendance, the BFASS welcomed Cardinal Lavigerie to address the horrors of the African slave trade. The meeting concluded with a call for the newly allied British and continental abolitionists to press their governments to act in concert to bring an end to the slave trade in Africa.[23]

On 21 April 1890, the BFASS launched a national petition, the Memorial to the Brussels Conference. Designed to convey the support of the political and social elite, it was unlike the monster petitions of the 1830s. It had just 746 signatures organised in a deferential hierarchical order: 37 executive officers and committee members of the BFASS; 10 eminent women including seven titled ladies and the three sisters of General Gordon; 26 peers including the two archbishops and eight bishops; 66 members of the House of Commons; 180 professionals including fifty-six clergy, thirty-four associated with universities or learned societies, six doctors, ten lawyers, and twenty-eight headmasters and teachers; 69 municipal politicians from twenty-two cities and including fourteen mayors; and 358 members of the general public of whom seventy-nine, or twenty-two per cent, were women. Imperial notables on the list included James Stevenson, Chair of the African Lakes Company, Joseph Thomson, an explorer into Masailand and other regions of Africa, and H. Rider Haggard.[24] Wishing to keep a singular focus on the slave trade and slavery and concerned about possible conflicts with its European humanitarian partners, the BFASS initially refused to join the APS and other lobby groups advocating restrictions on the liquor and gun trades in Africa.[25]

In its representation of support from the late Victorian elite, the Memorial to the Brussels Conference marked the high point of the anti-slavery society's lobbying through a well-organised public campaign. In the 1880s, with some variation from year to year, the BFASS had an annual budget of just over £1,500, a reserve fund accumulated from bequests, and its principal publication, the *Anti-Slavery Reporter*, had a circulation of 550 copies for members and 1,200 for subscribers.[26] By the 1890s, its revenues suffered a steady decline. In 1897, with the 'exhaustion' of funds, and the failing health of J. E. Teall, its assistant secretary, Arthur Pease, the president, asked the committee consider the society's future. Committee members rallied round the cause, though a supportive letter from Dr R. N. Cust and Richard Shore commented that 'whilst admitting slavery dies hard', they still wondered whether it was 'necessary any longer to keep up a special Agency to stamp out the dying embers'. Nonetheless, the committee decided there was still work to be accomplished, and put reinvigorated, if not altogether successful, efforts into restoring the society's finances.[27] From the origins of the anti-slavery movement, women had played an important role, and now with the BFASS in decline, its membership was largely maintained by the increase in the number of women members.[28]

With limited funds, the BFASS focused its attentions on East Africa. On a mutual understanding, the APS monitored developments in southern Africa and West Africa. With the acquisition of Zanzibar and Pemba as British protectorates in 1890, the BFASS could concentrate on familiar ground because in the new protectorates the clove plantations relied upon slave labour. Contrary to the empire's anti-slavery past, British authorities administered the import of slaves and their conditions of residence and labour. Through the 1890s, this British complicity with slavery became the principal issue in the society's *Anti-Slavery Reporter.*[29]

By keeping its focus on developments that fit its historic mission, the BFASS proved reluctant, even politically incapable, of expanding its mandate to address the newer forms of coerced labour introduced with the colonisation and economic development of Africa. It did not take up in any concerted fashion the recruitment and exploitation of African labour in railway or other construction projects, or in the South African mining industry. The *Reporter's* occasional article on African economic development favoured industrial training for Africans under missionary or other European supervision.[30] Its support for Leopold II's Congo Free State made the society, like the Baptist Missionary Society working among Congolese people, largely silent on the abuses of the concessionaire companies. This silence was not a result of ignorance. Even though the APS had supported Leopold and his commitment against slavery and the gun and liquor trades at Brussels in 1890, within a year, and a decade before E. D. Morel founded the Congo Reform Association (CRA), Fox Bourne began publicising abuses. It was only with Roger Casement's report in 1904 that the BFASS joined the critics of Leopold's Congo.[31] With the South African War (1899–1902) and the task of a post-war reconstruction, the BFASS followed the lead of the APS in its defence of the legal status and political rights of the brown and black majority.[32]

Beyond the question of slavery in Zanzibar and Pemba, the *Anti-Slavery Reporter* contained articles from other sources on developments in the United States, the West Indies and elsewhere. As a compendium of anti-slavery information, the editor of the *Anti-Slavery Reporter* regularly printed a caveat that the opinions expressed were not necessarily endorsed by the BFASS.[33] Reports from the United States of lynching and convict leasing called for action, for in the abolitionists' view, both were a reinvention of slavery. Commentaries in the *Anti-Slavery Reporter* on Reconstruction and the reassertion of white power in the South largely attributed these developments to the excesses of American democracy. It expressed concern about the growth of antipathy to African-Americans among whites in the north as well as the south. While critical of any suggestion of returning ex-slaves to Africa, and expressing its opposition to race separation, the *Anti-Slavery Reporter* made few specific comments about sharecropping and Jim Crow legislation. Its commentaries on English press reports on American race relations, while dissenting from extreme expressions of racism, largely accepted the state of racial inequality.[34] Surprised by the outrage in the American press over Theodore Roosevelt's lunch with Booker T. Washington at the White House, the *Anti-Slavery Reporter* praised Washington and his Tuskegee Institute for its programme of self-help and industrial training. It saw such a programme as the means for uplifting the black population from the legacy of slavery and as a model for development in Africa.[35]

While the interest in the American 'Negro Problem', as it was commonly called, was one legacy of earlier anti-slavery commitments, far less attention was paid to the West Indies. In 1888, the Golden Jubilee of the ending of apprenticeship, the real ending of slavery in the Afro-Caribbean historical consciousness, was celebrated in the West Indies, but the BFASS did not sponsor a celebration in the United Kingdom. From the West Indian press, the *Anti-Slavery Reporter*, in 1888 and again in 1898, reprinted speeches at official celebrations. As a direct challenge to J. A. Froude and others who reported a decline of ex-slaves into African savagery since emancipation, speakers celebrated the advance in education, professional accomplishments and status of the generation whose parents had been liberated in 1838. In 1893, the *Anti-Slavery Reporter* gave notice of a new journal of the Council of the West Indian Union, the *West Indian Journal and Civil Rights Guardian*. The purpose of the Union was to 'investigate cases of infringement of civil rights of members', and to use 'all proper political means to secure and enlarge the civil rights of British subjects in the West Indies'. The editor of the *Anti-Slavery Reporter* noted that the West Indian journal 'would no doubt claim the sympathy of the Anti-Slavery Society', though some of its concerns appeared 'to be of too political a nature' to fall under the mandate of the Society's constitution.[36] Still ready to celebrate 1834 and 1838 as the successful, if incomplete, achievement of British humanitarianism, their measured assessment of the outcome of the great experiment made them more aware of the complexity of the transition from slave to free labour. Less confident in the liberation of people from racial oppression, they put more trust in control exercised by imperial authority. This confidence in the British Empire as an instrument of progress rested upon the belief that the exercise of imperial authority would be subject to the scrutiny of those humanitarian agencies which still claimed to be the voice of the national conscience.

Trapped within its own history, and trusting to the benevolence of empire, the BFASS failed to take up the challenge of newer forms of racial oppression evident at the beginning of the twentieth century. In July of 1906, the BFASS committee reported receiving 'a letter from a coloured man in Liverpool' proposing a celebration of the centenary of the abolition of the slave trade. Unlike the orchestrated jubilee of 1884, in 1907 the BFASS determined that with the continued oppression of Africans, such as in the Congo, it would not be appropriate to celebrate the centenary.[37] Some of descendants of liberated slaves in Freetown, Sierra Leone, held their own celebration on the one-hundredth anniversary, 25 March 1907. In London, A. B. C. Merriman-Labor, a Sierra Leonean law student and writer, arranged for a party of Africans and persons of African descent to hold a private service in Westminster Abbey. At the memorials for Wilberforce and other abolitionists, representatives placed wreaths on behalf of Africans, on behalf of Africans in America and the West Indies, and on behalf of Africans in the United Kingdom.[38] This private service in 1907 is in striking contrast to the commemorations that occurred in 2007. Perhaps not deliberately, but symbolically in 1907, the principal agency of the anti-slavery movement turned the struggle against racism and empire over to other historical actors and agencies.

As we have seen in Chapters 5 and 6 on the language of race relations, the humanitarian organisation more directly involved in a dissenting racial discourse was the APS. Founded in 1836, and inspired by the parliamentary commission's strident condemnation of the destructive impact of colonialism, the APS more directly than the BFASS confronted its own government's colonial policies and administration. It endeavoured to give meaning to the principle of equality before the law in colonial jurisdictions, and saw itself as a watchdog over the process of transformation in which it assumed that non-European peoples over time would assimilate to British conditions of modernity. With the development of self-government for white settlement communities, and their political jurisdiction over aboriginal peoples, the role of the colonial office and the APS diminished. The humanitarians' attentions focused on crown colonies, especially the new colonial acquisitions in West Africa and the turbulent frontier of southern Africa.[39]

[269]

Though not directly engaged in the abolitionist campaign against American slavery, after 1865 the APS rather than the BFASS carried forward the legacy of the more radical branches of British abolitionism. This link was established through Frederick William Chesson, the secretary of the APS from 1866 to 1888. Dr Thomas Hodgkin, a Quaker physician and a founder of both the APS and the Ethnological Society of London, had alienated his abolitionist friends by supporting the American Colonization Society and its plans for the return of American slaves to Africa. Hodgkin had an interest in the liberated slave creole communities of Sierra Leone and Liberia. To promote trade and friendship he hosted meetings of African-American and African visitors in his home in London. Hodgkin supported the North in the American Civil War, and hosted the first meeting of the Freedman's Aid Society established to assist emancipated slaves. Chesson became Hodgkin's assistant secretary in 1855, and participated in these meetings with African and African-American visitors.[40]

Chesson recorded that he first became aware of racial injustice while visiting his stepfather in New York. There he had attended a meeting of 3,000 African-Americans protesting against the fugitive slave law. On his return to England, he assisted George Thompson, a lecturer on slavery, free trade and peace, and leader among British supporters of William Lloyd Garrison. Chesson and Thompson's daughter, Amelia, married in 1855 shortly before he took up his duties with the APS. As well as his work for the APS, Chesson was a journalist for the *Morning Star* and *Daily News*. For the rest of his life he was an organiser and lobbyist for various liberal causes. He directed publicity for the Emancipation Committee formed to support the North and oppose Confederate propaganda. He served a similar role for the Jamaica Committee in its prosecution of Governor Eyre. After 1867, he became a Gladstonian Liberal, especially noted as a leading organiser in the Bulgarian agitation of 1878 and forming the South Africa Committee to shore up the imperial presence there against settler resistance.[41]

An organisation like the APS, with a smaller membership and more limited funds than the BFASS, was heavily dependent on the work of its secretary in managing its meetings, publications and lobbying efforts. When Chesson died unexpectedly in 1888 at age 55, the executive committee proposed that for efficiencies in cost, organisation and membership, the APS should join forces with the BFASS. The anti-slavery society preparing for the Brussels Conference and anxious not to be distracted from its singular focus on slavery rejected the proposal.[42] The APS then searched for a new secretary, knowing that Chesson would be a difficult person to replace.

In their new secretary, Henry Richard Fox Bourne, they found someone who by family connection was similarly rooted in the abolitionist movement, and an experienced journalist of a radical liberal stripe. Fox Bourne was born in Jamaica in 1837, while his father, a Nonconformist abolitionist and publicist, served as a stipendiary magistrate dealing with the apprenticeship system. In 1841, the family moved to British Guiana and returned to England in 1848. After a private education, Fox Bourne attended the University of London and found employment in the War Office. While a civil servant he also worked as a journalist writing for *Dickens' Household Words* and the *Examiner*, a weekly with a distinguished radical past. Leaving the civil service in 1870, he took over ownership of the *Examiner*, hoping to restore its reputation. Among British journalists, Fox Bourne, informed by visits with Karl Marx, took the exceptional stance of defending the Paris Commune. His radical associations did not draw him toward socialism, for throughout his life he remained attached to a mid-Victorian radicalism closer to the liberalism of John Stuart Mill. He was not successful as a newspaper owner, and sold the *Examiner* in 1873 to become editor of the *Weekly Dispatch*, a radical newspaper for the working class. During this period, he wrote a number of romanticised histories of British overseas commerce and empire for adult and juvenile readers and a biography of John Locke, and in 1873 he edited a volume of tributes to John Stuart Mill. In 1887, he published his best-known and still useful work on the history of English newspapers, which provided an insider's look at the world of Victorian journalism.[43]

Although supportive of Gladstone and the Liberals, the *Weekly Dispatch* and its editor defended their own independent, radical position. The paper criticised the limits of the Third Reform Bill of 1884 and of the Redistribution Act of 1885. When Gladstone's conversion to home rule wreaked havoc in the Liberal ranks, Fox Bourne and the *Weekly Dispatch*, supporters of home rule but critics of Gladstone's bill, warned readers of the demagoguery of the GOM.[44] As a consequence, Fox Bourne lost his position as editor. After a couple of years as a writer and journalist, he gained the position of secretary of the APS.

Arriving at the APS, Fox Bourne immediately had to deal with a number of contentious issues. The APS's participation in meetings on the liquor and gun trades in preparation for lobbying at Leopold II's Brussels Conference ran afoul of the BFASS's insistence on a singular focus on the slave trade and slavery.[45] Fox Bourne had published a critical article on the conduct of British chartered companies in West Africa, and received a rebuke from Sir George Goldie of the Niger Company.[46] More significantly, Frank Mackarness, a Cape Town lawyer, and Flora Shaw, a journalist on imperial affairs for *The Times*, had picked up on Sir Hercules Robinson's parting remarks as High Commissioner on 'irresponsible' bodies in England. Independently, they each identified these 'irresponsible' bodies with the APS. Mackarness went so far as to repeat Premier Gordon Sprigg's comment that the APS was the greatest enemy of the black and coloured population in South Africa, and that the society preached disloyalty among the Queen's African subjects. Fox Bourne offered a vigorous defence of the APS, claiming that given settlers' treatment of Africans there was every need for the APS to intervene. Fox Bourne coupled this claim with a more controversial observation that the firm but paternalistic conduct of the Boers towards African servants and labourers was less abusive than the exploitive labour practices in British colonies.[47] The South African agitation came from critics of the ASP alliance with the Colenso family in defence of the Zulus and Cetshwayo and from supporters of Cecil Rhodes. In a public letter of March 1889, the APS had advised Lobengula not to make mining concessions to the British South Africa Company.[48] In 1891, some of Rhodes' friends attended meetings of the APS and made remarks defending the British South Africa's Company's dealing with Africans. Harriet Colenso rebuked Fox Bourne for inviting the Duke of Fife, vice-chairman of the company's board, and giving him the opportunity to claim that the company supported APS policies. In the *Anti-Caste*, Colenso and Catherine Impey criticised the APS for its association with Rhodes' company. Thereafter, Fox Bourne, largely in cooperation with Harriet Colenso, in special pamphlets and in the *Aborigines' Friend*, offered a sustained criticism of Rhodes and the conduct of his company's agents.[49]

Among APS informants, Fox Bourne relied upon western-educated Africans or persons of African descent who complained of racial discrimination, and reported the abusive conduct of colonial officials, white settlers and traders. In 1889, Fox Bourne wrote to the Reverend James Johnson to ask if he would serve as a local correspondent of the APS. Johnson, a leader among the CMS native pastorate and an early nationalist, expressed his appreciation of the work of the APS, for too many 'Christian and civilised people' did not understand that 'Might is not Right'. Giving a supportive yet realistic appraisal of the APS, he observed: 'Your Society's exposure of facts cannot but do much good if even it should not always succeed to produce imperial censure upon unjust unnecessarily severe and cruel proceedings on the part of those who exercise authority abroad for the Empire and others.'[50] The APS's African correspondents used their status as British subjects to defend their rights under the law. In 1891, 'coloured' migrants from the Cape complained that they were subject to pass laws in the Transvaal and, unlike African-Americans there, treated as 'natives', and denied their status as British subjects. Similarly, correspondents from British West African colonies working in the Congo Free State complained of their conditions of employment and offered early reports of abusive practices there.[51]

These informants confirmed Fox Bourne's confidence in assimilation to modern British ways, or what he described as 'civilised' conditions. On the other hand, he realised that the new, more assertive colonialism in Africa forced change by armed force and by the coercive power of administrative practices and the law. In the short term, these instruments of colonialism inflicted harm on African peoples, and in the longer term they created new obstacles to the goal of assimilation. While he respected and cited Mary Kingsley's more culturally relative and sympathetic view of African cultures, he did not share her contempt, and the contempt of many colonial officials, for westernised Africans put down as 'mimic' men – neither fully Europeanised nor authentically African.[52]

Beginning in 1891, Fox Bourne delivered a series of papers in which he attempted to identify conditions under which colonialism could be made compatible with the protection and improvement of African rights and interests. Still tied to the Victorian language of 'civilised' and 'uncivilised' conditions, and still describing Europeans and Africans as 'superior' and 'weaker' races, his attempted resolution of these issues articulated a set of 'native' rights. Rooted in his radical liberalism, his vision presumed that Africans and Europeans shared a common humanity. From his knowledge of West African engagement in overseas trade, he believed that, with new opportunities for the production of goods and commerce on a wider global market place, Africans would respond as projected by the 'rational' man of his political economy. Consequently, he believed, reflecting the Quaker origins of the APS, that the process of transition from 'uncivilised' to 'civilised' conditions could occur over time not by coercion but by the agency and consent of Africans themselves.[53]

Such a view may seem hopelessly utopian, though it bears closer resemblance to more recent development strategies than the coercive practices of colonial promoters in the 1890s. As an alternative vision, it grew out of the engagement of one of the best-informed critics of what he came to term 'European barbarism' in Africa. It was a vision wiped out by the new South Africa of 1910, by Lord Lugard's indirect rule in West Africa, and by the marginalisation of early proponents of African nationalism. Nevertheless, while retaining a belief in the civilising mission, he treated Africans not as a uniform 'race' but as a diverse people who by historical experience and opportunity, might be living under 'civilised' or 'uncivilised' conditions. Under Fox Bourne and the APS, this vision of Africa's transition to modernity sustained a critique of European colonialism from the 1890s to 1910. It served as the foundation for the defence of the political and legal status of Africans and coloureds during the reconstruction of South Africa, and contributed to a new international view of human rights then in creation under the Hague Convention.

The hard political reality was that the agency through which Fox Bourne and his associates attempted to promote the rights of Africans was in a state of serious decline. Through its principal parliamentary spokesman Sir Charles Dilke, the APS raised questions about abuses in the Congo Free State. Similarly, Fox Bourne maintained a critical commentary on Rhodes, the British South African Company and developments in southern Africa only to provoke increased hostility among white South Africans toward humanitarian opinion. The secretary of the APS directly challenged Joseph Chamberlain, the colonial secretary, whose plans for the economic development of the hinterland of West African colonies relied upon military force. From its foundation, the APS had articulated a creed of 'native' rights as a protection against the destructive impact of colonialism. With the partition of Africa and the coercive development strategies of Leopold II, Chamberlain and Rhodes, to name only the most famous, Fox Bourne's articulation of those rights in the language of his radical journalism received less of a considered hearing from Chamberlain and colonial office civil servants. There was some truth to Chamberlain's minute that the APS secretary's critical communications did not necessarily reflect the opinions of the society's members.[54]

Despite these differences, the APS secretary and members were in agreement on the challenge they faced – the expanding scope of problems demanding the society's attention and its diminished reputation and support among political leaders and the public. At its meeting of 7 April 1897 on 'The Treatment of Native Races', speakers surveyed the issues before them, paying most attention to developments in Africa. Leonard Courtney, the chair, and other MPs defended the role of the APS, but worried that recent developments had deviated from past principles. Sir Charles Dilke, the longest-serving APS supporter among members of parliament, commented that the 'doctrines of the Society' no longer had the general support they once had, and he called for a stand for the principles founded by the 'grandfathers of the present generation of the Society'.[55] Despite Dilke's appeal and despite the efforts of Dilke himself, Fox Bourne and other activists in the APS, they not only faced greater challenges with the new twentieth century, but failed to halt the forces eroding the principles of 1837.

Resistance – initiatives

While the two principal humanitarian organisations surviving from the anti-slavery movement of the 1830s were in a weakened condition, other historical actors, persons of colour who faced prejudice and discrimination directly, and others with roots in the abolitionist past, took up the challenge of confronting the intensified racialism of the late nineteenth century. From recent studies, we now know more about these initiatives to launch a sustained critique of racialism and empire from the 1880s to the First World War, though there are still untapped resources in the archives for a fuller historical narrative. My interest here is in the obstacles in the way of linking these new dissenting voices with institutions with a history of opposing racial oppression. Part of the equation that accounts for the power of the dominant racialist ideology, both in the science of race and in the language of race relations, rests upon the weaknesses of the dissenting discourse.

Dissent by its very nature implies weakness from its location outside the political mainstream. One such voice initiating, organising and sustaining a dissenting view of race and racialism for over a quarter of a century belonged to Catherine Impey (1847–1923), a Quaker spinster from Street, Somerset. Through her membership of the Society of Friends and from her Quaker relatives in Philadelphia, she had connections with the abolitionist movement and opportunities to visit the United States. There she witnessed how legacies of slavery – race prejudice and discrimination – affected the lives of African-Americans in northern cities as well as in the south. She formed friendships with influential African-Americans, most importantly with Frederick Douglass and his circle. When some of them visited England – William Wells Brown for example – they stayed with her in Street, Somerset. While Impey's views on racial injustice were shaped by her visits to the United States and her African-American friends, she recognised that comparable trends were at work within the British Empire, and she supported dissenting voices among persons of colour in Africa, India and the West Indies, and in the United Kingdom.[56]

Catherine Impey began her activism in 1878 by protesting against her Quaker temperance society, the Independent Order of Good Templars, for its acceptance of a colour bar in its American lodges. She conducted her campaign at Good Templar meetings in both the United States and England, and succeeded in having the Good Templars in the United Kingdom dissociate themselves from its American affiliates.[57] Her visits to the United States, and her failure to prevent a reunion of the Good Templars on the basis of accepting segregation in its lodges, led her to begin her more ambitious project against racialism.

In 1888, she launched the *Anti-Caste*, a monthly magazine dedicated to opposing racial prejudice and segregation and advancing the case for equal treatment. She dedicated her magazine to opposing 'the evils of Caste as it prevails in countries where our white race habitually ostracises those who are even partly descended from darker races'.[58] She relied upon the Society of Friends as her basis of support, and particularly upon a network of Quaker women many of whom had been activists in the anti-slavery movement. This network of subscribers provided financial support for distributing copies of the *Anti-Caste*, which were sold or circulated for free. The magazine attained a monthly circulation of 3,500 and was not just national in distribution: Impey had volunteers ready to circulate the magazine in Africa, India, the United States and the West Indies,. One of the founding purposes of the *Anti-Caste* was to provide a forum for articles by African-Americans and British subjects of colour so that readers could be introduced to their experience of racial injustice. Concerned that her magazine was too dependent on African-American sources, she wrote, as a member of the APS, to F. W. Chesson requesting articles about Africa or other news.[59]

Catherine Impey was also innovative in adopting the idea of caste from India and applying it to social relations between blacks and whites in the United States. In 1883, in a letter to Charles Allen of the BFASS, she describes racial separation as 'this caste system which is negro slavery in another form – robbing coloured people of the opportunity to rise artificially & systematically impoverishing them in mind, body and estate'.[60] In 1891, she provided a further definition of 'caste' in searching for a word to capture what a decade later would be termed 'racialism' – 'Caste is an arbitrary and systematic restriction of persons to particular ranks of life on grounds other than those of individual merit and fitness.'[61] Impey did not identify the source from which she adopted the language of caste, but she may well have been familiar with George Campbell's comparison of the southern United States with India based on his extensive administrative experience there. Some of her African-American sources also used the language of caste, though on hearing about the *Anti-Caste*, Ida B. Wells assumed it addressed British rule in India.[62] In adapting the language of caste, her focus was not on theories of racial inequality advanced by scientists but upon the social practices of racial separation and oppression which she described as both 'arbitrary' and 'systematic'. In other words, the discourse of the *Anti-Caste* was not about what has come to be known as 'scientific racism' but about what came to be known as 'race relations'. Here the influence of her African-American informants may be evident, for their engagement with racial discrimination occurred not in response to the armchair speculations of the white intelligentsia but through their everyday encounter with white privilege, racial exclusion and subordination.

In many ways, Catherine Impey was in advance of her time. Frederick Douglass wrote to her commenting that she was more needed in America than in England.[63] In the late nineteenth century, the United States pioneered new forms of institutionalised racial oppression in the aftermath of emancipation, within a modernised capitalist economy, and, at least from a British perspective, within a radical experiment with democracy. These innovative forms of racial oppression, especially in the practices of segregation and the collapse of the rule of law under the terror of the lynch mobs, not only denied the expectations for emancipation of British abolitionists like Impey but also gave an awful clarity to American exceptionalism, not too say deviation, from the norms of civil society. In her appeal to her supporters, Impey identified with the plight of largely educated, professional African-Americans who, by culture and lifestyle, had no more difficulty in accommodating themselves to the peculiar customs of Street, Somerset or England in general than did white American visitors. To their British hosts, their one distinguishing feature was the darkness of their complexion. Knowledgeable about American legal definitions of blackness and whiteness, and about white males' paternity of biracial offspring from the sexual exploitation of slave women in the past and of free women of colour in the present, Impey and her friends viewed African-Americans not so much as a race but as a hybrid people varying widely in colour. In other words, African-Americans were the model of a darker complexioned, English-speaking, Christian ethnicity capable of engaging the sympathy and support of British philanthropists. In this engagement against racial oppression there were none of the complexities of race and culture presented by colonial Africa as faced by Impey's friends in the APS. Attempting to protect Africans facing the destructive forces of colonialism, the APS believed the answer lay in assimilating over time to western, modern conditions, as had model African-Americans.

'Caste' or the system of race separation, according to the *Anti-Caste* and its sources, developed to prevent progress among freed slaves and to maintain a servile labouring class. American developments also had a larger international dimension with a comparable regressive purpose. In 1889, the *Anti-Caste* quoted an article from the *Spectator* of Natal opposing education for Africans and criticising newspapers such as Tengo Javabu's *Imvo* (*the native voice*), one of Impey's sources. In the opinion of the Natal journal, 'the raw native who doesn't even know his alphabet, makes a much more efficient labourer than does his so-called educated brother who sings in the choir on Sundays, and frequently at other times, when he ought to be at work, reads his newspaper and talks politics'.[64] What especially alarmed Impey was that the *Standard*, a London daily, took up the South African opinion and applied it to a recent uprising in Haiti, to black labour in the West Indies, and more extensively to relations between whites and blacks in the American South, paying special attention to alleged black male sexual aggression against white women. In her rebuttal, Impey pointed out that South African capitalists had an interest in a cheap and ignorant labour force, and, several years in advance of the campaign against lynching, she emphasised the history of white male sexual exploitation of African-American women. She concluded that 'there may be other demoralising influences to account for the so-called "relapse of the negro"... other than the inherent tendency of black nature to return to a former state of barbarism'.[65]

Aware of lynching and its ritualised brutalities, she sought confirmation of these reports on a visit to the United States. She arranged to meet Ida B. Wells, an African-American journalist who had recently fled from her home in Memphis under threats against her life for her newspaper reports on a local lynching. The meeting took place in Philadelphia in the fall of 1892, and Impey, shocked by Wells' accounts, thought that a campaign in the United Kingdom, reminiscent of campaigns by black abolitionists three decades earlier, might assist Wells in the United States. With the support of Frederick Douglass, Impey returned home and used her network of correspondents to propose a campaign against lynching.[66] Mailing copies of the *Anti-Caste* to a wide range of interested persons, Impey wrote to Isabella Fyvie Mayo, a novelist and essayist known under the pen-name of Edward Garrett. In Aberdeen, Mayo provided rooms for South Asian students attending university. As a young girl, she had been powerfully affected by the death of the Fyvie family's black butler, a former American slave who, out of memories of slavery and his isolation in London, had committed suicide.[67] After a correspondence exploring their mutual interests, Mayo invited Impey north to Aberdeen to plan the campaign against lynching.

At Isabella Mayo's, according to Catherine Impey's account, the two women worked on the next issue of the *Anti-Caste* and issued their invitation to Ida B. Wells. This invitation, based on Impey's original draft, was written by George Ferdinands, a doctor from Ceylon residing at Mayo's house. It sketched out a proposal for an 'Emancipation League' committed to remove 'all disabilities (inequalities) on the grounds of race', possibly international in scope with some eminent person such as Frederick Douglass as president. The invitation emphasised that Impey and Mayo hoped that Wells herself would be able to give a lecture tour on lynching: 'we think you as a *woman* would perhaps find a *readier* hearing among those who are densely ignorant of the whole situation'. No doubt, Impey had in mind her network of female subscribers to the *Anti-Caste*. Knowing that lynching often followed from accusations of sexual assault, and having met Wells, she may have also realised that the public discussion of such matters would be a delicate and challenging task requiring a skilled and knowledgeable presenter. The invitation advises Wells that 'we shant [*sic*] carry England with a rush but we can set the ball rolling'.[68]

Wells accepted the invitation, arriving in England on 13 April 1893, and she and Impey travelled to see Isabella Mayo to begin the campaign with a series of lectures in Scotland and northern England. In Edinburgh, before the startled presence of the American visitor, a stunning confrontation occurred between her two British hosts. Mayo charged Catherine Impey, then 45 years old, with forming a romantic attachment to George Ferdinands, and with having written a letter proposing marriage. The doctor, not returning Impey's affection, had sought Mayo's advice. Mayo accused Impey of having the kind of gross sexual interest in Ferdinands that some deranged white women have for men of colour, calling the Quaker spinster a nymphomaniac. Declaring that Impey was unfit to be involved in a public campaign, Mayo attempted without success to have Wells refuse to associate with her Quaker friend. The Scottish novelist sought to discredit Impey by writing letters to supporters of the anti-lynching campaign including Frederick Douglass and other African-American friends.[69] The rupture between Mayo and Impey interfered with plans for meetings in London, and Wells left England in June 1893 feeling that she had not accomplished as much as she had anticipated, and certainly less than she achieved in a second tour in 1894.[70] There is no record of Catherine Impey denying her romantic interest in Ferdinands or of her letter of proposal. Mayo's vindictive response is more puzzling. She was a non-denominational Christian; like Impey she participated in a variety of philanthropic causes; she had links to labour and socialist groups; and she formed friendships with Tolstoy and Gandhi. While not opposed to inter-racial marriage, she had fairly conventional ideas about sex and gender. Her essays of advice to servant girls warned that those who became pregnant posed a danger to the virtue of other servants and should be dismissed.[71]

Impey's own private account makes no reference to Mayo's accusation but claims the two women fell out over financial matters.[72] Recent scholarly studies have explored the dynamics of race, gender and sexuality both in the dispute between Mayo and Impey and in the discussion of lynching itself.[73] Despite some criticism from African-

American males, Wells insisted on making the controversial public statement that one of the causes of lynching was white women initiating adulterous relations with black men.[74] Both Impey and Mayo were independent women with firmly held convictions, but from Impey's correspondence, let alone from the confrontation over Ferdinands, Mayo appears as the dominant personality.

Mayo's hostility to Impey may have stemmed in part from the Scottish author's desire to gain control of the movement. If so, she did not anticipate the energy and political commitment of a third exceptional leader, Celestine Edwards (1858–94). This son of emancipated slaves in Dominica in the British West Indies had become a sailor at age 12, had settled in Edinburgh and the northeast of England for more than a decade and, as a largely self-taught and voracious reader, had became a temperance preacher for the Primitive Methodists. He graduated with a diploma in theology from King's College, University of London, and had plans to study medicine. From his home in the east end of London, he gained a national reputation as a popular lecturer for the Christian Evidence Society, founded in 1870 by the Church of England and Nonconformists to combat the growth of secularism among the working classes. He became the founding editor of *Lux*, the society's magazine.[75]

At Ida B. Wells' anti-lynching lectures in Scotland and England, and in the *Anti-Slavery Reporter*, Impey solicited support for a new 'Society for the Furtherance of the Brotherhood of Man'. As a London representative, Celestine Edwards participated in an informal organising conference in Birmingham, on 10 June 1893. Mayo was not in attendance at the Birmingham meeting, and those who participated, in addition to Impey and Edwards, came largely from Impey's *Anti-Caste* network. These initial plans for the SRBM were finalised at a conference in London on 11 August 1893. Once again, Mayo could not attend, and regrets were conveyed from Dadabhai Naoroji, a member of the Indian National Congress and formerly a Liberal MP, Ellen Robinson, the purchaser of Frederick Douglass' freedom, and Harriet Colenso. The Reverend Henry Mason Joseph of Antigua attended the London meeting and served a useful role in moving matters forward, such as differences between Impey and Edwards over the best passage of Scripture to express human brotherhood.[76] Joseph served on the council of the SRBM, and would be a continuing presence during the next decade or more. He was president of the African Association and participated in its Pan-African Conference held in 1900. Joseph had been Edwards' tutor back in Antigua, and had subsequently spent time in the United States and Canada. The black clergyman had come to England seeking support for the Wilberforce Institute, an educational centre established by American fugitive slaves in Ontario to provide improved education for black children subject to white prejudices in local schools.[77]

When he joined the newly founded SRBM, Edwards had at least ten years' experience as a lay preacher on temperance, and more recently as a lecturer and editor for the Christian Evidence Society. Edwards gained a national reputation filling lecture halls across the country with his combative, often humorous, debates with secularists. Styling himself as the 'Black Champion', or 'BC' he delighted in calling Charles Bradlaugh, J. M. Robertson and other secularist opponents 'the White Champion', or 'WC'.[78] His Christian apologetics gave him an opening for the condemnation of past evils such as slavery and its legacy of racial oppression, and for exposing current challenges to Christian teachings, including the drink trade in Africa, the slaughter of the maxim guns in colonial wars and the role of missionary societies in new imperialism. What Celestine Edwards brought to Impey, Mayo and the SRBM was a new black voice capable of exposing the institutionalised racial barriers evident in the United States and dramatised by Ida B. Wells' anti-lynching campaign. He also brought the British Empire onto his platform, challenging any pretence that Britons at home and overseas did not have their own racial prejudices and did not bear responsibility for the racial injustices which were part and parcel of the imperial mission.

In 1889, Edwards attended the annual meeting of the APS, and his remarks in thanking the chair struck a new discordant tone in the gentlemanly decorum of such gatherings. His condemnation of 'the misgovernment and cruel and cowardly treatment which British representatives were inflicting upon some Africans' was not unusual in such gatherings, but he then concluded with a threat: 'Africans did not come to this country for nothing. They frequented English slums and English palaces, and read English newspapers; and in proportion as they received an education, so would their future policy take form.'[79] In his preface to the biography of Bishop Hawkins of the British Episcopal Methodist Church, a small but independent African-Canadian church, Edwards described the experience of black people living in a racist culture: 'No nation can be expected to advance in so-called civilisation whose faults are continually being paraded before them, as ours are in the literature of the superior race'. These prejudicial comments were a result of deliberate policy, for 'in every country where the Negro has been sent as an exile', Edwards observed, 'his superior brethren have used every means and meanness, not only to make him feel his position, but to prolong his degradation'. As exemplified by

Bishop Hawkins, Edwards' faith lay in the belief that 'God ha[d] not sent him into the world as a mere toy to be kicked about by every and any one'.[80]

When Edwards founded *Lux*, this theme became a regular part of the magazine, just as it was of his popular lectures. The historian E. A. Freeman observed in his account of his trip to America: 'the eternal laws of nature, the eternal distinction of colour, forbid the assimilation of the negro'. Edwards challenged not only Freeman's racism but his assumption about assimilation: 'The imaginary assimilation of which Professor Freeman spoke is a bogey which exists in the mind of Negro-hating Americans, because the Negro neither craves nor demands such assimilation.' According to Edwards, African-Americans would be satisfied if they could 'live and be protected by the law of a country' which benefited from their 'industry and free labour'.[81] In addition to being editor for *Lux*, Edwards took on the editorship of *Fraternity*, the new publication of the SRBM.

When Ida B. Wells returned to England for her second tour, members of the SRBM advised her that the split between Impey and Mayo had caused difficulties. Edwards had taken over the leadership, and would supervise her second tour, at times travelling and lecturing with her.[82] In both *Lux* and in the first number of *Fraternity*, Edwards recognised Impey's contribution to the struggle against racial injustice through the *Anti-Caste*.[83] 'Unity our Aim' was the title of Edwards' first leader in *Fraternity* (July 1893). The headline identified the society's principle of human unity and indirectly the internal divisions of the SRBM. Recognising the contributions of Impey and Mayo, the article affirms that 'the human race – whatever be their creed, colour, or nationality – are from one common origin, with like feelings, ambitions and desires'. In contrast, Edwards points to the ill-treatment of 'English-speaking peoples' toward persons of colour in the United States, India, and Australia. This conduct he attributes to 'a feeling of superiority existing in the mind of the English race over his darker brethren, and this feeling breeds caste, and caste ends in reckless cruelty'.[84] In August 1893, Edwards pointed out that the SRBM faced a far larger challenge than that addressed by the anti-slavery society. Whereas many might work to liberate the slave, it would require the education of 'ourselves and others to do even more' – to establish for those 'however far removed in colour, country, and religion, equality of treatment'.[85]

Subsequent issues of *Fraternity* reaffirmed these principles and addressed specific instances of racial oppression. It reported regularly on lynching, including an illustrated article in August 1894, and ran a series on 'The racial war in America' which included a controversy in the Aberdeen press provoked by letters critical of the SRBM, Edwards and Isabella Mayo.[86] He provided a comparative study of race relations premised on the claim that racial antipathy in America and the British Empire was 'Anglo-Saxon'. He compared the status of persons of African descent in the smaller and larger islands of the West Indies, developed a fuller contrast with the status of former slaves in Brazil, Cuba, Guadaloupe and Martinque, and observed that the most rigid racial barriers existed in the United States and Canada. He promised further explorations of what he termed 'Anglo-Saxonism'.[87] In March 1894, *Fraternity* printed an article by a 'Brown Man', an Indian Christian convert married to an English woman. Beyond his wife's exclusion from Anglo-Indian society, and the refusal of missionary societies to employ Indian Christians, the author described the mistrust of missionaries. 'Shrewd Orientals', he commented, looked upon missionaries as agents of their own country, 'to preach the morality, or the excellence, of that race – to pave the way for the commercial, social, political, ecclesiastical usurpation of that nation'.[88] Informed by Fox Bourne's reports for the APS, Edwards condemned the conduct of Cecil Rhodes and the British South Africa in Matabeland and appealed to the British government to intervene under the headline 'Humanity before Politics'. In a leader 'Murder will out', he claimed that the maxim guns that slaughtered Lobengula's forces would never be used against white soldiers. Reporting that Rhodes had the support of missionaries, Edwards satirised the Cape Town dinner celebrating Rhodes' victory, for 'some murderers are hanged, others escape being hanged on the grounds of provocation; but there are others who kill so many that, either through fear or favour, they are neither hanged or transported, but are fested by their compatriots as heroes'.[89]

Eventually, Edwards' editorial tasks for two monthly journals and his busy lecture schedule took its toll on his health. On his doctor's advice, he announced in April 1894 his plan to return temporarily to the West Indies to recuperate. Wells continued on with her tour. Accompanied by Catherine Impey, she spoke and received the support of both the BFASS and the APS.[90] Edwards left for the West Indies in June, but his health never recovered, and he died, probably from consumption, on 25 July 1894.

Prior to the announcement of Edwards' death in the July 1894 issue of *Fraternity*, an advertisement and notice appeared of a novel, *Hard Truth*. The novel took the form of a dialogue between Christ and the devil, and its author, Theodore Thomas, was an African-American then resident in England. From internal evidence, the author was familiar with SRBM and its associated publications.[91] In all probability, Theodore Thomas was a *nom de plume*, and the author of *Hard Truth* was more than likely Celestine Edwards himself. The dialogue between

Christ and Satan occurs in three sections: the first provides a slave narrative in the American South with a young slave heroine subjected to sexual exploitation; the second narrates how emancipated slaves with signs of intelligence and progress are subjected to white terror and murder; and the third part, 'Britain leads the world', returns to England so that Christ can observe the agents of Lucifer, white Christian Britons, at work. In South Africa, where a black Christ experiences prejudice and discrimination, Lucifer observes that in a land once belonging to Africans, 'your Church ... has founded a civilisation based on slavery, brutality, race prejudice, hatred and destruction'.[92] Having taken the reader through racial exploitation under slavery in the New World and colonial rule in Africa, Edwards identifies racialism's place of origin. 'Here's my truth', he affirms. 'Britain is the birth-place of the very essence of the seed of prejudice against the negro race. And the little uncouth, rough shrub, when transplanted from its mother country, grows into a great tree in Gentile lands.'[93] The author also had some hard advice for the SRBM. 'The Society for the Recognition of the Brotherhood of Man', he advised, 'might as well stop pleading to your Church – that is to say, to your modern Chosen People – to be just towards the negro, and the editor of *Fraternity*, might as well cease beseeching his race and people to take their foot off the negro's neck, and give *him a chance to get up*. "Might is Right!"'[94] Suffering ill-health since at least the end of 1893, giving up his lecturing in April, profoundly alienated by more than two decades of activism in the United Kingdom, upon returning home to Dominica, he reconverted to the Catholicism of his family shortly before his death.

Edwards' departure left the SRBM and its journal, *Fraternity*, in disarray. What Mayo called the 'schism' became much more open. Impey had maintained a separate organisation, the west of England or Somerset branch. Its activities and finances, unlike with other branches, never appeared in the columns of *Fraternity*. Impey called upon her network of friends to reconstitute a provisional executive committee of the SRBM, while Mayo, not named to this committee remained in control of *Fraternity*. A series of articles in August through November of 1894, charged, without naming Impey directly, that the other branch of SRBM was under the leadership of a mentally disturbed female. Under the title 'The female accusation', Mayo linked the sexual fantasies of a deluded English woman with the mental illness of white women that led to charges of rape against black men. By November, Mayo openly called for branches loyal to the memory of Celestine Edwards to join with the 'Scottish branches' and not to associate with the English branches and their discredited leadership.[95]

Under a succession of editors appointed through Mayo's influence,

Fraternity continued publishing until 1897, but it could not repli-
cate the passion and personal commitment evident in Edwards' lead
articles. The magazine became more reliant on clippings from other
sources. It reported regularly on Ida B. Wells anti-lynching campaign
back in America, though it had fewer articles from African-American
writers. As the *Anti-Caste* had done in support of Dadahbai Noaroji
and the Indian National Congress, *Fraternity* criticised British rule in
India, paying more attention to developments there, including some
articles by Dr George Fernandes, who was now a vice-president of the
reconstituted SRBM. Under its new editors, *Fraternity* had closer links
to labour and socialist organisations, was less infused with Christian
ethics, and was more secular in its language. As under Edwards' editorship, Cecil Rhodes was still the ugly face of capitalism exploiting
African land and labour. Later issues began to address concerns of
international organised labour, though *Fraternity* from its founding
principles criticised anti-Chinese agitation in Australia.[96]

In the meantime, Catherine Impey kept alive her own section of
SRBM in pursuit of the original mission of the *Anti-Caste*. In fulfilment of an agreement with Edwards, the Somerset branch of the SRBM
purchased copies of *Fraternity* from his estate and distributed 22,000
copies world-wide during 1894. It requested that his executors instruct
the editor of *Fraternity* to cease claiming to be the official organ of
SRBM, and adopted the *Bond of Brotherhood*, a Quaker temperance
paper from the 1860s, as a vehicle for its reports.[97] This association was
short-lived, for Quaker temperance leaders were still ready to tolerate
segregation in American affiliates, and Impey and her supporters once
again severed their association. In 1895, Impey revived the *Anti-Caste*
producing two issues in March and July.

For four or five years in the early 1890s, through the anti-lynching
campaign of Ida B. Wells, through the foundation of the SRBM and
its new journal, *Fraternity*, and especially through its editor, Celestine Edwards, a new, articulate voice dissented from the hegemonic
racialism of the metropolitan culture. It expressed its dissent in the
rejection of new forms of institutionalised racism, most evident in
the United States; in its assertion of demands for political rights and
representation for persons of colour, most clearly in support of the
Indian National Congress; and in its opposition to the racial oppression associated with the new imperialism in Africa, most evident in
the conquest of land and recruitment of labour in southern Africa and
in King Leopold's Congo. Unlike established organisations such as the
BFASS and the APS, these voices of dissent did not act as a lobby to influence government policy but had a broader and less precise objective
of presenting an alternative liberating vision of human rights which

transcended differences of race or colour. Ida B. Wells thought that her campaigns in England prompted some American religious and political leaders to give her space for her campaign back home. In London, an anti-lynching committee chaired by Florence Balgarnie, a journalist and temperance advocate, and sixty original members of whom a quarter were women, kept a watching brief on developments across the Atlantic.[98] Any other measurable impact rests not upon a continuity of political organisations or institutions, but upon the continuity of individuals in a succession of attempts to launch a movement challenging the orthodox ideology of racial superiority and to advance the cause of racial equality.

In December 1895, the *Anti-Slavery Reporter* included a notice that 'Mr Henry Williams, a young man of colour from Trinidad', had received a favourable reception for several lectures he had given on 'the Negro question in the new world'. In September, 1897, Williams convened the first meeting of the African Association and initiated a more ambitious movement to address the global predicament facing Africans and those of African descent. Henry Sylvester Williams, a Trinidadian who had lived in the United States and attended Dalhousie University in Halifax, Nova Scotia, came to England to study law, being admitted to Gray's Inn. He maintained himself by lecturing on temperance and thrift, and while on his countrywide tours promoted his African Association. The Reverend Henry Mason Joseph of Antigua, who had been active in the SRBM, was affiliated with the Society for the Propagation of the Gospel and the curate at St Mark's, Old Street, in the City of London, assisted Williams and served as president of the African Association. From discussions at association meetings, Williams proposed a conference in London under the original title of a 'Pan-African' conference.[99]

Unlike earlier associations sponsored through the APS or BFASS, Williams' new African Association limited its membership to persons of African descent, while permitting persons belonging to other ethnicities to have associate membership. Most of its members were African, West Indian and African-American students in Britain, and among its associate members were Miss F. Balgarnie and Peter Claydon of the anti-lynching committee and Dadhabai Naoroji and Isabella Fyvie Mayo of the SRBM. Reports in the *Aborigines' Friend* welcomed an association created for and to be run by peoples of African descent.[100] Williams had written to the BFASS and the APS seeking support. As it had done with fugitive slaves and black abolitionists since the 1850s, the BFASS responded by offering cautious support but refusing any financial assistance.[101] Williams was more puzzled and disturbed by the similar response from the APS. Fox Bourne was an associate member and had given a supportive address at an association meeting. The APS secretary's initial response has not survived, but Williams, in writing to ask Fox Bourne to reconsider, objected to his claim that the conference went beyond the association's constitutional mandate. Williams defended the proposed conference, expressed surprise at Fox Bourne's response in the light of his record of promoting the interests of Africans, and, more importantly because, he wrote, 'I think the time is come when we ought to be heard and credited in our own affairs'.[102] As late as one month before the conference, in June 1900, Williams informed Booker T. Washington that he still was meeting 'slight opposition' from the APS.[103]

Since becoming secretary of the APS in 1889, Fox Bourne had established a good relationship with West African correspondents and had advanced many cases of alleged racial discrimination with the colonial office. His response was not likely a simple matter of race prejudice or paternalism. More likely the response came not from the APS secretary but from its committee.[104] Fox Bourne attended the conference, sponsored a luncheon at the Liberal Club and gave a donation to help defray expenses. The APS committee was strapped for funds and was defensive about its role of protector of 'uncivilised' as distinct from educated 'natives'. If Fox Bourne was behind APS opposition, the more likely reason was tactical. At odds with Chamberlain and the colonial office, the APS focused its attentions on the South African War and its aftermath. By May of 1900 it had commenced its promotion of a 'Suggested Charter of South African Native Rights', and on 3 July the APS held a conference on the 'Native Question in South Africa'. At the meeting, D. E. Tobias, an African-American who attended the Pan-African Conference, and Williams, identified as native of Trinidad, made supportive remarks. Williams called for consultation with the 'very many well-educated men of his race' about the 'future status of aborigines in South Africa'.[105] Fox Bourne may have thought that formal APS support of the Pan-African Conference might be a distraction, even a liability, for the society's lobbying on South Africa.

Despite the lack of financial support from the BFASS and the APS, about forty persons of African descent, mostly from the United Kingdom, the United States and the West Indies, attended the conference. Fox Bourne and Jane Cobden Unwin, the daughter of Richard Cobden, attended from the APS, and Travers Buxton from the BFASS. At a reception in the Houses of Parliament, Bishop Alexander Walters, of the American Methodist Episcopal Zion Church and president of the conference, reported meeting Catherine Impey. Among donors who helped meet the conference costs were the Impey sisters, Dadabhai Naoroji, Miss Balgarnie, Fox Bourne and Travers Buxton.[106] Williams planned to establish an independent agency to press issues of racial justice on an international scale, and for that purpose set up a permanent committee. Among its members resident in England were Samuel Coleridge Taylor, a black English classical composer and musician, J. R. Archer, the future black mayor of Battersea, and Jane Cobden Unwin, a member of the London County Council and advocate for women's suffrage. Plans were made for future conferences in the United States in 1902 and in Haiti in 1904 as a centenary celebration of the slaves' revolution. After the conference, Williams toured the West Indies promoting Pan-Africanism, and on his return to London, he found, much to his annoyance, that his committee pleading lack of funds had closed the association's operation.[107]

The experience of meeting in London in 1900, and the Pan-African vision captured in the conference's 'Address to the Peoples of the World' laid the foundation for the movement's historic rebirth in 1919. With Du Bois' famous prediction – 'the problem of the twentieth century is the problem of the colour line' – the address called for a recognition that as the nineteenth century came to its close, in a world becoming more closely bound together, 'the millions of black men in Africa, America, and the Islands of the Sea, not to speak of the brown and yellow myriads elsewhere, [were] bound to have a great influence upon the world in the future, by reason of sheer numbers and physical contact'. To describe the racial barriers to an improved understanding, the address used the language of 'caste' and appealed to the Jeffersonian language of universal human rights from the Declaration of Independence: 'Let the world take no backward step in that slow but sure progress which has successively refused to let the spirit of class, of caste, of privilege, or birth, debar from life, liberty and the pursuit of happiness a striving human soul.'[108] In contrast, it specified how the historical promise of the progressive liberation of all peoples was threatened by 'the greed for gold in Africa' and, in language reminiscent of Celestine Edwards, by 'the cloak of Christian missionary enterprise' which served 'so often in the past, to hide the ruthless economic exploitation and political downfall of less developed nations'. The address called on the international community to respect the 'integrity and independence' of the black states of Abyssinia, Liberia and Haiti. It appealed to the abolitionist past, calling on Britain to fulfil the work of Wilberforce and his generation by advancing 'the rights of responsible government to the black colonies of Africa and the West Indies'. Similarly, it appealed to the icons of the American anti-slavery movement – Garrison, Phillips, and Douglass – to reawaken the conscience of Americans and 'rebuke all dishonesty and unrighteous oppression toward the American Negro, and grant to him the right of franchise, security of person and property'.[109]

To a later generation of nationalists, the address was still deferential to western presumptions of cultural difference in its call for support of civilising, progressive development. It also deferred to the leadership of the great powers by paying tribute to their past record of humanitarian progress. This optimism was coupled with a pessimistic forecast: 'if by reason of carelessness, prejudice, greed and injustice, the black world is exploited and ravished and degraded, the results must be deplorable, if not fatal – not simply to them, but to the high ideals of justice, freedom and culture which a thousand years of Christian civilisation have held before Europe'.[110] In all likelihood these fears rather than the elevated hopes for progress motivated Williams, Du Bois and their colleagues in London in 1900. The address, with its more robust political observations intended for heads of states, was not sent to supportive humanitarian agencies. These agencies received resolutions acknowledging past achievements. The BFASS committee simply acknowledged the resolution and did not view it as a call for action to meet the global crisis of racial oppression. The *Anti-Slavery Reporter*, which reprinted the resolution, stressed affirmations of mutuality between whites and blacks and respect accorded to the abolitionist movement.[111] In its report on the conference, the *Aborigines' Friend* gave a more detailed and supportive account of plans for an autonomous African movement. Nonetheless, the APS journal did draw an important distinction. In its view the Pan-African Conference represented 'civilised' Africans largely from the United States and the West Indies, but not 'the uncivilised and oppressed millions in Africa itself'.[112]

In a more direct political initiative, the Pan-African Conference communicated an appeal to the Queen on behalf of black South Africans listing abusive practices, including the compound system in the mines, forced labour, racial separation and pass laws. There was a lengthy delay before Her Majesty's Government responded, and Joseph Chamberlain's reply did not address the points listed in the appeal, but only offered, as he did to the BFASS and APS, the bland assurance that the government would be mindful of 'native interests'.[113]

From a background and perspective similar to H. Sylvester Williams and his African Association and the Pan-African Conference, though not participating in either, Theophilus E. Scholes, (1856–1935), a Jamaican medical doctor, wrote extensively on Chamberlain's imperialism, and the empire divided between the white – or as he preferred, the 'colourless' – people and the coloured majority.[114] Educated at Glasgow, Brussels and Edinburgh, he toured Scotland and Ireland speaking on missionary work in Africa before spending two years in the Congo. Upon completion of his medical training in Brussels,

Scholes, along with Thomas L. Johnson, an African-American preacher who had participated in the anti-slavery Jubilee of 1884, toured Ireland promoting support for Africans engaged in missions to Africa. In 1893, Scholes attended the Colwyn Bay Institute, which trained persons of African descent for missionary work. From there he returned to Africa and worked for the institute in Nigeria.[115] *Fraternity* announced his departure from Colwyn Bay in 1894, and from Nigeria Scholes wrote to *Fraternity* in 1896 on lynching in the United States.[116]

Beyond the connection to *Fraternity* and the SRBM, Scholes' letter provides a sign that a new sharp intellect with an equally sharp pen has entered the struggle. He begins by asking if '*white men* are lynched for the same class of crime for which negroes are lynched'. He suggests that African-Americans are often lynched for their 'political opinions'. He sees lynching as part of the system of segregation, and 'the outcome of race hatred, a hatred that impregnates every layer of American society, and finds in the church a soil as congenial as it does outside it'.[117] While in Africa his advocacy of the native pastorate had aroused controversy. Upon his return to England, he studied in the British Museum reading on imperial policy and trade.

Scholes' first pamphlet on the West Indies and the sugar industry (1897) called for a more diversified agriculture, defended the black peasantry of Jamaica, and exposed the inequity of how consumer taxes on the black majority subsidised the sugar plantations and the Indian indentured labour of the white elite.[118] In a more substantial work in 1899, *The British Empire and its Alliances*, Scholes observed that the empire was entering a new phase with a more competitive international climate. Britain had created its empire by the conquest of lands and peoples and by the migration and settlement of British colonists. That process had created a divided empire, for in the temperate zones British people, institutions and culture prevailed, whereas in the tropical zone of the empire, the British ruled despotically over a numerically larger coloured, resentful population. Now Britain needed to consolidate its empire by building new cooperative relations with the coloured majority of its imperial subjects. Citing A. H. Keane, J. A. Froude and E. A. Freeman as British authorities who denigrated the capacity of Africans and their descendants in the West Indies and the United States, he recognised that the development of respect for coloured races would be a difficult challenge. Nonetheless, he saw colour prejudice as a delusion or superstition like witchcraft or slavery and affirmed that it could be overcome just as those past evils had been.[119]

That note of optimism could hardly withstand the direction of imperial policy under Joseph Chamberlain. In 1903, under the pen name of Bartholomew Smith, Scholes in *Chamberlain and Chamberlainism*

offered a critique of the colonial secretary's proposal for imperial pref-
erential tariffs. He also enumerated Chamberlain's failings in office, especially the South African War and its aftermath where policy-makers
found that a common white prejudice united British settlers and the
Boers at the cost of ignoring obligations to the 'natives'. In Sierra Leone,
coercive use of hut taxes only produced rebellion; in West Africa,
persons of African descent were excluded from appointments; and in
Jamaica, a £20,000 subsidy to the sugar planters reduced funding for
education and forced the closing of schools for black children. Scholes
took particular offence at Chamberlain's imperial preference based
upon an empire of 50 million white consumers living in the British
Isles and the self-governing dominions. The colonial secretary ignored
altogether the 350 million persons of colour who were subjects of the
empire and in the opinion of his West Indian critic, these neglected
subjects were greatly relieved by Chamberlain's exit from office.[120]

In his most substantial study of race and empire, *Glimpses of the
Ages*, Scholes devoted the first volume (1905) to the defence of the
peoples of Africa and the diaspora. Using his medical knowledge, and
his experience in Africa, he criticised A. H. Keane and his textbook,
Ethnology, for producing stereotypes based on prejudice and displaying
ignorance of the similarity of the bodily tissues and organs of all races,
including the structure of the skin and its pigmentation. In his opinion,
Keane was equally ignorant of the variation in colour and individual
diversity of the peoples of Africa. Beyond ridiculing Keane's racial science, Scholes challenged European claims of superiority in civilisation
by offering an Afrocentric account of the black origins of ancient Egypt
as the birthplace of a derivative western culture.[121] He objected to the
depiction of the entire 'Ethiopian race' as 'uncivilised' and affirmed,
not unlike Renner Maxwell of the Gambia, A. B. C. Merriman-Labor of
Sierra Leone or Fox Bourne of the APS, that there were both 'civilised'
and 'uncivilised' black peoples. In his view, the obligation of the state
in its policies and especially in its power to tax was to assist in progress
toward civilised conditions. In South Africa, the use of taxation under
the Glen Grey Act and new post-war taxes in the Transvaal aimed to
perpetuate an uncivilised, servile labour force.[122]

In the second volume (1908), he observed that the England of the
new twentieth century was unlike the England of 1860s and 1870s.
Two or three decades earlier it might have been possible to claim that
England was relatively free of racial prejudice. Now black residents and
visitors faced discrimination in the public services, and black students
from Africa, the West Indies and the United States faced harassment
from British students at universities. Qualified medical doctors were
denied employment in London hospitals because of their colour, and

opportunities in the colonial service, such as the West Africa Medical Service, were now only open to whites. The press, in his view, deliberately repeated common prejudices and insults against black people in a strategy of what a later generation would call 'blame the victim'.[123] In response, he repeatedly turned the accusation against the accuser. People who have a slave past should not feel shame; rather, the enslavers, the British, should be ashamed of their past. He pointed out that the accusation of black men raping white women came from the southern United States and not from the West Indies or Africa, yet the press accused all black men of being rapists. In response, he reported the number of convictions for rape and charges for sexual assault in the United Kingdom, and asked if this evidence proved that all white men were rapists.[124] Whether or not his direct responses were persuasive, many English readers were no doubt taken aback by his new assertive voice.

Scholes recognised that persons of colour could not help but be affected by the steady stream of 'malicious and mendacious aspersions by the great journalistic organs of Britain, of the colonies, and of the dependencies'; these were, he said, 'such acts as insults, disabilities, and humiliations to which persons of colour are subjected'. He was an advocate of the native pastorate, and in the Ethiopian movement to establish separate African churches, he saw a means to restore self-worth and dignity. In his opinion the missionary endeavours of white Christians were so 'impregnated with the spirit of Caucasian superiority' that this produced in the coloured races 'an unhealthy depreciation of themselves and an equally unhealthy exaltation of the colourless man'. Freed of this encumbrance, Ethiopianism provided 'the native right views of himself and right views of the white man'. Because it threatened white 'pretensions and their debasing interests, it is tabooed and anathematised by the colourless man'.[125]

The British Empire, or what he called the 'hegemonical state', rested its authority on the claim that the British had a special aptitude for good government. Scholes denied that British imperialism was different from any other. Holding white imperial rule up to his test of good government – the improvement of the lives of its subjects – he presented a catalogue of examples showing that imperial rule produced misgovernment. He had no difficulty producing a long list: European retaliation against the Boxers in China, the decline of Indian manufacture and trade, the drain on resources and increased incidence of famine under the Raj, the horrors of the Congo as documented in Casement's recent report, the failed promise to look after the 'native interest' in South Africa yet readiness to comply with the labour demands of the Rand capitalists including 'Chinese slavery', and in 1906 alone, risings in Northern Nigeria over taxation, the Bambatha rebellion in Natal, and nationalist insurgency in Egypt over the Denshawai incident.

For Scholes, British imperialism no longer adhered to Queen Victoria's declaration to her Indian subjects in 1858 promising a colour-blind empire. In his summary, he attributed the regressive change in imperial policy to the desire to exploit coloured labour, to the desire to show support for white colonists in self-governing states, and to the desire to secure the friendship of the United States.[126] According to Scholes, these three imperatives were not based on affinity or kinship or patriotism but upon power – the power of colonial employers in need of labour, the power of white electorates at home and in the self-governing dominions, and the power of the two principal English-speaking states in the international arena. In his concluding remarks, he identified the cost of these imperial imperatives. First, the coloured races had largely been forced into the empire by conquest, slavery or other forms of appropriation. Second, in cultivating the support of the coloured races, 'the hegemonical state pledged to them its word that they should be accorded equality of treatment with the colourless race, and should be prepared for autonomous government'. Those promises were broken. Third, he noted: 'the hegemonical state, endeavours to justify its unfaithfulness to these races, and at the same time to ensure their submission to its crimes by means of oppressive taxation, defective educational facilities, and ... by the systematic aspersion of their character with lies of the most abominable kind, and by degrading, humiliating, and deceiving them'.[127] Despite the evident alienation and anger in his analysis, Scholes still worked within an imperial framework, envisaging a colour-blind empire with equality of legal and political rights established, and colonies with black and brown majorities as self-governing parts of what one day would become a commonwealth. Prior to 1914, that was a radical and even utopian vision.

Although Scholes had plans to extend his *Glimpses of the Ages* to six volumes, no further volumes were published. Nonetheless, from his West Indian origins, his experience in Africa, his familiarity with *Fraternity* and the SRBM, and his witness of imperialism and its conflicts, he provided a substantial and influential analysis of race and empire. He was well-known among blacks in Edwardian London, including H. Sylvester Williams who asked him to speak at a dinner which the barrister organised in 1905 for Sapara Williams from Lagos. African, West Indian and African-American students met with him in London to discuss his works and ideas. Pixley Seme and Sol Plaatje, South African nationalists, visited Scholes, as did Alain Locke, the first African-American Rhodes Scholar, who became a leading figure in the Harlem Renaissance. Du Bois recommended Scholes' works to fellow

Pan-Africanists in the United States. In the 1930s, Jomo Kenyata and Ras Makonnen, a West Indian Pan-Africanist, visited him in London. In the second volume of *Glimpses of the Ages*, Scholes commented that a British reviewer had reacted unfavourably to a black writer critical of the empire and British superiority. There is little evidence of Scholes' work in the publications of 'colourless' writers on race and race relations prior to the First World War. His scientific critique of racism, his historical approach to the origin and development of world cultures, and his documenting of the abuses of colonialism were, nonetheless, significant contributions to the development of Pan-Africanism.[128]

Obstacles: South Africa, race and empire

The Pan-African Conference and Scholes' writing on race and empire took place during the crisis of the South African War and its aftermath. The war polarised the metropolitan public between the critical minority, labelled the pro-Boers by their opponents, and the patriotic majority whose jingoism, from the perspective of critics such as J. A. Hobson, revelled in the irrational psychology of the crowd. As the war became protracted and its conduct more brutal, the pro-Boers gained support as they focused on the army's scorched earth tactics and the children and women incarcerated in the concentration camps.[129] The historiography of the war no longer treats it as a white civil war between the British and the Boers, and recognises the role of Africans, coloureds and Indians as combatants and civilians. Nonetheless, in assessing the significance of the war, insufficient attention has been paid to how the war and post-war reconstruction between 1902 and 1910 transformed British discourse on race and race relations.[130] In the historical narrative of racist ideology it has a place as significant as the Indian Mutiny and the Jamaican Insurrection of 1865. The war and its aftermath tested the limits of resistance to racism. White power in South Africa did not just expose the weakness of the outworn liberal illusion of assimilation within a colour-blind empire. Along with the United States, it set the template for the ordering of racial exclusion and subordination as dictated by 'human nature' as constructed by the new social sciences.

From the beginning of the war, British observers realised that beyond the question of the control of the Boer republics and their mineral riches lay the issue of the place of the black and brown majority in post-war South Africa. While some commentators in their construction of the Boer enemy contrasted their treatment of Africans and their slave-holding past with British humanitarian traditions, few seriously believed that the British fought the war to protect African interests beyond Lord Salisbury's and Chamberlain's recognition that the 'native question' would have to be addressed in the peace. Nonetheless, the war opened up space for a new and more forceful critique of imperialism and of the link between empire and racial oppression.

While not all critics of empire extended their analysis to include forms of racialism, the catalogue of delusions and abuses set against imperialism included the exploitation of peoples of colour. Serious questioning of racial theory had commenced with studies of nationalism which concluded not simply that nationalities did not constitute races, but that race theory had little substance. J. M. Robertson, a leading secularist and Liberal MP, argued that 'the very concept of race [was] a relatively modern and factitious development'.[131] With Joseph Chamberlain's more assertive imperialism, critics challenged the association of patriotism with empire. Before the publication of Hobson's *Imperialism* (1902), but undoubtedly from the discussion of the economist's ideas at the South Place Ethical Society, J. M. Robertson in *Patriotism and Empire* (1899) identified the imperial classes – investors, bureaucrats and the military – as those who benefited from empire to the detriment of social reform at home. According to Robertson, a supporter of the APS, colonised peoples were denied liberties that were taken for granted in Britain. Consequently, the subordination of colonised peoples exposed the hypocrisy of humanitarian pretence of a civilising mission and protection for persons of colour.[132]

In *Patriotism and Ethics* (1901), John G. Godard, a regular contributor to the *Westminster Gazette*, ridiculed Chamberlain's claim that colonial conquests were only 'occasionally stained by crimes of rapacity'. As ironically enumerated by Godard, these colonial conquests never involved 'inhumanity', 'despotism' or 'cruelty', and 'abstain[ed] from coercing the natives'. In his view, Chamberlain's imperialism assumed 'that civilization [had] no fetishes – not even money or power'.[133] Godard affirmed individual diversity regardless of race in the fashion that would become commonplace after the Second World War: 'If racial peculiarities exist, so do individual idiosyncrasies; and the disparity between two men of different nationalities need not be so great as the disparity between two men of the same nationality'.[134] In *Racial Supremacy*, published during the 1905 election campaign, he called upon the Liberals to reject imperialism and return to liberal principles, including a belief in political equality. Godard began with Lord Rosebery, a leading Liberal Imperialist, who had pronounced, 'what is empire but predominance of race?' Identifying imperialism with 'the spirit of rule, ascendency, or predominance; the rule of one race or people by another race or people', Godard described the South African War as a 'grim catalogue of horrors'. Any claim that imperialism was of benefit to the conquered was simply a 'self-delusion', for imperialism rested upon 'asserting our own supremacy', upon 'the doctrine of the chosen nation', and had 'inequality' as its foundation.[135] Here the churches had lost their way, preaching not universal brotherhood but patriotism and racial supremacy, whereas protests against 'lust of conquest and the law of predominance' came from the secularists.[136] Concluding that imperialism was not in the British national interest, Godard affirmed: 'Our safety lies where our honour lies; not in fostering empire, dominion, predominance; but in promoting autonomy, liberty, brotherhood. Egoism, not less than altruism, bids us abjure the doctrine of racial supremacy.'[137]

In 1904, in *Democracy and Reaction*, L. T. Hobhouse more directly addressed post-war developments in South Africa, and how the imperial idea, liberal in origin, had been corrupted. The liberal principle of self-government only applied to colonies of white settlement and not to tropical dependencies which he claimed made up to seven-eighths of the population of the empire. According to Hobhouse, 'The literature of Imperialism is openly contemptuous — sometimes aggressively, sometimes patronisingly — of the "coloured" races, and scoffs at the old Liberal conception of opening to them the road to self-development, and alternates between a sentimental insistence on the duties owed to them by the white man, and invective against any one who inquires how those duties are being performed.'[138] The South African War and post-war reconstruction gave rise to an innovative discourse on legal and political rights within a new kind of multi-racial society, but it was not the sole issue attracting the attention of the critics and reformers of empire.

The BFASS and the APS, both with limited resources, faced the challenge of 'new slaveries' in cocoa production. Henry Nevinson charged that the British Quaker manufacturers of chocolate – Cadbury, Fry, and Rowntree – relied on slave-produced cocoa from plantations on São Tomé and Príncipe off the coast of Portuguese Angola. From the foundation of both humanitarian agencies, the Quakers had provided leadership and support. During the South African War, George Cadbury had purchased the *Daily News*, the one London daily that the BFASS and the APS could rely upon for favourable publicity. William Cadbury led the discussions of the chocolate manufacturers with the BFASS and the APS seeking to coordinate lobbying of the foreign office and the Portuguese government.[139]

At the same time, British and international opinion began to probe abuses reported from King Leopold's Congo Free State. Although the APS like the BFASS had supported Leopold II's proclaimed humanitarian objectives at Brussels, as early as 1890 Fox Bourne began collecting and investigating reported abuses. Beginning with Henry Stanley's exploits, the *Aborigines' Friend* reported on the Congo, and on behalf of the APS, Sir Charles Dilke had raised questions in parliament. Correspondence between Fox Bourne and E. D. Morel began in 1901, and in its early stages the APS secretary provided advice on lobbying parliament, and served as a link between Morel and Sir Charles Dilke.[140] Relations between Fox Bourne and Morel became difficult when Morel proposed establishing the Congo Reform Association (CRA). There were no doubt territorial imperatives at work. Fox Bourne's book *Crisis in Congoland* (1903) had just been published, and the APS committee and its secretary felt they had initiated the campaign. Partly due to the intervention of Roger Casement, whose 1904 report turned the public debate against King Leopold's colonial enterprise, the dispute was substantially resolved. While the APS maintained its own watching brief on developments, in effect the CRA became the principal agency lobbying on the Congo, and Fox Bourne, Dilke and Francis Fox from the APS served on the CRA executive.[141] Nagging differences remained, especially over Morel's disdain for the political work of the APS. Recent studies, some taking Morel's self-promotion at face value, have built a contrast between Morel as a successful publicist and Fox Bourne as a failure, largely due to an inability to focus on a single issue capable of a political resolution.[142] To put it simply, a satisfactory outcome for Africans, coloureds and Indians in South Africa was not possible. Fox Bourne and the APS exhausted their energies and political capital in this struggle for racial justice, and fittingly in 1909, a year before the new South African race-based constitution came into effect, Fox Bourne died and the APS ceased to exist as an independent organisation.

If one pursues a somewhat different question from whether the ASP was a success or a failure, the outcome of the APS campaign over South Africa takes on a different significance. While there were a host of issues engaging the humanitarian agency's attention, given its involvement with southern Africa since the 1870s, and given the challenge of a post-war settlement to the APS defence of its flawed vision of racial equality, neither Fox Bourne nor the APS could abandon the cause. In the history of colonialism and race, there were also some disturbing aspects to the Congo reform campaign. In its presentations, especially in the illustrated 'atrocity lectures' by John and Alice Harris at Nonconformist chapels, the Congolese were first of all victims of horrendous abuse, and their saviours were white British humanitarians.[143] While Leopold's officials were held responsible for outrages against the Congolese, the agents under European command were African mercenaries, often depicted as cannibals deliberately selected to carry out savage reprisals for failure to meet rubber quotas. The images of innocent victim and savage mercenary reinforced existing stereotypes of Africans. In 1919, the black mercenaries of the Congo would rematerialise in Morel's outcry of 'Horror on the Rhine' against the French use of African troops in Germany.[144] The Congo reform campaign also had a more immediate and longer lasting outcome for defence of the rights and interests of Africans. In 1910, E. D. Morel's associate in the CRA, the Reverend John Harris, became the secretary of the newly amalgamated Anti-Slavery and Aborigines Protection Society. Under his leadership, the leading British humanitarian organisation dealing with slavery and other forms of racial oppression became one of the principal advocates of imperial trusteeship.[145]

With the commencement of the South African War (1899–1902), Fox Bourne and the APS moved beyond statements affirming 'the claims of uncivilised races' to land, to the retention of customs and institutions, and to the adoption of western practices not by coercion but only by consent. In 1900, in *Blacks and Whites in South Africa*, Fox Bourne asserted that until the wrongs inflicted upon Africans in the Boer Republics and in British jurisdictions were addressed, 'there [would] be no equality of rights for black people and white in South Africa'.[146] For some time, he had advised his readers that contrary to British humanitarian conceit conditions for Africans under British jurisdictions were worse than their treatment by the Boers. Furthermore, the worst excesses under the Republics occurred under British employers in the gold mines. These opinions, which he conveyed in a letter to *The Times* in 1901, provoked a controversy with an old adversary, Charles Allen of the BFASS.[147]

Avoiding a contentious debate on the causes of the war, the APS made the politically intelligent decision to look forward to the end of the war, and the task of post-war reconstruction. Wishing to protect its non-partisan status, and aware of divisions over the war among its members, the BFASS decided to follow the lead of the APS.[148] Latching on to a statement by Lord Salisbury that a settlement would have to address the welfare of Africans, in 1900 the APS issued a nine-point charter of native rights as a basis for government policy. The charter and its explanatory notes reflected some of the earlier APS statements on the status of Africans placing less emphasis on race than on culture in which the key distinction lay between the 'civilised' and the 'uncivilised'.

In its charter of native rights, the APS grouped as 'natives', all who were 'not of the white race', including Africans, coloureds and Indians largely resident in Natal. This terminology had the political advantage of conforming to the common usage in South Africa, and of making the 'native' class an overwhelming majority that included both 'civilised' and 'uncivilised' peoples. All persons designated as 'natives' were to be wards of the imperial government and not subject to laws of local legislatures unless approved by the imperial authority. Within this native class, the charter addressed the legal status and rights of persons in three categories: first, the uncivilised; second, the civilised; and third, those in a state of transition between these two categories. For the 'uncivilised' the charter provided for the establishment of reserved territories, modelled on the Bechuanaland Protectorate. For persons choosing to live under traditional conditions on reserved lands, the charter called for protections for customary practices and institutions, an independent role for royal commissioners to oversee relations with the external white community and governments, and specific provisions for education, forms of taxation and the regulation of pass laws for travel and work outside of the reserved territories.[149] These terms were a product of the long history of APS attempts to construct a protected legal status for indigenous peoples, and of more recent developments in southern Africa in which the 'imperial factor' would regulate relations between whites and Africans. The explanatory notes reviewed existing territories under occupation by Africans within the Boer Republics and under the British crown, and called for such lands to be fixed for African residence. These lands were far more extensive than the reserves under the Land Act of 1913. Outside these territories, an initial estimate of 500,000 – or between ten and fifteen per cent of the 'native' population – resided under the 'civilised' conditions of white rule, including those working for white employers.[150] Contrary to some secondary accounts looking for the origins of apartheid, the reserved lands, in the APS design, were not a form of separate development. The report of the South African Native Affairs Commission, appointed by Milner and chaired by Sir Godfrey Lagden, became the blueprint for segregation by race. Its recommendations, according to the *Aborigines' Friend*, were a set of 'reactionary proposals'.[151] In APS thinking, over time those residing on reserved lands would choose to assimilate to civilised conditions, and the political challenge was to establish equality under the law for those 'natives' already assimilated, and to prevent the creation of obstacles to the assimilating process in the future.[152]

In addition to its reliance on the 'imperial factor', the charter's provisions for persons in transition to civilised conditions or living under civilised conditions were politically contentious, necessitating substantial reforms not only in the Boer Republics but in Natal and Cape Colony. Under the charter, persons in transition to civilised status were subject to regulations under civil not criminal law. Questions of employment and residence would come under municipal authorities not private companies, and there could be other special provisions, for example liquor laws and protections against indebtedness due to fraudulent contracts. Otherwise, such persons were not to be placed in a distinct legal category but were to have equal standing under the law. Persons living under civilised conditions would by their free consent give up all the rights and privileges of residence in reserved territories. Such persons would have equal standing with whites under the law, including the right to own and bequeath property, the right to enter trades and professions for which they qualified, and the right to the franchise at municipal and parliamentary elections.[153] Under the APS charter of native rights, the goal was eventual legal and political equality under assimilation to civilised conditions. It still made significant distinctions between peoples and their legal status, but these distinctions were based not on the fixed identity of race but on the malleable conditions of culture. The first and hardest test of the principles of the APS charter came with the negotiations for the new constitutions of the former Boer Republics of the Transvaal and the Orange Free State. The APS failure to influence the imperial government in these negotiations presaged its failure in the making of the constitution for the new South African Union.[154]

In 1903, the APS reissued its charter as an appendix to Fox Bourne's pamphlet on *Forced Labour in South Africa*. The controversies surrounding the origin and conduct of the war gave rise to a more radical political discourse on South Africa, its financial interests, particularly in the mining sector, and the efforts to recruit at first African labour, and failing that Chinese indentured labour. Whereas the charter of native rights published in 1900 had been formally approved at a meeting of the APS and aimed to provide a blueprint for government policy, Fox Bourne's pamphlet of 1903 on forced labour was not subject to such moderating influences. In fact, its stated intention was to fulfil the historical purpose of such special reports – to provide information and analysis in preparation for debates in parliament. By 1903, all indications suggested that Charles Dilke's warning prior to the end of the war might become a reality. Dilke had warned in 1902 that the peace 'might be a peace over the body of the native: there might be an inclination on both sides ... to make a peace in which native interests would be sacrificed or forgotten'.[155]

Quoting from government reports, submissions from the mining companies, and his own South African correspondents, Fox Bourne warned his readers of the intention of the 'Rand Capitalists' to reinvent conditions of slavery. Citing the mine owners' submission on their need for cheap labour and their description of the African labourer as 'an excellent and powerful muscular machine', he was particularly critical of Milner and Chamberlain for becoming the agents of the mining interests. Even though Milner had written that he accepted in principle the APS charter of native rights, Fox Bourne cited specific examples of how the High Commissioner's initiatives were in conflict with those principles. The APS secretary took Chamberlain to task for accepting the capitalists' claim that African men were inherently idle, relied on the work of their wives, and therefore needed coercive means to fulfil their duty to labour. Fox Bourne defended African marriage customs, claiming that the exchange of cattle between families gave women greater status and greater protection from abuse or abandonment than monogamy offered working-class wives in Glasgow.[156] He directed his sharpest rebuke to clergymen who had linked the discipline of the Gospel with the discipline of labour in the gold mines. The APS secretary observed: 'the highest function of the Church in South Africa is to co-operate with the State in forcing on the natives, under the name of education, a universal system of industrial training, by which the mines can be stocked with such an abundance of cheap labour as will satisfy even the capitalists of the Rand'.[157] Fox Bourne concluded his analysis by calling on his readers to recollect the anti-slavery commitments of Wilberforce and Clarkson, and challenged them 'to now prevent the setting-up of a new slave-trade and a new slavery under new names'.[158] Such APS appeals angered the society's critics at home, and carried little weight in South Africa.[159] Dissatisfied with the supply of African workers and seeking to reduce their wages, the mine owners – with the approval of the imperial authorities – imported 60,000 indentured labourers from China.

Despite the formation of a Liberal Government in 1906, the reconstruction of South Africa seemed to be headed in the direction Fox Bourne and the APS most feared. With the support of the APS Committee, Fox Bourne participated in a conference at the Hague in August 1907 to consider the rights of subject races and to establish principles as part of the international Hague Convention. The APS secretary clearly had a hand in drafting some of the resolutions, for the language was similar to comparable principles he had crafted in papers presented in the 1890s. In speaking to the resolutions, mindful that he had spent the previous two decades publicising the abuses of colonialism, and that the APS had failed in its efforts to protect the rights and liberties of Africans and persons of colour in the reconstructed South Africa, he observed:

> unhappily, no code of international law has yet been established for systematising, or even for humanising in any comprehensive sense, the relations of the nations that call themselves civilised with races and

communities that they brand as uncivilised, and it is not too much to
say that, as regards the relations between the so-called civilised and the
so-called uncivilised in our own times, the vaunted progress of civilisation has been marked, if not by unparalleled barbarism, at any rate by an
appalling, recrudescence of barbarism.[160]

In face of this situation, Fox Bourne, more unequivocally than he had
done before, set out the natural rights of indigenous peoples to land,
to control of their cultural, political and other institutions including
future reforms, and to participate on 'equitable terms' in any benefits
resulting from interventions of 'civilised' agencies.[161]

The international campaign over the Congo had disgraced King
Leopold and forced the Belgian government to intervene. Faced with
a British government impervious to humanitarian appeals, there was
always the hope that an appeal to an international tribunal might have
some sway against the appeal of Rand gold and the patriotic call to
king and empire. Concluding his remarks by reviewing the abuses of
colonialism beginning with the Congo and ending with British rule in
Africa, Fox Bourne puts his hope in 'an agreement being arrived at for
the bringing of offences against more or less savage communities, no
less than against other subject races, within the sphere of international
law – such an agreement as alone can effectively overcome the monstrous evils that now are rampant'.[162]

Fox Bourne was now seventy years old. He had hoped that a Liberal
Government might set a different course in South Africa, but the only
significant change was on the issue of Chinese indentured labour.
While the APS and the BFASS participated in the outrage over 'Chinese
slavery,' they were minor players in a public outcry from the electorate
led by the Liberal Party, from trade unionists protecting white labour,
and from whites in South Africa. Consequently, Milner's and the
mining employers' labour scheme had a short life.[163]

Frustrated in its efforts to influence the imperial government, the
APS supported petitions from persons of colour objecting to the racial
exclusions in the new constitutions of the Transvaal and Orange Free
State and under the terms of the new union government. The *Aborigines' Friend* printed the APS memorial to the colonial office and the attached petitions from organisations calling upon APS assistance. It also
gave a supportive report on petitions from the South African Native
Congress and the Transvaal Native Congress.[164] The society and Sir
Charles Dilke assisted Dr Abdurahman, the president of the African
Political Organization (Coloured People), in a meeting with MPs and
the colonial office to present the case for the franchise. The presentation impressed the politicians and the civil servants, but it made no
headway as votes for the coloureds meant that the franchise could not

be denied to qualified Indians in Natal, and white South African opinion, both Boer and British, was resolutely opposed. In Westminster, the priority was to achieve a settlement that British settlers and the Boers would accept. APS lobbying, regardless of the rightness of the cause or the effectiveness of Dr Abdurahman and his fellow petitioners, did not have the political clout of white South Africa.[165]

In the meantime, Fox Bourne faced a number of critical issues, and he became more radical in his response to the mounting evidence of racial oppression. The APS secretary grew impatient with diplomacy on the new slaveries in São Tomé and Príncipe. Early in 1908 and independently of the BFASS, Fox Bourne called for a consumer boycott of slave-produced chocolate. His action provoked William Cadbury to sever all connections with the APS.[166] Through his participation in meetings at the Hague he had become more aware of nationalist demands in central and eastern Europe, the Ottoman Empire and elsewhere. He worked with Henry Nevinson and Mrs N. Dryhurst of the Subject Races and Nationalities Committee. Its agenda had expanded from minorities in the empires of the old world to colonised subjects of overseas empires.[167] He joined J. M. Robertson's Egypt Committee, which kept a watch over Lord Cromer's administration and its censorship of the press and imprisonment of nationalists. On 13 June 1906 at the village of Denshawai, five British officers on a pigeon shoot were attacked by peasants, resulting in injury to three officers and the death of a fourth. In retaliation, a special tribunal sentenced four peasants to death and nine to penal servitude with flogging. Fox Bourne published a pamphlet entitled *Egypt under British Control* (1907) and a series, *Notes on Egyptian Affairs* (1907, 1908), offering a critique of Cromer's administration. The name of the APS appeared on the cover, but the APS committee had not approved the publications.[168]

At its meeting of 17 January 1908, the APS committee reviewed a proposal for the amalgamation of the APS, the BFASS, and the London District of the CRA. Discussions had taken place between Travers Buxton, the secretary of the BFASS, Francis Fox of the APS, and the Reverend John Harris. On learning that E. D. Morel had not been consulted, the APS dropped the idea.[169] On 2 March 1908, Fox Bourne submitted his resignation, claiming he did not have the united support of the APS committee. The APS minutes did not indicate any discontent with the secretary's performance, but the most likely reasons were his stand on the chocolate boycott and possibly his Egyptian pamphlets. The committee rejected Fox Bourne's resignation and assured him of its support.[170] In the last number of the *Aborigines' Friend* under his direction, in October 1908, he reiterated the principles of the APS, including political equality for those qualified as 'civilised', and more emphatically than in earlier statements, adopted the principles of the Hague resolutions giving peoples subject to colonial interventions the right to maintain their own customs and institutions.[171] Whether APS members would support this advance in defending the rights and autonomy of 'native' peoples was never tested. Within four months, Fox Bourne died of a heart attack on 2 February 1909.

The APS could barely keep itself financially solvent, and with the death of its secretary, the society bowed to the inevitable, and discussions commenced immediately on amalgamation with the BFASS. Some APS members opposed the merger for they feared that their larger agenda might be reduced to the diminishing scope of anti-slavery. The one contentious matter was an effort by BFASS members to exclude constitutional representation and self-government from the mandate of the new society. The APS committee managed to get that exclusion removed, though it was left for future discussions.[172]

The last issue of the *Aborigines' Friend* in May 1909 still protested against the 'colour bar' in the draft South African constitution.[173] In contrast, the new Anti-Slavery and Aborigines Protection Society reprinted the convocation address at the University of the Cape of Good Hope by Lord Selborne, the High Commissioner. Both the BFASS and APS had welcomed Selborne's warnings to white South Africans that they had to address the 'native' or 'colour' question now, or their children and children's children would reap the consequences. Despite this perceptive warning, and while open to a 'civilisation test' for the franchise, the pamphlet affirmed the essential racialised differences between blacks and whites, offered a weakened defence of that vestige of Cape liberalism, the coloured franchise, and asserted that Africans were not suited to parliamentary forms of government.[174]

Within a year the Reverend John Harris was hired as the secretary of the amalgamated society. He had fallen out with E. D. Morel and had left the CRA. As a former missionary and evangelical preacher, Harris and his wife Alice, as they had done for the CRA, relied on their Nonconformist connections to rebuild support for the newly amalgamated society. Some of the more radical and active members of the APS committee – for example, Jane Cobden Unwin – eventually resigned, and new members included a significant number of clergy. Fox Bourne, Morel and Dilke had recognised that their supporters included members of missionary societies but nonetheless distrusted religious influences on the political objectives of their organisations. Under Harris, the merged society more readily promoted imperial rule as a 'sacred trust', and its philanthropy had less space for the agency of colonised people. The society under Harris was more deferential in its relations with cabinet ministers, civil servants and colonial administrators, and supported Lord Lugard's policy of indirect rule. Despite the moderation of its criticism, the Anti-Slavery and Aborigines Protection Society lost its royal patron. George V could not be patron of a society even moderately critical of his own South African government. In an article on 'The South African Native Land Act', *Anti-Slavery Reporter and Aborigines' Friend* described the hostile reaction of Africans, and the society's assistance with a delegation to Westminster, but offered no critical appraisal of its own. Subsequently, Harris, who approved of segregation and the Land Act and had worked to frustrate the lobby of the African delegation, published a pamphlet in support of General Botha's modest reform proposal of 1916. As part of a long dispute, Harris sharply accused Sol Plaatje and the South African Native National Congress of a 'monstrous misrepresentation' of the 1913 Act. While supportive of Botha's unrealised reforms, even Harris acknowledged they provided a less than generous allocation of 40 million acres to 5 million 'coloured' and 260 million acres to 1.3 million whites.[175]

Like Fox Bourne, Harris also saw a need for international conventions on the treatment of subject peoples. Far less critical of British imperialism with its humanitarian tradition, and in his view preferable to the imperialism of other European powers, Harris, along with James Bryce and other British officials, participated in planning for mandated territories and trusteeships established under the League of Nations. His pamphlet on *Native Races and the Peace Terms* (1916) called for a 'just settlement for the child races of the world'.[176] In the *African Times and Oriental Review*, Dues Mohammed Ali accused Harris of being out of touch with 'progressive' native opinion and referred to the pamphlet as 'patronizing Anti-Slavery Society slime'.[177]

Historians of empire have largely seen the language of trusteeship as a positive accommodation of the humanitarian tradition to the imperialism of the twentieth century and as a bridge to the discourse of development.[178] They have largely overlooked the cost of this transition, especially when viewed through the lens of racial discourse. Notions of imperial trusteeship retained many of the illusions of the older civilising mission. Its exponents, such as the Reverend John Harris, envisaged a white guardianship over ageless brown and black children and did not anticipate that, in the face of colonial nationalism, imperial trusteeship would have a relatively short historical life. What was lost was the goal of racial equality and the language of 'native' or human rights. Rooted in the more radical branches of the anti-slavery movement, this language was given an extended life by Catherine Impey through the SRBM and by Fox Bourne through the APS. More direct challenges to race and empire came from Celestine Edwards, Dadabhai Naoroji, H. Sylvester Williams, T. E. S. Scholes and other colonial nationalists who faced the sharp end of racism. On the other hand, the discourse of trusteeship accommodated the obsolescent racial types of the scientists, and more significantly for enduring defences of inequality, readily adopted the newer language of race relations. A few British radicals still used the language of human rights, but resistance to racism would be largely sustained, and its political analysis and practice largely developed by colonised subjects of colour living under an imperial regime bifurcated by race.

Notes

1 *The News of the World* (5 June 1887), 5b; another report in *The Weekly Dispatch* (5 June 1887), 11b.
2 RH, Anti-Slavery Papers. Brit. Emp. S18. Correspondence. C159/77, James R. Maxwell to Earl of Derby, 23 May 1883; on Bryce, see Chapter 6.
3 RH, Anti-Slavery Papers. Brit. Emp. S18. Correspondence. C58/23–23a, D. G. Garraway to C. H. Allen, 7 February 1882.
4 Douglas Lorimer, 'Black resistance to slavery and racism in eighteenth-century England', in J. S. Gundara and I. Duffield (eds), *Essays in the History of Blacks in Britain* (Aldershot: Avebury, 1992), pp. 58–80.
5 See discussion of Celestine Edwards and T. E. S. Scholes below.
6 Blackett, *Building the Anti-Slavery Wall*; Spiers, 'Black Americans in Britain', pp. 81–98; Lorimer, *Colour, Class*, pp. 45–56; on Pan-African Address, see below.
7 Holt, *Problem of Freedom*; Hall, *Civilising Subjects*; Richardson (ed.), *Abolition and its Aftermath*; Seymour Drescher, *The Mighty Experiment*.
8 Blackburn, *Overthrow of Colonial Slavery*, pp. 436–57; Drescher, *Abolition*, pp. 248–66.
9 BFASS. *Sixty Years against Slavery. A Brief Record of the Work and Aims of the British and Foreign Anti-Slavery Society, 1839–1899* (London: 1899); Temperley, *British Anti-Slavery*; David Turley, *The Culture of English Antislavery, 1780–1860* (London: Routledge, 1991).
10 Fox Bourne, *Chapters*, pp. 3–13; Heartfield, *Aborigines' Protection*, pp. 9–41.
11 Evans *et al.* (eds), *Equal Subjects, Unequal Rights*.
12 See Chapter 2.
13 'Good word for the anti-slavery society', *ASR*, 4th ser., 15 (1895), 40.
14 *ASR*, 4th ser., 28 (1908), 67–8.
15 *ASR*, 4th ser., 28 (1908), 35.
16 Heartfield, *Aborigines' Protection*, pp. 61–9; Fox Bourne, *Chapters*, p. 48.
17 J. Eastoe Teall, *Slave Trade and Slavery, 1889: Facts and Memoranda compiled from the Slave-trade Papers, the Statutes at large, and other Sources* (London: British and Foreign Anti-Slavery Society, 1889).
18 Teall, *Slave Trade and Slavery*; Charles H. Allen, 'What is Great Britain doing to suppress slavery and the slave-trade?', *ASR*, 4th ser., 13 (1893), 247–259; Suzanne Miers, *Britain and the Ending of the Slave Trade* (New York: Africana Publishing, 1975).
19 J. Eastoe Teall, *A Brief Account of the Results of Compensation to the West India Slave-holders and the Continuation of Slavery after Apprenticeship* (1897); Howard Temperley, 'The Deregulation of Slavery in British India', *After Slavery*, pp. 169–87; Frederick Cooper, 'Conditions Analogous to Slavery: Imperialism and Free Labor Ideology in Africa', in F. Cooper, T. C. Holt and R. J. Scott, *Beyond Slavery: Explorations of Race, Labor, and Citizenship in Post-Emancipation Societies* (Chapel Hill, NC: University of North Carolina Press, 2000), pp. 107–49.
20 Report of 1884 Jubilee celebration, *ASR*, 4th ser., 4 (1884), 171–92; Thomas L. Johnson, *Twenty-Eight Years a Slave, or the Story of My Life on Three Continents* (Bournemouth, 1909), pp. 158–9, 167–8.

21 *ASR*, 4th ser., 5 (1885), 279–85.
22 *ASR*, 3rd ser., 20 (1876), 144–7; 4th ser., 10 (1890), 41–2, 81–5; 11 (1891), 12–13; A. G. Hopkins', Explorers' Tales: Stanley Presumes – Again', *Journal of Imperial and Commonwealth History* 36 (2008), 669–84.
23 'Anti-Slavery Crusade', *ASR*, 4th ser., 8 (1888), 91–117.
24 *ASR*, 4th ser., 10 (1890), 31–9.
25 *ASR*, 4th ser., 10 (1890), 5–9.
26 *ASR*, 4th ser., 7 (1887), 37–41; 10 (1890), 28; 1 (1881), 12.
27 RH. Anti-Slavery Papers. Brit. Emp. S20 E2/11 BFASS Minute Book (1887–1901), #755 30 July 1897; #986 4 January 1901; for 1900, the minutes reported a deficit of £102; in 1902 and 1903, the revenues had declined to less than £800, or to fifty per cent less than fifteen years earlier.
28 Between the 1880s and 1907, the proportion of women subscribers and donors in the BFASS increased from thirty per cent to forty per cent – *ASR*, 4th ser., 7 (1887), 37–41, and 22 (1907), 15–21; in 1905, the society allowed for the election of women on the executive committee; Clare Midgley, 'Anti-Slavery and the roots of imperial feminism', in Midgley (ed.), *Gender and Imperialism* (Manchester: Manchester University Press), pp. 161–79.
29 'Slavery under the British flag', *ASR*, 4th ser., 15 (1895), 147–61, and BFASS dispute with the *Pall Mall Gazette*, 189–202; BFASS, *Memorial of the British and Foreign Anti-Slavery Society. Documents Connected with Slavery and the Slave Trade in the Sultinate of Zanzibar* (London: 1897); F. Cooper, *From Slaves to Squatters: Plantation Labor and Agriculture in Zanzibar and Coastal Kenya, 1890–1925* (New Haven, CT: Yale University Press, 1980), pp. 24–68.
30 *ASR*, 4th ser., 5 (1885), 300–1, and 13 (1893), 129–35.
31 *ASR*, 4th ser., 21 (1901), 183–5; 22 (1902), 6; 24 (1904), 11.
32 RH, Anti-Slavery Papers. Brit. Emp. S20 E2/11 BFASS Minute Book, #932, 4 May 1900; *ASR*, 4th ser., 20 (1900), 100–1.
33 For example, *ASR*, 4th ser., 20 (1900), 156.
34 'The emancipated people and the Southern States', *ASR*, 3rd ser., 21 (1879), 171–6; 'The negro question in the United States', 4th ser., 11 (1891), 30–3; 'The negro future', 4th ser., 15 (1895), 249–51; on lynching and convict leasing, 4th ser., 22 (1902), 65–8, 95, and 24 (1904), 31–3.
35 'The race problem in the United States', *ASR*, 4th ser., 21 (1901), 168–71.
36 'The West Indian Journal and Civil Rights Guardian', *ASR*, 4th ser., 13 (1893), 98.
37 RH, Anti-Slavery Papers. Brit. Emp. S20 E2/12 BFASS Minute Book, #1406, 6 July 1906; 'Annual report, 1907', *ASR*, 4th ser., 27 (1907), 4 (separately paged), and 'Centenary of the abolition of the slave trade', 3; *The Times* (23 March 1907), 3f.
38 Merriman-Labor, *Britons*, pp. 152–6; *ASR*, 4th ser., 27 (1907), 41–5; about three hundred people attended including the descendants of the heroic first generation of abolitionists and representatives of the BFASS, the APS and the CRA.
39 RH, Anti-Slavery Papers. Brit. Emp. S18. Correspondence C153/36 (Copy), H. R. Fox Bourne to Arnold White, 24 February 1890.
40 *The Colonial Intelligencer and Aborigines' Friend*, new ser., 1 (1855–8), 347–8, and 2 (1859–66), 292–6, 524; Laidlaw, 'Thomas Hodgkin's critique of missions and anti-slavery', 133–61. See also Chapter 5.
41 H. C. Swaisland, 'Chesson, Frederick William (1833–88)', *NODNB* (2005) [www.oxfoddnb.com]; [H. R. Fox Bourne], 'Frederick William Chesson', *AF*, new ser., 3 (March 1889), 513–23. See also Chapter 5.
42 Fox Bourne, *Chapters*, p. 44.
43 H. C. Swaisland, 'Bourne, Henry Richard Fox (1837–1909)', *NODNB* (2004), [www.oxforddnb.com]; 'H. R. Fox Bourne', *AF* new ser., 8 (May 1909), 245–55; *The Times* (6 February 1909), 13d; Ernest Belfort Bax, *Reminiscences and Reflections of a Mid and Late Victorian* [1918] (New York: August M. Kelly, 1967), pp. 30–1, 228–9; Heartfield, *Aborigines' Protection*, p. 33.
44 Fox Bourne, *English Newspapers: Chapters in the History of Journalism* (London, 1887), vol. 2, pp. 348–54.

45 This split between the two societies created a lengthy, combative correspondence and public dispute, e.g., RH, Anti-Slavery Papers. Brit. Emp. S18. Correspondence C150/12 and 12a, Charles Allen to Fox Bourne, 13 January 1890, and C150/114, S. Buxton to Fox Bourne, 28 January 1890; *AF*, new ser., 4 (1890), 3–10, 11–21.

46 H. R. Fox Bourne, 'Our West Africa possessions', *Gentleman's Magazine*, 267 (October 1889), 379–90; RH, Anti-Slavery Papers. Brit. Emp. S18. Correspondence C151/60, George T. Goldie to Fox Bourne, 7 November 1889.

47 Frederick Mackarness, 'South Africa and irresponsible government', *Contemporary Review*, 56 (August 1889), 234–43; Flora Shaw, 'Dry-Nursing the colonies', *Fortnightly Review*, new ser., 46 (September 1889), 367–79; Fox Bourne, 'South Africa and the Aborigines Protection Society', *Contemporary Review*, 56 (September 1889), 347–69; 'The society on its defence', *AF*, new ser., 4 (February 1890), 31–5; on Spriggs' remarks, *Pall Mall Gazette* (9 September 1887).

48 Secondary sources mention the letter but rarely cite it directly; reprinted in *AF*, new ser., 3 (1889), 585; Åke Holmberg, *African Tribes and European Agencies: Colonialism and Humanitarianism in British South and East Africa, 1870–1895* (Göteborg: Scandinavian University Books, 1966), pp. 202–23.

49 Fife chaired the APS annual meeting, *AF*, new ser., 4 (1891), 196–7; RH, Anti-Slavery Papers. Brit. Emp. S18. Correspondence C150/203, Harriet Colenso to Fox Bourne, 1 June 1891; *Anti-Caste*, 4 (July 1891), 1–2, 4; H. R. Fox Bourne and Harriet Colenso, *The Story of Dinuzulu* (London: Zulu Defence Committee, 1890); H. R. Fox Bourne, *Matebeleland and the Chartered Company* (1897); H. R. Fox Bourne, *The Bechuana Troubles: a Story of Pledge-Breaking, Rebel-Making and Slave-Making in a British Colony* (1898); Jeff Guy, *The View across the River: Harriet Colenso and the Zulu Struggle against Imperialism* (Charlottesville, VA.: University of Virginia Press, 2002).

50 RH, Anti-Slavery Papers. Brit. Emp. S18. Correspondence C151/173–173a, James Johnson to Fox Bourne, 18 July 1889.

51 RH, Anti-Slavery Papers. Brit. Emp. S18. Correspondence C165/75, Mutual Protection Association to ASP, July 1890; 'Coloured British Subjects in the Transvaal', *AF*, new ser., 4 (1890), 130–1; 4 (1891), 148–9; 4 (1892), 258–63; H. R. Fox Bourne, *Civilisation in Congoland: A Story of International Wrong-Doing* (London, 1903), pp. 124–5, and *Chapters*, pp. 52–3.

52 H. R. Fox Bourne, *Blacks and Whites in West Africa: An Account of the Past and Present Condition of West African Natives under European Control* (London: P. S. King, 1902), pp. 5–6, 38–43 (critique of Chamberlain), and pp. 55, 68–70, 77, 80 (citations to Kingsley).

53 H. R. Fox Bourne, 'The duty of civilised states to weaker races', *AF*, new ser., 4 (April 1891), 169–76; 'The civilising of Africa', *AF*, new ser., 4 (February 1893), 330–8; 'Natives under British Rule in Africa', *AF*, new ser., 5 (December 1896), 96–105. On his criteria for 'civilised' and 'uncivilised' conditions, see Chapter 6.

54 TNA, CO96/284 APS Memorial on British Administration in West Africa, 28 March 1896, H. R. Fox Bourne to Rt Hon. Joseph Chamberlain, Secretary of State, Colonial Office [printed]; CO291/65 APS to Lyttleton, 25 November 1903, minute signed FG [Frederick Graham] 27 November 1903.

55 'The treatment of native races', *AF*, new ser., 5 (May 1897), 154–5.

56 *Anti-Caste*, 1 (March 1888), 1; David M. Fahey, 'Impey, Catherine (1847–1923)', *NODNB* (2004) [www.oxforddnb.com]; Vron Ware, *Beyond the Pale*, pp. 169–224.

57 *ASR*, 3rd ser., 21 (1879), 148–9; Fahey, *Temperance and Racism*.

58 *Anti-Caste*, 1 (March 1888), 1.

59 *Anti-Caste*, 5 (March 1892), 4, and 6 (January 1893), 4; RH, Anti-Slavery Papers. Brit. Emp. S18. Correspondence C138/173, Catherine Impey to F. W. Chesson, 1 March 1888.

60 RH, Anti-Slavery Papers. Brit. Emp. S18. Correspondence C61/4, Catherine Impey to Charles Allen, 8 March 1883.

61 *Anti-Caste*, 4 (April 1891), 2.

62 Ida B. Wells, *Crusade for Justice: The Autobiography of Ida B. Wells*, ed., Alfreda M.

Duster (Chicago, IL: University of Chicago, 1970), p. 82. On Campbell, see Chapter 5.
63 RH, Anti-Slavery Papers. Brit. Emp. S20 E5/7 'Minute Book of C. Impey for the Society of the Brotherhood of Man' enclosing Frederick Douglass to Catherine Impey, 9 July 1888.
64 *Anti-Caste*, 2 (October 1889), 4.
65 *Anti-Caste*, 2 (October 1889), 2, 4; 'The relapse of the negro', *Standard* (20 September 1889), 3. Robert Brown may be the author of the *Standard* leader (see Chapter 4).
66 RH, Anti-Slavery Papers. Brit. Emp. S20 E5/7 'Minute Book of C. Impey for the Society of the Brotherhood of Man' enclosing [Private] To whom it may concern. Catherine Impey, 17 August 1893; Wells, *Crusade*, p. 82.
67 Lindy Moore, 'The reputation of Isabella Fyvie Mayo: interpretation of a life', *Women's History Review*, 19 (2010), 71–88; Emma Plaskitt, 'Mayo Isabella (1843–1914)', *NODNB* (2004) [www.oxforddnb.com], Isabella Mayo, *Recollections: What I saw, What I lived through and What I learned* (London: 1910), p. 18.
68 RH, Brit. Emp. S20 E5/7 'Minute Book of C. Impey' enclosing 'To whom it may concern', 17 August 1893.
69 Wells, *Crusade*, pp. 105–10; Ware, *Beyond the Pale*, pp. 190–7.
70 Wells, *Crusade*, pp. 109–13.
71 Mayo, *Recollections*, pp. 348–9; Moore, 'Mayo'.
72 Impey and Mayo had agreed to share equally in paying for any debts incurred from Wells' campaign, and according to Impey, Mayo reneged on the promise and left her to pay the £37 owing. RH, Anti-Slavery Papers. Brit. Emp. S20 E5/7 'Minute Book of C. Impey', 17 August 1893.
73 Ware, *Beyond the Pale*; Sandra Stanley Horton, 'Segregation, racism and white women reformers: a transnational analysis', *Women's History Review*, 10 (2001), 5–26; Caroline Bressey, 'A strange and bitter crop: Ida B Wells' anti-lynching tours, Britain 1893 and 1894', *Centre for Capital Punishment Studies: Occasional Papers*, 1 (December 2003), 8–28; Moore, 'Mayo', 71–88; unfortunately most accounts do not make use of Catherine Impey's papers and minute books in the Anti-Slavery Collection at Rhodes House Library.
74 Wells, *Crusade*, pp. 137, 220.
75 Jonathan Schneer, 'Edwards (Samuel Jules) Celestine (1857?–1894)', *NODNB* (2006) [www.oxforddnb.com.]; Schneer, *London 1900*, pp. 205–12; Peter Fryer, *Staying Power*, pp. 277–9.
76 *ASR*, 4th ser., 13 (1893), 155–6; RH, Anti-Slavery Papers. Brit. Emp. S20 E5/7 'Early Record of Brotherhood Society', June 10 – August 11, 1893, and 'Minute Book of C. Impey', 17 August 1893.
77 *Lux*, 5 (22 September 1894), 124; *Anti-Caste*, 1 (October 1888), 2.
78 *Lux*, 1 (31 December 1892), 344.
79 *AF*, new ser., 3 (1889), 567.
80 Celestine Edwards, *From Slavery to a Bishopric, of the life of Bishop Walter Hawkins of the British Methodist Episcopal Church Canada* (London: John Kensit, 1891), p. xii, in *Documenting the American South* (Chapel Hill, NC: University of North Carolina, 1999), [www.docsouth.unc.edu/edwardsc/edwards.html].
81 *Lux*, 2 (20 May 1893), 241.
82 Wells, *Crusade*, pp. 124–6.
83 *Lux*, 2 (20 May 1893), 250; *Fraternity* (July 1893), 1.
84 *Fraternity* (July 1893), 1; there was no further mention of Impey by name in the paper.
85 *Fraternity* (August 1893), 1.
86 *Fraternity* (August 1893), 5–7, 12–13, 15.
87 *Fraternity* (October 1893), 4.
88 *Fraternity* (15 March 1894), 10–11.
89 *Fraternity* (15 January 1894), 1, 10, and (15 December 1893), 1.
90 *ASR*, 4th ser., 14 (May–June 1894), 168–71; *AF*, new ser., 4 (1894), 421–3.
91 *Fraternity* (1 July 1894), 1–2 and advertisement facing page 1; another advertisement on (1 December 1894); the book was available from the editor of *Fraternity* at the same address as the Lux publishing company.

92 Theodore Thomas [Celestine Edwards], *Hard Truth* (London: Lawrence and Symcox, 1894), p. 50.

93 Thomas, *Hard Truth*, pp. 52–3.

94 Thomas, *Hard Truth*, p. 58.

95 *Fraternity* (August 1894), 4–5, and (September 1894), 4–5; Ware, *Beyond the Pale*, pp. 190–7; this newly constituted branch of SRBM had an executive largely drawn from Mayo's circle in Aberdeen.

96 *Fraternity* (January 1897), 78.

97 RH, Anti-Slavery Papers. Brit. Emp. S.20 E5/8 West End Branch SRBM, Minute Book (C. Impey) 4 October 1894; E5/8 encl., Society for the Recognition of the Brotherhood of Man, *Annual Report of 1894*, pp. 8, 10; *Anti-Caste* (March 1895), 7.

98 Wells, *Crusade*, p. 216; most of the women had met Wells on her tours and no doubt encouraged their husbands, including a distinguished collection of Liberal newspaper editors and MPs, to join. Among those who were part of Catherine Impey's *Anti-Caste* network were Dadabhai Naoroji, Frederic Harrison, Mr and Mrs Moncure Conway, and Miss Wigham of Edinburgh; Tom Mann and Ben Tillet came from labour organisations.

99 *ASR* 4th ser., 15 (1895), 262; Marika Sherwood, *Origins of Pan Africanism: Henry Sylvester Williams, Africa and the African Diaspora* (London: Routledge, 2011); Marika Sherwood, 'Williams, Henry Sylvester (1869–1911)', *NODNB* (2009) [www.oxforddnb.com]; Owen C. Mathurin, *Henry Sylvester Williams and the Origins of the Pan-African Movement* (Westport, CT: Greenwood, 1976).

100 *AF*, new ser., 5 (1897), 297–8, and 5 (1898), 348–9; Sherwood, *Pan Africanism*, pp. 31–62; Schneer, *London 1900*, pp. 212–20 discusses the links between C. Edwards, the SRBM and Williams' African Association.

101 RH, Anti-Slavery Papers. Brit. Emp. E2/11, BFASS Minute Book (1887–1901), #942, 1 June 1900.

102 RH, Anti-Slavery Papers. Brit. Emp. S18. Correspondence C153/40, H. S. Williams to Fox Bourne, 11 November 1899.

103 H. S. Williams to Booker T. Washington, Grey's Inn, London, 29 June 1900, Louis R, Harlan *et al.* (eds), *The Booker T. Washington Papers* (Urbana, IL: University of Illinois Press, 1972), vol. 4, pp. 569–70.

104 Sherwood, *Pan Africanism*, p. 68, charges him with racism; Schneer, *London 1900*, p. 166, 220–1, with paternalism.

105 The APS sent its charter to the government on May 11, and issued a pamphlet with its text on 25 May 1900 – APS [H. R. Fox Bourne], *The Native Question in South Africa* (London, 1902), pp. 3–6; 'The Native Question in South Africa', *AF*, new ser., 5 (1900), pp. 529–50, and Tobias and Williams' remarks, p. 542; unfortunately the APS Committee minutes prior to 1902 have not survived.

106 Alexander Walters, *My Life and Work* (New York: Fleming H. Revell, 1917), pp. 253–64; Sherwood, *Pan Africanism*, pp. 99–100; Mathurin, *Williams*, pp. 76–82; Imanuel Geiss, *The Pan-African Movement: A History of Pan-Africanism in America, Europe, and Africa*, trans. Ann Keep (New York: Africana, 1974), pp. 192–4.

107 Sherwood, *Pan Africanism*, pp. 126–8; Geiss, *Pan-African*, pp. 195–8.

108 'Address to the Nations of the World by the Pan-African Conference in London, 1900', in J. Ayodele Langley (ed.), *Ideologies of Liberation in Black Africa, 1856–1970: Documents on Modern African Political Thought from Colonial Times to the Present* (London: R. Collins, 1979), pp.738–9; the address was also printed in the conference proceedings and in Walters, *My Life*, pp. 257–9.

109 'Address', pp. 738–9.

110 'Address', p. 738.

111 RH, Anti-Slavery Papers. Brit. Emp. S20 E2/11 BFASS Minute Book (1887–1901), #963, 5 October 1900; *ASR*, 4th ser., 20 (1900), 139–41.

112 *AF*, new ser., 5 (1900), 559–60.

113 Walters, *My Life*, pp. 256–7; Sherwood, *Pan Africanism*, p. 101; J. R. Hooker, *Henry Sylvester Williams: Imperial Pan-Africanist* (London: Rex Collins, 1975), pp. 35–7; Mathurin, *Williams*, pp. 79–82.

114 Kim Blake, 'T. E. S. Scholes: the unkown Pan-Africanist', *Race and Class*, 49 (2007), 62–80; Jeffrey Green, 'Scholes, Theophilus Edward Samuel (c.1858 – c.1940)', *NODNB* (2004) [www.oxforddnb.com]. Scholes' dates of birth and death are uncertain; the British Library Catalogue lists (1856–1935) for both Scholes and his pen-name Bartholomew Smith.

115 Jeffrey Green, *Black Edwardians: Black People in Britain, 1901–1914* (London: Frank Cass, 1998), pp. 241–6; Johnson, *Twenty-eight Years*, pp. 169, 176–8.

116 *Fraternity* (4 August 1894), 8, and (1 June 1896), 156.

117 *Fraternity* (1 June 1896), 156.

118 T. E. S. Scholes, *Sugar and the West Indies* (London: 1897).

119 T. E. S. Scholes, *The British Empire and its Alliances; or Britain's Duty to her Colonies and Subject Races* (London: 1899), pp. 251–329, 374–400.

120 Bartholomew Smith [T. E. S. Scholes], *Chamberlain and Chamberlainism: His Fiscal Proposals and Colonial Policy* (London, 1903), pp. 39–42, 81–9.

121 Scholes, *Glimpses*, vol. 1, pp. 5–12, 144–53, 191–209, 312–38.

122 Scholes, *Glimpses*, vol. 1, pp. 355–73.

123 Scholes, *Glimpses*, vol. 2, pp. 176–82, 232–6, 249–63.

124 Scholes, *Glimpses*, vol. 2, pp. 91, 220–3.

125 Scholes, *Glimpses*, vol. 2, pp. 282, 292.

126 Scholes, *Glimpses*, vol. 2, p. 312; as an example of the cultivation of good relations with the United States, he cited James Bryce's Romanes Lecture of 1902 (pp. 308–11).

127 Scholes, *Glimpses*, vol. 2, p. 487.

128 Blake, 'Scholes', 76–8; Jeffrey Green, *Black Edwardians*, pp. 241–6; Sherwood, *Pan Africanism*, p. 159; Geiss, *Pan-African Movement*, pp. 110–12.

129 J. A. Hobson, *The Psychology of Jingoism* (London: 1901); Stephen Koss, *The Pro-Boers: The Anatomy of an Anti-war Movement* (Chicago, IL : University of Chicago Press, 1973).

130 Shula Marks, 'Rewriting the South African War', H-SAfrica@h-net.msu.edu (June 2003); Bill Nasson, *The War for South Africa: The Anglo-Boer War, 1899–1902* (Cape Town: Tafelberg, 2010); Peter Warwick, *Black People and the South African War, 1899–1902* (Cambridge: Cambridge University Press, 1983).

131 Robertson, *Saxon and Celt*, p. 63; see also Babington, *Fallacies of Race*.

132 John Mackinnon Robertson, *Patriotism and Empire* (London: Grant Richards, 1899), pp. 182–93, 193–201, and *Wrecking of Empire* (London: Grant Richards, 1901), pp. 28–31, and *Our Relation to India* (London: 1904), pp. 3–4; Porter, *Critics of Empire*, p. 199.

133 John G. Godard, *Patriotism and Ethics* (London: Grant Richards, 1901), pp. 280–1.

134 Godard, *Patriotism*, p. 236.

135 Godard, *Racial Supremacy*, pp. 4–5, 12–14, 58.

136 Godard, *Racial Supremacy*, p. 212–13.

137 Godard, *Racial Supremacy*, p. 310.

138 Hobhouse, *Democracy and Reaction*, pp. 36–7.

139 Henry W. Nevinson, *A Modern Slavery* [1906] (New York: Schoken, 1968); RH, Anti-Slavery Papers. Brit. Emp. S20 E5/10 APS Minute Book 4 June 1903; 4 July 1907; 5 November 1907; RH, Anti-Slavery Papers. Brit. Emp. S18. Correspondence C150/121, W. Cadbury to Fox Bourne, 9 February 1905; C150/123, W. Cadbury to Fox Bourne, 6 June 1905; Lowell J. Satre, *Chocolate on Trial: Slavery, Politics and the Ethics of Business* (Athens, OH: Ohio University Press, 2005); Kevin Grant, *A Civilised Savagery*, pp. 109–34.

140 "The Congo atrocities', *AF*, new ser., 4 (April 1891), 155–64; "The Congo Free State' *AF*, new ser., 6 (December 1896), 66–83; Fox Bourne, *Congoland*, pp. vii–x; LSE. Morel Papers F8/67: #4, H. R. Fox Bourne to E. D. Morel, #5, 17 April 1901, #70, 8 July 1902, and #191, 11 January 1904; *ASR*, 4th ser., 24 (1904), 11, 14–22.

141 LSE, Morel Papers F8/67 #194, Fox Bourne to Roger Casement, 4 March 1904; #195 (Copy), Morel to Fox Bourne, 7 March 1904; #206, Fox Bourne to Morel, 29 May 1904; RH, Anti-Slavery Papers. Brit. Emp. S22 G261/B vol. 2 #3, Roger Case-

ment to Fox Bourne, 25 January 1904, and #7 (Copy), Charles Dilke to Fox Bourne, 25 January 1904; and S20 E5/10 APS Minute Book, 4 February 1904 and 2 June 1904; W. Roger Louis and Jean Stengers (eds), *E. D. Morel's History of the Congo Reform Movement* (Oxford: Clarendon, 1968); Cline, *Morel*, pp. 41–3.

142 RH, Brit. Emp. S22 G414. Newspaper clipping from *West African Mail*, 23 March 1906; H. R. Fox Bourne to editor of *West African Mail*; Morel to Fox Bourne, 26 March 1906; Fox Bourne to Morel, 27 March 1906; E. D. Morel, *Red Rubber: The Story of the Rubber Slave Trade Flourishing on the Congo* (London: T. Fisher Unwin, 1907), pp. 8–9, 13; Hochschild, *King Leopold's Ghost*, pp. 187–94; Grant, *A Civilised Savagery*, pp. 32–7, 60–3; Dean Pavlakis, 'The development of British humanitarianism and the Congo Reform Campaign', *Journal of Colonialism and Colonial History*, 11 (2010).

143 Grant, *A Civilised Savagery*, pp. 66–78.

144 Morel, *Horror on the Rhine*; Cline, *Morel*, pp. 126–8; Reinders, 'Racialism on the Left', *International Review of Social History*, 13 (1968); Fryer, *Staying Power*, pp. 316–19.

145 Wm. Roger Louis, 'Sir John Harris and "Colonial Trusteeship"', *Bulletin des Séances Académie Royale des Sciences d'Outre-Mer*, 14 (1968), 832–5.

146 Fox Bourne, *Blacks and Whites in South Africa*, p. 93.

147 H. R. Fox Bourne to the editor, *The Times* (26 August 1901), 9; C. H. Allen to the editor, *The Times* (11 September 1901), 10; H. R. Fox Bourne to the editor, *The Times* (12 September 1901), 4; Charles Swaisland, 'The Aborigines Protection Society, 1837–1909', *Slavery and Abolition*, 21 (2000), 271–3.

148 APS, *Native Question in South Africa*; RH. Anti-Slavery Papers. Brit. Emp. S20 E2/11 BFASS Minute Book #932, 4 May 1900; 'The native question in South Africa', *ASR*, 4th ser., 20 (1900), 155–8.

149 APS, *Native Question*, pp. 7–10.

150 APS, *Native Question*, pp. 12–17.

151 'South African problems', *AF* new ser., 7 (March 1906), 484; Heartfield, *Aborigines' Protection*, pp. 279–86, provides an incomplete analysis of the APS charter and the society's position on South African legal and political questions; for the Lagden Commission see Cell, *Highest Stage of White Supremacy*, pp. 196–215.

152 'South African questions', *AF* new ser., 7 (July 1905), 354–7; 'South African problems' pp. 484–9; 'Native grievances in Natal', *AF*, series, 8 (October 1907), 61–70.

153 APS, *Native Question*, pp. 9–10, 17–20.

154 TNA, CO291/33. 'Natives'. APS to Secretary of State for the Colonies, 11 January 1901; 'Natives in the Transvaal', *AF*, new ser., 6 (March 1902), 161–76; 'South African Natives and the Transvaal Constitution', *AF*, new ser., 7 (August 1906), 602–15.

155 H. R. Fox Bourne, *Forced Labour in South Africa* (London, 1903), p. 5.

156 Fox Bourne, *Forced*, p. 22. Chamberlain's charge of African male indolence was a common argument of defenders of coercion of African males for mine work; see *The Times* (10 February 1903), 7b–c.

157 Fox Bourne, *Forced*, pp. 19–20.

158 Fox Bourne, *Forced*, p. 43.

159 *Globe and Traveller* (11 April 1906), 1, and (27 April 1906), 1.

160 'The rights of subject races', *AF*, new ser., 8 (October 1907), 82 (see 80–8).

161 'Subject races', 84.

162 'Subject races', 88.

163 TNA, CO291/78 APSW to Lord Lyttleton, 15 December 1904; 'The Transvaal and Chinese labour', *AF*, new ser., 7 (February 1904), 1–16; with an occasional lapse into prejudicial statements against the Chinese, most APS commentary followed Charles Dilke's observation that they opposed not the Chinese but conditions of the indenture and labour – *AF*, new ser., 7 (March 1904), 32; Swaisland, 'Aborigines Protection Society', pp. 273–5; Grant, *A Civilised Savagery*, pp. 79–107.

164 *AF*, new ser., 7 (August 1906), 602–15 printed petitions from the Political Organization of Coloured British Subjects in South Africa, from a group of British subjects resident in Cape Colony led by J. Tengo-Jabavu, editor of *Imvo*, and from the Lovedale Missionary Institute.

165 TNA, CO417/434 APS, New Constitution. Protection of Rights of Natives and Coloured People, 13 July 1906.
166 RH, Anti-Slavery Papers. Brit. Emp. S18. Correspondence C150/125–125b (Copy), W. A. Cadbury to the APS, 6 February 1908; Satre, *Chocolate*, pp. 101–3.
167 'Subject races', *AF*, new ser., 8 (October 1907), 80–1; N. F. Dryhurst (ed.), *Nationalities and Subject Races. Report of Conference held in Caxton Hall, June 28–30, 1910* (London, 1911).
168 H. R. Fox Bourne, *Egypt under British Control* (London: P. S. King and Son and the Aborigines Protection Society, 1907); Fox Bourne, *Notes on Egyptian Affairs, no. 1 – 5* (London, 1907, 1908); RH, Anti-Slavery Papers. Brit. Emp. S22. APS Letters G415, F. W. Fox to H. R. Fox Bourne, 14 March 1907.
169 RH, Anti-Slavery Papers. Brit. Emp. S20 E2/12 BFASS Minute Book, #1534, 3 January 1908; S20 E5/10 APS Minute Book, 17 January 1908.
170 RH, Anti-Slavery Papers. Brit. Emp. S20 E5/10 APS Minute Book, 2 March 1908, and 21 March 1908.
171 'Native franchise in South Africa', *AF*, new ser., 8 (October 1908), p. 188; see also 'Native rights in South Africa,' *AF*, new ser., 8 (January 1909), 225–6.
172 RH, Anti-Slavery Papers. Brit. Emp. S20 E5/10 APS Minute Book, 11 March 1909; S22 APS Letters G415, Travers Buxton to A. F. G, Bryant, 3 April 1909.
173 *AF*, new ser., 8 (May 1909), 257–62.
174 Earl of Selborne, *The Native Question in South Africa* (London: Anti-Slavery and Aborigines Protection Society, 1909); *AF*, new ser., 8 (October 1908), 185.
175 'South African Native Land Act', *Anti-Slavery Reporter and Aborigines' Friend*, 5th ser., 3 (January 1914), 76–9, 172–3; John H. Harris, *General Botha's Native Land Policy* (London: Anti-Slavery and Aborigines Protection Society, 1916), pp. 11–14; Brian Willan, 'The Anti-Slavery and Aborigines Protection Society and the South African Natives' Land Act of 1913', *Journal of African History*, 20 (1979), 83–102; Brian Willan, *Sol Plaatje: South African Nationalist, 1876–1932* (London: Heinemann, 1984), pp. 176–83, 190, 199–201; Rich, *Race and Empire*, pp. 37–41.
176 John H. Harris, *Native Races and the Peace* (London: Anti-Slavery and Aborigines Protection Society, 1916), p. 8; Louis, 'Harris', 842–7.
177 *African Times and Oriental Review*, new ser., 4 (June 1917), 111–13.
178 Andrew Porter, 'Trusteeship, anti-slavery and humanitarianism', *OHBE*, vol. 3, pp. 198–221; B. Porter, *Critics of Empire*.

CHAPTER EIGHT

Conclusion

Many years ago when I began my studies of the Victorians and race, I started by looking at the experience of black residents and visitors in the United Kingdom during the 1830s–1860s, when the anti-slavery movement could still lay claim to the sympathy and support of a broad cross-section of the society. Towards the end of that period the abolitionist vision of 'racial equality', ambiguously and imperfectly constructed as it surely was, began to lose its purchase, partly through disillusionment with the mighty experiment in emancipation, and partly from external events like the Indian Rebellion (1857), the American Civil War, and the Jamaica Uprising (1865). The more substantial change was less visible. Social and cultural changes in the metropolitan society transformed the Victorians themselves, losing, in particular, the liberating reform enthusiasms of the 1830s. Some historians pointed to the emergence of modern scientific racism as a significant intellectual influence, though I remained sceptical, especially from the evidence of the 1860s. Nonetheless, a regressive change in the discourse on race, and its associated expressions in the popular culture, was underway. Therefore, I began this study of the period after 1870 with the historian's usual question – 'what happened next?'

What happened next was an explosion in new studies and new methods for understanding constructions of race and culture. The range and variety of these studies, even if overwhelming, were exciting and informative; the best of them reshaped the intellectual landscape. Nonetheless, as mentioned in the introduction, I had a nagging concern that our scholarship allowed us to select our Victorians and focus on historical or literary exemplars of a racist archetype. A more adequate representation of the Victorians and race needed to encompass a broader range and diversity of opinions, and to recognise that race continued to be a contested territory, as it had been from the 1840s to the 1860s, and as it continued to be in the twentieth and twenty-first centuries.

I began with the scientists recognising that the growth in the professional and intellectual standing of the sciences had a profound effect on the production and authority of what was deemed to be 'real' knowledge. Anthropology, the academic discipline especially devoted to the study of race and culture, experienced a protracted and at times difficult process to get itself accepted among the sciences. Part of the problem was the inseparable mix of race and culture. Even the physical anthropologists and comparative anatomists – those practitioners who come closest to being biological determinists – could not escape culture. Their method involved establishing a correlation between anatomical features (for example, the cephalic index) and the psychological and cultural traits of their constructed types (traits which they presumed but did not subject to scientific enquiry). While one can find a few scientists espousing polygenesis in the late nineteenth century, the scientific consensus favoured monogenesis. The legacy of Victorian racial scientists for the twentieth century was a certainty about the inequality of 'races' and uncertainty about how they defined 'race'.[1] Crude racial typologies were more common in popular science at the beginning of the twentieth century, and the chief populariser, Professor Augustus Keane, was a linguist.

At the Anthropological Institute, culture not biology dominated proceedings. The most innovative theorists developed the applications of Darwinian evolution to culture. Schemes of cultural evolution, developed by E. B. Tylor and others, incorporated the extension of human time established by archaeology, separated cultures farther apart in time, and ranked peoples and cultures according to states of progress toward a civilised Victorian norm. Similarly, in popular science representations of 'races', cultural differences and rankings were well-established, drawn from the common culture and even in some cases from missionary publications, before the rigidities of biologically determined race types became more common. Victorian anthropology's principal contribution was to the study of cultural differences rather than biologically determined differences. The next generation of anthropologists, that of Bronislaw Malinowski and Alfred Radcliffe-Brown, liberated their discipline from the evolutionary paradigm, and their cultural science gained recognition as a practical guide to colonial administration.

Prior to 1914, the anthropologists claimed they did not engage in political questions, and consequently their studies did not address the political dimensions of relations between European colonisers and colonised peoples. The theoretical constructions of race by the scientists placed their human objects in an illusionary state of nature uncontaminated by the colonial context. Scholars compound this error when they study the scientists' race types without considering contemporary understandings of the identities and relations created by the negotiated inter-reactions between the colonisers and the colonised. In contrast, the abolitionist movement and related humanitarian agencies offered a more critical scrutiny of the conditions of slaves and aboriginal peoples within a colonial context, and originated a new language of race relations.

Inspired by the abolitionists, the language of race relations began with the presumption of 'racial equality' and a need to explain, critique or justify deviations from that standard. Given the inequalities of class and gender in early Victorian society and their incorporation into the law and its jurisprudence, and government policies and administration, what 'racial equality' might actually mean in practice is difficult to determine. It may well have had an evocative appeal to members of the middle class, especially Nonconformists, who thought they had recently established something approaching equality in their own society despite its visible ranks and privileges. The aspiration for achieving some form of equality lay behind the belief in the imperial mission and its call for the eventual assimilation of all peoples to Victorian civilisation. In many ways, such an aspiration was comparable to the missionary movement's goal of conversion. By 1850, this original abolitionist vision was under serious attack, and as the pace of colonial acquisition and conflict accelerated after 1870, the discourse addressed the question of the legitimate as distinct from the illegitimate forms of racial inequality in law and practice in colonial regimes. Needless to say, disputes did not get resolved, but they expanded the vocabulary of race relations. The descendants of the abolitionists still proclaimed the ideal of racial equality and assimilation, whereas white settlers and their supporters claimed that colonial circumstances required a different social order, with the separation and subordination of the 'native', and restrictive laws against non-European immigrants. Developments across the Atlantic in the post-emancipation, post-reconstruction United States provided an alternative, if contentious, model of 'modern' race relations.

By the beginning of the twentieth century, forecasters saw a future with a more integrated world, with racial groups in closer contact, and with the cultural differences between such groups lessened, but nonetheless with intensified conflict from the demands of the racially oppressed and from whites instinctively drawn to defend their privileges. The South African War, especially the public discourse on the post-war settlement, provided the occasion for the airing of the 'colour question' and the development of the concept of 'race relations'. The defenders of the old idea of 'racial equality' were clearly in the minority, and regardless of all the light and heat exchanged, the resolution was a political settlement in which white power in South Africa ruled.

Who participated in this debate on the colour question is of greater interest. Outside of humanitarian lobbyists like Fox Bourne, many of the participants moved between journalism, politics, and the academy. They belonged to the founding generation of the new social sciences such as such as sociology, psychology and politics. Like the scientists whose methods they emulated, they too claimed to be producers of knowledge. Their knowledge, though, was not simply about the natural inequality of human races, but about the management of race relations seeking how racial subordination could be made compatible with social and political stability.

A third group was more directly engaged in the politics of resistance to one, some, or all forms of racial oppression. By history, by experience and by ethnicity, they were a diverse group, differentially placed in the political arena, and with differing political agendas. Those with the most continuous history of engagement and greatest political influence worked within established humanitarian agencies, principally the BFASS and the APS. Both were committed to the civilising mission and were pro-imperialist, believing in positive benefits from western intervention in the non-western world. Of the two organisations, the BFASS, as the embodiment of the anti-slavery movement whose achievements were built into the mythology of the empire, had an easier relationship with Her Majesty's Government. After 1865, issues such as the slave trade and slavery involved relations with foreign governments, and in the 1880s included lobbying the British government to act in concert with other European powers in the partition of Africa. Despite its caution and its attempt to restrict its focus to slave-related issues, political and economic developments in Africa forced the BFASS to address newer forms of coerced labour and the survival or reinvention of slavery. From its origin, the APS focused on British colonial possessions, and consequently, it engaged in a more direct criticism of colonial policy and practices. Its title, 'aborigines' protection', was something of a misnomer, for while it set out to protect aboriginal peoples from harm from white settlers, the society's longer term perspective anticipated that aboriginal cultures would be assimilated to norms of British modernity. Its fear was that colonial administrators and white settlers would place obstacles to that transition by racially oppressive practices. More directly than the BFASS, especially in southern Africa, the APS confronted new and extensive practices in regard to land and labour that obstructed paths to assimilation.

As forms of racial oppression intensified in multi-racial colonies, and as the United States introduced new kinds of institutionalised segregation, individuals began a number of initiatives to revive old

[317]

abolitionist commitments of the past and to counter the regressive trends of the present. When Catherine Impey launched the *Anti-Caste* in 1888, she was inspired to do so by her friendship with African-Americans, and by the recognition that the most effective voice against racial injustice would come from persons of colour who were the targets of racial prejudice. Between 1893 and 1900, from the foundation of the SRBM to the Pan-African Conference, there was a remarkable rebirth of a movement committed to racial egalitarianism, and engaged in exposing racial oppression in the United States and the British Empire. On the lecture tour and in print, the public face of this racial egalitarianism belonged to such persons of colour as Ida B. Wells, Celestine Edwards, T. E. S. Scholes, H. Sylvester Williams and others who toured extensively round the British Isles. Out of their experience of directly confronting racialism, they challenged the presumed superiority of not only the imperialists but also British humanitarians. Ultimately their insights would have a greater influence upon the development of colonial nationalism than upon resistance to racialism within the metropolitan society.

As these initiatives got underway, the nation's attentions fixed on the South African War and its aftermath. The APS led the humanitarian agencies in developing a charter of native rights as a blueprint for addressing the 'native' interest. Fox Bourne and the APS used cultural rather than racial markers of difference by distinguishing as they had done in the past between the 'uncivilised' and the 'civilised' among the 'native' populations including all non-whites in South Africa. Their charter failed to come to grips with South African realities. It relied on the imperial factor as protector of the 'natives', which neither the Boers nor the British would accept. Even with the Cape coloured franchise, Fox Bourne's 'uncivilised' and 'civilised' categories, cumbersome to implement in law or policy, would never replace the existing racial markers in South Africa. After all, in South Africa in the 1820s, Robert Knox had learned, 'race is everything'. Frustrated by the inability to move either the Tories or the Liberals to address the 'native question', Fox Bourne became more radical in his analysis of racial oppression. He turned his energies to the Hague Convention where he had some influence on drafting international conventions on subject races. He also dared to criticise an imperial pro-consul, Lord Cromer, in support of Egyptian nationalists. When he died in 1909, the APS died with him.

The newly amalgamated Anti-Slavery and Aborigines Protection Society came under the leadership of the Reverend John Harris, a more successful lobbyist respectful of the imperial state. The new society kept a low profile on South Africa, supported Lord Lugard's policies of indirect rule, and looked to the international arena to continue its abolitionist work and to promote imperial trusteeship. Such a strategy avoided confrontations with the government yet kept alive the humanitarian legacy of the anti-slavery movement as an adjunct to the imperial mission.

What had been lost in the process was that old, archaic abolitionist ideal of racial equality. Another loss was the radical abolitionist strategy of relying on persons of colour as the most effective voices against racial oppression. The APS inherited this strategy through F. W. Chesson; it was kept alive by Fox Bourne through his African correspondents; and it was publicised by Catherine Impey through her African-American friends. When Ida B. Wells made her tours in 1893–94, the greatest of these spokespersons against racial oppression, Frederick Douglass, was still remembered. Persons of African descent by their visible presence and by their itinerant lectures conveyed a powerful message against racial prejudice and oppression, but after 1909 the institutional basis for such a message needed to be reconstructed.

After 1910, there were signs that there might be a revival of an alliance between British activists and persons of colour. In July of 1911, the Universal Races Congress met at the University of London. As many as a thousand or more attended for four days to discuss the theme of cultivating improved relations between the races. The Congress has attracted some recent attention among scholars interested in the meetings as window into an emerging cosmopolitan world prior to 1914.[2] For someone more familiar with the nineteenth century it has the appearance of an end rather than a beginning. Its limitations stemmed from its origins in the ethical reform movement, for it did not have the capacity to develop a critical or unified political analysis. The anti-slavery society, caught up in the arrangements for amalgamation and dubious about Gustav Spiller, the Congress organiser and his plans, decided not to participate.[3] Many of the papers were exercises in the analysis of race relations by colonial administrators, humanitarian reformers and distinguished academics after the fashion of what had taken place in the previous decade. What was new about the Congress was its international representation from a great variety of persons of colour and from virtually all continents, with a special concentration of participants from Asia and the Middle East.[4] The effort to limit or exclude participation from anthropologists whose science of race types was in conflict with the ethical goals of the Congress occasioned some controversy.[5] Gustav Spiller at the Congress and in his publications championed racial equalitarianism and the role of environment over biology in explaining human differences.[6] Even though this response to the science of race impressed W. E. B. Du Bois, A. C. Haddon, speaking as an anthropologist, thought that race, an 'academic' subject, was not suitable for such a large assembly. He dissented from Spiller's environmentalism and claimed that while scientists recognised 'races' were mixed and not pure, nonetheless there were significant human differences, especially in the 'psychology of different peoples'.[7] Most press reports expressed support of the Congress objectives and scepticism about any practical outcome. On the other hand, the *Standard* defended the reality of racial distinctions and saw in the Congress the danger of philanthropy in 'conflict with human nature' provoking 'an explosion of fanaticism'.[8] Spiller and the Universal Races Congress may have given a sign of future directions, but race and race relations remained a contested territory. There were plans for further meetings, but war in 1914 put an end to such good intentions.

What was missing in 1911 was the historic appeal of anti-slavery tradition weakened by its struggles between 1900 and 1909. The abolitionist movement and its various branches had championed some form of the ideal of racial equality since its origins with Granville Sharp in the 1770s. As the historical context changed, its coalition of engaged reformers had shown the capacity to change as circumstances demanded, so abolitionism did not end in 1807, or 1833, or 1838, or 1865. After 1870, the abolitionists and their colleagues engaged in the struggle against newer forms of racial oppression associated with colonialism and the emergence of multi-racial, modern democratic states. As the members of the APS realised in 1900, their task was far larger than the challenge their founders had faced in 1837. They had more limited resources and a public less engaged in the cause of racial justice. Their prospects were even worse by 1910.

The professionalisation of the production of knowledge gave less scope for the amateur enthusiasts and lobbyists pleading for special causes. There were now professional experts in the academy, producing knowledge not only in the natural sciences but also in the social sciences. Of the two, the social scientists adopting and developing the Victorian language of race relations would have a longer-term significance in the maintenance of racial inequality. Both kinds of producers of knowledge saw their expertise as useful for the imperial state. The Anti-Slavery and Aborigines Protection Society, the one surviving agency from the abolitionist past, out of the bruising experience of confronting white power in South Africa, opted under new leadership for a strategy of imperial trusteeship more in harmony with colonial policies. Any dissenting voices, most evident among early colonial nationalists from Africa, Asia and the West Indies, would have to invent new political objectives, new political strategies and new institutions to contest what T. E. S. Scholes called the 'hegemonical' state.

Notes

1 This confusion was evident in responses to the Universal Races Congress of 1911: H. H. Johnston, 'Racial problems', *Views and Reviews*, pp. 200–42, and 'Black and white in South Africa,' *Colonial Office Journal*, 5 (January 1912), 214–22.
2 'Forum', *Radical History Review* 92 (2005), 99–152; Paul B. Rich, *Race and Empire*, pp. 44–9.
3 RH, Anti-Slavery Papers. Brit. Emp. S 22 G441, Correspondence re-Universal Races Congress (30 March – 22 December 1909).
4 Lake and Reynolds, *Drawing the Global*, pp. 251–62; Susan D. Pennybacker, 'The Universal Races Congress, London political culture, and imperial dissent, 1900–1939', *Radical History Review* 92 (2005), 103–17.
5 *Daily News* (29 July 1911), 4d.
6 G. Spiller, 'The problem of race equality', in G. Spiller (ed.), *Papers on Inter-Racial Problems communicated to the First Universal Races Congress* (London: P. S. King, 1911), pp. 29–39; and 'Science and race prejudice,' *Sociological Review* (October 1912), 1–24; *The Mentality of Australian Aborigines* (London: Sherratt and Hughes, 1913); *Darwinism and Sociology* (London: Sherratt and Hughes, 1914).
7 W. E. B. Du Bois, *Dusk of Dawn: An Essay toward an Autobiography of a Race Concept* (New York: Harcourt Brace, 1940), pp. 229–31; David Levering Lewis, *W. E. B. Du Bois: Biography of Race, 1868–1919* (New York: Henry Holt, 1993), pp. 439–43; A. C. Haddon's remarks in *Record of the Proceedings of the First Universal Races Congress* (London: P. S. King, 1911), pp. 25–6.
8 'The problems of race', *Standard* (26 July 1911), 6e–f.

SELECT BIBLIOGRAPHY

Bibliography and reference

Dabydeen, David, Gilmore, John and Jones Cecily (eds). *The Oxford Companion to Black British History* (Oxford: Oxford University Press, 2007).

Lewin, Evans. *Subject Catalogue of the Library of the Royal Empire Society: Volume One: The British Empire Generally and Africa* (London: Royal Empire Society, 1930).

Oxford History of the British Empire

Brown, Judith, and Louis, Wm. Roger (eds). *The Twentieth Century* (Oxford: Oxford University Press, 1999).

Etherington, Norman (ed.). *Missions and Empire*, OHBE Companion Series (Oxford: Oxford University Press, 2005).

Levine, Philippa (ed.). *Gender and Empire*, OHBE Companion Series (Oxford: Oxford University Press, 2004).

Morgan, Philip D., and Hawkins, Sean (eds). *Black Experience and the Empire*, OHBE Companion Series (Oxford: Oxford University Press, 2004).

Porter, Andrew (ed.). *The Nineteenth Century* (Oxford: Oxford University Press, 1999).

Primary sources

Manuscript

British Library
- Additional Manuscripts: Dilke Papers, Wallace Papers
- British Publishers Archive

Imperial College, London
- Huxley Papers

London School of Economics
- Morel Papers

The National Archive
- CO885/19 Miscellaneous No. 217 Confidential. *Native Races in the British Empire* [CPL] (31 December 1907), pp. 23–6 (cited as [Lucas], *Native Races*).
- CO886/1 Dominions No. 1. Confidential. The Self-Governing Dominions and Coloured Immigration [CPL] July 1908.

- CO886/1 Dominions No. 2. Very Confidential. Suggestions as to Coloured Immigration into the Self-Governing Dominions [CPL] July 1908.
- APS Correspondence with the colonial office in series CO96, 291, 417.

Rhodes House Library, Oxford
- Anti-Slavery Papers including minute books and correspondence of BFASS and APS, and minute books and letters of Catherine Impey and the SRBM

Royal Anthropological Institute Archives
- Council minutes, membership lists and attendance books

University College, London
- Galton Papers
- Archival records relating to the appointment of Professor A. H. Keane

Official publications

British Parliamentary Debates
British Parliamentary Papers. Report of the Select Committee on Aborigines (British Settlements) [1837], *British Parliamentary Papers* (Shannon: Irish University Press, 1968).

Books and articles

Alston, Leonard. *The White Man's Work in Asia and Africa: A Discussion of the Main Difficulties of the Colour Question* (London: Longmans Green, 1907).

APS. 'Address', *Regulations of the Society and Address* (London: 1837).

APS. *Report of the Parliamentary Committee on Aboriginal Tribes reprinted with comments by the Society* (London, 1837).

APS. *The Native Question in South Africa* (London: P. S. King, 1900).

Archer, William. *Through Afro-America: An English Reading of the Race Problem* (London: Chapman Hall, 1910) [reprint Westport, CT: Negro Universities Press, 1970].

Babington, William Dalton. *Fallacies of Race Theories as Applied to National Characteristics* (London: Longmans Green, 1895).

Bancroft, Francis [Frances Charlotte Slater]. 'White women in South Africa', *Englishwoman* (March 1911).

Baring, Evelyn, Earl of Cromer. *Ancient and Modern Imperialism* (London: John Murray, 1910).

Beddoe, John. *The Races of Britain: A Contribution to the Anthropology of Western Europe* (London: 1885).

Beddoe, John. *Memories of Eighty Years* (Bristol: J. W. Arrowsmith, 1910).

Besant, Annie. 'Coloured races in the Empire', *The Indian Review*, 14 (April 1913), 288–94.

BFASS. *Sixty Years against Slavery. A Brief Record of the Work and Aims of the British and Foreign Anti-Slavery Society, 1839–1899* (London: 1899).

British Association for the Advancement of Science. *Anthropometric Investigation in the British Isles* (London: Royal Anthropological Institute, 1909).

Brown, Robert. *The Races of Mankind: Being a Popular Description of the Characteristics, Manners and Customs of the Principal Varieties of the Human Family* (London: Cassell, Petter and Galpin, 1873–76), 4 vols.

Brown, Robert. *The Peoples of the World* (London: Cassell, Petter and Galpin, 1881–86), 6 vols.

Brown, Robert. *The Countries of the World: Being a Popular Description of the Various Continents, Islands, Rivers, Seas, and Peoples of the Globe* (London: Cassell, 1884–89), 6 vols.

Brown, Robert. *The Story of Africa and its Explorers* (London: Cassell, 1892–95), vol. 4.

Bruce, Sir Charles. *The Broad Stone of Empire: Problems of Crown Colony Administration, with Records of Personal Experience* (London: Macmillan, 1910), vol. 1, pp. 306–69.

Bruce, Sir Charles. *True Temper of the Times* (London: Macmillan, 1912).

Bryce, James. *Impressions of South Africa* (London: Macmillan, 1897).

Bryce, James. *The Relations of the Advanced and the Backward Races of Mankind* (Oxford: Clarendon Press, 1902) The Romanes Lecture 1902 [facsimile University Microfilms International, Ann Arbor, MI, 1979].

Campbell, Sir George. *Black and White: The Outcome of a Visit to the United States* (New York: R. Worthington, 1879).

Campbell, Sir George. *The British Empire* (London: Cassell, 1887).

Clodd, Edward. *The Childhood of the World. A Simple Account of Man's Early Years* (London: Macmillan, 1873).

Clodd, Edward. *The Childhood of Religions: Embracing a Simple Account of the Birth and Growth of Myths and Legends* (1875) (London: Kegan Paul Trench, 1889).

Clodd, Edward. *The Story of Creation: a Plain Account of Evolution* (London: Longmans, 1888).

Clowes, W. Laird. *Black America: A Study of the Ex-Slave and his Late Master* [1891] (Westport, CT: Negro Universities, 1970).

Darwin, Charles. *The Descent of Man, and Selection in Relation to Sex* (London: John Murray, 1871), 2 vols.

Dilke, Sir Charles. *Greater Britain: A Record of Travel in English-Speaking Countries during 1866 and 1867* (New York: Harper, 1869).

Dilke, Sir Charles. *Problems of Greater Britain* (London: Macmillan, 1890), 2 vols.

Dilke, Sir Charles. *The British Empire* (London: Chatto and Windus, 1899).

Edwards, Celestine. *From Slavery to a Bishopric, of the life of Bishop Walter Hawkins of the British Methodist Episcopal Church Canada* (London: John Kensit, 1891), in *Documenting the American South* (Chapel Hill, NC: University of North Carolina, 1999) [www.docsouth.unc.edu/neh/edwardsc/edwards.html].

[Edwards, Celestine] Thomas, Theodore. *Hard Truth* (London: Lawrence and Symcox, 1894).

Finot, Jean. *Race Prejudice* (London: Archibald Constable, 1906).

Finot, Jean. *The Death-Agony of the 'Science' of Race* (London: Stead Publishing, 1911).

Flower, W. H. 'The Comparative Anatomy of Man', *Nature*, 20 (1879), 222–5, 244–6, 267–9 and 22 (1880), 59–61, 78–80, 97–100.

Flower, W. H. 'Opening Address, Section D: Biology – Department of Anthropology, Report of the British Association ', *Nature*, 24 (1881), 436–9.

Flower, W. H. 'On the aims and prospects of the study of anthropology', *JAI* 13 (1883–4), 488-99.

Fox Bourne, H. R. *English Newspapers: Chapters in the History of Journalism* (London, 1887), 2 vols.

Fox Bourne, H. R. *The Aborigines Protection Society: Chapters in its History* (London, 1895).

Fox Bourne, H. R. *Blacks and Whites in South Africa: An Account of the Past Treatment and Present Conditions of South African Natives under British and Boer Control* (London, 1900).

Fox Bourne, H. R. *Blacks and Whites in West Africa: An Account of the Past and Present Condition of West African Natives under European Control* (London: P. S. King, 1902).

Fox Bourne, H. R. *Civilisation in Congoland: A Story of International Wrong-Doing* (London, 1903).

Fox Bourne, H. R. *Forced Labour in South Africa* (London, 1903).

Fox Bourne, H. R. *Egypt under British Control* (London: P. S. King and Son and the Aborigines Protection Society, 1907).

Fox Bourne, H. R. *Notes on Egyptian Affairs, no. 1 – 5* (London: P. S. King and Son and the Aborigines Protection Society, 1907, 1908).

Fox Bourne, H. R. 'Our West Africa possessions', *Gentleman's Magazine*, 267 (October 1889), 379–90.

Fox Bourne, H. R. 'South Africa and the Aborigines Protection Society', *Contemporary Review*, 56 (September 1889), 347–69.

Fox Bourne, H. R., and Colenso, Harriet. *The Story of Dinuzulu* (London: Zulu Defence Committee, 1890).

Froude, J. A. *The English in the West Indies* (London, 1888).

Galton, Francis. *The Narrative of an Explorer in Tropical South Africa* (London: John Murray, 1853).

Galton, Francis. *Englishmen of Science: Their Nature and Nurture* (London: Macmillan, 1874).

Godard, John G. *Patriotism and Ethics* (London: Grant Richards, 1901).

Godard, John G. *Racial Supremacy: Being Studies in Imperialism* (London: Simpkin, Marshall, 1905).

Haddon, A. C. *The Study of Man* (London: Bliss, Sands, 1898).

Haddon, A. C. *The Races of Man and Their Distribution* (Halifax: Milner [1912]).

Harris, John H. *General Botha's Native Land Policy* (London: Anti-Slavery and Aborigines Protection Society, 1916).

Harris, John H. *Native Races and the Peace* (London: Anti-Slavery and Aborigines Protection Society, 1916).

Hobhouse, L. T. *Democracy and Reaction* [1904] ed. P. F. Clarke (Brighton: Harvester 1972).

Hobson, J. A. *The Psychology of Jingoism* (London: 1901).

Hobson, J. A. 'The negro problem in the United States', *Nineteenth Century*, 54 (October 1903), 581–94.

Huxley, T. H. 'On the geographical distribution of the chief modifications of man', *Journal of the Ethnological Society*, n.s., 2 (1869–70), 404–12.

Jebb, Richard .'The imperial problem of Asiatic immigration', *Journal of the Royal Society of Art* 56 (24 April 1908).

Johnson, Thomas L. *Twenty-Eight Years a Slave, or the Story of My Life on Three Continents* (Bournemouth, 1909).

Johnston, H. H. *Views and Reviews: From the Outlook of an Anthropologist* (London: Williams and Norgate, 1912).

Keane, A. H. *Ethnology* (Cambridge: Cambridge University Press, 1896).

Keane, A. H. *Anthropological, Philological, Geographical, Historical and Other Writings* (London: privately printed, [1897]).

Keane, A. H. *Man: Past and Present* (Cambridge: Cambridge University Press, 1900).

Keane, A. H. *The Boer States: Land and People* (London: Methuen, 1900).

Keane, A. H. *The World's Peoples* (London: Hutchinson, 1908).

Keane, A. H., and Lydekker, R. (eds). *The Living Races of Mankind* (London: Hutchinson, 1905).

Keane, A. H. 'On the relations of the Indo-Chinese and Inter-Oceanic races and languages', *JAI*, 9 (1879–80), 254–89.

Kidd, Benjamin. *Social Evolution* (New York: Macmillan, 1895.

Kidd, Benjamin. *The Control of the Tropics* (London: Macmillan, 1898).

Kingsley, Mary. *Travels in West Africa* [1897] (London: Virago, 1982).

Knox, Robert. *The Races of Men: A Philosophical Enquiry into the Influence of Race over the Destinies of Nations* (London: Henry Renshaw, 1862).

Lydekker, R. 'Introduction', in A. H. Keane, R. Lydekker *et al.* (eds), *The Living Races of Mankind* (London: Hutchinson, 1905).

Lucas, C. P. *Greater Rome and Greater Britain* (Oxford: Clarendon, 1912).

MacDonald, J. Ramsay. *Labour and Empire* [1907], reprint in *From Serfdom to Socialism: Labour and the Empire*, ed. Robert F. Dowse (Warbury, NJ: Associated Universities, 1974).

Mackarness, Frederick. 'South Africa and irresponsible government', *Contemporary Review* 56 (August 1889), 234–43.

Marshall, Newton H. 'Empires and races', *The Contemporary Review*, 96 (September 1906), 304–13.

Mayo, Isabella. *Recollections: What I saw, What I lived through and What I learned* (London, 1910).

Merivale, Herman. *Lectures on Colonization and Colonies* [1861] Reprints of Economic Classics (New York: Augustus Kelly, 1967).

Merriman-Labor, A. B. C. *Britons through Negro Spectacles* (London: Imperial and Foreign, 1909).

Morel, E. D. *Horror on the Rhine* (London: Union for Democratic Control, 1920).

Morel, E. D. *Red Rubber: The Story of the Rubber Slave Trade Flourishing on the Congo* (London: T. Fisher Unwin, 1907).

Murray, Gilbert. 'The exploitation of inferior races in ancient and modern times', in Francis Hirst, G. Murray and J. L. Hammond (eds), *Liberalism and Empire* (London: 1900).

Nevinson, Henry W. *A Modern Slavery* [1906] (New York: Schoken, 1968).

Olivier, Sidney. *Letters and Selected Writings*, ed. with memoir by Margaret Olivier (London: George Allen and Unwin, 1948).

Olivier, Sidney. *White Capital and Coloured Labour* (London: Independent Labour Party, 1910) (Westport, CT: Negro Universities Press, 1970).

Pan-African Conference. 'Address to the Nations of the World by the Pan-African Conference in London, 1900', in J. Ayodele Langley (ed.), *Ideologies of Liberation in Black Africa, 1856–1970: Documents on Modern African Political Thought from Colonial Times to the Present* (London: R. Collins, 1979).

Pearson, Charles H. *National Life and Character: A Forecast* (London: Macmillan, 1893).

Robertson, John Mackinnon. *Patriotism and Empire* (London: Grant Richards, 1899).

Robertson, John Mackinnon. *The Saxon and the Celt: A Study in Sociology* (London: University Press, 1897).

Robertson, John Mackinnon. *Wrecking of Empire* (London: Grant Richards, 1901).

Rosebery, Lord [Primrose, Archibald Philip]. *Miscellanies: Literary and Historical* (London: Hodder and Stoughton, 1921), 2 vols.

Scholes, T. E. S. *Sugar and the West Indies* (London: 1897).

Scholes, T. E. S. *The British Empire and its Alliances; or Britain's Duty to her Colonies and Subject Races* (London, 1899).

[Scholes T. E. S.] Bartholomew Smith, *Chamberlain and Chamberlainism: His Fiscal Proposals and Colonial Policy* (London, 1903).

Scholes, T. E. S. *Glimpses of Past Ages, or the 'Superior' and 'Inferior' Races, so-called, discussed in the light of Science and History* (London: John Long, 1905, 1908), 2 vols.

Seeley, J. R. *The Expansion of England* [1883], ed. John Gross (London and Chicago, IL: University of Chicago, 1971).

Selborne, William Palmer (Second Earl of). *The Native Question in South Africa* (London: Anti-Slavery and Aborigines Protection Society, 1909).

Shaw, Flora. 'Dry-Nursing the colonies', *Fortnightly Review*, new ser., 46 (September 1889), 367–79.

Shaw, G. B. (ed.). *Fabianism and Empire: A Manifesto of the Fabian Society* (London: Grant Edwards, 1900).

Silburn, P. A. *The Governance of Empire* [1910] (Port Washington, NY: Kennikat, 1971).

Spencer, Herbert. 'The comparative psychology of man', *JAI* 5 (1875–6), 301–15; in Biddiss (ed.), *Images of Race*, pp. 187–204.

Spiller, Gustav (ed.). *Papers on Inter-Racial Problems communicated to the First Universal Races Congress* (London: P. S. King, 1911).

Spiller, Gustav. *Science and Race Prejudice* (London: Sherratt and Hughes, 1912).

Spiller, Gustav. *Darwinism and Sociology* (London: Sherratt and Hughes, 1914).

Tyler, E. B. *Primitive Culture* (London: John Murray, 1871), 2 vols.

Tyler, E. B. *Anthropology: An Introduction to the Study of Man and Civilization* (London: Macmillan, 1881).

Universal Races Congress. *Record of the Proceedings of the First Universal Races Congress* (London: P. S. King, 1911).

Wallace, A. R. 'The origin of the human races and the antiquity of man deduced from the theory of "natural selection"', *Journal of the Anthropological Society of London*, 2 (1864), in Biddiss (ed.), *Images of Race*, 37–54.

Wallas, Graham. *Human Nature in Politics* (1908) (London: Constable, 4th edn, 1948).

Walters, Alexander. *My Life and Work* (New York: Fleming H. Revell, 1917).

Ward, James L. *Colonization and its bearing on the extinction of the Aboriginal Races* (Leek: 1874).

Weale, B. L. Putnam [Bertram Lennox Simpson]. *The Conflict of Colour: Being a Detailed Examination of Racial Problems throughout the World with Special Reference to English-Speaking Peoples* (London: Macmillan, 1910).

Wells, Ida B. *Crusade for Justice: The Autobiography of Ida B. Wells*, ed., Alfreda M. Duster (Chicago, IL: University of Chicago, 1970).

Wood, John G. *The Boy's Own Book of Natural History* (London: Routledge, Warne, and Routledge, 1861).

Wood, John G. *The Natural History of Man, being an Account of the Manners and Customs of the Uncivilised Races of Man* (London: Routledge), vol. 1 (1868), vol. 2 (1870).

Periodicals and newspapers

General
See endnotes

Science
- *Cassell's General Storehouse of Information* (1890–94)
- *English Mechanic and World of Science*
- *Knowledge*
- *Journal of the Anthropological Institute of Great Britain and Ireland*
- *Man*
- *Nature*
- *Science Monthly*

Humanitarian lobby and resistance
- *Aborigines' Friend*
- *Colonial Intelligencer and Aborigines' Friend*
- *African Times and Oriental Review*

- *Anti-Caste*
- *Anti-Slavery Reporter*
- *Anti-Slavery Reporter and Aborigines' Friend*
- *Fraternity*
- *Lux*

Secondary sources

Books and articles

Abrams, Philip. *The Origins of British Sociology, 1834–1914* (Chicago, IL: Chicago University Press, 1968).

Adas, Michael. *Machines as the Measure of Men: Science, Technology, and Ideologies of Western Dominance* (Ithaca, NY, and London: Cornell University Press, 1989).

Balibar, E. 'Is there a "Neo-Racism"?' in E. Balibar and I. Wallerstein, *Race, Nation, Class: Ambiguous Identities* (London: Verso, 1991), pp. 17–28.

Ballantyne, Tony. *Orientalism and Race: Aryanism in the British Empire* (Basingstoke: Macmillan, 2002).

Banton, Michael. *The Idea of Race* (London: Tavistock, 1977).

Barkan, Elazar. *The Retreat of Scientific Racism: Changing Concepts of Race in Britain and the United States between the World Wars* (Cambridge: Cambridge University Press, 1992).

Bayly, C. A. *The Birth of the Modern World, 1780–1914* (Oxford: Blackwell, 2004).

Beinhart, William, and Dubow, Saul (eds). *Segregation and Apartheid in Twentieth-Century South Africa* (New York: Routledge, 1995).

Bell, Duncan. *The Idea of Greater Britain: Empire and the Future of the World Order, 1860–1900* (Princeton, NJ: Princeton University Press, 2007).

Benedict, Ruth. *Race, Science and Politics* (New York: Modern Age, 1940).

Biddiss, Michael D. (ed.). *Images of Race* (Leicester: Leicester University Press, 1979).

Blackburn, Robin. *The Overthrow of Colonial Slavery, 1776–1848* (London: Verso, 1988).

Blackett, R. J. M. *Building the Anti-Slavery Wall: Black Americans in the Atlantic Abolitionist Movement, 1830–1860* (Baton Rouge, LA: Louisiana State University Press, 1983).

Blake, Kim. 'T. E. S. Scholes: The unkown Pan-Africanist', *Race and Class*, 49 (2007), 62–80.

Bolt, Christine. *Victorian Attitudes to Race* (London: Routledge and Kegan Paul, 1971).

Bressey, Caroline. 'A Strange and Bitter Crop: Ida B Wells' Anti-lynching Tours. Britain 1893 and 1894', *Centre for Capital Punishment Studies: Occasional Papers*, 1 (December 2003), 8–28.

Burrow, J. W. *Evolution and Society: A Study in Victorian Social Theory* (Cambridge: Cambridge University Press, 1970).

Cain, P. J., and Hopkins, A. G. *British Imperialism: Innovation and Expansion, 1688–1914* (London: Longman, 1993).

Cannadine, David. *Ornamentalism: How the British Saw their Empire* (Oxford: Oxford University Press, 2001).

Cell, John W. *The Highest Stage of White Supremacy: The Origins of Segregation in South Africa and the American South* (Cambridge: Cambridge University Press, 1982).

Cline, Catherine A. *E. D. Morel, 1873–1924: The Strategies of Protest* (Belfast: Blackstaff, 1980).

Coombs, Annie E. *Reinventing Africa: Museums, Material Culture and Popular Imagination in Late Victorian and Edwardian England* (New Haven, CT: Yale University Press, 1994).

Cooper, Frederick. *Colonialism in Question: Theory, Knowledge, History* (Berkeley, CA: University of California Press, 2005).

Cooper, Frederick, Holt, T. C., and Scott, R. J. *Beyond Slavery: Explorations of Race, Labor, and Citizenship in Post-Emancipation Societies* (Chapel Hill, NC: University of North Carolina Press, 2000).

Curtin, Philip. *The Image of Africa: British Ideas and Action, 1780–1850* (London: Macmillan, 1964).

Darder, Antonio, and Torres, Rodolfo. *After Race: Racism after Multiculturalism* (New York: New York University Press, 2004).

Darwin, John. *The Empire Project: The Rise and Fall of the British World-System, 1830–1970* (Cambridge: Cambridge University Press, 2009).

Davis, David Brion. *Slavery and Human Progress* (London: Oxford University Press, 1984).

Desmond, Adrian, and Moore, James. *Darwin's Sacred Cause: Race, Slavery, and the Quest for Human Origins* (London: Allen Lane, 2009).

Dirks, Nicholas B. (ed.). *Colonialism and Culture* (Ann Arbor, MI: University of Michigan Press, 1992).

Drayton, Richard. *Nature's Government: Science, Imperial Britain and the Improvement of the World* (New Haven, CT: Yale University Press, 2000).

Drescher, Seymour. *The Mighty Experiment: Free Labor Versus Slavery in British Emancipation* (Oxford: Oxford University Press, 2002).

Drescher, Seymour. *Abolition: A History of Slavery and Antislavery* (Cambridge: Cambridge University Press, 2009).

Dubow, Saul. 'Race, civilisation and culture: the elaboration of segregationist discourse in the inter-war years', in Shula Marks and Stanley Trapido (eds), *The Politics of Race, Class and Nationalism in Twentieth-Century South Africa* (London: Longman, 1987).

Eddy, John, and Schroeder, Derek. *The Rise of Colonial Nationalism: Australia, New Zealand, Canada and South Africa First Assert their Nationalities, 1880–1914* (Sydney: Allen and Unwin, 1988).

Edwards Elizabeth (ed.). *Anthropology and Photography* (New Haven, CT: Yale University Press, 1992).

Evans, Julie, *et al. Equal Subjects, Unequal Rights: Indigenous Peoples in British Settler Colonies, 1830–1910* (Manchester: Manchester University, 2003).

[330]

Fahey, David A. *Temperance and Racism: John Bull, Johnny Reb, and the Good Templars* (Lexington, KY: University Press of Kentucky, 1996).

Field, H. J. *Toward a Programme of Imperial Life: The British Empire at the Turn of the Century* (Westport, CT: Greenwood, 1982).

Foner, Eric. *Nothing but Freedom: Emancipation and its Legacy* (Baton Rouge, LA: Louisiana State University Press, 1983).

Fryer, Peter. *Staying Power: The History of Black People in Britain* (Atlantic Highlands, NJ: Humanities Press, 1984).

Geiss, Imanuel. *The Pan-African Movement: A History of Pan-Africanism in America, Europe, and Africa*, trans. Ann Keep (New York: Africana, 1974).

Getzina, Gretchen H. (ed.). *Black Victorians/Black Victoriana* (New Brunswick, NJ: Rutgers University Press, 2003).

Gilroy, Paul. *Against Race: Imagining Political Culture beyond the Color Line* (Cambridge, MA: Belnap, 2000).

Goldberg, David T. *The Threat of Race: Reflections on Racial Neoliberalism* (Malden, MA: Wiley-Blackwell, 2009).

Goldberg, David Theo (ed.). *Anatomy of Racism* (Minneapolis, MN: University of Minnesota, 1990).

Gould, Stephen Jay. *The Mismeasure of Man* (Harmondsworth: Penguin, 1984).

Grant, Kevin. *A Civilised Savagery: Britain and the New Slaveries in Africa, 1884–1926* (London: Routledge, 2005).

Green, Jeffrey. *Black Edwardians: Black People in Britain, 1901–1914* (London: Frank Cass, 1998).

Gundara, J. S., and Duffield, Ian (eds). *Essays on the History of Blacks in Britain* (Aldershot: Avebury, 1992).

Guy, Jeff. *The View across the River: Harriet Colenso and the Zulu Struggle against Imperialism* (Charlottesville, VA: University of Virginia Press, 2002).

Gwynn, S. and Tuckwell, G. M. *Life of Sir Charles Dilke* (London: John Murray, 1917), 2 vols.

Hall, Catherine. *Civilising Subjects: Metropole and Colony in the English Imagination, 1830–1867* (Cambridge: Polity, 2002).

Hall, Catherine, McClelland, Keith, and Rendall, Jane. *Defining the Victorian Nation: Class, Race and Gender and the Reform Act of 1867* (Cambridge: Cambridge University Press, 2000).

Hall, Catherine. 'Introduction: thinking the post-colonial, thinking the empire', in Hall (ed.), *Cultures of Empire: Colonizers in Britain and the Empire in the Nineteenth and Twentieth Centuries* (New York: Routledge, 2000), 1–33.

Hall, Catherine. and Rose, Sonya (eds). *At Home with the Empire: Metropolitan Culture and the Imperial World* (Cambridge: Cambridge University Press, 2006).

Halliday, R. J. 'Social Darwinism: a definition', *Victorian Studies*, 14:4 (1971), 389–405.

Hay, Douglas, and Craven, Paul (eds). *Masters, Servants, and Magistrates in Britain and the Empire, 1562–1955* (Chapel Hill, NC: University of North Carolina Press, 2004).

Heartfield, James. *The Aborigines' Protection Society: Humanitarian Imperialism in Australia, New Zealand, Fiji, Canada, South Africa, and the Congo, 1836–1909* (New York: Columbia University Press, 2011).

Heyck, T. W. *The Transformation of Intellectual Life in Victorian England* (New York: St. Martin, 1982).

Hobsbawm, E. J., and Ranger, Terence (eds). *The Invention of Tradition* (Cambridge: Cambridge University Press, 1983).

Hochschild, Adam. *King Leopold's Ghost: A Story of Greed, Terror and Heroism in Colonial Africa* (New York: Houghton Mifflin, 1998).

Holmes, Colin. *John Bull's Island: Immigration and British Society, 1871–1971* (London: Macmillan, 1988).

Holt, Thomas. *The Problem of Freedom: Race, Labor, and Politics in Jamaica and Britain, 1832–1938* (Baltimore, MD: John Hopkins University Press, 1992).

Holt, Thomas. *The Problem of Race in the 21st Century* (Cambridge, MA: Harvard University Press, 2000).

Howe, Stephen. *Anticolonialism in British Politics: The Left and the End of Empire, 1918–1964* (Oxford: Clarendon, 1993).

Huttenback, Robert A. *Racism and Empire: White Settlers and Colored Immigration in the British Self-Governing Dominions, 1830–1910* (Ithaca, NY: Cornell University Press, 1976).

Hyam, Ronald. *Elgin and Churchill at the Colonial Office, 1905–1908: The Watershed of the Empire-Commonwealth* (London: Macmillan, 1968).

Hyslop, Jonathan. 'The imperial working class makes itself "white": White labourism in Britain, Australia, and South Africa before the First World War', *Journal of Historical Sociology*, 12 (1999), 398–421.

Jenkins, Roy. *Sir Charles Dilke: A Victorian Tragedy* (London: Fontana, 1968).

Jones, Greta. *Social Darwinism and English Thought: The Interaction between Biological and Social Theory* (Brighton: Harvester, 1980).

Kubicek, R. V. *The Administration of Imperialism: Joseph Chamberlain at the Colonial Office* (Durham, NC: Duke University Press, 1969).

Kuklick, Henrika.*The Social History of British Anthropology, 1885–1945* (Cambridge: Cambridge University Press, 1991).

Kuper, Adam. *Anthropologists and Anthropology: The British School, 1922–72* (Harmondsworth: Penguin, 1975).

Laidlaw, Zoë. 'Heathens, slaves and aborigines: Thomas Hodgkin's critique of missions and anti-slavery', *History Workshop Journal*, 64 (2007), 133–61.

Lake, Marilyn and Reynolds, Henry. *Drawing the Global Colour Line: White Men's Countries and the International Challenge of Racial Equality* (Cambridge: Cambridge University Press, 2008).

Lee, Francis. *Fabianism and Colonialism: The Life and Political Thought of Lord Sydney Olivier* (London: Defiant, 1988).

Lorimer, Douglas. *Colour, Class and the Victorians: English Attitudes to the Negro in the Mid-Nineteenth Century* (Leicester: Leicester University Press, 1978).

Lorimer, Douglas. 'Science and the secularization of Victorian images of race', in B. Lightman (ed.), *Victorian Science in Context* (Chicago, IL: University of Chicago, 1997).

Lorimer, Douglas. 'From Victorian values to white virtues: Assimilation and exclusion in British racial discourse, c. 1870–1914', in P. Buckner and D. Francis (eds), *Rediscovering the British World* (Calgary: University of Calgary Press, 2005).

Lorimer, Douglas. 'From natural science to social science: Race and the language of race relations in late Victorian and Edwardian discourse', in Duncan Kelly (ed.), *Lineages of Empire: The Historical Roots of British Imperial Thought*, Proceedings of the British Academy, 155 (Oxford University Press/The British Academy, 2009).

Louis, Wm. Roger. 'Sir John Harris and "Colonial Trusteeship"', *Bulletin des Séances Académie Royale des Sciences d'Outre-Mer*, 14 (1968), 832–56.

Louis, Wm. Roger, and Jean Stengers (eds), *E. D. Morel's History of the Congo Reform Movement* (Oxford: Clarendon, 1968).

MacKenzie, John M. *Propaganda and Empire.The Manipulation of British Public Opinion, 1880–1960* (Manchester: Manchester University Press, 1984).

MacKenzie John M. (ed.). *Imperialism and Popular Culture* (Manchester: Manchester University Press, 1986).

MacKenzie, John M. (ed.). *Imperialism and the Natural World* (Manchester: Manchester University Press, 1990).

MacKenzie, John M. 'Missionaries, science and the environment in nineteenth-century Africa', in A. Porter (ed.), *The Imperial Horizons of British Protestant Missions, 1880–1914* (Cambridge: William B. Eerdmans, 2003).

Macleod, Roy M. 'Centenary review, 1869–1969', *Nature*, 224 (1 November 1969), 417–76.

Malik, Kenan. *The Meaning of Race: Race, History and Culture in Western Society* (New York: New York University Press, 1996).

Mamdani, Mahood. *Citizen and Subject: Contemporary Africa and the Legacy of Late Colonialism* (Princeton, NJ: Princeton University Press, 1996).

Mandler, Peter. *The English National Character: The History of an Idea from Edmund Burke to Tony Blair* (New Haven, CT: Yale University Press, 2006).

Mandler, Peter. '"Race" and "nation" in mid-Victorian thought', in S. Collini, R. Whatmore and B. Young (eds), *History, Religion and Culture: British Intellectual History*, (Cambridge: Cambridge University Press, 2000).

Mathurin, Owen C. *Henry SylvesterWilliams and the Origins of the Pan-African Movement* (Westport, CT: Greenwood, 1976).

McClintock, Anne. *Imperial Leather: Race, Gender, and Sexuality in the Colonial Contest* (London: Routledge, 1995).

Midgley, Clare (ed.). *Gender and Imperialism* (Manchester: Manchester University Press, 1998).

Miers, Suzanne. *Britain and the Ending of the Slave Trade* (New York: Africana Publishing, 1975).

Miles, Robert. *Racism after 'Race Relations'* (London: Routledge, 1993).

Moore, Lindy. 'The reputation of Isabella Fyvie Mayo: interpretation of a life', *Women's History Review*, 19 (2010), 71–88.

Nasson, Bill. *The War for South Africa: The Anglo-Boer War, 1899–1902* (Cape

Town: Tafelberg, 2010).

Oppenheimer, Stephen. *Out of Eden: The Peopling of the World* (London: Robinson, 2003).

Pennybacker, Susan D. 'The Universal Races Congress, London political culture, and imperial dissent, 1900–1939', *Radical History Review*, 92 (2005), 103–17.

Porter, Andrew. *Religion versus Empire? British Protestant Missionaries and Overseas Expansion, 1700–1914* (Manchester: Manchester University Press, 2004).

Porter, Bernard. *Critics of Empire: British Radical Attitudes to Colonialism in Africa* (London: Macmillan, 1968).

Porter, Bernard. *The Absent-Minded Imperialists* (Oxford: Oxford University Press, 2004).

Price, Richard. *British Society, 1680–1880: Dynamism, Containment and Change* (Cambridge: Cambridge University Press, 1999).

Price, Richard. *Making Empire: Colonial Encounters and the Creation of Imperial Rule in Nineteenth-Century Africa* (Cambridge: Cambridge University Press, 2008).

Price, Richard. 'One big thing: Britain, its empire and their imperial culture', *Journal of British Studies*, 45 (2006), 602–27.

Rich, Paul B. *Race and Empire in British Politics* (Cambridge: Cambridge University Press, 1986).

Richards, Evelleen The Moral Anatomy" of Robert Knox: The inter-play between biological and social thought in Victorian scientific naturalism', *Journal of the History of Biology*, 22 (1989), 373–436.

Richards, Jeffrey (ed.). *Imperialism and Juvenile Literature* (Manchester: Manchester University, 1989).

Richardson, David (ed.). *Abolition and its Aftermath: The Historical Context, 1790–1916* (London: Frank Cass, 1985).

Robinson, Ronald. 'Non-European foundations of European imperialism', in E. R. Owen and B. Sutcliffe (eds), *Studies in the Theory of Imperialism* (London: Longman, 1972).

Said, Edward. *Orientalism* (1978) (Harmondsworth: Penguin, 1985).

Said, Edward. *Culture and Imperialism* (New York: Alfred A. Knopf, 1993).

Satre, Lowell J. *Chocolate on Trial: Slavery, Politics and the Ethics of Business* (Athens, OH: Ohio University Press, 2005).

Saunders, Kay (ed.). *Indentured Labour in the British Empire, 1834-1920* (London: Croom Helm, 1984).

Schneer, Jonathan. *London 1900: The Imperial Metropolis* (New Haven, CT, and London: Yale University Press, 1999).

Searle, G. R. *Eugenics and Politics in Great Britain, 1900–1914* (Leyden: Noordhoff International, 1976).

Sherwood, Marika. *Origins of Pan Africanism: Henry Sylvester Williams, Africa and the African Diaspora* (London: Routledge, 2011).

Stepan, Nancy. *The Idea of Race in Science: Great Britain, 1800–1960* (Hamden, CT: Archon, 1982).

Stocking, Jr., George W. 'What's in a Name? The origins of the Royal Anthropological Institute (1837–71)', *Man*, n.s., 6 (1971), 369–90.

Stocking, Jr., George W. *Victorian Anthropology* (New York, Free Press, 1987).

Stoler, Ann Laura. *Carnal Knowledge and Imperial Power: Race and the Intimate in Colonial Rule* (Los Angeles, CA: University of California Press, 2002).

Street, Brian V. *The Savage in Literature: Representations of 'Primitive' Society in English Fiction, 1858–1920* (London: Routledge Kegan Paul, 1975).

Swaisland, Charles. 'The Aborigines Protection Society and British Southern and West Africa', DPhil, University of Oxford (1968).

Swaisland, Charles. 'The Aborigines Protection Society, 1837–1909', *Slavery and Abolition*, 21 (2000), 265–80.

Tabili, Laura. 'Race is a relationship not a thing', *Journal of Social History*, 37 (2003), 125–30.

Taylor, Miles. 'Imperialism and libertas? Rethinking the radical critique of imperialism during the nineteenth century', *Journal of Imperial and Commonwealth History*, 19 (1991), 1–23.

Temperley, Howard. *British Anti-Slavery, 1833–1870* (London: Longman, 1972).

Temperley, Howard (ed.). *After Slavery: Emancipation and its Discontents* (London: Frank Cass, 2000).

Thomas, Keith. *Man and the Natural World* (Harmondsworth: Penguin, 1984).

Thompson, Andrew. *The Empire Strikes Back: The Impact of Imperialism on Britain from the Mid-Nineteenth Century* (London: Longman, 2005).

Thorne, Susan. *Congregational Mission and the Making of an Imperial Culture in Nineteenth-Century England* (Stanford: Stanford University Press, 1999).

Trapido, Stanley. '"The friends of the natives": merchants, peasants and the political and ideological structure of liberalism at the Cape, 1854–1910', in Shula Marks and Anthony Atmore (eds), *Economy and Society in Pre-Industrial South Africa* (London: Longman, 1980).

Turner, Frank. M. *Between Science and Religion: The Reaction to Scientific Naturalism in late Victorian England* (New Haven, CT: Yale University Press, 1974).

Ware, Vron. *Beyond the Pale: White Women, Racism and History* (London: Verso, 1992).

Willan, Brian. *Sol Plaatje: South African Nationalist, 1876–1932* (London: Heinemann, 1984).

Willan, Brian. 'The Anti-Slavery and Aborigines Protection Society and the South African Natives' Land Act of 1913', *Journal of African History*, 20 (1979), 83–102.

Winnant, Howard. *The World is a Ghetto: Race and Democracy since World War Two* (New York: Basic Books, 2001).

Young, Robert. Darwinism is social', in David Kohn (ed.), *The Darwinian Heritage* (Princeton, NJ: Princeton University Press, 1982).

Young, Robert M. *Darwin's Metaphor: Nature's Place in Victorian Culture* (Cambridge: Cambridge University Press, 1985).

INDEX

Note: 'n.' after a page reference indicates the number of the note on that page.